PRINCIPLES OF
PSYCHOTHERAPY
WITH
CHILDREN

Series in Scientific Foundations of Clinical and Counseling Psychology
Eugene Walker, Series Editor

PRINCIPLES OF PSYCHOTHERAPY WITH CHILDREN

SECOND EDITION

John M. Reisman
Sheila Ribordy

DePaul University

LEXINGTON BOOKS

An Imprint of Macmillan, Inc.
NEW YORK
Maxwell Macmillan Canada
TORONTO
Maxwell Macmillan International
NEW YORK OXFORD SINGAPORE SYDNEY

Library of Congress Cataloging-in -Publication Data

Reisman, John M.
  Principles of psychotherapy with children / John M. Reisman
Sheila Ribordy. -- 2nd ed.
    p. cm. -- (Scientific foundations of clinical and counseling
psychology)
  Includes bibliographical references.
  ISBN 0-669-28055-0
  1. Child psychotherapy. I. Ribordy, Sheila. II. Title
III. Series: Scientific foundations of clinical and counseling
psychology.
  [DNLM: 1. Psychotherapy -- in infancy & childhood.   WS 350.2 R377p
1993]
RJ504.R44   1993
618.92'8914 -- dc20
DNLM/DLC
for Library of Congress   93 - 1430
                                                                      CIP

Copyright © 1993 by Lexington Books
An Imprint of Macmillan, Inc.
Copyright © 1973 by John M. Reisman

Lexington Books
An Imprint of Macmillan, Inc.
866 Third Avenue, New York, NY 10022

Maxwell Macmillan Canada, Inc.
1200 Eglinton Avenue East
Suite 200
Don Mills, Ontario M3C 3N1

Macmillan, Inc. is part of the Maxwell Communication
Group of Companies.

Printed in the United States of America

printing number
1 2 3 4 5 6 7 8 9 10

Contents

Preface

The major aim of this book is to make clear how one practices an integrative form of psychotherapy with children and their parents. It begins by arriving at seven principles that guide the conduct of virtually every kind of psychotherapy with both children and adults, and illustrates the working of these principles in actual cases.

Inevitably, this book draws heavily upon the authors' clinical experiences. Although names and identifying information have been changed, the cases and quotations represent what happened and what was said.

We wish to express our gratitude to those who helped to make this book possible, in particular to DePaul University for making time available to devote to this project.

1
Children and Psychotherapy

This is a book about how to do psychotherapy with children and families. Childhood covers a wide range of development, from preschool youngsters to older adolescents. Nevertheless, there are principles of psychotherapy that apply to every client regardless of age; this book emphasizes seven of them and illustrates their applications.

Psychotherapy is a complex field consisting of many different methods and procedures, some of which contradict and dispute the techniques and practices of others. Kazdin (1988) estimated there were at least 230 kinds of psychological treatment used with children, and it would not be incorrect to assume there has been an increase in the number since his estimate was given. No single therapist could be competent in all the aspects of psychotherapy; fortunately, however, no single therapist needs to be competent in every aspect of the field. It is possible to be an effective therapist by becoming familiar with psychotherapeutic principles and skilled in their use.

Some Misconceptions About Child Psychotherapy

Before we consider these principles, it is important to make explicit our understanding of child psychotherapy, to evaluate the scientific evidence for its effectiveness, and to examine some pertinent attitudes. There are adults who believe there is a correspondence between the size of the client and the seriousness of the problem, as well as the ease with which that problem can be treated. In other words, small children have smaller worries and concerns than big adults, and so their problems are more easily solved. This is sometimes construed to mean that therapists who deal with the problems of children need not have the professional qualifications and training of those who work with adults. During the period from 1925 to 1929, for example, there was a controversy within psychoanalytic circles

1

about whether analysts needed to be trained first as physicians. Freud's position was that psychoanalysis was not part of medicine, and so medical training was unnecessary; however, he was strongly opposed by analysts within the United States. A temporary compromise was achieved when the New York Psychoanalytic Society conceded that lay analysts could be appropriate for children but not for adults (E. Jones, 1957). The position that child therapists require less rigorous training than those who work with adults is definitely not held today (Tuma, 1989).

Skepticism is often expressed about the validity of children's problems. Many of these problems do appear to follow a developmental course in which their severity or frequency is reduced over time without any specific treatment. Thus, parents may simply be advised to be tolerant and patient, in the belief that the child's troublesome behaviors will simply go away by themselves (Lapouse & Monk, 1964).

Compounding difficulties in understanding children are the many differences noted between them and adults. How to communicate with a child is a puzzle for many adults because they assume there are differences in language that they must bridge. A certain amount of awkwardness in being introduced to a youngster can be observed at almost any large, "mixed" gathering (Rautman & Rautman, 1948). This is evident by the adult speaking in a singsong manner, raising the pitch of his or her voice, increasing its volume, and exaggerating gestures. Consider the enormous popular success of the books by Ginott (1965, 1969) teaching fathers and mothers how to comprehend and converse in "childrenese," a strange and peculiar language supposedly spoken by their offspring.

More to the point of this book are the differences in psychotherapy and psychopathology that are alleged to be peculiar to children. To take one example, it is often stated that psychologically troubled children are seldom able to express their distress in words, but instead communicate their need for help by their actions (A. Freud, 1965). Thus, they cry and they demand; they cling and they rebel; they fail in school, break laws, and act in a hundred different ways to bring about disaster for themselves and thereby compel attention from adults. In contrast, grown-ups can seek assistance directly and give verbal expression to their needs.

There is much truth to this observation, as there is to the many others that have been made about how children tend to differ from adults. Yet it is also true that many adults behave so as to be judged as disturbed by professionals, although these same adults would deny emphatically that they have psychological problems. Furthermore, it is also true that many children are able to state what troubles them and that they desire help—in fact, some do so repeatedly in an effort to get some adult to take their complaints seriously. The contention that children deny their psychological problems is not true of all children, nor is it true only of children.

The range of development covered by childhood (from infancy

through adolescence) makes it possible to raise a similar argument with many of the other differences noted between children and adults. But the aim here is not to minimize the merit of generalities or to deny that differences exist. It is, for example, simple fact, and highly important for a child psychotherapist to keep in mind, that children have a great deal to learn and are most dependent upon their parents and other adults. Nevertheless, the consequences of our awareness of such facts should be to enhance our understanding of children and to decrease the psychological distance that exists between them and us.

Accordingly, the point of view of this book with regard to the differences between children and adults is to be mindful of them, but not intimidated by them; to be aware of special considerations, but not to see them as obstacles to being of help; and to see a continuity of development and a similarity of needs between children and adolescents and adults. Consistent with this point of view is the thesis that the principles of psychotherapy, though described in relation to children, are the same as those used with adults.

Professional Psychotherapy with Children

Professional psychotherapy with children is a relatively new field that can trace its origins to the early days of psychoanalysis at the beginning of the twentieth century. The first published case describing the use of a psychological method of treatment—psychoanalysis—with a child was Freud's report in 1909 ("Little Hans") of the treatment of a phobia in a 5-year-old boy (S. Freud, 1959).

Although the treatment was actually conducted by the boy's father under Freud's supervision by mail, the case was monumental in its theoretical significance because Freud regarded his young patient's unreasonable fears as an expression of unconscious conflicts (that is, as indications of psychological disturbances in the child's relationships with his parents that were not within his awareness). Surprisingly, that a child might have such conflicts and emotional problems was a new concept even to Freud. At that time, so far as the public was concerned, children behaved as they did because they were wicked, ill-bred, naughty, ill-mannered, overimaginative, foulmouthed, high-strung, distempered, and untutored. The prevalent view among professionals, meanwhile, was that the disorders of childhood were indicative of deficiencies in the child's education and training. Therefore, in treatment the emphasis had been on the teaching of proper habits and on persuading the child to overcome immorality and to behave correctly (Reisman, 1991). Freud's ideas suggested that some children were deeply troubled by their own feelings and wishes, and that they could best be helped by being made aware of these and becoming reconciled to their existence—that is, by becoming more integrated as a person through an acceptance of feelings and thoughts that had been frightening or abhorrent.

Within a few years of the publication of this case a female, nonmedical psychoanalyst, Hermine Hug-Hellmuth, began to see children in play therapy in Vienna (E. Jones, 1957); she is generally credited with originating play psychotherapy. It is sad (but important because of its ethical implications) to note that Hug-Hellmuth was murdered by a nephew whom she raised as her son, and while she herself was treating him for emotional problems (Haizlip, Corder, & Ball, 1984, p. 143).

The psychoanalytic approach to the understanding and treatment of children was presented in a series of lectures by Freud's daughter Anna at the Vienna Institute of Psychoanalysis in 1926 and 1927 and in books written by her in 1928 and 1946. At approximately the same time, Melanie Klein (1932) described her method of psychoanalytic treatment with children. Both of these analysts were influential in directing professional attention to the use of play in psychotherapy with children. Klein's method, which has generally been regarded in the United Sates as more speculative and less credible than Freud's, is based on a theoretical system that sees extensive psychological conflict occurring in early infancy. Kleinians also assume that virtually every act of the child is expressive of the unconscious; hence, they advocate immediate interpretations of play activities, which are almost always construed as symbolic. Though Anna Freud agreed play might express unconscious fantasies and impulses, she also saw it serving many other purposes (Gerard, 1952). She and Klein promoted the use of play as a natural medium of communication for children and as a means for adults to acquire an understanding of the problems and concerns within this age group.

These concepts revolutionized prevailing attitudes toward behavior disorders in childhood and methods of treatment. The term *emotionally disturbed* was applied to children, apparently for the first time, in an article that appeared in 1932 (Despert, 1970). The literature about disturbed children grew quickly, with numerous case studies informing professionals of youngsters who had fallen far behind their classmates in their schoolwork but made rapid progress once the unconscious conflicts that blocked their learning were uncovered.

By the end of the 1930s the psychoanalytic position was widely accepted in the United States and England as a progressive and sound explanation for psychological disturbances, juvenile delinquency, and a variety of other troublesome behaviors. So widespread was its acceptance that in retrospect it now seems probable that some children who had learning disorders caused by central nervous system dysfunctions were treated instead for emotional problems. The emphasis among professionals shifted from the use of remedial tutoring or training to psychotherapy as the treatment of choice.

As a result of this professional interest, other psychotherapeutic approaches were quickly developed and enlisted enthusiastic proponents. One of the enduring and influential methods of treatment was that of the child psychiatrist Frederick Allen (1942), whose work was derived from the theories of Otto Rank and, in turn, had a significant influence on the development of Carl Rogers's client-centered therapy. Allen was convinced that children should be regarded as persons with the strength to alter their behaviors constructively. Time and again, Allen repeated his belief that when the therapist consistently conveyed confidence in children's ability to help themselves, the children responded by demonstrating growth in their development. Allen's concept of the role of the therapist was that it consisted in large measure of providing conditions of freedom and respect that would allow the client to abandon a defensive posture and resume forward progress: "I am interested in creating a natural relation in which the patient can acquire a more adequate acceptance of himself, a clear conception of what he can do and feel in relation to the world in which he continues to live. . . . I am not afraid to let the patient feel that I am interested in him as a person" (Allen, 1934, p. 201).

Allen's system of psychotherapy stressed the importance of creating a special kind of human relationship between the therapist and the child. It was held that this relationship was what was therapeutic, rather than the bringing of unconscious conflicts into awareness and the communication of insight. Since Allen's time it has become appreciated by therapists of almost every orientaton that the relationship between themselves and their clients is of great significance; basically, the relationship is seen to involve cooperation, in which both client and therapist work together to bring about change. There are, however, some therapists who believe psychotherapy is the particular relationship they form with their clients. In support of their belief, they point to many instances in which neither the therapist nor the client dealt directly with any symptoms, yet the frequencies of these behaviors were reduced. It seemed plausible to conclude, in the absence of any symptom-reduction techniques or any insights offered or gained, that the warm, accepting, friendly therapist-client interaction was what made psychotherapy effective (Rogers, 1962).

Beginning in the 1960s, though, such a humanistic conception of psychotherapy has been increasingly challenged by treatment approaches based on the straightforward application of learning principles to the modification of behavior problems with children. Although the significance of the relationship between client and therapist is not dismissed, behavior therapists give greater emphasis to the judicious use of conditioning techniques and reinforcements.

Education and training procedures were employed by clinical psychologists from the very inception of their profession in 1896 (Reisman, 1991). In that year, Lightner Witmer established the first psychological clinic—

and arguably the first child guidance clinic—in the world at the University of Pennsylvania and began to see and teach children who had difficulties in their schooling and development. One 3-year-old child who seemed to respond well to Witmer's "pedagogic" method evidenced autistic behaviors (Witmer, 1919–1922). A much more frequently cited case in the behavior therapy literature, however, is that of Peter, a 3-year-old boy who had an unreasonable fear of rabbits and other furry objects. Mary Cover Jones (1924) described how this fear was extinguished by the pairing of the noxious stimulus (a caged rabbit) with pleasurable stimuli and responses (food and eating) so that only the latter were elicited. The rabbit was placed at some distance from Peter and was gradually moved closer and closer, without triggering alarm, until finally it could be released at the child's table.

The professional response to Peter's recovery was at first mild when compared to the surge of enthusiasm for psychoanalytic concepts and the view of children having emotional disorders rather than mere problems in learning. In time, though, there occurred a decline in the importance of Little Hans's case and an increase in the significance of Peter's, helped along their respective paths by sober and discomfiting appraisals of psychotherapy with children (Eysenck, 1961, Hood-Williams, 1960; Levitt, 1957, 1960). These critiques undoubtedly heightened the receptivity of a new generation of professionals to conditioning and behavior modification (Gelfand, 1969; Staats, 1971; Ross, 1981).

The professional field of psychotherapy with children today has more different kinds of procedures than it ever did. There are not only divisions among different systems of psychotherapy, but also the increasing numbers of other kinds of therapies whose relationship to psychotherapy is not altogether clear. For example, to many psychotherapists, behavior therapy is a form of training, not psychotherapy. There are some behavior therapists who agree with this point of view, though many others disagree. This ambiguity is not directly relevant to the public, but it indicates what has been a central problem for the profession: no consensus about the meaning of certain terms (in this instance, psychotherapy). Because this book is about psychotherapy, it is appropriate to make clear what we mean by the term.

The Definition of Psychotherapy

First, psychotherapy is best defined according to what those who make use of this method do, rather than what they intend or hope to accomplish. This reasonable stipulation takes intended effects of the treatment—the improvement of the client's condition, the creation of a special learning process or relationship—and divorces them from being definitive of psychotherapy. By so doing, it leaves open for investigation or research the conditions under which a given form of psychotherapy may be effective, as well as what the effects of this treatment may be for given clients. It emphasizes the distinction between what is psychotherapy (which refers to some particular procedure or activity of the therapist) and what is merely psychotherapeutic (anything that has some favorable effect on a person's psychological well-being). Eating ice cream, taking a brisk walk on a warm day, and watching a football game may be psychotherapeutic, but they are not psychotherapy.

Furthermore, this stipulation makes the aims or goals of psychotherapy separate from its definition. By doing this, it becomes possible to determine the existence of psychotherapy wherever it may occur, without depending upon the practitioner for a statement of intent. Thus, the way is open for conceiving of psychotherapy outside of professional relationships and for identifying it in varying amounts in many forms of human interaction.

Second, although legal and ethical considerations require that the public practice of psychotherapy be restricted to qualified professionals, it should be recognized that because psychotherapy is something that is done, there are probably people who do it without being professional therapists. This means its definition should not stipulate its being performed only by mental health personnel. In this way it can be thought of as being produced by anyone who performs this type of activity, and it can be recognized when the professional therapist is not engaged in its practice.

This point immediately suggests distinctions between psychotherapy as it is practiced professionally and as it may be discovered to occur "naturally." Professional psychotherapy would be expected to be a deliberate effort by the practitioner to perform this activity; therefore, its occurrence with a client would probably be frequent, consistent, deliberate, and systematic. In contrast, its occurrences in everyday situations would probably be haphazard, casual, infrequent, and unintegrated. But this prediction, if confirmed, should be little cause for professionals to be content. Rather, it can be argued that a major task for the professional is to help the public to make use of psychotherapy more often in their dealings with one another.

Third, the activity of psychotherapy must be made explicit. Some definitions of psychotherapy err by being too vague. Unsatisfactory definitions lead to the conclusion that everything psychotherapists do during their meetings with clients is psychotherapy, or that beneficial psychological changes are the only evidence that psychotherapy has been conducted. Neither conclusion makes much sense.

Mindful of these considerations, Reisman (1971) defined psychotherapy in a very broad and fundamental sense as *the communication of person-related understanding, respect, and a wish to be of help*. This definition makes clear the basic type of activity that is psychotherapy, and it offers a means for determining when the communications of a given person may be instances of this method of treatment.

The terms of the definition are straightforward in their meanings, though research may suggest qualifications and refinements. *Person-related understanding* refers to all communications that attempt to comprehend the client's or other person's thoughts, feelings, and behaviors, regardless of whether this understanding is based on Freudian, Skinnerian, or any other theory. *Respect* denotes a positive regard for the individual's dignity, rights, uniqueness, and capacities for constructive change. *A wish to be of help* is simply that, and it implies that the professional is motivated by the desire to assist the person; this is usually assumed to be the case in the therapist-client relationship.

Insofar as psychotherapy with children is concerned, the definition proves its value by pointing out the limits of the subject matter. For example, play, art, dance, and work are not psychotherapy, though they may be therapeutic, unless there is someone to communicate an understanding of what the child is feeling, thinking, or doing while engaged in that activity; it is that communication that is psychotherapy. Some therapists describe their role as one in which they sit quietly while providing a warm, friendly, accepting presence—their only communication may be to say, "Time's up." Although this too may be therapeutic, it is probably not psychotherapy, unless of a very low order. Nor is it psychotherapy when the therapist seeks to intrude on a psychotic child's awareness and compel attention to an outside world by forcing eye contact. It is also not psychotherapy when the therapist tries to inhibit the impulses of the child or to teach the child a particular behavior. Despite the merit of these activities, the definition specifies that psychotherapy is a certain kind of communication. Presumably, for this communication to be meaningful and effective, the child should be able to attend to it and to understand it. To the extent that the therapist does or does not engage in this form of communication, psychotherapy is or is not being practiced, though its effectiveness depends also on the extent to which it is perceived by the child.

Definitions of behavior therapy generally state that its procedures and understanding are based on learning principles derived from experimentation, with the aims of modifying specific presenting behaviors and monitoring the effectiveness of the interventions (Linehan, 1980). There is nothing to preclude behavior therapists from using psychotherapy, or psychotherapists from using behavioral techniques. It should be understood, however, that the training and tutoring of a child are no more psychotherapy than would be the training or tutoring of a dog or parrot.

Although this definition of psychotherapy excludes some behaviors, it includes all theoretical systems of understanding. It is to be hoped that as evidence about psychotherapy accumulates, refinements in the definition will be introduced, such as which systems or types of understanding are particularly effective in increasing people's understanding of themselves, enhancing their self-esteem, and making their attitude and behaviors more positive.

Moreover, although this definition promotes the development of psychotherapy as a form of everyday communication, this book is addressed to the professional use of psychotherapy. It seeks to describe the conduct of this kind of communication and the ways in which it may be used in a deliberate and systematic manner. Therefore, issues must be considered that are not properly part of psychotherapy as communication, but are germane to its offering as a professional service. For instance, although we encourage psychotherapy in the communications that take place between all human beings, we recognize that when this communication occurs as a professional service, there must be some discrimination in deciding for whom it is appropriate. This is a most important consideration not only for practitioners but also for parents, who after all are expected to pay for the psychotherapy their children receive. It is this issue, which involves the question of the effectiveness of psychotherapy, that will be examined next.

Indications for Professional Psychotherapy

The pioneering therapists who worked with children in the early twentieth century filled the literature with glowing reports of their successes and enthusiastic endorsements of psychotherapy. The children of analysts-in-training were often seen in play therapy as a combination of "prophylactic analysis" and baby-sitting while their parents were undergoing their own analyses (Astor, 1989). Up until about the middle of the century, it was not uncommon to see play therapy recommended for normal children as a healthful experience that could do no harm and might do some good (Moustakas, 1953).

Over the next decade reports about child psychotherapy became increasingly cautious, and evaluations of its effectiveness were highly skeptical. Reviews of the effectiveness of child psychotherapy (Eysenck, 1961; Hood-Williams, 1960; Levitt, 1957, 1960) generally concluded that the numbers of children who benefited from psychotherapy were not significantly different from the numbers who improved without psychotherapy. There was much criticism and unhappiness about these conclusions, because they argued that even though the majority of children improved during psychotherapy, they would have improved in any event.

Some critics attacked the quality of the studies in the reviews; some argued the percentage of children who were in the nontreatment comparison group who were thought to be improved was spuriously inflated; and some felt better research was needed. It could also be argued that though the percentages of improvement in treatment and comparison groups were about the same, the children in the treatment group improved with greater speed or comfort (just as people who fly first class pay a premium for the service though they arrive at their destination no sooner than those who fly coach). Nevertheless, despite the exceptions taken to the findings about the effectiveness of child psychotherapy, these findings generally stood for close to 20 years (Barrett, Hampe, & Miller, 1978).

Beginning in the 1970s and extending into the 1980s, the research seemed to take a turn for the better, or at the least there appeared to be more studies in which treatment groups were compared with control groups on the same dependent measures. Of even more significance was the emergence of *meta-analysis,* a relatively new statistical procedure for comparing the results from different studies (Smith & Glass, 1977). A meta-analysis is basically a means for converting data into standard scores: the mean for the control group is subtracted from that for the treatment group, this result is divided by either the standard deviation (*SD*) of the control group or the pooled *SD* of the groups in the study; the statistic that emerges from this computation is called the *effect size,* which is computed for each of the studies being compared.

When Smith and Glass (1977) and Smith, Glass, and Miller (1980) reported their meta-analysis of psychotherapy outcome studies, the judgment of the effectiveness of psychotherapy changed from "ineffective" or "inconclusive" to "psychotherapy produces significantly greater improvements than occur in no treatment control groups." Put another way, significantly more of the people seen in treatment had better outcomes than people who were not in treatment. There quickly followed reviews of outcome research with children and adolescents employing meta-analyses. One review examined 75 studies of treatment with children 12 years old and younger (Casey & Berman, 1985). For the major analysis there were 64 studies, of which 40 involved behavioral therapies and 24 involved client-centered and psychodynamic psychotherapies. The conclusions from this review were that treatment was effective (the mean effect size was .71.), and behavioral therapies were significantly more effective than nonbehavioral (mean effect size of .91 vs. .40). The reviewers cautioned, however, that behavior therapies frequently have training programs directed at the same specific performances as those used as measures of outcome (for example, a child is trained to be less fearful of school, and the measure of improvement is fearfulness of school). When such studies were removed, the effect sizes for behavioral and nonbehavioral therapies were not significantly different.

A second review with similar results was based on 108 studies of children and adolescents in treatment (Weisz, Weiss, Alicke, & Klotz, 1987). This review suggested that children responded better to treatment than adolescents (mean effect size of .92 vs. .58), but it is difficult to know whether the two age groups presented problems of comparable difficulty. There was also evidence found for greater effectiveness of treatment to be associated with greater training of the therapist: the mean effect size for professional therapists was 1.03; for graduate students, it was .71; and for paraprofessioonals, it was .53. This is a predicted (though seldom obtained) finding, and further research is needed to determine its reliability.

In any case, by the latter half of the 1980s, and despite some misgivings about the validity of the studies (Weisz, Weiss, & Donenberg, 1992) it was generally accepted that psychotherapy was an effective method of treatment for children and adults. It reduced the severity of symptoms, speeded the process of healing or recovery, and helped people acquire new techniques for coping with their personal problems. There was also agreement that the evidence showing the greater effectiveness of one therapy over another was meager, and that in every system of therapy, relationship factors of therapist warmth, wisdom, acceptance, and trust are crucial.

Moreover, given further research and time, the early enthusiasm for behavior therapies had moderated. There was no question about the effectiveness of behavioral techniques, but there were questions about the duration of improvements, the generalizability of gains made in training, and the value of certain procedures (Ollendick, 1986). It was even acknowledged there could be failures in behavior therapy for many of the same reasons once thought peculiar only to psychotherapy: clients dropping out and failing to cooperate, inexplicable relapses, and the treatment evidently being inappropriate for the person (Foa & Emmelkamp, 1983).

To summarize, the consensus is that psychotherapy and behavior therapy are effective interventions with children, adults, and families (Gurman, Kniskern, & Pinsof, 1986). There is still much, however, that needs to be learned from research about enhancing the effectiveness of these procedures (Kazdin, Bass, Ayers, & Rodgers, 1990), including about when psychotherapy should be offered.

Psychological problems are present in varying degrees and are tolerated and dealt with differently by different people. Their very commonness makes it uncertain how seriously to take them. Because almost everyone has some sort of psychological problem and experiences periods of unhappiness and personal dissatisfaction, it is usually not the presence or absence of difficulties that is the primary factor in determining whether psychotherapy is sought and received. Instead, a number of factors are involved in determining the appropriateness of psychotherapy: (a) the severity of the disorder, with the most disabling disturbances tending to compel professional intervention but often to contraindicate the use of individual psychotherapy; (b) the attitude of the client toward psychological services and practitioners, with a favorable attitude being more likely to elicit a constructive responsiveness from professionals; (c) the attitude of the client toward the problems and what can be done about them (an old joke: How many clinical psychologists does it take to change a light bulb? One, but the light bulb has to want to change.); and (d) the availability of services for the given individual.

With children, the issue is complicated further by the fact that they are dependent upon adults for seeing to it that they receive the help they need. This dependence may prevent some children from receiving professional assistance, even though they desire it and professionals believe it is appropriate and are willing to make it available. At the same time, this dependence may bring some children to a psychotherapist despite their strong opposition to help. Probably every child psychotherapist has seen children who begin by saying they have very little understanding of why they are being seen and who profess to be quite satisfied with their behavior and life circumstances, whereas there may be other children who want to be seen in psychotherapy but whose parents refuse to permit it. This emphasizes the great importance of the parents (or of the adults who have parental responsibilities) in the practice of psychotherapy with children and in the determination of whether professional psychotherapy is considered and employed.

A study of children referred to a guidance clinic in Great Britain attests to the significance of the variables just discussed (Shepherd, Oppenheim, & Mitchell, 1966). One group of 50 children who had been treated in the clinic was compared with a group of 50 youngsters, matched for age and symptom patterns, who had not been referred for psychotherapy. For example, a 5-year-old boy who received treatment for enuresis was matched with a 5-year-old boy in the general population who was enuretic and whose parents had not requested treatment for him. One of the interesting questions raised by this study was why one child with a given problem was referred, whereas another was not. The authors found that the major factor relating to referral in their sample was the personality functioning of the mother. The mothers who went to the child guidance clinic tended to be depressed, anxious, easily upset by stress, and perplexed by their children's problems. Not surprisingly, they were worried and uncertain about what to do and turned to professionals for help. The mothers of children in the other group, however, were comparatively casual about the disturbed behaviors of their offspring. They tended to see their children's difficulties as temporary, minor upheavals or setbacks that would be outgrown with patience and time. These results suggest that mothers who are apt to seek professional assistance for their children are likely to be unsure of themselves and their roles, whereas mothers who do not try to get help include those who have self-confidence and believe they have the stability and competence to tolerate the mild to moderate disturbances of youth and to deal with them on their own.

A most important qualification to the study just cited is that approximately 25% of the children treated in the clinic had disorders so severe that it was not possible to match them with children in the general population not receiving help. In other words, the researchers found that another significant variable in determining referrals was the severity of the disturbance; some disorders are so profound that parents are compelled to obtain the aid of professionals. Among the seriously handicapping problems of childhood are two worthy of specific mention: schizophrenia and autism.

Although, fortunately, both autism and schizophrenia in children are relatively rare, they are so very disabling that when they occur, the parents' anguish may arouse communitywide concern. Justification for this concern is apparent from a consideration of the symptoms used in establishing the diagnoses of these disorders.

When first described by Leo Kanner (1943, 1944), early infantile autism was diagnosed on the basis of three essential symptoms: (a) withdrawn and avoidant behaviors from all human contacts, noticed by the parents during the first year and seeming to exist virtually from birth; (b) speech disorders such as mutism, echolalia, or some other failing to make use of language in normal communication; and (c) an insistence upon following routine or engaging in repetitive acts, with great distress when there are changes or disruptions. Kanner estimated there might be 1 child in 10,000 who fit this symptom picture. In later years the age of onset was broadened, and in the current nomenclature (American Psychiatric Association, 1987), *autistic disorder* has an age of onset up to 36 months and may even be diagnosed as of *childhood onset* when the symptoms occur between the ages of 3 to 7 years. With the change in age of onset there have been increases in the estimates of prevalence. Wing, O'Connor, and Lotter (1967) reported an incidence of 4.5 per 10,000, and the criteria of DSM-III-R are certain to lead to greater prevalence figures and probable overdiagnosis of the disorder (Volkmar, Bregman, Cohen, & Cicchetti, 1988). Thus, there is a likelihood in the 1990s of a "tightening" of the criteria, particularly with regard to the onset of symptoms. Whatever happens, it is obvious the symptoms associated with autism present a formidable obstacle to being of help with psychotherapeutic techniques.

Schizophrenia is diagnosed when, after a relatively normal period of development, the following incapacitating symptoms appear: (a) disorganized or bizarre use of speech; (b) hallucinations or delusions; and (c) markedly impaired relationships with people. These symptoms are required to last for a period of at least 6 months to qualify for diagnosis. As might be expected, both schizophrenia and autism are characterized by many secondary symptoms resulting from the pronounced handicaps that these children have in dealing with educational situations and interacting with others.

That these children need help cannot be disputed. It is questionable, however, whether the help they need is professional psychotherapy. As previously indicated, psychotherapy is a method of treatment predicated on the use of communication, and the hallmark of these disorders is extreme impairment in the communicative process. One of the few psychotherapists who reported some success in treating these children with psychotherapy was Bruno Bettelheim (1967), but this was under conditions (placement in a residential therapeutic setting for several years) that are not readily available, and that in similar settings have not been found to yield similar results (Kemph, 1964). A prudent conclusion has been that professional psychotherapy is not a particularly effective means for the initial treatment of autism and schizophrenia (Knowlton, 1967), but that it may be appropriate after behavioral techniques (Lovaas, 1968, 1987) or other methods of treatment (DesLauriers & Carlson, 1969; Zaslow & Breger, 1969) have helped the child become accessible to it.

Psychotherapy seems to be a more suitable treatment for dealing with the comparatively mild to moderate problems of childhood and for initiating and maintaining a cooperative therapeutic stance, regardless of the treatment. Its use is associated, at times with dramatic suddenness, with the occurrence of favorable changes in attitudes and behaviors. It should be noted, though, that these problems are "mild" from the perspective of the professional, who is knowledgeable about the wide spectrum of disorders. For children who experience fears, unhappiness, inhibitions, immature habits or behaviors, difficulties in getting along with others, and failures in school, as well as for their involved parents, such problems are serious and extremely troubling.

These minor to moderate disturbances constitute the great majority of those that occur in childhood. If clinical appraisals of adults and adolescents are any guide to the prevalence of mild to moderate psychological problems among children, then perhaps 80% of children would be found to have one or more of them (Weiner, 1970, p. 52). Even this estimate, large though it seems, may actually err on the side of conservatism. Whenever surveys of symptoms among children are conducted (Cummings, 1944; Lapouse & Monk, 1964; Miller, Hampe, Barrett, & Noble, 1972), virtually every child is reported to have a symptom or two, including laziness, restlessness, and daydreaming. Jersild (1960) calculated that the symptom of unreasonable and persistent fears and worries alone is manifested by some 50% of children.

Indeed, as mentioned earlier, the very prevalence of these disorders prompts many professionals to doubt that they are of pathological significance. Generally, the arguments advanced to view them benignly are of two types. The first is simply that because most children have psychological problems, then in a statistical sense they represent what is normal, whereas the happy and successful child is the one who is abnormal (Valentine, 1956). It is therefore concluded that because it is statistically normal for children to have problems, nothing really needs to be done about them. This line of reasoning, which is an excursion into sophistry more than into good sense, may be countered by noting that it is also statistically normal for people to have colds, headaches, eye defects, and dandruff, and yet these disorders are not ignored. Moreover, the prevalence of a behavior is only one factor in weighing its significance: "Normality . . . is an informed judgment concerning the age-specific effective handling of life's difficulties and challenges, the satisfactory development in feelings about oneself and others, and the modulated expression of behavior" (Reisman, 1986, p. 29).

The second type of argument against regarding the troubles of childhood as indicative of pathology to be treated is based on observations that many seemingly well-adjusted adults showed disorders of behavior in their youth. For example, Kanner (1960) reported that in his sample of apparently successful men, some admitted they had been enuretic up to 13 years of age without being seen in psychotherapy. A similar favorable course of development was found for other men in connection with other symptoms. These results are not unlike those found by Robins (1966) in a follow-up of "neurotic" child guidance clinic patients, and those obtained when treated groups are compared with controls on percentages of improved patients, as in the Shepherd et al. (1966) study. What is typically found is that about two thirds of children (and about two thirds of adults, for that matter) with mild to moderate problems improve with or without professional intervention.

Psychotherapists respond to this argument by emphasizing that, first, it is of value to facilitate and contribute to a recovery process, and second, many clients are in great distress and experience relief when someone attends to their complaints and endeavors to be of help to them. As Kessler (1966, p. 70) asked rhetorically, "Does the medical profession ignore the usual childhood diseases because all children have them and they ordinarily run their course without permanent aftereffects?"

Furthermore, even if these disorders improve with time—and there is some reason to question this assumption (Masterson, 1967)—this would not mean that they are *best* dealt with by being complacently ignored. It is a fact of the human condition that every problem is eventually put to rest. *Thus, any professional intervention is always a matter of values and priorities.* Who can deny that our society has the resources to address psychological disturbances and that the problems experienced by any child are of significance?

In this book, we assume that mild to moderate difficulties in the adjustment of children may merit professional assistance in order to bring about improvement in the best possible manner. At the same time, we recognize that not every psychological problem requires psychotherapy or responds well to this method of treatment. In order to make discriminations among these problems, the professional therapist must in assessing the situation take into account the assessments and wishes of the child, the parents, and often other involved parties as well (such as the family physician and school personnel). These various understandings of the "same" psychological problem will now be considered.

The Professional's Assessment of Disturbance

The client of the professional child psychotherapist does not live in isolation. The child is a member of a family, or is in some setting where adults are obliged by law to exercise control and parental responsibilities. Therefore, a child is compelled to depend upon adults for survival and must somehow come to an accommodation with them.

The adults with whom children interact reward some of their behaviors, are indifferent to others, and may be extremely punitive with regard to acts they find objectionable. These responses shape much of the children's behaviors, influence their self-concepts and their attitudes toward their world, color their expectations of how people will treat them, and are important in determining the nature of their disturbances.

In almost every case of mild to moderate disorder, the problem exhibited by the child has not been dealt with effectively by important adults. Frequently they have tried to compel the child to perform up to their standards in circumstances over which they actually have no control, such as by demanding the attainment of certain grades in school and then feeling personally defeated by anything less. Often they have unknowingly encouraged undesirable behaviors in the child by their protestations of frustration and helplessness in being able to control him or her. Many times they have heard but not listened to, or talked to, but not with, their child.

All of this is commonplace to professionals, but it constitutes a unique, baffling, disheartening problem for the parents in question. Although therapists have no interest in assigning blame and exacting retribution, they must be sensitive to the possibility that this is what some parents may fearfully expect. They may ask for an explanation of what is wrong—and it would not be unusual for the therapist to have a fairly complete understanding of much that is involved rather quickly—but rarely would it be wise to share more than one or two of these insights at any one time, or very early in the treatment.

The therapist may see the child's disorder as an expression of inadequate parental training, as an assertion of autonomy in a world of enforced obedience, or as a means of communicating the depth and intensity of emotions and wishes. Whatever the understanding of the therapist may be, the context in which the behavior occurs (and, in particular, the actions and attitudes of family members) must be assessed to determine what can be used to modify the child's adjustment for the better.

The therapist sees three major kinds of psychological problems in childhood. Each involves some disruption of the course of development, and therefore its assessment is predicated on knowledge of normal psychological growth.

Retardations

The first kind of problem is a slowing or retardation in development. Despite stimulation and opportunities for learning provided by their environment, children with mental retardation display markedly less progress in language skills, visual-motor coordination, and memory than do their peers. Moreover, even when provided with extra tutorial assistance in these areas, they do not improve sufficiently to reach the level of achievement more readily attained by their normally developing classmates. These children are sometimes called "slow learners," an unfortunate euphemism because it often misleads parents to believe that their child is limited only in speed of acquisition and not in eventual accomplishment.

Identification of the problem, however, does not mean parents need be discouraged. It is essential to the assessment to determine the degree of retardation and to remember that skills other than academic ones may enable the child to enjoy considerable success in adulthood. Retardation covers a broad range of behaviors that are in part determined by the values, complexities, and demands of our society. Although most children who are retarded continue to show intellectual limitations throughout their lives, they can be useful, productive, reasonably happy citizens.

Most children diagnosed as mentally retarded seem to have no physical anomaly that can account for their disorder. In previous times it was hypothesized that such children were emotionally disturbed, their low intellectual functioning for no apparent physical reason being prima facie evidence of neurosis. Today, the prevailing view is these children represent the lower end of the normal continuum of intellectual functioning, and that many of them may have been deprived of adequate stimulation and educational experiences. Thus, environmental enrichment and compensatory training are advocated for their benefit.

Although there may be rare exceptions, there is little support for the hypothesis of neurosis; in fact, many retarded children seem well adjusted. Of course, some of these children may have emotional problems, but this may be no more a function of their retardation than the problems of persons at the other end of the intellectual continuum are attributable to their superior abilities. Accordingly, the mentally retarded or intellectually subnormal child is not by that fact alone in need of psychotherapy.

Special educational help for these children is a parental and community responsibility. Given parents, teachers, and peers who are understanding and accepting of these children, and given a satisfactory plan for their schooling, it is unlikely that the services of the professional psychotherapist will be desired or required. When retardations are thought of in a subtle and broad sense, however, many of the behaviors that are so distressing to parents and other adults may be found to be determined in large part by failures to train children properly. Enuresis, encopresis, disobedience, and many other disturbances may be behaviors that adults have handled ineffectively.

A mother will tell of her son walking away from her and her commanding him again and again to return. But he does not; he just keeps walking. This mother will complain that her son does not listen to and obey her, and she says she has no idea about what to do to get him to mind. She appears to have no appreciation for the fact that children must learn that words have meanings associated with their consequences, and so it is necessary for her to get up and move actively to bring about her son's compliance with her commands. In situations where parents are obviously ineffective in dealing with their child and are asking for information about what to do, a first step (and perhaps the only necessary one) may be to inform or train the parents regarding how to handle their children.

Fixations

A second major indication of disturbance takes the form of fixations, or developmental arrests. A fixation is an unreasonable persistence of some behavior, wish, emotion, or means of gaining satisfaction beyond the age when it is appropriate and accepted. The stipulation that the persistence is unreasonable refers to the judgments of the adults concerned, and perhaps of the child as well.

Professionals suggest a number of reasons for the continuance of a particular behavior. Psychodynamic formulations assume excessive frustrations or gratifications at a relevant stage of development are involved. Behaviorists postulate a problem in learning or training: someone may inadvertently be rewarding the child for performing the act or adults may have been unreliable in their teaching. Within the psychiatric nomenclature are a number of disorders where a distinction is made between primary and secondary types. *Primary* here refers to the child's persistence in a behavior (fixation), while *secondary* refers to the child resuming the age-inappropriate behavior after an interval of normal performance (regression).

To a degree, all people are fixated in the sense that they remember their past, there is continuity in their growth, and old pleasures and wounds act to determine future behaviors. Thus, fixations in and of themselves are not regarded as pathological. It is only when they are so extensive that they prevent the child from being able to deal with the problems and demands of the moment, or when they persist in virtually unmodified and inflexible forms, that the professional regards them as indicative of abnormality.

Knowledge of the range of variability for the behavior in question is essential to the distinction that the professional makes between fixated and normal behavior. Temper tantrums and a refusal to share toys are not unusual for a 3-year-old, but they are out of the ordinary for a child of 8. Bed-wetting is common among 2-year-olds, but not among children who are 4 or 5. Imaginary playmates are usually not to be found among children who have entered school, though they are frequently found among preschoolers in need of peer relationships.

The professional also has to assess what has been done to try to modify the behavior; this information is helpful in deciding whether the behavior requires psychotherapy or further educational efforts. Care must be exercised in obtaining specific data from the parents. It is not uncommon for a professional to hear parents say that they have tried valiantly to train their child, only to learn that what they mean is they did their best for a day or so and then gave up. Probably every child therapist has encountered a family with an enuretic boy whose mother describes years of dutifully changing the bed linen each morning while allowing the child to drink several glasses of water at bedtime each night because he is thirsty.

Although there are times when it appears that one or both of the parents—and not the child—are fixated, it is best to approach the parents at first as a consultant, rather than as a therapist. In other words, assume the parents who ask for your recommendations want them and may be able to implement them. But proceed slowly and with flexibility in this plan; after giving a suggestion to the parents, note whether they regard it as helpful. Do they show some eagerness to carry it out, or do they doubt it will work? Are they silent, uncomprehending, sullen, unenthusiastic, or perhaps even hostile? If the parents recognize their need for change and the rightness of the therapist's recommendations, but show signs of being unable to cooperate in a treatment program, then probably some time will have to be set aside for their counseling in order to ensure they can be of help to their child. Some of these points are illustrated in the following case.

Bill's parents were not especially responsive to suggestions when they were first seen, and yet they eventually proved to be quite effective in following some simple bits of advice. Their son, a strikingly handsome 8-year-old, was doing so poorly in school that he was in danger of being required to repeat the third grade. He had been doing mediocre work ever since the first grade, and this was proving to be more and more of a handicap to him. Examinations by physicians and by the school psychologist suggested Bill could do better, and that certainly he should not be failing. He was well behaved and likable, and so everyone was distressed by his learning problems—as, supposedly, was Bill by the disappointments he was causing his parents. At home Bill had never been a problem; in fact, his parents proudly reported he was a big help to them around the house. Both described him as a nice, obedient, quiet child who had been struck down by some mysterous malady.

Bill's impression of what was wrong differed considerably from that of his parents. Although he recognized his failures in school, his immediate concern was to have someone who would listen to him and begin to take his complaints seriously: "I have to do the dishes and take out the garbage every night, and every Saturday I have to mow the lawn when there's cartoons on. And we have a big hill in our back with leaves and sticks. It's hard for me to push that mower with all that smoke and everything. I sure wish my father would do it, but he says I have to." More than anything else, Bill wanted the therapist to bring the mowing to the attention of his parents, and the therapist agreed to do so.

The therapist speculated that Bill's interactions with his parents had fallen into a pattern, in terms of which it might be said that Bill was fixated. Despite his feelings that he was exploited and that impossible demands were being made upon him, Bill did very little to make his objections known openly. Instead, he would seem to do what was expected of him but actually perform in a manner that he recognized was unsatisfactory. He exhibited a similar pattern in school, where in addition he displaced much of the resentment he felt toward his parents onto his teachers, all of whom he described as unfair and overdemanding.

Bill's parents knew about his dislike of lawn mowing, but they claimed not to realize that he was so bothered by it he would tell the therapist about it. His mention of the mowing to a professional underscored its importance and caused them to regard it more seriously than they had. His father admitted that he was always critical of Bill's work, and that he knew the hill area of his property was both dangerous and physically burdensome for a child of 8. Nevertheless, he said, "I told Bill he had to mow the lawn, even though he doesn't do a good job, because I'm too busy."

The therapist proposed a compromise whereby Bill would mow the large flat portion of the lawn, and his father would mow the hill. It was also suggested that the parents distinguish between Bill's efforts to comply with authority and the results of his efforts—that they praise him for trying to do well whether or not he was successful and encourage him to do his best in school regardless of what marks he might achieve. Psychotherapy for Bill and counseling for his parents were also recommended. Within a month after this program of treatment began, Bill's parents reported that he was getting A's and B's on his papers in school, and that a decided improvement in his work was noticed by his teacher.

Regressions

A third major indication of disturbance is regression in behavior. The child seems to be developing normally and then displays relatively immature behavior, usually after a crisis or unwanted change. The birth of a sibling, divorce or separation of parents, the death of a relative, a move to a new neighborhood or school, abuse of the child, demands to engage in hetero-sexual relationships, and the breaking away from parents are typical situations that can elicit regressive reactions. It is common to hear parents observe that following the birth of their baby, one of their other children began to wet the bed or to bother them for affection. It is less common for parents to recognize that the emotional upheavals of adolescence are often regressed behaviors to familiar conflicts about limits and rules.

Regressions in the child's development can be normal, both in the sense that most people find it appropriate from time to time to relax and to indulge in less mature behavior, and in the sense that temporary reactions of this kind occur quite frequently in response to stress, illness, and fatigue. What distinguishes pathological from normal regression is the former's persistence, its maladaptive nature, its inappropriateness, and the child's feeling that the behavior is not under control. Because a regression is by definition a departure from a behavior already acquired and well practiced (or a return to conflicts previously mastered), it is obvious to the parents or teacher that something is wrong, and they may become very alarmed.

"What's gotten into her?" is the sort of question parents ask of the therapist. They express puzzlement about the change in their child's attitudes, and they profess a willingness to cooperate so things can be made right again. With the alleviation of the symptom, however, there is the feeling of everything having returned to normal. Often psychotherapy comes to an abrupt end, though not necessarily a disappointing one if the therapist can take satisfaction in doing the best job possible under the circumstances. The crisis experienced by Joan and her parents illustrates much of what has been said.

Joan's problem became apparent in the middle of her freshman year in high school. She had never had difficulties before and was described as "a model student" and "a teacher's dream." Her grades were always high, practically all A's, and she excelled in creative writing and dramatics. In the opinion of her parents, Joan could easily have all the friends she wanted, but for some reason she had been cutting herself off from social contacts for the past year. Of more immediate concern was that for several months she had been refusing to go to school. She would complain of headaches, stomach pains, and nausea each morning before school and plead to remain at home. The family physician could find nothing medically wrong with Joan, and a variety of special arrangements had been tried in order to help her attend class (such as having her parents or a social worker take her, and arranging her program so she would only have to attend half days). None of them had worked.

Joan was a stunningly pretty adolescent, with large, dark eyes and long black hair. Although she wore a very short skirt, her head was tilted down as if to say she was a sweet, innocent little girl who was embarrassed by the exposure of her legs. Throughout her interview with the therapist, she maintained an attitude of primness, speaking softly with eyes lowered. On occasion she would look up quickly to scrutinize the therapist's face in order to ascertain the impact of her words, thus seeming to be suspicious and testing.

The problem, as Joan saw it, was that her classmates were preoccupied with sex: "That's all they talk about, and that's all they're interested in." She was convinced that all the smiling and giggling that took place in school had to do with sex. Moreover, she was certain that notes and whispered conversations were sexual in content. The pervasiveness of this topic at school gave her a "dirty feeling" she could not tolerate and which "makes me sick." Furthermore, her peers' sexual monomania estranged Joan from them. Her own interests were fine and noble, things like good literature and the writing of poetry. She was particularly proud of a sonnet she had written that described a girl's enduring love for a tree, a tree that would soon die because of old age.

At an interview with Joan's parents, her mother sat quietly and said little other than to express concern about her daughter being in the house all day. Her father, however, agreed with his daughter's evaluation of her peers and suggested that, if anything, his daughter's assessment of the situation was conservative: "Isn't she right! Isn't it true! Look around you in this world. I hate to say it, but that's what you see all over. Filth and sex!" Nevertheless, he agreed to allow Joan to be seen in psychotherapy and to cooperate with efforts to have her return to school. Two weeks later Joan began her second regularly scheduled session with her therapist by announcing that since she had been attending school regularly, she wished to stop the meetings. Despite the therapist's misgivings about the abruptness of this decision, her parents agreed with her, and the sessions were terminated.

Joan's behavior illustrates not only a regression and a problem of some seriousness, but also a controversy in the evaluation of outcome. Some therapists would see her return to school as an indication of success in crisis intervention, brief therapy, or a behavioral treatment such as in vivo desensitization. After all, she was no longer sick in the morning, and she had been in school every day for two weeks. But other therapists would wonder about the peculiar attitudes expressed by Joan and her father, and how they could possibly be modified in so short a time with so little effort. If we assume these attitudes were not modified (not an unreasonable assumption), they might well be expected to interfere with Joan's social relationships and effectiveness. Yet, we must admit, Joan represents an extreme more than an exception. At the end of psychotherapy the therapist sees many clients who still have problems (though perhaps not the ones for which they originally sought help), so that termination is often a compromise between standards of ideal functioning and practical demands. This is an issue that will be discussed throughout this book.

A Professional's Point of View

The professional's assessment of disturbance is also a matter of some controversy among therapists. Rogers (1951), for one, contended that a diagnostic assessment and preoccupation detract from a proper empathic attitude and have little redeeming value. This assertion has no research to support it and is contradicted by the many therapists who believe empathic understanding depends upon perceiving the client within the context of a history, a situation, and previous remarks, among other variables. A pragmatic criticism of diagnosis is to question its value when the treatment plan is about the same for everyone. Such a criticism is particularly cogent when quibbling about the diagnosis and insisting upon additional evaluations may delay the client from receiving prompt and desired treatment. Certainly we do not intend that decisions about whether behaviors are fixations or regressions should be paramount concerns.

Nevertheless, although an argument to do away with diagnosis may have some validity with relatively well-integrated adults who voluntarily seek out psychotherapy for help in dealing with their worries and concerns, it becomes untenable when dealing with children. A child is usually referred for help because of failure to satisfy the expectations of adults, and this failure may be determined by the unreasonableness of the expectations just as well as by problems of the child. Although it may be safe to assume that the poor work of a college student is brought about by psychological conflicts (and one could easily question even this assumption), the failures of young children in school can have a variety of determinants with a number of different treatment plans.

In every case the professional must evaluate the behavior in question, the situation or context in which it occurs, and the circumstances in which the child lives in order to determine what treatment plan is indicated or most feasible. This evaluation, however, proceeds with some degree of flexibility. Sometimes psychological tests and procedures are selected to address the questions posed by this individual. For example, an adolescent who is referred for disobeying her parents by staying out late at night is a diagnostic problem of a different order from the 3-year-old who still does not talk.

In other words, a psychological assessment is always of importance, but it is a means to an end, not an end in itself. Its purpose is to aid in the formulation of a treatment plan. Because people differ, the assessment procedure should differ. It should not become a routine, and it should not persist to the detriment of helping the child. Absurd as it may sound, some diagnostic evaluations are so prolonged that by their conclusion the parents have become discouraged and have sought help elsewhere, leaving the diagnostician with a fine understanding but no one with whom to share it. Diagnosis and treatment are complementary activities that should be regarded not as separate phases, but as interrelated functions that are subject to revision so long as contacts with and about the client are maintained.

The Child's Assessment of Disturbance

As can be seen in the discussions of Bill and Joan, the child's understanding of what is wrong may be quite different from the assessments of parents and other adults. It is rare to find children who believe their behaviors are unreasonable and self-defeating. Quite the contrary is true: children usually believe that they have good reasons for behaving as they do in matters important to them. In this respect, they are not so different from adults who have characterological problems. Such adults project their attitudes and fears, and thus see a world that provides ample justification for their behaviors. So do many children, who complain bitterly of the mistreatment inflicted upon them by others and do not recognize their own responsibilities in bringing it about.

The child's denial of problems is often mentioned as a difference between the adult and child patient (A. Freud, 1965). It must be remembered that the child (unlike the adult) is brought to the therapist, perhaps with no explanation or some half-truth provided by apprehensive parents. There are times when the child really does not have a problem other than being in a situation where people are making unfair demands. Some children are brought more because of the problems of the adults than any problem of their own.

There are some children, however, whose statement that nothing is wrong is made with little conviction. When the concerns of their parents are mentioned, they may acknowledge difficulties in school or home but profess to be unconcerned about these matters. They sit quietly—like bridge players saying, "I pass"—whenever what they might do is mentioned. Yet they express no indignation about being seen by a therapist and usually indicate a willingness for continued interviews in psychotherapy when this is offered to them.

The Child's Problems

At times, the actions of children will immediately refute their denials and demonstrate the difficulties they have. A girl may hurl curses at her mother for leaving her with the therapist, while screaming at the therapist who reflects her feelings, "I love her, you son of a bitch!" A boy may have a violent temper tantrum in the office when he meets with some minor frustration, but yell that there is nothing wrong with him and that he does not know why he is being seen.

Almost every child who has siblings has complaints about them. If they are older, they are bullies. If they are younger, they are pests. Often children will state that improved relations with siblings is what they want most.

From the point of view of some children their major difficulty is with their parents, and this problem often translates into "They won't let me grow up." These children see their parents as overcontrolling, regardless of how permissive their parents believe themselves to be, and they want some relaxation of restrictions and expectations. A problem frequently encountered in trying to help them is that they may see the therapist as one more attempt by the parents to be controlling and to stifle their individuality.

Other children may feel "nervous" but will be unable to explain why. They have no complaints to offer about anyone, and they see their problems as centering around their own feelings. Some of these children may welcome a behavioral approach (such as relaxation training), and some may welcome the prospect of psychotherapy in part because they enjoy being with the therapist and experiencing a sense of safety and freedom.

The child's perception of what is wrong is of greatest importance because the child is the therapist's client. The therapist should arrive at some understanding with the child about why therapy is being offered and what its purposes or goals will be, and it is the child's assessment of the disturbance that serves as the basis for this understanding.

For example, Mary, 9 years old, was referred for help by her mother because she had been doing poorly in school and was "anxious and over-affectionate" with men. Her mother said Mary talked in a "nervous, giggly way" and would run up to strange men in supermarkets, hug them about their legs, and kiss them. Understandably, she had concerns that her daughter might be sexually exploited. She could not fully understand the reasons for Mary's behavior, though she supposed it might have something to do with her husband being away in the army.

In first meeting the therapist, Mary expressed her fear by shrinking herself in size and acting very immature. She was utterly, coyingly sweet, delightedly squealing about the "beautiful" toys in the office (which, as a matter of fact, were a rather battered and worn collection). At once she began playing with them, chattering all the while and bombarding the therapist with questions, thereby preventing him from asking any questions of his own. Her play centered around the family of dolls. She moved them about while assuming the role of a stern, scolding mother. From time to time she suddenly grabbed a toy pistol, "shot" the therapist, and laughed with great satisfaction.

At length, the therapist interrupted her play in order to assess her understanding of why she was being seen. Mary acknowledged her problems in school, especially with arithmetic, brushed off her mother's concern about the men, and stated what worried her most was her lack of friends: "The girls don't seem to like me. I don't know why, but they don't like me." It was on the basis of receiving help with her peer relationships and schoolwork that she eagerly sought additional appointments. Except to mention improvement in these problems, though, Mary discussed neither of them in the psychotherapy meetings that followed. Her sessions with the therapist dealt largely with the ways she attempted to structure and to dominate their relationship. As she became more honest and flexible in her dealing with him, she reported one day that she now had friends and was being invited to parties, so that this problem no longer existed.

The Parents' Assessment of Disturbance

It often happens that the behaviors that are of significance to the professional are of little importance to the parents. The behaviors of concern to the parents, however, must always receive the careful attention of the professional. Mary's mother was most worried about her daughter running up to and embracing strange men. If this behavior persisted, then regardless of how satisfied the therapist and Mary might have been with the outcome of therapy, Mary's mother would have been bitterly disappointed. As it turned out, during the course of psychotherapy Mary did attempt to engage in this behavior with the therapist, and thus it could be responded to and understood. But she ceased to do this outside the therapy, so the mother's concerns were addressed to her satisfaction.

In general, parents are most troubled about behaviors that increase the burdens and demands upon them. If their son is a problem in school but does what he is supposed to do at home, the parents, though sympathetic, are inclined to believe this is "his teacher's fault, because we don't let him get away with anything at home." A similar attitude may be expressed by parents whose children are involved in delinquent or antisocial acts. They see authorities as lax in discipline and too soft on children, and they argue if everybody would just be more punitive, the child would behave. Such parents are reluctant to profit from professional services, since they stoutly assert their competence and argue all would be well if others came around to their way of thinking. They have been urged or compelled to see the therapist by some authority in the community, not because they feel any need for assistance.

Other parents, however, may display an opposite (but also extreme) reaction to the matter of their responsibility. Sensing that difficulties in their child's adjustment may signify the existence of covert problems within the family, they are too quick to assume that they have failed totally as parents. Their readiness to blame themselves can interfere with their ability to attach the proper significance to events outside the family that may be damaging to their son or daughter. Parents who deny their influence and those who too readily accept their guilt are hampered in helping their children. Both may interefere with their children getting the assistance they need, the former by refusing to participate in treatment and the latter by interposing themselves in the treatment process to the exclusion of their children.

Probably the most constructive attitude for parents to have is an inquisitive and receptive one in which they are willing to investigate, to question, and to consider the various options and possibilities that professionals may advance, as well as to speculate and explore their own thoughts and hunches. This is not unlike the attitude that professionals who are trying to be of help to them and to their children will have.

Some parents fear encounters with professionals because they dread having their own disturbances uncovered. Over a period of years they reject one referral after another, only to find that the problem has not gone away and that their child will soon attain the status of an adult. At this crucial juncture in development they may reluctantly turn to professional assistance, hoping the experts can do something with their adolescent to ensure independence and the assumption of adult responsibilites. This was the situation with Michael and his parents.

Michael was 17 and had never done well in school, even though tests by school psychologists over the years indicated he was of average intellectual functioning and capable of satisfactory work. He was quiet and well behaved at home and at school, so his parents, who did not think he was particularly bright anyway, did not feel any compelling reason to follow recommendatons that he be seen at a child guidance clinic. Because he fell further behind his classmates in achievement each year, the school authorities finally concluded that if he were to have any chance at all to catch up, he should be in a special class for the mildly retarded. It was in this special, ungraded program that Michael remained from his later childhood through his adolescence. When he was on the verge of receiving a certificate attesting to his completion of high school, his parents began to wonder what kind of work he might be able to do and whether he could be self-supporting.

When first seen by the therapist, Michael was seated in the waiting room reading a copy of the *New York Times*. He claimed to prefer that paper and the *Christian Science Monitor* because they provided broader coverage of current events than was available locally. His speech had the quality of a sneering mumbling, and though his eyes were alert and furtive, his lips were pressed tight, and his face was empty of expression.

Michael described a lonely childhood, without friends or social activities except for the condescending companionship of elderly neighbors and trips to concerts with relatives. Yet he had no complaints about being lonely, nor did he share his parents' worries about getting a job. These were trivial matters in comparison with the problems that bothered him most: he was worried about the world coming to an end and about making his getaway as soon as possible. He explained that the only means of escape was by journey into space, but he recognized his special class education had not prepared him to be an astronaut. Therefore, Michael confided, he was prepared to accept a janitorial position with the National Aeronautics and Space Administration, sweeping out rocket hangars and launch pads at first and eventually working up to a position in a space vehicle.

It was possible for Michael to accept further appointments in order to consider alternative vocational plans in the likely event that NASA would not hire him. The therapists's diagnostic impression was of a schizoid personality, so the goals and expectations were modest; yet the therapist hoped that contacts would help Michael to feel less apprehensive about his future and more involved with people outside his immediate family. These hopes were realized. Several months after the treatment began, Michael enrolled in a training program conducted by the state's department of vocational rehabilitation to prepare him for an appropriate job.

Michael's parents did not become involved in his treatment. They could only see the problem as his, and they wished to distance themselves from him and from the therapist. Although their fear of the therapist is not very common, many parents are ambivalent about psychotherapy, and this can be destructive unless the therapist addresses their concerns and establishes a cooperative relationship with them.

Despite protestations and affirmations of wanting only to see their children helped, there are parents who actually fear that the therapist may be successful in accomplishing what they have failed to do. They have presented their child as stubborn, unwilling to listen, and insistent on doing things in a self-defeating way. They have pictured years of frustration and futility with a youngster who will not mind, will not listen, will not behave, and will not be motivated. They have offered their child as a supreme challenge to the therapist, and they have conveyed the conviction that here at last is the one child who cannot be reached.

After the child's meeting with the therapist, these parents are eager for a bad report and are disappointed if the child has discussed problems. If their child is seen in psychotherapy, they may be distressed by signs of improvement, seeing this progress as proof of their own inadequacies. Under these circumstances, the parents' resentment toward the psychotherapist and their own child may build. The therapist may be perceived as aloof, arrogant, and patronizing, and the child may appear to be an ingrate who would not confide in the parents but would run off at the mouth to a stranger.

Such a situation is not helped by professionals who believe they are showing their humanity and skills to parents who are truly inept. Therapists must be sensitive to parental ambivalence and their own ambivalent feelings. They must look at the situation and at themselves realistically, keeping in mind the advantages that they have that the parents do not.

Advantages of Child Therapists

One advantage that child psychotherapists have that parents do not is that the former are not personally responsible for the children's behaviors or their consequences. Children are brought to them exhibiting disorders, and the therapists know they themselves had nothing to do with bringing these problems about. Thus, they do not have to contend with feelings of guilt. Moreover, therapists, unlike parents, can be somewhat detached about children's failures and misbehaviors. When children do poorly in school or are arrested by the police, parents may be so distressed that they are unable to meet these crises effectively. Yet therapists can address these events with some equanimity and objectivity and so better understand their implications and the measures necessary to deal with them.

A second advantage is that children's difficulties may correspond exquisitely to problems their parents find particularly troublesome. Therapists, however, may not find the same behaviors quite so distressing, and hence may be better able to deal with them.

A third advantage is that therapists' contacts with children are limited in time. Ordinarily they see a child for about an hour an day, perhaps one or more times a week for a year or so. In most cases, their interactions with the child are far less frequent and protracted than those of the parents. These limited contacts enable therapists to be accepting of activities that might be tolerated less readily if exposure to them were prolonged.

A fourth advantage is that the space in which the child is seen by the therapist is intended specifically for this purpose. A playroom or play area is intended to allow the child freedom of expression by containing a minimum of fragile articles that could be damaged, by being designed for easy cleaning and durability, and by providing toys and materials that are sturdy, attractive, and inexpensive. Therefore the therapist is able to permit a wider range of behaviors than is possible in other settings (such as the home) where generally there are concerns about breakage, damage to furniture and valuables, and possible injury.

A fifth advantage is that psychotherapists reserve the appointed time exclusively for the child; they have nothing else to do but to be attentive to their clients. This is probably quite different from the experiences parents must provide, in which the child must compete with other children and other activities and interests for their notice.

A sixth advantage is that psychotherapists need make few demands upon the child. Unlike the parents, therapists are not held accountable for the child's grooming, dress, nourishment, health, safety, values, choice of language, and much more. They do not have particular chores or tasks they wish children to perform around the office, nor do they expect certain moral and religious beliefs. There is thus less occasion for them to become engaged in conflict with the child, as well as fewer opportunities for conflicts to arise.

A seventh advantage is that child therapists have been intensively trained for their field of work. They have become knowledgeable about human development and have acquired a familiarity with a number of different approaches to treatment, in addition to possessing special skills in the ones they ordinarily practice. They have read about and seen psychopathology. Their sensitivity to feelings has been sharpened, and they have been trained in the communication of their understanding, their respect, and their wish to be of help. Unlike parents, who may be quite puzzled by the child's behaviors and find them totally outside the realm of their own experiences, therapists have acquired a background in dealing with children who present similar problems.

With these advantages, is it so remarkable that psychotherapists can be patient, accepting, and understanding, and that they can offer the children they see a unique adult relationship? Of course, this is not to say that these advantages are not important—and perhaps essential—to the success of treatment. As can quickly be seen in the problems exemplified by Bill, Mary, Joan, and Michael, child psychotherapists can expect to see children who span the years from early childhood through adolescence. They must be prepared to assess a wide range of difficulties from a number of different perspectives, all the while giving thought to the influences of others and their possible role and involvement in bringing about a successful outcome. Child psychotherapists have a task that is not simple, and they are not born equipped to perform it. Their knowledge and skills are acquired, which suggests the purpose of this book: to promote such acquisitions and to communicate the practice of child psychotherapy.

In succeeding chapters the work of the child psychotherapist will be described in detail. Particular attention will be given to the principles that can be said to guide this work, for these principles provide direction in situations that are not discussed and that may be novel and strange. The major aim is to make clear what child psychotherapy is and what it may accomplish, not only for children but also for entire families and for those who wish to practice it.

2
Principles of Pyschotherapy

Many therapists of differing orientations agree that the same principles of psychotherapy apply to children and adults (Alexander, 1950; Rogers, 1951; White, 1964; Freud, 1965; Glasser, 1965; Szurek, 1967; Truax & Carkhuff, 1967; Clarizio & McCoy, 1970). The principles, however, are seldom presented according to what the therapist does. They are sometimes presented as generalities derived from research:

1. Patients who are intelligent, anxious, verbal, insightful, aware of their problems, and interested in changing them are more amenable to treatment than those who are not.
2. If treatment is comprehensive and addresses more of the relevant problems, the outcome is better.
3. There is more likely to be significant improvement when the treatment is of sufficient duration and intensity (at least 11 sessions over a period of 3 months; Heinicke, 1990).
4. In trying to be of help, "the steps of listening, understanding, clarifying, and articulating alternate perceptions of and solutions to the difficulties in the parent-child interaction are similar to the same steps used in relation to issues of personal adaptation" (Heinicke, 1990, p. 717).

The principles we are going to discuss, however, are related specifically to the activities of the psychotherapist.

Principle I: The Therapist Assesses the Client as a Precondition to Psychotherapy and as an Integral Part of the Process of Psychotherapy

Chapter 1 presented a case for the importance of assessment in psychotherapy, especially with children. Alexander (1950) commented that there are

31

many advantages to the evaluation of clients, not the least of which is its demonstration that the complaints are taken seriously and a thorough and sensitive effort is under way to alleviate them. Of course, in behavior therapy, the functional analysis of the target problems strives to identify the variables associated with their occurrence and maintenance (Haynes & O'Brien, 1990). This lays a sound foundation for what the professional may suggest or recommend. Assessment, however, should be construed not as a phase that precedes psychotherapy or treatment but as an integral part of what a psychotherapist does. The client is understood not once and for all by a certain point in time, but rather from moment to moment. This continuous and changing understanding of the client is also what is meant by assessment.

Because professional psychotherapy is often a lengthy and demanding process for both the therapist and the client, it should be offerred only when it is appropriate and after serious consideration has been given to viable alternatives (Kessler, 1966, p. 399). Behavior therapy can be particularly effective in dealing with specific symptoms and problems (Weisz, Weiss, Alicke, & Klotz, 1987). If the child wants help with a circumscribed problem amenable to a behavioral intervention, then behavior therapy might well be recommended as a desirable option.

Many children who are referred for misbehaving describe a home life and neighborhood that are chaotic. They speak of not getting enough to eat, of constant intimidation by adults, siblings, and peers, of confused relationships, and of abuse and neglect. Under such circumstances there is little wonder they have psychological problems, but there is reason to question whether child psychotherapy—no matter how skillful—is the sole or even the best answer. Ideally, improvements in environmental conditions and modifications in the behaviors of others would be made, and the effects of these changes evaluated, before undertaking formal psychotherapy.

Ross (1959) noted conditions when presumably disturbed children may not be in need of professional psychotherapy. Sometimes youngsters are brought to the therapist by parents whose major aim is to obtain help for themselves. At other times, a child may be sent to the therapist as a disciplinary measure or in an attempt by some adult in a position of authority to shift responsibility for the problem to someone else. The situation with Steve came about because a professional discounted the seriousness of his complaint and opted to blame unconscious variables for bringing about his behavior instead of accepting the parsimonious explanation readily available.

Steve had been doing very well in school until he reached the seventh grade. Then he began to complain of stomachaches and pains in his head so severe that he refused to go to school. His pediatrician could find nothing medical that would account for his somatic complaints, but the school social worker believed oedipal problems (stimulated by pubertal changes and impending entry into high school) had disrupted his adjustment. As frequently happens in these circumstances, Steve was regarded as a truant.

Both he and his parents were warned that unless he returned to school immediately, he would be suspended; in fact, his suspension occurred shortly after his parents phoned the therapist for an appointment.

When Steve arrived for the evaluation, he appeared to be a robust, rather chubby youngster. With very little encouragement, he described the beginning of his problems as follows:

> *Steve:* Three boys grabbed me in the hall in school and told me if I didn't give them money, they'd beat me up. They showed me this knife they had. I was really scared, 'cause I knew they hurt other kids.
>
> *Therapist:* I see. So, being very scared, what did you do?
>
> *Steve:* I didn't know what to do. I told my parents, but they said I had to go to school, and then I got sick.
>
> *Therapist:* So getting those headaches and stomachaches kind of made it easy to stay out of school. But what about Miss _____, your social worker? I understand you had some meetings with her. Didn't you tell her about the boys and what happened?
>
> *Steve:* Yes. She told me not to worry about it and to go to school, because they wouldn't dare hurt me in school.
>
> *Therapist:* And that didn't help?
>
> *Steve:* No, she didn't know those guys. They'd beat you up in school. They don't care what happens to them, and I didn't have the money to give them.

If what Steve said were taken seriously, his symptoms could be understood as brought about by his being placed in an anxiety-arousing conflict that was aversive no matter what he did, and which he handled by avoidance. Although a possibility of disruptive oedipal feelings could not be entirely discounted, a simple and prudent first step was to discuss with his parents how they viewed the situation. They supported their son's account and, in considering options, suggested it would be possible to send Steve to another school where he was not likely to be a victim of extortion. Within a few days they informed the therapist that they had arranged for Steve's transfer; he had returned to his classes, and he no longer had physical ailments. Several months later they reported Steve was still attending school regularly, and they expected no further problems.

Principle II: The Therapist Listens to the Client and Allows Ample Opportunity for the Expression of Feelings and Beliefs

What happened to Steve all too frequently happens to children. They are asked to identify their problems by responsible adults who then proceed to discount the veracity or significance of their explanations. The psychotherapist must not make the same mistake: the child's understanding of the problem must be respected. Even when the child makes statements that the therapist knows are exaggerations or untruths, care must be exercised not to dismiss them hastily and to explore gently the basis for the child's beliefs.

Professional psychotherapy provides a setting in which the person is relatively free to discuss at considerable length whatever is of personal interest. Although it has been thought of as a kind of friendly relationship (Fiedler, 1950a, 1950b; Schofield, 1964), there are a number of differences that should be made explicit.

Sociologists emphasize the voluntary nature of friendship (Bell, 1981). People choose their friends and seek to spend as much of their free time together as they can (Hartup, 1975). They are usually public about their friendship, acknowledging it both to each other and to anyone interested enough to ask. What is particularly distinctive about a close friendship is that the parties treat one another as equals and base their relationship on a mutual feeling of fondness (Reisman, 1979). Such friends expect loyalty and intend to maintain their relationship for as long as possible. Further, during the early phase of getting acquainted there is an almost immediate reciprocity; if, for example, one person discloses information to the second, the second very quickly discloses something to the first (Argyle & Henderson, 1984).

Clearly, virtually every aspect of friendship mentioned above is not characteristic of the psychotherapist-client relationship. Unlike ordinary conversation, the therapist does not reciprocate disclosures. Clients tell their problems and feelings; the therapist listens patiently, does not interrupt unless there is some compelling reason to do so, and makes comments that facilitate the client's elaboration and understanding of what has been said.

Implicit in this second principle is the idea of freedom for expression and thus the idea of limits—the restrictions that exist on the freedom of the child and of the therapist. These restrictions are intended to be reasonable and to be kept to a minimum, and they are supposed to have a number of therapeutic effects. In fact, in writing about this subject, Bixler (1949) went so far as to title his article "Limits Are Therapy." Limits are supposed to reduce children's misconceptions about the therapist and about psychotherapy by making clear that some of their expectations and fantasies cannot be fulfilled (Brammer & Shostrom, 1960). In normal development, they serve to teach children that their parents have ideas and standards that differ from their own, and they often convey an attitude of caring.

Limits are supposed to be helpful and comforting in enabling the child to feel genuinely respected and accepted (Singer, 1965), since the therapist continues to communicate respect despite the child's attempts to express some intolerable behaviors. They are also supposed to provide a feeling of security (Moustakas, 1953), probably for both child and therapist, by affording some assurance and guidance that certain things simply cannot be done. Finally, because they are usually invoked concerning behaviors and not verbal expressions, they may help children to exercise restraint over what they do and to put their feelings into words or some other acceptable outlet.

What are some commonly accepted limits? Therapists generally agree to prohibit the child from being destructive or physically aggressive toward them (Dorfman, 1951). Similarly, they do not permit children to hurt themselves or innocent bystanders (as they might do if allowed to throw things out windows), nor do they allow children to be demonstrative of intimate physical affection. Beyond these restrictions, however, there are disagreements among therapists about many of the other limits that have been proposed.

Questions are raised as to how necessary it is to have every appointment end at the specified time and whether therapists cut themselves off from meaningful information by refusing to attend social events with the child outside the treatment session (Singer, 1965). Some therapists suggest there are times when it is helpful to take a nap during the session (Whitaker, Felder, Malone & Warkentin, 1962), which others would consider quite disrespectful, irresponsible, and foolhardy. Ginott (1961) believed it best to refrain from playing with a child seen in play therapy and not to give or accept gifts.

With respect to limits about which there are or might be disagreements, the position taken here is that therapists should do what is most congenial to their natures within commonly accepted professional guidelines. When therapists feel uncomfortable about imposing limits or restrictions, and assuming they are within ethical bounds, they are best advised to be true to their own convictions. There is something to be said for the existential-humanistic notions of genuineness and authenticity, though it is mainly when they lead to what most professoinals would endorse. In that spirit, it may be helpful to make clear our views on controversial limits.

First, it seems less of a problem to begin and end appointments when scheduled rather than to do so haphazardly; in cases where other parties are involved, this is a necessity and an indication of respect for their time constraints.

Second, without question there are more sources of valuable information about the client than are tapped ordinarily by the therapist. Yet two considerations restrain therapists from gathering every bit of data that may be of value. One is that there are practical limitations. Unlike therapy as it may be portrayed on television programs or in the cinema, therapists have not one client at a time to whom all attention can be directed, but several clients every day. It would be difficult for therapists to engage in social activities with all their clients, even assuming the absence of other considerations. But other considerations do exist, and chief among these is the very nature of psychotherapy as we are describing it. The relationship that therapists have with their clients is a professional, not a sociable one (Reisman, 1986), and this would limit attendance at parties or school events.

The implications of the professional therapist-client relationship help children to adhere to its primary purpose, which is to assist them toward improved self-understanding and behavior (Brammer & Shostrom, 1960; Strupp, Fox, & Lessler, 1969). It is also important in resolving some of the many disputes about limits. Should therapists give children gifts at Christmas or on their birthdays? Some therapists believe it is appropriate and suggest that those who do not exchange presents have unconscious conflicts about giving and taking. Other therapists contend with equal sincerity that what they have to offer their clients is their professional skills, and that to give anything material would be competitive with the parents and subversive of the true nature of the relationship. Suffice it to say that it is possible to accept small, inexpensive presents from children (such as drawings, clay knickknacks, or a piece of candy) with graciousness, to give nothing material at Christmas or on holidays, and to receive anger and disappointment and understanding . . . and to do all this because it is consistent with professional self-respect and respect for the client.

In keeping with the professional nature of the relationship, it would be absurd for the therapist to request a gift of any kind, no matter how trivial or inexpensive. It is generally best to inform children who wish to display their drawings or paintings on the walls of the office or playroom that this is not permitted; to do so runs the risk of transforming the setting into a classroom, with attendant competition and comparisons among the children. When given artistic productions, the therapist should allow the child to see they are being put away for safekeeping. Therapists should not allow themselves to be bound and gagged while playing cowboys and Indians with their clients, nor is it such a good idea to be blindfolded. On the other hand, there are games (such as checkers and cards, or play with puppets or a ball) in which the therapist's cooperation may be requested and can be given without the loss of dignity or integrity, and with the gain of the child's confidence and meaningful communication and interaction. The therapist should not allow children to listen to radios or other gadgets during the session.

Similarly, therapists should not evade their responsibilities. When the child is with the therapist, the latter is responsible for the safety of the child. It is difficult to see how taking a nap or daydreaming would be consistent with meeting this responsibility.

In most settings, leaving the door of the office or playroom open destroys privacy, whereas allowing the child to leave the room for whatever reason (usually to get a drink of water or to go to the bathroom) diminishes the already limited time of the session and can become a recurrent evasive or manipulative tactic. Unless there is some exceptional justification for acting otherwise, the child should be encouraged to remain. Children may be allowed to leave the first time if they insist it is necessary, but informed that this will not be permitted in subsequent sessions and that such matters should be attended to before or after meeting with the therapist. It is highly probable that the child will make the same request in the next session and will threaten to die of thirst or to wet or soil himself or herself. It is very unlikely, however, that any of these misfortunes will happen. At the end of the session the child usually will not make a dash for the bathroom or water fountain; when reminded of these urges, he or she will announce that they have passed.

Most therapists agree that limits should not be mentioned until the need to mention one arises. The child is not given a list of prohibitions, because for many children this would be irrelevant and insulting; for some, it would be an invitation to test what happens when the limits are violated. Hence, therapists proceed on the assumption that children are capable of reasonable behaviors and of conforming to limits when they are brought to their attention. When children persist in breaking a limit, the therapist has to deal with the situation. In so doing, the therapist may be leaving the area of psychotherapy and entering the area of training the child in self-control. The enforcement of limits will be discussed in detail in Chapter 5.

Principle III: The Therapist Communicates an Understanding of the Client, Respect, and a Wish to Be of Help

There is substantial agreement among therapists about the importance of this kind of communication (Allen, 1942; Glasser, 1965; Heinicke, 1990; Reisman, 1971; Schmeideberg, 1960; Shaw, 1948; Truax & Carkhuff, 1967; Woody, 1969). Disagreements exist, however, concerning the personality characteristics essential to psychotherapists and the nature and content of the understanding that is to be communicated.

In general, therapists must be knowledgeable, ethical, responsible, dedicated to the welfare of their clients, concerned about their professional integrity, and respectful of their clients as human beings with rights and dignity. They must be sufficiently mature that their own needs and beliefs do not corrupt their interactions with their clients. Ideally, they should be able to act naturally and do what they want to do, and what they want to do should be ethical and in the best interests of their clients.

Lippman (1956) stated that "the therapist must enjoy his work with children and be fond of them" (p. 283), but Palmer (1970) observed that "it does seem unreasonable to expect a therapist to 'like' the child from the outset or even feel friendly toward him" (p. 397). Why therapists should demand of themselves what they know cannot be demanded of others— that they be obligated to feel only a certain way—is difficult to answer. It seems sufficient for therapists to be aware of their feelings and to be in control of them, to recognize that something is wrong if they dislike many of their clients, but not to be too upset when a child's actions arouse anger. What is essential is that they respect (not necessarily like or love) their clients and guide their own actions by what seems likely to be of help.

Weiner (1970, pp. 367–368) recommended that therapists who work with adolescents should be familiar with their language and interests. A similar recommendation could be made for clients of all ages who have distinctive subcultures (American Psychological Association, 1993), and certainly there is no harm in the therapist striving to understand a particular group or type of slang. In fact, therapists who seek to serve a certain population have an ethical obligation to gain familiarity with that clientele (American Psychological Association, 1992). Yet it should not be assumed that all is lost if the therapist does not talk like a rock fan, drug addict, Valley girl, Trekkie, or what have you. Clients in psychotherapy, after all, have a responsibility to communicate so they can be understood by their therapists, just as therapists have a responsibility to make themselves understood by their clients. When therapists do not understand, then clients have some obligation to explain themselves, assuming they want the therapist to be of help and are not playing some game or trying to prove that professionals can be ineffective.

There are a number of other attributes that are supposed to characterize the therapist, such as warmth, friendliness, persuasiveness, self-confidence, empathic ability, spontaneity, humor, faith, unconditional positive regard, genuineness, and congruence. After some consideration of this list, Reisman (1971) concluded that the qualities of a good therapist depend, to some extent, on being compatible with a given client.

A large research effort was undertaken to test Rogers's contention (1957, 1962) that the effective therapist must be high in genuineness, accurate empathy, and unconditional positive regard. Early studies supported Rogers (Truax & Carkhuff, 1967), but later research with therapists of many differing orientations found little or no relationship between ratings on these variables and therapeutic effectiveness (Mitchell, 1974; Parloff, Waskow, & Wolfe, 1978). Although there is still a need for research to determine what kind of therapist is appropriate for which clients under what circumstances, the evidence indicates that within limits, therapists can vary in their personality characteristics and be effective in helping some clients, though perhaps not others.

The understandings arrived at by therapists are determined by their formulations about personality, treatment, and psychotherapy. Some therapists believe the child's behaviors are learned and maintained by reinforcement, and that they should be altered or developed primarily by the use of learning principles (Woody, 1969; Staats, 1971; Ross, 1981). These therapists tend to minimize or ignore what other therapists believe to be extremely important, namely, unconscious motivation and conflict (A. Freud, 1965; Szurek, 1967; Wolberg, 1967) and the human relationship that the therapist provides for the child (Allen, 1942; Dorfman, 1951; Moustakas, 1953, 1959; Raskin, 1985; Truax & Carkhuff, 1967). It is not possible within the scope of this book to set down in detail these differing views of personality, but it is appropriate to make explicit a few observations that can be helpful in understanding psychotherapy and treatment with children.

An Integrative View of Personality

The behavior of any person is a function of internal and external conditions. The internal conditions are physiological states, genes, perceptions, expectations, feelings, beliefs, wishes, impulses, and attitudes that operate consciously and unconsciously to influence behavior. External conditions are social and environmental stimuli, pressures, demands, rewards, threats, punishments, obstacles, and deprivations that have a bearing on the elicitation, shaping, extinction, and direction of behavior.

These conditions interact to determine behavior, although many professionals adopt a strategy in which their attention is focused upon only one class of variables. Thus, behaviorists know people have thoughts and beliefs and that human relationships are important, but some choose to concern themselves exclusively with adjustments of conditions of rewards in order to see how much can be accomplished by this strategy alone. Analysts or Rogerian therapists may suspect a client's behavior is being maintained by the reactions of others but strive to bring about change somewhat indirectly by improving the self-concept. To an extent, then, there is simplification in any single approach, if for no other reason than that the therapist chooses not to explore all that may be involved. Moreover, there is validity and the ring of truth in almost every approach, given that each is based on observations of people.

The development of children begins before their birth, and as they grow they must very early become aware of themselves as beings separate from others, though not independent of them. With time, the circle of social relationships that becomes of importance to them expands, from mothering persons to the immediate family to neighbors to teachers and classmates. All these persons interact with children, respond to them, and evaluate them, but the early relationships are of special significance because they set the tone or predispose the perception and behaviors in subsequent ones. Further, these early relationships are likely to follow a pattern, so that they may be thought of as frequent trials of learning, repeated countless times because they involve relatively permanent figures in the lives of children—the mother, the father, and siblings. Through their interactions and communications of their feelings and beliefs, the families of children influence and determine the concepts, expectancies, and emotions children have about themselves and their world.

So pervasive, natural, and informal is this family "training" that few children pause to reflect on the origins of their attitudes. They simply think of these attitudes as their own, as likes and dislikes expressive of themselves. Yet children learn what impulses, acts, wishes, feelings, and beliefs are approved and disapproved within their circle of social relationships. They learn that biting, wetting and soiling clothes, fondling their genitals in public, hitting, running about wherever they wish, and breaking items are behaviors that are not tolerated indefinitely. Accordingly, they must learn to inhibit themselves, to exercise self-control or restraint, to delay, and to judge the appropriateness of what they want to do within the context of the time and place wherein they want to do it.

Along with personal development and the acquisition of this kind of information come a deepening awareness of themselves in relation to adults, who are bigger, stronger, more knowledgeable, and freer than children. It is inevitable that to some extent children will feel less adequate than adults, but it is hoped that their inadequacy will not be so intense that they will be crippled by feelings of inferiority or that they will strive to overcompensate by attempts to prove their superiority. Parents can help by being loving of their children but firm in the setting of limits that prohibit hurtful and harmful behaviors, and by encouraging the development of respect and consideration for the rights and feelings of others. Similarly, parents must respect their children's rights to have feelings, wishes, and beliefs that differ from their own. Insofar as it is possible, they must not only allow their children to make decisions of their own, but also seek opportunities where their children can be given this freedom. They should welcome open disagreements by their sons and daughters and the frank discussion of differences. They must distinguish, however, between what children need and what they want. Children should be given what they need; they should not always be given what they want.

Children see in their parents sources of love, care, pleasure, and comfort. To lose them is frightening, and in fact children are lost without them. Nevertheless, parental orders, requests, and demands thwart children repeatedly. It is hoped that there is a healthy balance between the giving and the limiting, and an overall affection and acceptance. Through these sorts of interactions children learn to assert themselves and to develop their individuality without fearing this will jeopardize their security and being loved. They learn to submit to adults and accede to their wishes without feeling that in the process they have sacrificed their autonomy. They gain a sense of what they want, what is expected of them, what they can do, and who they are.

This identity or concept of self is a growing, changing system of beliefs, but it has continuity and consistency. Its beginnings lie in very early parent-child interactions, perhaps in the comfort and pleasure that the mother has in the caring and holding of her infant. Certainly this concept or schema is affected by the disciplining and training that are necessary in responsible child rearing: "Why did you do that?" "A good boy puts his toys away and does what he is told." "Isn't she sweet!" "Only a bad child would say that he hates his mother and would make a mess all over his nice, clean room." Over and over again children hear evaluations about the goodness and badness of their actions, feelings, and opinions; these teach them about their own goodness and badness, about the values of certain inclinations and thoughts, and about what can be expected from people.

Most parents seek deliberately to influence and determine the beliefs, values, behaviors, and attitudes of their children. They ask their children to perform and to believe as they do—not only to inhibit and restrain themselves, for example, but to feel that such inhibitions and restrictions are good, necessary, and proper. Children are expected to deal with social situations according to their parents' rules of etiquette, to speak as they do, to learn in school, and to uphold standards and traditions favored by the family.

When children move outside their families, they encounter different beliefs, demands, values, and attitudes. For many children this is a broadening experience that serves to modify their concepts and to increase their tolerance and respect for beliefs unlike their own. For some children, however, this new information is distressing and unacceptable. In both obvious and subtle ways they are compelled to distort it, to shape it so that it is consistent with their concepts, or else to block it from awareness.

This new information may originate not only from situations outside the family, but also from within the family and within the child. Wishes, impulses, and feelings that the child cannot accept may somehow be stimulated or provoked, with the consequence that they may be put into action, suppressed, or given some distorted expression. Should the child or responsible adults be distressed by these consequences, professional intervention may be sought.

As has been suggested, from some points of view, disturbed children have not been trained properly and need to acquire appropriate behaviors and eliminate the actions that are troublesome (Ross, 1981); are trying to cope with some external and internal stresses ineffectively but valiantly (Menninger, Mayman, & Pruyser, 1963); they are striving to express themselves under conditions of threat and need a safe environment in which to resume their normal growth (Allen, 1942, 1962); are behaving consistently with their negative and unflattering concepts of themselves (Rogers, 1951); are seeking to satisfy their needs to feel worthwhile and important at the expense of others (Ansbacher & Ansbacher, 1956; Glasser, 1965); or have erroneous beliefs that need to be made explicit and corrected (Beck, 1976). Regardless of the therapist's particular system of understanding, there is agreement that this understanding should be communicated with respect for the client's right to disagree and dissent.

Person-Related Understanding

Person-related understanding refers to communications with content that conveys comprehension of the client's feelings, beliefs, or behaviors. It is a major and definitive task of the psychotherapist to offer this kind of communication consistently, and yet this function is often minimized and misunderstood. Part of the difficulty comes about because of confusion between what is psychotherapy and what is simply therapeutic. A therapist sees a client; the client gets better. During the entire contact period, neither speaks a word to the other. Some professionals might say that such a relationship is psychotherapy. It would be more accurate to say that the contacts seem to have been therapeutic, but there is no evidence that psychotherapy was practiced. In other words, without the communication of person-related understanding, there is no psychotherapy.

There are five types of statements that fall under the category of person-related understanding. One is *empathic,* a communication that expresses what the client seems to be saying, feeling, experiencing, or believing. A second is *responsive,* where the therapist indicates by a simple word ("Yes"), expression ("I see"), or comment ("Um-hum") that the client's message has been received and understood (There are therapists who have made careers largely out of responding responsively.). A third type is *interpretative;* this has to do with statements in which the therapist points out possible relationships between seemingly unrelated feelings, thoughts, and situations. Fourth are *interrogative* comments, or questions and requests by the therapist for clarification and additional information. The fifth type consists of *expository* statements, which try to present an expert analysis or explanation of the client's behavior, problem, or possible course of action (Reisman, 1971).

Statements that are empathic were thought once to constitute the cornerstone of effective psychotherapy. As Truax and Carkhuff (1967) used empathic understanding in their research and training programs for psychotherapists, the category also included responsive and interpretative comments, though the drawing of relationships between past and present were not emphasized in the latter. Accurate empathy was thought to be the major, if not only, way therapists should communicate. Subsequent research did not find empathic communication to be essential for effective psychotherapy.

Briefly, this research found that people do not generally like empathic communicaton, judging it to be unnatural and irritatingly repetitive (Reisman & Yamokoski, 1974; Nelson-Jones, 1990). There is some basis in fact for this negative reaction. Not only is the level of empathy in non-professional interventions less than what a client-centered therapist communicates (Carkhuff & Berenson, 1977, pp. 30–33; Rogers, 1980, p. 148), but it is also exeedingly rare to find friends (Reisman & Yamokoski, 1974), married couples (Barker & Lemle, 1984), children and adults (Reisman & Shorr, 1980), and even some therapists (Reisman, 1982) making use of many empathic statements. In ordinary discourse, people tend to respond with disclosures of their own personal experiences ("You and me both"; "That reminds me of what happened to me"), evaluative judgments ("Smart"; "Good idea"; "That's a dumb thing to do"), and suggestions or advice—types of statements that are used infrequently and judiciously by professional psychotherapists.

When people are at a loss as to what to say or advise (and this happens to them more often than it does to psychotherapists), they lapse into silence or change the subject, minimize the importance of the problem, or suggest that the person seek professional help (Barker & Lemle, 1984; Cowen, 1982; Reisman & Yamokoski, 1974; Strupp & Hadley, 1979). Thus, empathic responses can be very helpful to clarify, to verify, and to insure understanding. But it would be an error to use them continuously and rigidly or to deny that there may be times when it is appropriate to ask questions, note consistencies and inconsistencies, give explanations, and provide advice or information. Moreover, Carkhuff and Berenson (1977) argue that giving information or advice under some circumstances may be the most empathic of all responses.

Respect

Therapists should respect all with whom they come into contact. It is particularly important, however, that they convey respect for children and parents (Szurek, 1967). Therapists and parents should not feel they are in competition for the child's affection; everyone should seek to work cooperatively for the child's benefit. One prominent exception to this principle was furnished by Rosen (1964), who based his treatment of schizophrenics and neurotics on the belief that the patient's affliction was an attempt to deny or distort bad mothering. Rosen advocated that the therapist assume the role of a good mother and compel the patient to face the badness and deficiencies of the actual mother; he believed this so strongly that he felt even deception was justified (for example, telling the patient that the mother's failure to visit proved her indifference, when in reality the therapist had issued orders against her visits). Rosen's procedure is unethical and indefensible.

The communication of understanding and respect is both essential for therapy and ethical. It is often because children's wishes and opinions have not been respected that they are disturbed in their behaviors. The therapist must take seriously what children say and would like to do and must encourage other adults to do the same. The child's wishes and preferences must be solicited and given careful consideration in deciding among treatment options or whether treatment should be offered at all (Melton, 1991).

Yet therapists cannot ignore the dependency of children. Children are dependent upon adults in actual fact for their food and shelter; they are dependent as a matter of law; they may feel dependent because of their own concerns and weaknesses; and they may be dependent because they lack sufficient knowledge and understanding. There are legal restrictions intended to benefit and protect children (such as school attendance and labor laws) that often frustrate and seem inappropriate to them. Child psychotherapists have to be familiar with these laws so that they can inform children of the legality or possible consequences of actions they report or contemplate. The therapist can always respect the child's wishes but cannot always grant them, because there may be occasions when what the child would like to do is unrealistic or illegal.

The decisions of children may be based on misinformation or ignorance, and it is the responsibility of the therapist to be informative. Children may not know where they are, who or what a psychotherapist is or does, why they are being seen, what behaviors are appropriate in a given situation, what the facts are concerning a given event, or how something that seems very simple to others should be done. In other words, there is the possibility that a child's errors, plans, distortions, denials, and misbehaviors may be attributable to lack of training and knowledge. Therefore, we cannot assume children know why they are being seen or what services psychotherapists offer. So many sources of confusion and error are possible, including explanations by parents that are incorrect or misunderstood, distorted or denied, contradictory of others provided by various adults or members of the family. The therapist must check the child's understanding of what the reasons are and, if necessary, ensure that there is some common understanding between the child, the therapist, and the parents about the purpose of the visits.

Therapist: Do you know why you're here?
Client: No.
Therapist: Well, could you tell me why your mother brought you to see me?
Client: I don't know.
Therapist: She didn't give you any reason?
Client: She just said, "Get your coat on. We're going to see a doctor about you today."

Therapist: So that's the way she does it. Just picks you up and brings you down here and you have to go along . . . and you don't know why. *(pause)* Well, your mother mentioned to me that you haven't been doing too well in school. *(pause)* Is that right?

Children frequently claim not to know why they are being seen. At times this is a way of expressing their anger and resentment about being brought for help for a problem about which they have little or no concern. At other times it may be a way of determining how much the therapist has been told about the situation and whether any of that information has been retained. Whatever the reason, the therapist's aim is not to demonstrate cleverness or agility by avoiding being taken in by a game. Instead, the therapist wants to come across to the child as a person interested in communicating understanding, respect, and a wish to be of help. Accordingly, the therapist shares information with the client.

Principle IV: The Therapist Negotiates with the Client a Purpose or Goal for their Meetings

The purpose of child psychotherapy is to be of help to the child, and the child and the therapist should feel that they are working together toward some common desired end. Their specific objective may not be the same as that desired by the parents or referring adults. For example, in the therapist-client interaction cited above, the parents are concerned about their child's performance in school, but the child and the therapist may agree that a legitimate goal would be for the child to be more assertive when his mother tells him to do something (to the extent that he might question why he should be seen in psychotherapy if he does not feel the need for it).

Particularly when a long period has elapsed from the occurrence of the presenting problem until the child is seen, children sometimes report that they used to misbehave, but now they recognize it was foolish of them to have done so, and they are determined to change for the better. In the recent past, they may add, their behaviors have been exemplary, yet their parents do not believe in their good intentions, do not trust them, and will not give them the opportunity to prove themselves. Here the therapist must respect the child's wishes to be responsible and must also respect the concerns of the parents. The therapist can accomplish this by offering to meet with the child and the parents in order to see whether there is some basis for mutual faith and trust and to assess the effects of the client's good intentions.

In negotiating a purpose or goal, the therapist should make clear to the child what the treatment options might be. For example, one child complained to the therapist about feelings of anxiety for which there was no attributable cause. One option was to try to figure out if there was anything that might be upsetting. A second option was to teach the child relaxation techniques and have the child practice them at home; if this did not prove effective, then the first option would be explored. The child picked the second option, which promoted not only relaxation but a feeling of control over the body and behavior that was very effective in alleviating the problem.

The presentation of options is an issue of some concern in the professional literature. What brought this matter into prominence was a lawsuit filed by a Dr. Osheroff against the Chestnut Lodge, a psychiatric inpatient facility where he had been a patient. Osheroff claimed he had been damaged by his treatment, since during his hospitalization he had lost his practice and been divorced. Moreover, he contended he had not been informed of treatment options that would not have involved long-term, inpatient psychoanalytic therapy. Although this suit was settled out of court, it implies that patients have the right to be informed what treatments exist for their problems and to decide which they might prefer. More controversially, it is argued that treatments whose effectiveness has been established by research should be given preference over those that are less effective or that still await studies demonstrating their efficacy (Klerman, 1990; Stone, 1990). Complicating this issue is the fact that therapists are not equally proficient in every treatment and that they have values and possibly biases, usually consistent with their training, about various treatments.

On two grounds, this issue is even more complicated with children than it is with adults. The first is that there are children who, by reason of their development or disturbance, are not able to communicate, weigh alternatives, and negotiate a purpose or goal. In such cases the therapist may communicate a wish to be of help and receive no acknowledgement or response, because to these children the situation with the therapist is nonexistent or utterly confused. Under these circumstances, because psychotherapy is dependent for its effectiveness on communication, attention, and cooperation, it is highly questionable that it would be an appropriate treatment, even though there may be therapists who would still choose to practice it (Truax, 1970). There may also be children who are too young to make a reasoned decision about treatment options, though it is better to err in giving them the opportunity to express a preference than to assume they are incapable of the choice. In any case, with young children (and, very often, older ones) the therapist should discuss the treatment options with the parents or other responsible adults.

A second basis for complications with children is derived from the theoretical positions of some humanistic therapists who believe they should not bring into their sessions anything that is not first introduced by their clients, a very literal interpretation of Axline's principle of psychotherapy (1947) that the child leads the way and the therapist follows. When pursued faithfully and blindly, this doctrine can lead to a situation of great absurdity, as is illustrated by the following account.

A therapist had been seeing a young boy in play therapy for about a year. Each week the child would play quietly with the toys and smile pleasantly or utter an appropriate comment when the therapist made some reflection of feelings. When told there were only a few minutes left in the session, he would stop his play, put everything back in order, and clean up the room. He was a perfect gentleman and provided the therapist with a pleasant, relaxing interlude. The only trouble was that his mother complained each week to her social worker that her son was rude to her and disobedient at home, at school, and throughout the neighborhood. With reluctance and misgivings about the betrayal of principles, the therapist eventually asked the boy his understanding of the purpose of their meetings. The boy explained that he had experienced trouble in summer camp the previous year and that the therapist's job was to make sure that he could now play quietly with toys and put them away neatly, or else he might not be able to go to camp again. As a matter of fact, he thought it was about time for the therapist to write the recommendation and for the meetings to come to an end. This experience convinced the therapist of the importance of negotiating a purpose or goal.

A very important point to make about negotiating a purpose is that the goal should be legitimate, which is to say it should be attainable given the efforts of the client and therapist. It is not legitimate to have a goal that depends upon the feelings and behaviors of others (such as becoming popular, obtaining certain grades on a report card, or winning the affection or approval of someone). It would be valid, however, to work toward the modification of behaviors that have interfered with achieving those goals, such as being aggressive and not studying; the development of these study habits and prosocial behaviors should be of value in and of themselves. Thus, the therapist may have to explain to a child that what he or she wants is outside their control, but they can work out for their meetings some different purpose that is amenable to their efforts. It is with this in mind, as well as to suggest that goals may be added or modified as psychotherapy progresses, that the word *negotiates* is used in stating the fourth principle.

For example, an adolescent of about 13 was referred for not doing well in school. He claimed to be unconcerned about his mediocre grades, but what did concern him was that he had no friends and one of his classmates was constantly picking on him. He wanted to become better liked by his peers. The therapist explained there could be no guarantees about getting others to like him; however, it might be possible to consider how he acted with his classmates and see if handling himself in a different way would be better (social skills training), or just to talk about it and see if there was something he might do. The boy chose to talk about the situation and try to come up with ideas of his own. Two sessions later, he told the therapist that he had asked the boy who was picking on him to come to his house for lunch. The other boy, quite startled by the offer, accepted; the two of them found they enjoyed their time together, and they decided to become friends. In subsequent meetings the young client reported getting along well with his classmates and, incidentally, doing better in his schoolwork.

Principle V: The Therapist Makes Clear What Is Unusual or Inconsistent in the Client's Behavior, Feelings, and Beliefs

Perhaps in the first meeting, and certainly at times during the meetings that follow, therapists point out to children ways in which their behaviors are ineffective, inconsistent, and inappropriate given their professed beliefs, feelings, goals, and intentions. The professed aim of psychoanalysts in doing this is to help the client to become aware of the existence of conflicts and the futility of certain patterns of behavior (Wolberg, 1967). They also trust that the therapeutic handling of clients who are inconsistent will be quite different from the reactions these clients have previously aroused, so that their attitudes and convictions can be appreciated and recognized in their fullness instead of being rejected and distorted (Szurek, 1967).

Some therapists have made the pointing out of inconsistencies in behaviors and beliefs the foundation of their psychotherapy (Beck, 1976; Ellis, 1973; Lecky, 1969). They note the contrast between the person's ideals and aspirations and current performance, the differences between feelings toward someone at one time and at another, the discrepancies between how people claim to feel and how they look and behave, and the contradictions that exist between beliefs. Their aim may be to reduce the tyranny of misconceptions or to help clients to become more accepting of their own complexity and to make informed choices between the person they are and the person they might be.

In general, then, many therapists of differing orientations believe that they should call to the attention of their clients aspects of the latter's behaviors, feelings, and beliefs that are contradictory and self-defeating (Freud, 1965; Glasser, 1965; Schmeideberg, 1960; Shaw, 1948; Truax & Carkhuff, 1967). Their theoretical purposes and aims in following this policy differ, but in a broad sense all are pursuing what has been suggested as the goal of all systems of psychotherapy: helping the client toward self-interpretation or self-learning (Brammer & Shostrom, 1960; Heinicke, 1990; Strupp et al., 1969). An illustration of this principle is the following exchange from the first interview with a 9-year-old boy referred because of his anxious, irritable, negativistic, passively aggressive behavior:

Therapist: You seem to feel very angry.
Client: [Seems to agree but says nothing.]
Therapist: Can you tell me why?
Client: The kids at school make fun of me.
Therapist: Oh, in what way?
Client: They say I don't try in sports, and that I'm no good in baseball.
Therapist: And this kind of hurts your feelings . . . and makes you feel angry with them.
Client: No. I don't care. They're not my friends, so I don't care what they say.
Therapist: (Pause) Well, I wonder in what ways you might like me to help you.
Client: (Pause) I'd like to have more friends at school.
Therapist: (Pause) On the one hand you're saying you don't care about them, and on the other you're saying you would like them to be your friends.
Client: (begins to cry quietly) I do want them to be my friends.

Principle VI: When Dealing with Behaviors That Are Supported Within a Given Social System, the Therapist May Modify the Behaviors by Modifications and Negotiations Within the Social System

This principle is based on the assumption that there are deviant behaviors that are shaped and maintained by the system of social relationships in which the child lives. The system may consist of peers, who attend to or reinforce deviant or antisocial behaviors; the professional staff of a school, hospital, institution, or treatment center; or neighbors or members of the community (Klein, 1968). The system that will receive most attention in this book is the family, which is taken to mean the members of a given household. In the United States this is usually a nuclear family, made up of parents and their offspring, though at times parent figures, grandparents, and other relatives may also be in residence.

Some therapists like to get a handle on the family system very quickly and seek to schedule all its members for at least one interview together during the assessment. Some therapists insist that as part of the assessment they be invited to attend a dinner of the family within the home, and some refuse to treat a child whose parents are unwilling to participate in the treatment.

Although there are as many (if not more) theories of family therapy as there are theories of individual psychotherapy, to a large extent family diagnosis and a functional analysis of behavior are similar. It is important to determine how the members of the family respond to the child's misbehaviors, which members are aligned and mutually supportive and which may be criticized or ignored, who seems to benefit from the child's disturbance, and what function the disorder seems to serve for the child and family system.

A family diagnosis or assessment often moves without much further ado into family therapy, in which who is identified as the client becomes a rather meaningless distinction. When negotiating with the family about a purpose for the meetings, the therapist may point to a common desire for more harmonious relationships and a recognition that each member bears some responsibility in achieving that goal. Nathan Ackerman was among the first family therapists, and enthusiasm for this approach has grown since his early publications (Ackerman, 1958, 1961). Nevertheless, the evidence supporting the effectiveness of most types of family therapy has yet to be produced—behavioral or functional family therapy seems effective in helping in the alleviation of conduct disorders (Alexander & Parsons, 1982), and structural family therapy appears to improve eating disorders and problems in substance abuse (Minuchin, 1974)—and research in this area is sorely lacking (Gurman, Kniskern, & Pinsof, 1986).

Though proponents of family therapy frequently argue that it is the treatment of choice for almost any problem, the following considerations do seem pertinent in deciding whether this method should be used:

1. There should be some expressed wish or need on the part of the family members to work together or attain some semblance of mutual respect and cordiality; conversely, if the parents are on the verge of divorce, or want to be rid of their child, or if the child or adolescent wants as little to do with the parents as possible, family therapy does not seem particularly appropriate (at least initially).
2. Family members who are too young or too old or too handicapped for meaningful participation—or who are about to leave the home to go to college, the service, and so on—might well be excused from the meetings.
3. Members should feel there is some problem they have in getting along with one another (such as poor communication, provocative behavior, stubbornness, getting across their ideas, or telling what they really think and how they really feel).
4. A child who is quiet or fearful and whose major problem involves the suppression or repression of thoughts and feelings might better be seen in individual psychotherapy. Work with parents might be an adjunct treatment, and family therapy may eventually be used.
5. Parents who are very unsure of their own roles and their own adequacies, or who have marital problems that might better be discussed without their children present, could be seen in couple or marital therapy.

Chapters 10 and 11 in this book are devoted to family therapy, so here our emphasis is on presenting some historical perspective and discussing its relevance to the principle. Within a few years after its introduction, there were two major approaches in family therapy (Zuk, 1971). The first was influenced by psychoanalytic concepts and stressed dealing with unconscious processes, the influence of the past on current functioning, transference effects, and the fostering of insights. Ackerman (1958, 1961) was psychoanalytic in his orientation, and he saw the child as the scapegoat for the family's troubles, the person upon whom the family could heap all blame while avoiding the issues that otherwise would greatly distress them.

The other approach partook of systems analysis and communication therapy, and hence was concerned with establishing what members have power in the family and why, the nature of the communication that is transmitted from one member to another, and the kind of feedback (if any) that the sender receives, as well as with promoting negotiation. Satir (1967, 1968) suggested that a major reason for problems in communication was that the sender of the message was in conflict. On the one hand, the sender was trying to act in accord with certain values and ideals, with reasonableness, understanding, fairness, and respect for the other person's right to be different. On the other hand, he or she had already reached a conclusion and had a hostile feeling toward the recipeint of the message. The sender knew what should be done and was angry that the receiver probably would not do it. In this approach, the role of the family therapist is to be an expert in communication and a model of clear, congruent message transmission. The therapist directs each person's attention to what has just been communicated, to what might have been intended, to discrepancies between intention and commission, and to the impacts and effects that the message has upon family members. The aim is to develop honest expressions of feelings and beliefs in a family atmosphere of mutual respect.

In the analytic approach, silent members of the family tended to be ignored. In the communication approach, the members who talked were asked for their understanding of the silence of someone else and what effect it had upon them. In the analytic approach, suggestions were rarely offered; in the systems approach, family members might be asked to imagine what problems they might have if the client improved, and siblings might be encouraged to be "more of a problem" so as to relieve the client's burden in that regard (Jackson & Yalom, 1964). Because the two approaches were not mutually exclusive, there was no reason why they could not be combined, and many practitioners often did just that.

For years before the advent of family therapy, it was recognized by professionals that an important aspect of psychotherapy with children involved modification in the attitudes and response patterns of parents, teachers, or other adults so that they would be receptive to the changes that might take place in the child's behavior and so that they might help to promote them (Allen, 1942, 1962; Ross, 1959). In child guidance clinics, this recognition took the form of one professional seeing the child while another pforessional met with one or both of the parents, an admittedly expensive method of providing service. Family therapy, aside from its distinct advantages as a treatment, can be an economical approach to being of help.

A professional in private practice, however, may choose to act in accord with the principle by seeing the child and the parents in separate interviews. Brammer and Shostrom (1960) recommended that when this procedure is followed, the scheduling of interviews with the parents should be guided by the age of the child: with a child under the age of 6 years, for every session with the child the parent should be seen once; and with a client over the age of 12, the parents should be given one interview for every two sessions in which their child is seen. Although this scheme has a symmetrical progression that is most appealing, there is no research evidence for or against it.

Dorfman (1951) commented that there had been reports from therapists who were effective in helping young clients without working with the parents. Because in many settings it was de rigueur to work with parents when the child was in treatment, Dorfman's comment aroused professional interest. Principle VI suggests that when behaviors are not supported within a given system, it may be possible to see a child in effective individual psychotherapy without the parents also being seen. The following clinical experience illustrates such a circumstance.

Andy was 11 years old when his mother phoned a child guidance clinic to refer him for help. She claimed he was a reasonably happy, well-adjusted boy until about 2 months before the phone call. At that time his father, with whom he was close, abandoned the family and ran off with another woman. Immediately Andy became depressed. His marks in school dropped, and he began to hit and mercilessly tease his 9-year-old sister.

When offered an appointment, Andy's mother explained she could not come during the hours the clinic was open. She had taken a job after her husband's departure, thought herself fortunate to get it, and was certain her employer would not welcome any absences. She was now the sole support of the family, and if Andy had to be seen during clinic hours, he would be brought by his aunt. Her sister could relay any messages, and if need be, the therapist could phone her at her place of employment.

While the therapist puzzled over whether he or the mother was inflexible, he decided to go ahead and see Andy. This boy was, as described, depressed. He wept softly as he spoke of his love for his father and of his father's love for him, and he talked repeatedly in great detail about their fishing and hunting trips and of why he could never forget him. In the sessions that followed, it became clear that Andy blamed his sister for his father's abandoment of him. He expressed the conviction that his father would surely have taken him along, since he was the favored child, except that his father did not wish to hurt the girl's feelings so cruelly.

Andy saw his troubles in school as brought about by being unable to concentrate on the work. Everything seemed to remind him of his father; also thoughts of his father came to him unexpectedly. Andy did not like hurting his sister, and he wanted to do better in school, but he felt unable to control himself. He wanted help in being better able to deal with his feelings.

A dramatic point in Andy's psychotherapy sessions came during the sixth meeting. In his struggle to understand why his father had left him, he speculated that perhaps his father never really did like him.

Therapist: You mean you think now that maybe all along your father really hated you.
Client: Yes.
Therapist: Gee, that seems hard to believe after all you told me about how much you liked each other. I wonder if that's possible. Could it also be possible that maybe there are times when you don't like him?
Client: (pause) Yes. *(begins to weep softly)* I hate him for what he did to me. I hate him for what he did to my mother and sister. *(long pause)* I'll never see him again.
Therapist: (pause) And yet there were times when you loved him.
Client: (pause) Yes.

Andy was seen for 12 interviews. During the course of those meetings his aunt reported that he was no longer hurting his sister and that his grades in school had improved. Just before his last interview, his mother stated over the phone that he was once again reasonably happy and well adjusted. At his last session with the therapist, which took place while Andy was on his summer vacation from school, he stated that he might hop on his bike each week, come to the clinic, and just see the therapist; however, he apparently did not do this.

What seemed to be a key variable in Andy's case was that he was a relatively normal youngster undergoing a crisis situation. Similarly, Levy (1938, 1939) thought his "release therapy" (a form of play with puppets and dolls where the child is encouraged to express feelings) was most suited for children under 10 years of age whose symptoms were acute and in response to a specific trauma. He went on to hypothesize that a child's immediate reactions to a crisis can be modified successfully without parental involvement in psychotherapy.

A system can be a dyad, a family, a group, a class, a community, a culture, and so on. Negotiations within a system can refer to behavior modification, token economies, and changes in contingencies, ecological or community psychology, and efforts at primary prevention, as well as alterations within the structure of the family by clarifying expectations and roles and bettering communication. Although these are fields of specialization within themselves, they are mentioned explicitly to show the range of systems and services implied by Principle VI.

Principle VII. The Therapist Negotiates Termination with the Client When the Advantages of Ending the Meetings Outweigh What May Be Gained by Their Continuance

The question of when long-term, unlimited psychotherapy ends has received no more definitive discussion than that by Sigmund Freud (1959), which was originally published in 1937. Freud recognized that for practical purposes, an analysis might come to an end when the symptoms for which the client originally sought help were substantially reduced or eliminated and the therapist believed there was little likelihood of their recurrence. Freud also supposed that therapy never really did end, since the client could be expected to continue throughout life to examine and strive to understand behavior. Moreover, he recognized that standards or ideal goals for treatment existed, but these were difficult to achieve, seldom attained, and (if attained) not easily assessed: "We often feel that, when we have reached the wish for a penis and the masculine protest, we have penetrated all the psychological strata and reached 'bedrock' and that our task is accomplished" (S. Freud, 1959, pp. 356–357). Because it was not easy to determine whether these conflicts were truly resolved, Freud concluded that the therapist simply had to be consoled with the knowledge that the best had been done to bring the client face-to-face with these issues.

For therapists who are psychoanalytic in their orientation, and for many that are not, Freud's practical standards are satisfactory. Ideal goals are recognized, such as the self-actualizing or fully functioning person (Rogers, 1961), but it is also acknowledged that for most persons even Freud's presumably modest aims are sufficient (Brammer & Shostrom, 1960; Lippman, 1956; Strupp et al., 1969). Psychotherapy often ends with the alleviation of some symptoms, an awareness of the existence of other problems, and the feeling that the client is better able to deal with concerns than before and is progressing in the right direction. Nevertheless, there is considerable variation among therapists. Some are satisfied to reduce the severity of presenting symptoms, whereas others aspire to more theoretical and lofty goals (Reisman, 1971). In negotiating with the client about a purpose or goal for the meetings, such matters should be discussed.

Some therapists believe it is important to set a limit on the duration of the treatment at its outset. They may favor brief (10 or so sessions) or time-limited interventions to mobilize the resources of their clients, to bring issues of separation into immediate focus, or because they do not have much more time available. There is some evidence to suggest there are diminishing returns as the number of psychotherapy sessions increase beyond a certain number (Howard, Kopta, Krause, & Orlinsky, 1986). About 10% to 18% of clients improve while waiting for their 1st session; 50% improve by the 8th to 13th session, 75% by the 26th session, and 85% by the 52nd session. These data indicate a certain futility in planning psychotherapy interviews that extend beyond 52 meetings.

Unquestionably, therapist attitudes about termination play an important part in their approach to this phase of treatment. Some regard termination as a kind of wrap-up during which little more needs to be accomplished than to relieve any client anxieties about being independent. Others such as Allen (1942, 1962), who was heavily influenced in his approach by Otto Rank, see termination as a potentially constructive experience and a representation of a crucial human conflict. For these therapists, termination is not the culmination of their efforts but perhaps the most taxing and rewarding phase of psychotherapy. It is in ending that the courage, faith, and confidence of both the client and the therapist are put to the test.

Thus far we have been discussing termination as if it occurs only under the therapist's control. This is not always true. Regrettably, in many circumstances the decision to end treatment has nothing to do with the therapist's appraisal of the client's condition but is determined instead by needs of the setting, such as the rotation of interns or trainees or the departure of staff. Furthermore, there are therapists, notably those who are humanistic or Rogerian, who try to allow clients to make the decision about when therapy should end. These therapists contend termination should occur when the client feels ready for it. Yet their position, simple and straightforward though it seems, raises three questions: (1) How soon after therapy begins can such a decision be accepted? (2) Can such a decision be accepted when the client is a child whose parents are also involved in the treatment? (3) What does the therapist do if the client seems ready for termination but shows no sign of broaching the subject?

The first question gets into the matters of whether the client is terminating prematurely and client motivation for treatment, a special issue with children. Anna Freud (1946) believed the early phase of treatment was the time to establish and build the child's admiration and respect for the therapist; this might be accomplished by the therapist demonstrating skills beyond the child's abilities or by gaining favors for the child that had been previously denied at home or at school. She believed the positive feelings engendered were necessary to create a relationship valued by the child and thus not easily given up. Yet many therapists would question the wisdom and ethicality of some of her techniques, as well as motivational tactics such as scolding (Lippmann, 1956), the therapist pretending that the purpose of the sessions is to teach delinquent clients how to be more effective criminals (Strean, 1968), and threatening (Whitaker, Felder, Malone, & Warkentin, 1962). Put another way, this first question raises the problem of the therapist's responsibility for motivating the client if the latter seeks to terminate treatment shortly after it begins. This in turn raises the broader issue of the therapist's responsibilities in psychotherapy and how they relate to respect for the client's dignity and decisions.

It is reasonable to assert that the major aim of the therapist is to help the client. Therefore, in evaluating any decision or proposal, the therapist must weigh its consequences. Given a choice between uncertain alternatives, the therapist must help the client consider which is more likely to be of benefit than the other. Thus, when the client makes a decision or suggestion to terminate treatment or not to begin it, the therapist's responsibility is to ensure that the client has examined the alternatives and has an awareness of their implications: what are the reasons entering into this decision; whether it is consistent with the goals agreed upon for the psychotherapy and with the therapist's understanding of the client's problems and symptoms; and whether sufficient time has elapsed for treatment to be effective. Here knowledge that research indicates a minimum of 11 sessions for effectiveness (Heinicke, 1990) must be tempered by the recognition that many clients experience improvement in fewer meetings and by admonitions that the therapist must be "ever ready" to accept the client's decision about termination (Szurek, 1967).

When the client is a child, the therapist has the added responsibility to determine the acceptability of the decision to the parents. Should they be in accord with the decision, and if their agreement is soundly based, it would appear that the therapist has acted responsibly and the decision can be accepted. Should the parents disagree with the decision or have doubts about it, however, their reasons and concerns must be considered. Under such circumstances a possible outcome might be to have the child and parents meet with the therapist to arrive at a mutually agreeable solution, to see the parents in counseling or consultation for a period after the child stops treatment, or to decrease the frequency of sessions and see if all still goes well.

Moreover, in the case of children it is possible that the child's refusal of psychotherapy is a test of the therapist's interest, may be prompted by a belief that the therapist is in alliance with the parents, or may be occasioned by a lack of proper information. What should the therapist do if a 5-year-old girl says that she does not want to see the therapist anymore? It depends on whether the child has ever been willing to see the therapist (if she has, then this is a new decision that merits evaluation), on the nature of her problem (if she has been brought into the office screaming her defiance by parents who claim that she is uncooperative in everything, then this is a continuation of the same attitude), and most importantly, on her plans and intentions (whether she is planning to continue in patterns of behavior that are irresponsible and self-defeating or sees herself interacting more cooperatively with others).

Child psychotherapists must remember that children are their clients, that their aim is to help their clients by fostering psychological growth, and that respect for their clients' decision may in and of itself be more constructive and effective than anything else could be. For it is often by the therapist's respect and acceptance of such a decision, and by a willingness to meet with the parents to communicate this respect and acceptance of the child, that an interactional process is initiated between parents and child that is positive and based on understanding and a mutual recognition of strengths.

Because the therapist is usually aware of problems that remain and of crises that are still to come, however, there is frequently doubt about whether the client's decision has been accepted too readily. For example, a 17-year-old boy, Warren, had been referred for psychotherapy because he was doing poorly in school. Though of superior intellectual abilities, he had never fulfilled his promise, and there was now serious question about his acceptance at any college. His parents, both teachers who were very active in political and union affairs, claimed to be too busy to be seen by the therapist even once.

At first, Warren was at a loss to explain why he did poorly in school. Eventually he came to understand that his failures were an effort to embarrass his parents and to compel them to attend to him. To punish them by his mediocre grades seemed the only course open to him; he had told them recently of his feelings of rejection and hostility, and "they were too busy and too much in a rush to take them seriously." It was only when he brought his report cards home that they seemed upset for the moment and recognized he was alive and living in opposition to them and their values.

Warren claimed he could see no personal advantage in striving for success in his last year in high school. His blasé attitude toward grades won him acceptance and admiration from his classmates for being "cool." Furthermore, Warren doubted he had the skills to compete with them:

> If I try to do well and I don't, everybody'll know that I'm not really so bright. Right now they keep telling me that I'm college material and that I'm smart without really trying. And suppose through some miracle and a lot of hard work I do well, who'll get the credit? My teachers and my parents will be taking the bows, saying that they finally motivated me. I have nothing to gain and everything to lose by trying.

Warren took a job in a movie theater as an usher and stated that he wanted to terminate treatment. He claimed to understand now why he was doing poorly in school and thought he might try harder in his senior year, although he doubted it. After all, he explained, his parents had not changed, so why should he? There still seemed too much to be lost and too little to be gained, though he did appreciate his therapist's efforts and help in making things clearer to him. He also gave another reason for terminating the therapy: because his parents were not bringing him and there was no public transportation between his suburban home and the therapist's office, he had to hitch rides, and this was bothersome and time-consuming. Despite having little choice but to accept this decision, the therapist wondered what might have happened had there been more encouragement for continuance or some different handling of the case.

The third situation involves a client who seems ready for termination but does not broach the subject. Here the therapist feels with some certitude that treatment is no longer needed; he or she may have come to this feeling from evidence that the goals set for psychotherapy have been reached or because a greater investment of time and effort is not justified. In either case, the therapist must be mindful of responsibilities not only to the present client, but also to potential clients who might effectively make use of treatment. The therapist is obligated, both to the client and to the public, to introduce the subject of termination when an end to services is indicated.

This must be done with tact and skill. It is most important that the client not feel the therapist is rejecting him or her. Probably a statement such as "It sounds as though things are going a lot better for you, is that right?" or "We've been seeing each other for some time now, and I wonder how you feel about it" could serve to lead into the topic. These statements should be delivered slowly, deliberately, and matter-of-factly, so that the client does not feel compelled to respond to them in a certain way. There should be room for the client to express opinions that may change the therapist's assumptions.

If it is agreed that termination is appropriate, a date for the last meeting is negotiated. Clients should be asked when they would like their meetings to end. Ordinarily four to six more meetings are sufficient, although some clients, especially children, may select a birthday or an auspicious occasion that may be some distance in the future. The point is that whenever possible, the client should select the termination date.

Of course, there are treatment and training programs where the number of sessions are fixed at the outset or where the attainment of certain specified goals determines the duration of the meetings. These circumstances seldom make for the emotional involvements and uncertainties that we have been discussing in connection with a course of psychotherapy of unspecified length. From what we have been saying about termination, it is clear that for many clients long-term psychotherapy ends not with a joyous rush into a bright new day, but with a sober appraisal of accomplishments and a resolve to deal with problems as they come. For the therapist this means there is often no major personality transformation to signal services are not longer needed, but instead minor triumphs and gains. "The only thing a therapist can do for anyone . . . is to help that person gradually to be himself, to help him gain a sounder evaluation of his own difference" (Allen, 1942, p. 54).

It must also be recognized that the termination of psychotherapy, like the beginning, involves variables over which the therapist may have no control. The child may be removed from treatment by a parent who cannot tolerate the expression of certain feelings, by the family's move to another community, by the mother's pregnancy, or by family crises that are given precedence over the needs of the child. The summer vacation, with its travels, departures for camps, and disruptions in professionals' schedules, has probably precipitated termination for many clients. A discussion of termination in greater detail is the subject of Chapter 8.

3
Behavior Therapy: Operant and Classical Conditioning Models

There is an abundant literature that espouses the use of behavior therapy techniques as primary interventions with children (Graziano & Mooney, 1984; Johnson, Rasbury, & Siegel, 1986; Morris & Kratochwill, 1983). In this book, however, behavior therapy techniques will be discussed primarily as adjuncts to the conductance of child psychotherapy. There has been general agreement in the child clinical training literature that the child clinician should be trained eclectically in theoretical orientation and practice (Shirk & Phillips, 1991; Tuma, 1985). This electicism allows for a degree of flexibility often necessary to deal with a variety of child, family, and environmental variables that impact on children's behavior. Regardless of theoretical orientation, a familiarity with behavioral techniques and family therapy will enhance the repetoire of the child clinician. This and the next chapter will summarize basic learning theory principles, introduce the reader to the four main areas of behavior therapy (operant conditioning, classical or respondent conditioning, social learning, and cognitive-behavioral therapy) in terms of both theory and practical applications. First, however, a brief history of the development of behaviorism is in order.

Historical Perspective

The individual most identified with the origins of behavioral practice as it is known today is John B. Watson (1913). The first half of the twentieth century saw learning theory primarily utilized within experimental psychology and usually with animals. Although there were some attempts to apply behavioral theory to human conditions during this time (Dunlap, 1932; Jones, 1924; Salter, 1949; Watson & Raynor, 1920), it was not until the 1950s and 1960s that interventions based on learning theory were widely advocated (Skinner, 1948, 1953; Wolpe, 1958). These application efforts were based on operant and classical conditioning research and followed from the earlier work of Watson and the work of the Russian physiologist Ivan Pavlov (1927). The 1950s and 1960s were a time in the history of psychological treatment that was marked by isolationism for behavioral practitioners. Because learning theory and its variety of operant and classical conditioning techniques were presented as diametrically opposed to traditional approaches (at that time, psychodynamic and client-centered approaches prevailed), practitioners often felt that they had to choose one or the other of these orientations exclusively. Integration of these various approaches to treatment was not viewed as possible or desirable.

Since that time, there has been gradual acceptance of behaviorally based interventions by the traditional camp (American Psychiatric Association Task Force on Behavior Therapy, 1974) and vice versa (Goldfried & Merbaum, 1973). This acceptance was no doubt facilitated by the emergence of social learning theory in the late 1960s and 1970s (Bandura, 1969, 1977) and by the development of the cognitive-behavioral therapy area in the 1970s (Kanfer & Karoly, 1972; Mahoney, 1974; Meichenbaum, 1977). That relationship variables and cognitions were now considered by some behavior therapists as legitimate aspects for which interventions could be developed helped to facilitate behaviorism's acceptance by more traditional practitioners. This broadening of the definition of what behaviors were acceptable for behavior therapists to be concerned about brought the application of behaviorism from the strict S-R model (in which stimulus leads directly to a response) to an S-O-R model, with the "organism" now given credit for interpreting and affecting the environment (as well as being affected by the environment). At which point in this cycle of cause and effect a behaviorist chooses to intervene can vary from one practitioner to another. That is, interventions can be designed to alter environmental conditions (S), how an individual interprets events (O), or a symptom or a response directly (R). Still, there are primary principles, based in learning theory, that most behaviorists would espouse regardless of the point of intervention.

General Learning Principles

Behaviorists tend to downplay or minimize intrapsychic motivations and unconscious processes. Instead, there is an emphasis on what is observable (behaviors) or explainable (cognitions). The context in which an individual functions is viewed as directly influencing behavior. It is toward this context that interventions are often developed (for example, getting parents to be more consistent in their rewards and punishments, or minimizing distracting features of a classroom for a child with an attention deficit).

The role of a thorough and complete assessment is regarded as critical not only before an intervention is attempted, but throughout the treatment process. There should be an ongoing evaluation of an intervention's impact. When an intervention has not been effective, rather than assume that a client is being resistant or displaying transference phenomena, the behaviorist tends to assume that an inaccurate assessment was made and, therefore, an inappropriate intervention was attempted. Thus, the behaviorist usually returns to the assessment to determine which variables (often secondary-gain issues or the inconsistent delivery of the intervention by parents and teachers) did not receive sufficient attention. The behavior therapist might then develop a new treatment strategy. This process of trying an intervention, assessing its effectiveness, and altering it (if the first try has not been entirely successful) constitutes an empirical methodology and relates to behaviorism's early developmental years in the field of experimental psychology. The practice of behavior therapy has been characterized as hypothesis testing in nature, and critical to this approach is a thorough and ongoing assessment. Behavioral assessment procedures will be discussed in more detail later in this chapter.

Another principle that most behaviorists would espouse is that pathology is not an appropriate model for understanding problems; instead, it is believed that inappropriate behavior, feelings, and cognitions are learned. These troublesome behaviors or "symptoms" are acquired and maintained by the same principles as are appropriate responses. Furthermore, it is believed that these troublesome reactions can be altered by similar learning principles. The behavioral approach would intervene directly with the symptom or external conditions related to it, with little concern for underlying motivations and unconscious processes. There is often a direct cause-and-effect mentality among behaviorists, in which they believe responses are directly triggered by environmental stimuli. As the cognitive-behaviorists have become more prominent, behaviorists have acknowledged that the cause-and-effect connection is not always so simple. Intervening variables such as cognitions (how one interprets a stimulus) and vicarious learning histories also have to be considered.

Behavioral Assessment

Behavior therapists' emphasis on a thorough and ongoing assessment is quite compatible with our own Principle I. Similarities and differences between traditional assessment and behavioral assessment are discussed by Hartmann, Roper, and Bradford (1979). Whereas traditional assessors would be interested in information that represents underlying dynamics and unconscious processes as well as historical information, the behavioral assessor concentrates on here-and-now information regarding the conditions (stimuli) that precede or elicit dysfunctional behavior, the conditions that maintain or follow the dysfunctional behavior, and the context in which the behavior occurs. Context for the behaviorist can refer to a variety of dimensions outside the individual, such as one's family or other relationships (for children, teacher and peer relationships are usually important to assess) and environmental influences (such as noise, crowdedness, violence, or prejudice). Thus, a *functional analysis of behavior* is an examination of the relationships between inappropriate behaviors and various contextual or environmental factors that precede or elicit these behaviors.

One of the most commonly cited examples of a model for doing a behavioral assessment is the SORKC model (Kanfer & Saslow, 1969). Each of the initials in this anachronism represents an aspect of a functional analysis of behavior. The *S* refers to external stimuli (which typically precede or signal an inappropirate reaction); the *O* represents any unique characteristics of the individual (organism) that may intervene in how the external stimuli affect subsequent responding (typically these are biological, physical, or cognitive factors); the *R* refers to the individual's responses (these can be motoric, cognitive, or physiological); the *K* represents contingent relationships between the inappropriate reaction and its consequences, especially as it pertains to maintenance of the problematic response; and the *C* refers to specific consequences that follow the response. Behaviorists are interested in information regarding the frequency, intensity, and durations of problematic responses, and they would acknowledge that consequences can be other than specific, overt events (for example, feelings of relief or guilt, or social disapproval or approval).

Behaviorists rely heavily on self-report and reports of others (parents, teachers, and so on) when doing child assessments. The information generated from self (the child) and others is most likely to be gathered through interviewing and a variety of questionnaires. These questionnaires elicit information on the occurrence of specific behaviors, and often ask for judgments regarding frequency or intensity. Child behavior problem checklists, fear survey schedules, and skills deficits questionnaires (social skills, study skills, and so forth) are commonly used. There are a number of specialized texts that discuss the use of behavioral interviewing and questionnaires. The reader is referred to these sources for a more thorough discussion of this aspect of behavioral assessment (for example, Bellack & Hersen, 1977, 1988; Ciminero, Calhoun, & Adams, 1986; Cone & Hawkins, 1977; Hersen & Bellack, 1976; Kestenbaum & Williams, 1988; Mash and Terdal, 1982; Ollendick & Hersen, 1984).

Unlike projective test assessors, behaviorists are interested in collecting information within the context in which the problematic behavior occurs. The interest often takes the form of behavioral observations (in the class-

room or at home) or behavior rehearsal, in which the child is asked to sim-
ulate a situation in which the problematic behavior occurs. As behaviorists
do not accept that behavior is necessarily consistent and traitlike, there is
interest in collecting data from a variety of settings. In fact, it may be critical to discover that certain behaviors (such as distractibility) do not occur
in all settings in which the child functions (such as in a chaotic and over-
crowded classroom, but not at Sunday school or home). The following
case serves as an example of a typical behavioral assessment.

Case Example

Carrie was a 7-year-old second grader who was brought to treatment by
her parents as a result of complaints from school that she was not paying
attention in class and was in conflicts with her classmates and teacher. The
initial session was conducted with only the parents present. During this
time, they were interviewed thoroughly about the present situation as well
as for relevant developmental information from Carrie's former years. It
was discovered that these complaints were not new; in kindergarten and
first grade she was also described as inattentive and "bossy" with peers.
The parents reported a history with Carrie in which she had always required much attention from them to keep her focused and out of trouble.
They said they often felt like bad parents because they were always reprimanding her or anticipating that she would misbehave. When in public,
they reported being "on edge" regarding whether or not Carrie would act
appropriately.

The parents felt Carrie was less inattentive at home (she could watch a
television program without becoming distractible, listen as they read a
story to her, or play Nintendo for a period of time). They felt, however,
that she did not use good judgment and often reacted without thinking
about what she was doing. When she had a friend over to play, she often
demanded to be first and to determine what was played, and she became
easily frustrated if not given her way. At the same time, she wanted to
have friends and would feel hurt if things did not work out well with one.
The parents reported a good marital relationship, adequate finances, and
no unusual stresses in the family. Carrie was described as having a "normal sibling relationship" with her 10-year-old brother.

When the parents were asked to describe Carrie's assets, they beamed
and reported her athletic abilities, her excellent academic skills, and her
creative imagination. Both parents felt her to be affectionate and empathic
within the family. No unusual fears or anxieties were reported. The parents said that in general they were consistent in their expectations for
Carrie, and that time out was the most effective punishment to use with
her. They felt at times Carrie would even impose "time out" on herself
when she became overstimulated (when at a church function at which chil-

dren were running around and being loud, Carrie came over to where her parents were talking with other adults and asked if she could sit with them for a while). At bedtime, she frequently requested back rubs and gentle physical massaging; these acts seemed to relax and calm her. She clearly behaved best when she had a predictable routine and would become upset if she was surprised by some change in her schedule. Nevertheless, she periodically would test to see if limits were still enforced. She would drop her testing behavior once she knew the same rules were in effect.

The parents were each asked to complete the Connors Rating Scale (a questionnaire that is particularly helpful in identifying attention-deficit hyperactivity disorder symptoms) and the Peterson Behavior Problem Checklist. They were instructed to bring with them to the next session all academic paperwork that they had collected on Carrie (report cards, teacher notes, awards, standardized tests, and the like). As Carrie's academic performance was excellent, the school had never advised that Carrie be formally assessed for learning problems.

Before the parents left this first session, they were asked to sign a permission form that would allow the therapist to speak to Carrie's teacher. Before the next session, which was the first meeting with Carrie, the therapist had a lengthy phone interview with the teacher and sent through the mail a Connors Rating Scale for the teacher to complete. As the therapist also knew the social worker at this particular school, she called him to ask if he might do a behavioral observation of Carrie. The teacher reported that early afternoons were particularly difficult for Carrie, as were recesses. The school social worker agreed to observe Carrie during several class periods and at recess.

Finally, the first session with Carrie was held. She presented herself as a delightful, very talkative child who was very curious about the therapist and the therapy room; she was immediately all around the room investigating the games and toys. With great reluctance, Carrie agreed to forgo playing with them while she and the therapist talked. This agreement was very hard to keep, however, and soon she was greatly distracted by the toys and games and unable to concentrate on the questions being asked. When allowed to play with the toys, Carrie went from one set to another rather than settling on one thing. When the therapist suggested playing a game, Carrie demanded to go first, and she became visibly upset when she was not doing well in the game relative to how the therapist was doing. When this happened, she chose to discontinue the game. During the play, the therapist was able to ask questions of Carrie. She was not defensive and responded openly to the questions; there were, however, times when she was not paying enough attention to hear the question accurately.

Carrie reported that she was sad that she did not have enough friends, and she did not understand why her teacher was always calling her down or asking her to get back to her work (she felt her teacher did not like her).

She agreed that she was easily distracted when other children in the room talked, walked about, or made noises. Carrie also said that she did not like the desk to which she had recently been moved; instead of being on the edge of the classroom, she was now in the middle and surrounded by children on all sides. She felt she had gotten into more trouble since making this move. (A later call to the teacher indeed did verify that her inattentive behavior had worsened in the past 2 weeks, a time comparable to the move in the classroom. The teacher also reported that she was now sitting closer to one of her friends, and the two were frequently in trouble for talking.)

This case illustrates the multiple dimensions of assessment that a behavioral therapist would find important. Reports of the child and relevant others, behavioral observations in the school, the therapist's own observations during the session, and objective records of past school performance were all seen as valuable in the assessment effort. It is important to point out that assessment did not stop at this stage. Indeed, several weeks later, arrangements were made for Carrie to be evaluated by a pediatric neurologist, as attention-deficit hyperactivity disorder (ADHD) was suspected and medication might be indicated. Further assessment occurred as various interventions were attempted. Additional details about the interventions used in this case will be discussed later in this chapter.

Operant Conditioning

Operant conditioning theory (Skinner, 1953) is concerned primarily with how behaviors (operants) are contolled (increased or decreased) by the consequences that occur after the behaviors. Those operants or behaviors that are followed by reward and positive consequences have the likelihood of being maintained or increased in frequency. Those operants or behaviors that are followed by punishment or negative consequences are likely to be decreased. Much of the control that parents and teachers exert over children falls into the category of operant conditioning. It is likely that parents and teachers do not often plan to use these consequences deliberately; nevertheless, their positive and negative reactions (consequences) following various child behaviors will serve to maintain, increase, or decrease the likelihood of these behaviors in the future.

Interventions that are used with children and are based on operant conditioning theory attempt to alter the nature of the consequences following a child's behavior so that the desired behaviors result. Kazdin (1984) and Graziano and Mooney (1984) provide excellent detail on how various behavioral techniques, including operant techniques, can be devised and delivered. In this chapter, the frequently used operant interventions will be briefly examined; these include interventions based on the Premack principle, the use of time-out procedures, and various contingency management techniques (including charting, home-school note systems, and contingency or behavioral contracting).

Premack Principle

The Premack principle is a rule stating that a higher-probability behavior can reinforce a lower-probability behavior; a desirable event or object can be used to increase the occurrence of an aversive event if access to the desirable event or object is withheld until the aversive event is completed. Parents use this principle when they say, "You cannot watch television until your homework is done," "You cannot have dessert until you eat your vegetables," and, "You must clean up your room before you can play with Jimmy." In each of these examples, the parents want the child to complete a task that the child experiences as negative or aversive. To accomplish this goal, a desirable event or object is promised as a consequence for getting the aversive task completed. The key to establishing an intervention based on the Premack principle is that the desirable event or object that is being withheld must indeed be viewed by the child as attractive—and importantly, as more attractive than the aversive task is negative. If the children in the above examples hate vegetables more than they like dessert, dread cleaning their room more than they enjoy playing with a friend, or do not believe that there is anything of interest on television this particular night, then the interventions would likely fail. Thus, when establishing an intervention of this sort, it is important (usually with the parents' help) to find out which behaviors, events, or objects are sufficiently attractive or rewarding for the particular child under question. If this is difficult to do while interviewing the child and/or parents, a Children's Reinforcement Survey Schedule (Phillips, Fischer, & Singh, 1977) can be used. This survey lists a variety of things, privileges, and events that children typically find appealing and enjoyable. Children are instructed to mark which items are pleasurable and to rate how positive the item is for them.

When an intervention has been used over time, what was once a very attractive event loses some of its appeal. Therefore, there should be a periodic reassessment to determine whether the desirable events or objects continue to be "stronger" than the aversive event. Interventions based on the Premack principle are often carried out by parents and teachers; an example of a teacher intervention would be "You can work on the computer once you have your math problems completed." Whenever the therapist is reliant on the parents or a teacher to deliver an intervention, care must be taken to be certain they understand the rationale for the intervention, know what exactly it is that they are to do, and are capable of consistently and appropriately implementing the intervention. Other issues related to working with parents and teachers in the development and delivery of behavioral techniques will be discussed throughout this chapter.

Time Out

Time out is a specific punishment procedure in which an individual is removed from the setting, person, or activity that he or she finds positively reinforcing. The removal of the individual is typically for a brief period of time, and the individual's ability to return to the original setting is dependent on the reestablishment of appropriate behavior in the meantime. Parents commonly use time out in a variety of forms—sitting a child on a specific chair or on the steps leading upstairs, sending a child to his or her room, and so on. Teachers, too, may utilize time out by having the child removed to the hallway or to a specially designated time-out area in the classroom. Time out is typically used for the management of out-of-control behavior such as temper tantrums; however, it can be effectively used if a child refuses to stop performing any behavior that is deemed undesirable by the adult. It is usually the attention and reaction of the adult to the undesirable behavior that is serving as a reinforcer for the child's continuance of the behavior. Thus, a parent who pleads, gives in, or even yells back may be serving as reinforcement for the negative behavior. It is very important that the removal or time out should not itself be rewarding.

Something to keep in mind when prescribing time-out procedures for use with children is that, in general, the younger the child, the less time spent in time out. Patterson (1976) maintains that 3 minutes can be as effective as 30 minutes. Consistent enforcement is probably more important than the amount of time in time out, so the duration should not be so long that it defeats the purpose of the procedure. For the youngest of children, partial removal from the setting (having the child sit on a chair in the same room) may be effective. Complete removal of the child from the adult's vision should never occur if there is any concern about the safety of the child. Also, a child should never be put in a room in which there are potential hazards (a bathroom in which medicines, razors, or the like might be used by an upset child).

Before time out is instituted, the child should be given a warning to quit the negative behavior and told that continuance of the negative behavior will lead to removal or time out. If the behavior does continue, then the child should be removed or put in time out without further warnings. A parent who continues to give warnings without consequences will likely not get the desired behavior from the child and may inadvertently reinforce the undesirable behavior.

Young children may have to be physically placed in time out. Older children can be instructed that if they do not go when told, then extra minutes will be added to the time-out period. If a parent is unable to get a child into time out with these efforts, then time out is probably not the best aversive procedure to be using. Once in time out, children should be told how long they will be there (with a child who is too young to understand time, a timer can be used) and told of the behavior that is expected of them in order for them to get out. If the child continues with unacceptable negative behavior when the timeout period is over, additional minutes can be added, or other negative consequences can be applied. Sometimes it is necessary to warn the child a priori that additional negative or destructive behavior while in time out will lead to further minutes of exclusion. Depending on the child's age, when time out is over and the child (and adult) are again relatively calm, it is a good idea to discuss the events that led to the time out. For young children, talking may be less helpful; actually showing the child what alternative behavior is desired may be more effective.

Within the therapy room, time out may be necessary if a child has become out of control or refuses to abide by the rules. The child can be made to sit in a chair, toys can be removed, or in extreme cases, the session may be prematurely terminated. As described above, before any of these occur, the child should be given adequate warning of impending time out if the undesirable behavior persists.

A milder version of time out is *ignoring*. This is not always powerful enough to change entrenched behaviors, but it may be effective with negative behaviors that are emitted specifically to elicit a reaction. For instance, once children enter school, they are introduced to a variety of words with which to expand their vocabularies. Some of these words will make a parent's chest expand in pride; others, usually of four letters, will make a parent see red. Often a child will experiment with curse words around a parent. If the parent's reaction is one that delights the child, the parent may have inadvertently reinforced the further utterance of the profanity. When it is apparent that a child persists in a negative behavior in order to provoke a certain reaction from another person (shock, negative attention, embarrassment, and so forth) then ignoring the child's behavior may serve to extinguish the behavior. In this case, the child is not physically removed from the reinforcing condition, but the reinforcing condition is removed from the child. Sometimes it is difficult to ignore a child while staying in close proximity; the physical removal of the adult may then be necessary. (Adults, too, can effectively use a sort of time out for themselves, which is helpful when the adult is becoming overly negative in reaction to the child.) In any case, the child is left without the reinforcing conditions that were supporting the negative behavior. Behaviors that are particularly amenable to ignoring are whining, pouting, and insincere crying.

Contingency Management Procedures

Contingency management procedures entail the purposeful use of positive and negative reinforcement and punishment. Positive reinforcement is used to increase the incidence of a desirable behavior. Positive reinforcement can also decrease the incidence of an undesirable behavior by encouraging a competing behavior that is more appropriate. Negative reinforcement also increases or strengthens a behavior, but does so by the escape principle; if the performance of a behavior leads to the cessation of an aversive condition, the behavior will be reinforced. Putting on one's seat belt in order to stop the buzzer in a car is an example of negative reinforcement. A parent's nagging may have a negatively reinforcing effect if a child finally performs their chores in order to "get Mom off my back." Punishment is a consequence that is aversive and is intended to decrease the occurrence of a behavior. Punishment can also take the form of the removal of a positive condition (with ignoring equal to removal of attention) until a negative behavior is decreased or eliminated. Three contingency management approaches that are frequently used with children will be discussed here.

Charting. This is a simple way to apply contingent consequences and is most effective for young children. When using charting, one needs to identify behaviors that are to be altered. Some of these identified behaviors are to be increased; others are to be decreased. The behaviors should be specifically defined so that there is no confusion on the part of the child and the adult administering the program about whether a behavior occurred or not. Next, a monitoring system (or chart) is established so that a record can be kept of whether or not, when, and to what degree the targeted behaviors occurred. A typical chart would have a line for each target behavior and columns for each of the days of the week. In some cases, charts used at school may be further divided into morning and afternoon periods.

For very young children, the use of colorful stickers is sufficient to interest and motivate the child to change behavior. For older children and some young children, the tallies (stickers) that appear on the chart can be traded in at a later time for a reward. Thus, a given number of points, checks, or stickers can lead to the child being rewarded once they have been earned. Rewards can be physical (such as toys, candy, money, or music tapes), social (an opportunity to play with friends, have a sleepover, or go out to breakfast with Dad), or involve privileges (a number of hours of playing Nintendo, staying up longer before bedtime, or renting a videotape). Physical rewards tend to be least preferred but may work best with the youngest of children. Social and privilege awards are more valuable because they involve the child in interacting with others or exercising age-appropriate freedoms.

Social rewards are particularly intriguing in that they can serve a secondary benefit in addition to the primary one of increasing desirable behavior. For instance, if a boy's reward for completing homework for a week is lunch at McDonald's on Saturday with his normally unavailable father, then the father may be involved in a way with his son that would not have occurred otherwise. Thus, the father-son relationship might be strengthened if the father is involved in the reward. Taking this particular example, it may even be advisable for the therapist to suggest that the father instead of the mother (particularly if the mother has a history of having conflict with her son regarding the completion of homework) should be the primary monitor of the charting procedure. In this case, the mother will be let off the hook (which may reduce negative intensity between her and her son), and the father may be pulled in to relate to his son more frequently than before. Furthermore, the mother and father may have to discuss their son's situation and work as a team—an experience that may not have been occurring enough. Thus, beyond the effects of getting this boy to complete his homework, family relationships can also be affected by the implementation of this simple charting system.

If possible, the child (and definitely the parents) should be involved in deciding what the rewards are to be. If the child is unlikely to select rewards that are acceptable to the parents and therapist, the child should be presented with several possible rewards, all of which are acceptable to the adults, and asked to select from this list. The child's involvement increases the chances that the rewards are in fact appealing to the child, and thus may increase the interest and motivation of the child to earn the rewards. Likewise, if the parents are not in agreement with the rewards, they may not cooperate or deliver the program as intended. Finally, in selecting the behaviors to be changed, not only should they be very specifically defined, but care should be taken that the child has the skills needed to perform the behaviors. Initially, it may be advantageous to set a standard for obtaining the reward that is easily within the reach of the child. Once the child has attained some success, the conditions for further rewards can be renegotiated. One of the forms that this takes is to offer little rewards more frequently at first, then move to larger rewards that are earned over a longer period of time. Whenever using charting with children, frequent evaluations of the effects of the program should be conducted. It would not be unusual for old behaviors to be taken off the list or new behaviors added, or to have rewards or the conditions under which they are earned altered, over time.

Home-School Note System. This system of intervention is useful when school behavior—either academic performance or conduct—is the target of change. It involves the teacher monitoring the child's behavior and recording it in some fashion in a form that is sent to the parents at home, with the parents then reinforcing or punishing in accord with preestablished rules. In some cases, the behavior recorded on the home note is converted by the parents into points that can later can be exchanged for specific rewards.

As with charting, the behaviors being targeted need to be specifically defined, the child's cooperation with the program should be encouraged, and the child and parent need to agree on the rewards. A necessary element of the home-school note system is the cooperation of the teacher. One of the possible outcomes of such a system is increased communication between parents and teacher. If the child is assigned responsibility for carrying the note home, there should be a rule in effect at the beginning of the program about what will happen if the note does not make it home. Some children will be reluctant to present their parents a note detailing a bad day, and a variety of excuses will be offered instead of the note. Parents and teachers should think about how they can assist the child in being successful with such a program. As with most behavioral programs, rewards or positive incentives are preferable to punishments. When punishments are used in charting or a home-school note system, they are often penalties that reduce the amount of credit that the child has earned toward a reward; the primary emphasis thus remains on positive results.

A home-school note system was used with Carrie, the case reported earlier in this chapter. Three behaviors in need of change were identified by the teacher and Carrie: completes work, plays well with children, and works well with children. For the first several weeks the teacher made ratings on the form that Carrie carried home each day. After that, and because of her positive response to the program, Carrie conducted her own ratings; she then discussed these with the teacher, who "signed off" on the form. This increased Carrie's sense of responsibility and *self-monitoring* for her own behavior. Once the notes were presented to her parents, they awarded predetermined points that could be traded in later for special privileges. Interestingly, the tangible rewards seemed less important to this 7-year-old than the social reinforcement from her teacher, parents, and therapist. Figure 3-1 is an approximation of the note used with Carrie.

Contingency Contracting. Also known as behavioral contracting, this involves an agreement between two parties stating that if one party performs certain behaviors, then the other will respond in a certain way. Often contracting is valuable with older children, because they can play an active role in establishing the conditions of the contract. Contracts should be written, all parties to the contract should understand and agree to its particulars, and all parties should sign the contract. A good behavioral contract details the behaviors and responses expected, provides "bonuses" for exceptionally positive behavior, may contain a modest penalty for undesirable behavior, includes the means to monitor the conditions of the contract, and details a renegotiation or reevaluation process.

As with charting, initial behaviorial contracts should contain few rather than many behaviors, cover a brief period of time, and be designed to promote early success. The therapist can ask the family to post the contract in a highly visible area so that all parties are frequently reminded of

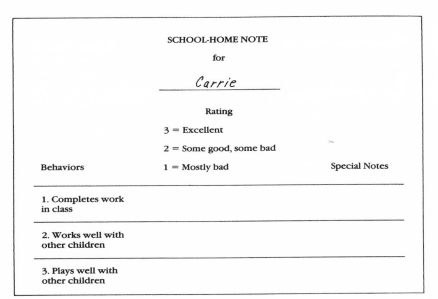

Figure 3–1

their roles in the intervention. As contracts require the cooperation of both parties, mutual agreement is needed for the abolishment or renegotation of the contract. Although contracts are most often established between a child and parents, contracts can also be used between the child and therapist or between a child and teacher. Figure 3-2 is an example of a behavioral contract.

General Issues Involved in Implementing Operant Conditioning Techniques

When utilizing operant conditioning procedures, one should keep in mind a number of informal rules. These include the following:

1. Whenever possible, use positive reinforcement procedures rather than punishment procedures.
2. Actively involve the child and parents (or teacher) in the devising and implementation of the procedures.
3. Start with interventions that are likely to succeed, then gradually move to more complicated ones.
4. Individualize the contingency plan. Each child should be evaluated differently, as no two children will have exactly the same response to various contingencies.

BEHAVIORAL CONTRACT

I,_____, promise to be ready (all dressed, hair combed, teeth brushed, and breakfast eaten) at 8:15 A.M. each school morning so that I will not be late for the school bus. If I can meet the conditions stated above for an entire week (5 consecutive school days), then my parents,_____, agree that I can have a sleepover with a friend on Friday or Saturday night. The sleepover can be either at my house or a friend's house, depending on my parents' plans. I understand that my parents must approve of the friend with whom I will have the sleepover and the night on which it is to occur. If I am successful at meeting the bus on time for 4 weeks in a row, I understand that I will be permitted to invite a friend (with my parents' approval) to go with me and my parents to a movie and out to eat afterward (my parents and I must all agree on which movie and which restaurant).

I understand that for each day that I am not ready to catch the school bus (defined as having met the conditions stated above) and my mother is required to drive me to school, I will owe her 1 hour's worth of chores after school in order to compensate her for her time. Which chores are to be done is to be decided by my mother, and regardless of how slow I work, she is to give me what in her opinion is 1 hour's worth of work. Furthermore, I understand that if I am not ready on each of the 5 school days in the week, I will not be able to have a sleepover on the weekend. During each weekly session with Dr. Ribordy, I and/or my parents will have the opportunity to discuss the specifics of this contract. In signing this contract, I understand its conditions and agree to abide by them.

Signature	Date

We,_____, the parents of_____, have read, understand, and agree to abide by the conditions of this contract.

Signature	Date

Signature	Date

I, Dr. Ribordy, have made certain that all parties to the above contract understand its conditions and have agreed to abide by them. Furthermore, I will provide opportunities for all parties to discuss the conditions of this contract at our weekly therapy sessions. If there is disagreement about how the contract should be implemented, I am willing to serve as an arbitrator for the parties involved.

Signature	Date

Figure 3-2

5. Periodically evaluate the continued effectiveness of the behavioral plan; be prepared to modify the intervention from time to time.
6. Rewards should occur more frequently initially, then less frequently over time. Moving from a continuous reinforcement schedule to an intermittent reinforcement schedule is likely to enhance maintenance effects.
7. Social and privilege rewards are preferable (where appropriate) to tangible rewards. When tangible rewards are used, they can be paired with social rewards, and tangible rewards can be gradually discontinued in favor of social and privilege rewards.
8. Rewards that are artificial are less preferred than those that are naturally occurring.
9. Plan systematically to discontinue an operant conditioning program to ensure the greatest chance for both maintenance of treatment gains and generalization.
10. Be certain that the behaviors that are to be developed are within the skill repertoire of the child.
11. Be certain that the adult (parent or teacher) who will administer the operant program is motivated and consistent in carrying out the program plan.
12. When developing an operant plan, anticipate and actively utilize the possible secondary effects on the relationship between the child and the adult(s) implementing the program.

Much of behavioral parent (or teacher) training involves the education of adults in the specifics of learning theory and various behavioral management techniques. There are some excellent books designed for this purpose (e.g., Crary, 1979; Fine, 1973; Parkinson, 1985; Patterson, 1976; Stumphauzer, 1977). In utilizing parents to carry out a behavioral intervention, one must remember that the parents bring their own issues to the child's treatment. Part of any good assessment will include an evalaution of the strengths and weaknesses of the parents, as well as the child. The later chapters on family therapy and working with parents will provide further guidance about dealing with parents.

An aspect in the treatment of Carrie, whose assessment was outlined earlier in this chapter, serves as a good example of this issue. Because Carrie's parents were feeling that they were bad parents for always reprimanding their daughter, a simple intervention was used that helped them to feel more positive about themselves and their daughter. The intervention consisted of a "good behavior chart" that the parent was to complete each evening at bedtime with Carrie. On the chart was to be written several good things that Carrie had done that day, with the parent taking particular care to communicate his or her pride in the child. After the first week of using the chart, Carrie proudly presented it to the therapist as evidence that she really was not so bad. The parents likewise reported it helped them focus less on Carrie's misbehavior and enabled them to put the negative behavior in perspective. After several weeks of using the chart, the therapist "forgot" to include it as a specific assignment for the following week. Upon leaving the session, the mother herself requested more forms, as the chart had become an enjoyable task for Carrie and her parents that they wanted to continue on their own. Although this particular intervention was not specifically focused on the inappropriate behaviors Carrie was exhibiting at school or at home, it helped create in all parties a positive attitude that facilitated later interventions more directly related to the misbehaviors. Carrie's self-esteem was enhanced, and her parents felt more hopeful about her and more positive about their own parenting.

Classical Conditioning

Procedures based on the theory of respondent or classical conditioning focus on the stimuli that elicit undesirable responses. These responses are regarded as automatic because they are reflexive and often are not learned. An example of a reflexive response is the fear reaction of an individual on an airplane that is going through extreme turbulence. He or she is fearful of the plane falling, of being confined and not being able to get out of the situation, and so forth. An individual's fear response to this particular situation is relatively unlearned. When other situations that are related but not the same start to elicit the same fear response, though, classical conditioning has occurred. These subsequent situations that can now create anxiety/fear are called *conditioned stimuli.* For instance, the individual may later experience similar fear on plane flights that are not turbulent, become inexplicably anxious when confined to small spaces such as elevators or moving trains, or refuse to venture higher than the second story of a building because of anxiety about being high above the ground.

In this particular example, an initial anxiety-provoking stimulus (unconditioned stimulus) experience is known (the turbulent flight), but in many cases of classically conditioned anxiety/fear, one never is able to specify the original unconditioned stimulus. Furthermore, anxiety and fear reactions can occur with just the imagination or anticipation of the conditioned stimulus event occurring. Thus, the individual may become anxious upon merely hearing about family plans that will require a plane trip months in the future, or delay getting dental care because the dentist's office is on the 12th floor. In classical conditioning, innocuous events or stimuli acquire the power to elicit or control subsequent responses.

Interventions based on classical conditioning theory attempt a reconditioning process in which the conditioned stimulus or event is made to lead to a more appropriate response. The most frequently used version of classical conditioning procedures attempts to teach or train an individual to remain relaxed in the face of formerly anxiety-provoking situations. Thus, following repeated pairings with relaxation responses, the situation is associated with the relaxation response instead of anxiety. This repeated pairing procedure diminishes the conditioned association between the stimulus and the anxiety that typically followed. The remainder of this chapter will discuss two commonly used procedures based on classical conditioning theory—the use of relaxation techniques and systematic desensitization with children. Readers are referred to other sources for a detailed discussion of the bell-and-pad procedure, another procedure based on classical conditioning theory that is designed solely for the treatment of enuresis (Mowrer & Mowrer, 1938; Walker, Milling, & Bonner, 1988). Another respondent technique, *stimulus control,* has been successfully used with obese children (Epstein & Squires, 1988).

Relaxation training procedures can be used for a variety of problems with children, including anxieties and fears (Barrios & O'Dell, 1989; Morris & Kratochwill, 1983), the overstimulation common in ADHD children (Barkley, 1990), anger management (Barkley, 1990, Novaco, 1978), obsessive-compulsive symptoms (Milby & Weber, 1991), and some somatic complaints like headaches (Siegel & Smith, 1991). Although the application of relaxation techniques can vary from one target population to another, there are relaxation procedures that can be discussed that generalize across practices.

The most frequently used relaxation training procedure for both adults and children is deep muscular relaxation, developed by Jacobson (1938). This form of training requires the child to practice tensing and then relaxing various muscle groups of the body. Initially, the therapist guides the child through the procedure; thereafter the child is asked to practice at home, most likely with the aid of directions on an audiocassette. Parents can also be trained to guide their child's relaxation sessions at home. After several weeks of conscientious practice, most children will be able to relax without the need for adult guidance or the instructions of the tape. Jacobson's relaxation training is most appropriate for older children, since it requires good attentional skills and some self-discipline. For younger children, training in deep muscular relaxation is enhanced by incorporating imagery exercises into the procedures. Koeppen (1974) was one of the first to adapt relaxation procedures originally developed for adults for use with children. For instance, rather than asking a child to tense his or her fists, the Koeppen instructions ask the child to imagine squeezing a whole lemon in the hand. Cautela and Groden (1978) also provide a fine manual on the use of various relaxation techniques with children.

Below is a verbatim relaxation training exercise used with youngsters. It is a compilation of progressive deep muscular relaxation procedures and imagery exercises. Before beginning the relaxation procedure, the therapist should give the child a rationale for why learning to relax will be helpful, explain to the child what will be happening, and answer any questions the child (or parent) may have. The child is then asked to sit in a comfortable chair (on which the head can be rested) or to lie flat on a comfortable surface, to close his or her eyes, and to concentrate on the therapist's instructions. The specific relaxation training instructions are then given in a slow, quiet manner.

> First thing I would like for you to do is to close your eyes and try to push everything out of your mind. . . . Try to be relaxed. What can help you be relaxed is to take a deep breath. I want you to breathe in very slowly, take in as much air as you can, fill your lungs all the way up, and now push the air all the way out. . . . Now I want you to do that several more times. Take in the air very slowly and deeply . . . hold it for a moment . . . then let all the air out. Do that again—fill the lungs very fully until it feels like they might burst . . . hold it . . . now let out all the air—push all the air out that you can. Already you may be feeling that your body is slowing down—kind of like a robot that is moving in slow motion—your body is starting to work slower.
>
> The next thing I want you to do is to hold your arms out in front of you and clench your fists tightly. Hold them very tightly until it almost feels like it is going to hurt. Notice how tight you can make your fists. . . . Now let your arms relax and come back to your lap. They are now losing that tightness and tension. . . . Now I want you to again put your arms out in front of you. This time I want you to imagine you are squeezing a tennis ball in each of your hands. You are squeezing a tennis ball. Your hands aren't closed all the way, but they are squeezing a tennis ball. Keep squeezing . . . OK, now let your hands relax. Let them come back down into your lap and let them relax. . . . One more time, I would like you to hold your hands out in front of you. This time I want you to open your hands and bend your fingers backward as far as possible. Notice how that makes the muscles in your hands feel real tight. . . . Now relax; let your arms come back down to your lap and be relaxed. . . . This time I want you to raise your hands out in front of you and flap your hands around. Take both hands and flap them, like you are shaking away any tightness or tension. It feels good to shake them around. Flap them around a little bit more. . . . Now let your arms relax in your lap again.
>
> Next I want you to take your right arm and make a muscle, like you were showing someone how strong you are. Bend your arm and make a muscle—make it as hard as you can. Hold it like that. . . . Now let that arm relax in your lap. . . . This time take your left arm and do the same thing. Hold it out in front of you, bend your arm at the elbow and make a muscle—and hold it tightly. Make a muscle and hold it tightly. . . . Okay, let that arm relax now. Let both arms relax now. . . . If you think about your arms, they may feel a little bit tingly—that means that they are starting to feel nice and relaxed.

Next I want you to arch your shoulders backward as if you were trying to touch your shoulder blades together. Arch your shoulders backward. I want you to hold that position for a moment. . . . Notice how tight your back feels when you do that. . . . OK, now relax. Let the shoulders come back down to a natural position. . . . This time I want you to hunch your shoulders forward. Try to touch your shoulders together in front of you. This time you hunch your shoulders forward. . . . Notice how tight it makes those muscles feel. . . . Now relax; let your shoulders come back to their natural position and relax.

This time I want you to turn your head to the right—turn your head as far to the right as you can. Hold it there and notice while you do that it tightens and tenses the neck muscles. . . . Now I want you to turn your head as far as you can to the left. Hold it there and again notice how tight you have made those muscles when you do that. . . . Now bring your head forward in a natural position . . . and now bend your head back as far as you can. Hold it there for a moment. . . . Now bend your head forward as if you were trying to touch your chin to your chest. Hold it there for a moment. . . . Now bring your head up, and to help your neck and shoulders relax a bit, I want you to make a circle with your head—a nice, slow circle with your head. Keep doing this for a bit. This helps the neck and shoulders relax. . . . Now let your head rest back against the chair and just relax for a moment.

Next I want you to open your mouth as far as possible. Open your mouth as wide as possible and hold it there. Notice how this makes all the muscles around the lips get very tight. . . . Now relax—close the mouth and let it be relaxed. . . . Now I want you to clench your mouth tightly closed. Close your mouth as tight as possible. I want you to imagine that someone is making you take medicine that is bitter, and there is no way you are going to let them get that medicine in your mouth. . . . Now relax—let your lips relax. . . . This time I want you to make a frown. Wrinkle up all the muscles on your forehead, around your eyes, and around your nose. Pretend that you just saw the yuckiest thing. All those muscles get all wrinkled up as you frown. Hold it there . . . now relax. Let all the wrinkles from your forehead disappear, relax the muscles around your eyes and nose.

We're going to stop for a moment, and I want you to just relax. Just sit there [or lie there] and try to relax. . . . Sometimes we can relax more if we try not to think of anything. Try to clear your mind. Imagine your mind is a blackboard and you have an eraser and you can make all your thoughts disappear by erasing the blackboard. . . . Now I want you to put something up on your blackboard. . . . I want you to have a picture. I want you to imagine something positive—something like, your parents love you . . . or a friend telling you that they like your new clothes . . . or maybe the next picture you could put on the blackboard is you eating your favorite food in your favorite restaurant or place with your favorite friends. . . . How about imagining you are getting a good grade on a paper at school and your teacher gives you a compliment. . . . Sometimes when we think of positive things it helps us relax. While you sit [lie] there and try to relax just think of a few things that make you feel good. [long pause]

Now we are going on to a few more of the exercises. Next, take a couple more of those deep breaths that we started with. To do this, breathe in real slow, take in as much air as you can, hold it for a second, then let it all out. Push all the air out that you can. . . . Once more; breathe in slow, hold it, and then let all the air out. . . . One more time; breathe in real slow, hold it, and push it all out—let it all go.

This time I want you to pretend you are lying on the carpet watching television and your baby sister or brother or a child who is visiting your house comes waddling along and they step on your stomach. Now protect yourself! Make your stomach real hard so when the child steps on your stomach it won't hurt. Make your stomach muscles real hard. . . . Relax now. Take a deep breath again—that will help those stomach muscles relax. . . . Next I want you to push your stomach out. Start from your back and push the back of the stomach out so your stomach is pushed out. Hold it for a little bit . . . now relax.

Next I want you to raise your feet a little bit off the floor and hold them out in front of you. Hold them there for a moment. . . . Notice how tight that makes your stomach and your legs. . . . Now relax—let your legs fall back on the floor. Just let them be relaxed. . . . Next I want you to take your feet and bend your feet up toward your knees. The feet can stay on the floor, but bend both feet at the ankles up toward your head. Like you were trying to point your feet upward. Hold it there for a bit and notice how tight you have made them. . . . Now relax and let them come back to a natural position. Let them be comfortable again. . . . Next I want you to curl your toes under. Curl your toes under on both feet. Notice how tight that makes the muscles of the feet feel. . . . Now relax.

We've now almost gone over your whole body. We've made everything a little bit tight and then we've let it relax, so now your whole body should be feeling nice and relaxed. Before you get up, take a few more minutes to just sit there and be relaxed. Remember and think about some of those positive thoughts that you imagined before. Go back and think about your parents telling you they love you . . . or a friend tells you they like your new clothes . . . or a teacher gives you a compliment about a good grade you got on a paper . . . or picture yourself eating your favorite food, in your favorite restaurant, with your favorite friends. . . . Perhaps you can think of some more positive things. Take a few more minutes, sit there and be relaxed, and think about some other things that make you feel happy and good.

We're almost done now. To end this relaxation exercise, what I want you to do is to open your eyes . . . look around you . . . shake your arms . . . shake your legs . . . and sit up from the chair. We are all done now, and you should still be feeling nice and relaxed but ready to go on with whatever comes next.

Some special considerations in using relaxation training with children are important to discuss. Some children may feel reluctant to close their eyes initially. They should be reassured that it is possible to do the procedure with their eyes open, but that since it will work better with their eyes closed, maybe they will at a later point want to try it that way. A child who has trouble trusting and needs to be in control is most likely to pose this issue. Parents can experience the relaxation procedure alongside their child; this may help the child feel more comfortable and will prepare the parent to assist the child when they practice at home. Early in the use of progressive muscular relaxation training, the therapist may need to show the child how to do the various tensing exercises. A therapist who performs the exercises along with the child may help a reluctant child feel more at ease.

With older children, a self-consciousness is possible as they wonder what they look like as they contort their facial muscles, hold their feet off the ground, and so on. A relaxed, nonchalant delivery on the part of the therapist will usually short-circuit these issues. If a child should complain of muscle cramping while doing the tensing exercises, ask him or her not to tense so hard. If this does not eliminate the cramping, further use of this particular relaxation procedure may not be advised. Instead, relaxation exercises that rely more on deep breathing and imagery procedures may be appropriate. When instructing the child in deep breathing, one should make sure the breathing pattern is slow and deliberate, thereby avoiding hyperventilation.

Although in general children can make good use of imagination, they do not always have the control over imagery that is needed to keep an image in place for a time. Thus, images should be dynamic and unfolding, rather than static. For those children who have trouble either imagining or keeping a picture in mind, the therapist can be helpful in providing a running commentary on the scene. In order to do this in a meaningful way for the child, however, the therapist should ask the child beforehand to describe several scenes that elicit positive and relaxing feelings. The therapist can then use the basic description for a foundation and further develop the scene for the child. When the relaxation procedure has been completed, the child should be asked for any reactions, positive or negative. Some children who have never experienced a deeply relaxed state while awake may feel uncomfortable with this new sensation. Reassurance on the therapist's part is usually sufficient for them to know that nothing is wrong. Children who are distractible may require a shorter procedure (perhaps one that uses breathing exercises more and imagery less) and more description from the therapist in order to maintain their attention.

No amount of relaxation training is helpful if the child is not also instructed in how and when to use the relaxation skills that they have learned. Thus, after relaxation training has been mastered, the therapist helps the child recognize critical situations and conditions in which to utilize the relaxation skills. Many children are relatively insensitive to body sensations that signal anxiety, fear, and anger. Some efforts should be taken by the therapist to assist the child in recognizing and labelling these conditions.

Relaxation skills can be most effective when utilized early in a troubling situation. In order for this to occur, however, the child (or someone else who prompts him or her) must recognize and react to early signs of upset. Although the therapist may have success at using his or her own language and procedures to accomplish this sensitization, it is also important to listen to the child. For instance, a ten-year-old boy who was having anger control problems had a unique description of his increasing anger, which usually led to an outburst. He described it as similar to what he had seen in cartoons in which a character was "so mad they turned purple and had smoke coming out of their ears." This particular image, which was his own, was then utilized to describe a sensation in which "turning purple" did not occur all at once, but was a gradual process. His job was to learn how to reverse the transformation process that led to dark purple all over and eventually having smoke coming out of his ears. He was instructed to apply his relaxation skills when he felt increasingly purple, and as he applied the skills he was to visualize a process in which he was able to drain away the "angry" color gradually from the tip of his head to the soles of his feet. This was not an analogy which was accessible to the therapist until she listened and learned from the child about his own personal reaction to getting upset.

Relaxation training procedures are used with children as primary procedures in and of themselves, and they are also used with a variety of systematic desensitization techniques. The following section will discuss the use of systematic desensitization with children.

Systematic Desensitization

The procedure of systematic desensitization was developed by Joseph Wolpe in the 1950s (Wolpe, 1958); however, his work was preceded by the work of Mary Cover Jones in the 1920s (Jones, 1924). Jones succeeded in eliminating a child's fear of rabbits by pairing the presentation of a rabbit with mealtime. Thus, the repeated association of the rabbit with the pleasure of eating was successful at eliminating a strong fear response to the rabbit. Interestingly, little was done clinically with this deconditioning procedure in the intervening 30 years until Wolpe developed his method of desensitization or reciprocal inhibition. It was another two decades until systematic desensitization was commonly practiced with children, primarily for children's fears and phobias (Morris & Kratochwill, 1983).

The basic theory of systematic desensitization (reciprocal inhibition) is that a fear/anxiety response can be inhibited by substituting a feeling or experience that is antagonistic to fear. Typically, the antagonistic or inhibiting response is relaxation, although humor (Smith, 1973), food (Jones, 1924; Lazarus, 1960), assertion (Wolpe, 1958), and emotive imagery (the imagination of a pleasant event or experience; Lazarus & Abramovitz, 1962) have also been used. Though the fear and pleasure responses are incompatible, the pleasure response must be stronger than the fear response when paired with the feared object/experience. Often this is accomplished by gradually introducing the feared object or keeping it at a distance so that little anxiety or fear is experienced. This insures that the child's relaxed or pleasant state is greater than the anxiety elicited by the fear experience/object. Gradually, then, as the child has success at maintaining relative calm when faced with the minor fear-provoking items, the more serious elements of the feared object/experience are presented.

Although systematic desensitization is commonly administered through an imagined hierarchy of items, in vivo systematic desensitization is also used with children (Morris & Kratochwill, 1983). In fact, in vivo desensitization may be the treatment method of choice with young children. While it may not be practical to do in vivo systematic desensitization for a fear of flying because of the expense involved, after some initial imagery-based systematic desensitization has been successful there may be opportunities to move to an in vivo procedure (for example, visits to the airport, walking on a plane without taking a trip, talking to a pilot).

The steps in a systematic desensitization plan of treatment for a child are as follows:

1. Do a thorough behavioral analysis to determine when, where, how, and to what degree fear reactions occur.
2. Interview the child and parents about the specifics of the child's fear reaction and the circumstances in which it occurs in order to get information for either an imagery hierarchy or an in vivo hierarchy.
3. Determine the degree to which the parents are able and willing to assist the child in learning relaxation skills, practicing imagining, and in vivo experiences.
4. Teach the child relaxation skills or some other anxiety-inhibiting response.
5. Once the child has mastered relaxation or some other pleasurable response, gradually introduce the child to the lower items (less anxiety-producing items) of the hierarchy.
6. Once the child is able to experience all the hierarchy items without undue fear or anxiety, efforts should be taken to enhance the possibility of generalization and maintenance of treatment gains. This typically requires having the child engage in *actual* experiences (and a variety of them that would have previously caused great fear or anxiety.

Typically, learning relaxation takes 3 to 4 weeks, during which the child practices not only with the therapist in session, but also at home. During this period the therapist is also gathering specific information from the child and parents so that a hierarchy of fear items/events can be established. Thereafter, the actual counterconditioning occurs. The length of this phase will vary from child to child, largely depending on factors such as motivation, the ability of the child to listen to directions, the willingness of the parents to assist, the severity and generality of the child's fear, and cooperation with the treatment regimen. For children, 15 to 30 minutes a session on systematic desensitization is usual. This allows the covering of 2 to 4 hierarchy items per session; a typical hierarchy may vary from 10 to 25 items. With children, systematic desensitization is not usually performed in isolation (that is, the remainder of the session might be spent on other activities or interventions).

The procedure for presenting a hierarchy for traditional systematic desensitization, starting with the least anxiety-provoking item, includes describing it in detail to the child while he or she is relaxed, usually with eyes closed. The child is then told to signal in some manner when and if the imagining of the scene causes any discomfort. At the point at which the child signals anxious or fearful feelings, he or she is instructed to discontinue the imagining of the fear-inducing scene and to concentrate on reestablishing a sense of relaxation. Once that has been achieved, the same scene is presented once more in similar fashion. The same scene (hierarchy item) is presented over and over until the child is able to tolerate imagining it without a fear or anxiety reaction. Once this occurs, the therapist moves up the hierarchy to present the next item to the child, using a similar procedure. The treatment proceeds this way until the entire hierarchy can be tolerated without undue fear or anxiety.

Some of the common problems that arise in conducting systematic desensitization with children include the child's inability to imagine the hierarchy items clearly, the child's failure to master a relaxation/pleasure response, proceeding too quickly through the hierarchy (thereby overwhelming the pleasure response with the fear response once again), and not helping the child generalize treatment gains to real-life experiences.

As mentioned earlier, in vivo systematic desensitization is especially attractive with younger children, as it does not require the child to have self-controlled imagery skills. Although most young children can actively use fantasy, the imagining required in systematic desensitization necessitates being able to create an image on demand and to sustain it in place over time, skills that are rare for young children (Morris & Kratochwill, 1983). Traditional systematic desensitization is usually most effective with older latency and teenage children, whereas in vivo or modeling systematic desensitization is best for younger children. Modeling procedures are also useful in the reduction of anxiety and fear. Vicarious systematic desensitization is one variant of modeling that will be discussed in the next chapter.

Another variant of systematic desensitization used with children includes combining an operant conditioning and shaping procedure with the desensitization. For instance, Danny was a 7-year-old mentally retarded boy who had severe dental problems; however, he had such extreme fear reactions whenever he visited the dentist that no dental work could be done. His mother sought help for this fear when his need for dental care could no longer be delayed. Because of Danny's limited abilities to follow directions and sustain images, it was clear that a more active desensitizing procedure was necessary. With the mother's help, a pseudo in vivo hierarchy was established that used food as the reciprocal inhibitor/reward.

The entire hierarchy presentation was conducted by the mother at home. The lowest item on the hierarchy involved sitting Danny in a high chair and placing a protective "bib" around his neck as a dental assistant would do. If Danny cooperated without becoming fearful or aggressive, then he was given some of his favorite food (in this case, either cereal or peanut butter crackers). Next the mother required Danny to lay his head back and open his mouth. Again, once he was able to do this without undue alarm, he was rewarded with food. The mother gradually worked through additional hierarchy items until Danny was compliant while she not only had her fingers in his mouth but used a utensil much like a dentist would use.

After playing the dentist "game" for a week, Danny made a visit to his actual dentist. The dentist was cooperative in that this visit was only for Danny to be examined, and no intrusive or painful procedures were performed. Danny first watched as the dentist examined his mother; he then took her place in the dentist's chair. The mother brought a supply of rewarding food, which Danny was given when the exam was finished. The dentist was also instructed to take particular care to make the visit a pleasurable one for Danny. This was accomplished, and Danny was later able to begin a long series of dental procedures. No doubt the length of this work related to Danny's somewhat limited tolerance for the dental procedures (especially when they became painful), but the work was nevertheless completed.

In dealing with a similar fear, a 9-year-old girl was taught to use emotive imagery after she was unable to master a relaxation procedure. This case provides another example of involving the child actively in developing the treatment. This child was asked to create her own pleasurable images that she could use instead of relaxing. At this particular time, the English rock star Boy George was popular, and this girl liked him—much to the dismay of her father, who was shocked at the singer's unusual appearance. One of the "funny" images this child chose to use was imagining her father dressed as Boy George and performing at her school. Because one image may lose some of its pleasurable effects after time, the girl created a list of images that the therapist then described for her as she was introduced to the various hierarchy items related to visiting dentists and doctors.

Traditional systematic desensitization procedures can be combined with variant procedures, such as in vivo homework assignments. Melissa was an 11-year-old who was brought for treatment because her lifelong fear of snakes had generalized to the point where it was infringing on healthy functioning. Melissa's history included early years in which her older brother enjoyed tormenting her with rubber snakes and various other reptiles. For some time, she had refused to visit the reptile house at the zoo; shortly before her referral, she would not go on a class trip to the zoo for fear she would be confronted with snakes or other reptiles. Other signs of generalization included becoming upset when her mother wore new shoes and carried a matching handbag made of reptile skin. Also, as an April Fool's joke, boys at Melissa's school had planted a rubber snake in her desk. When she found it, she had to be taken to the social worker to be calmed, and she now showed signs of school refusal (not getting ready on time, and complaining of stomachaches in the morning). Not only was she afraid that the boys would plant more surprises for her, but she was also embarrassed at the emotional outburst she had shown in front of peers.

By the time she came for treatment, Melissa was nervous about watching television shows because pictures of snakes or other reptiles might appear, and she refused to walk in her neighborhood (which was somewhat wooded) without someone with her. Most striking was the fact that Melissa could not tolerate hearing anyone use the word *snake*. She certainly could not utter the word herself! Other things of note about Melissa included her being an excellent student, a worrier about doing well, and in general a "perfectly" behaved young girl. There were no obvious family problems, other than the fact that both parents had long participated in protecting Melissa from her fears; in the process, they had encouraged a variety of dependent behaviors. Rather than help Melissa face her fears, they were primarily motivated to help her avoid fearful situations so that she would not feel frightened. Thus, there had been a long history of avoidance behaviors. When treatment began, Melissa was motivated to change because she could see that her fears were having social implications—she was now embarrassed about her emotional loss of control and was afraid to do certain things with friends because of her fears. She was afraid to go to her best friend's house because the friend's brother had a pet snake in a terrarium.

Melissa was taught both a relaxation exercise (similar to the one outlined earlier) and a list of positive scenes that were created early in treatment. These emotive images later served with the relaxation response as the antagonistic responses to fear. Among Melissa's positive images were shopping with her mother, a recent birthday party with friends, a trip to New York with her family, playing an acting game with her best friend, going to the movies with her father, meeting Joan Rivers, sitting at a table with hundreds of chocolate items that she was eating, being the star in a play and getting audience applause, and putting vaseline on her brother's comb as a prank. The mother agreed to assist Melissa in practicing the progressive muscular relaxation exercises at home with the help of an audiotape. In fact, the mother was actively involved in Melissa's treatment. She became the primary monitor of homework assignments, and in the process had to confront her own overly protective style with Melissa.

Because Melissa'a fear was most intense for snakes, it was decided to begin imagery desensitization to other creatures that she also found repulsive, but not to the degree to which she feared snakes. Thus, in the third session a hierarchy was established with Melissa's help. The items on this hierarchy, ranked from lowest to highest, were as follows:

1. Being in McDonald's with a friend and seeing a small spider on the wall.
2. Being in McDonald's with a friend and seeing a large spider on the floor a safe distance away.
3. Being in McDonald's with a friend and seeing a large, hairy spider on the floor crawling close to her feet.
4. Being with her family in a museum with a display consisting of dried butterflies, flies, insects, and spiders.
5. Being with her family in a museum with an insect display that features a large tarantula.

The following session, these five hierarchy items were successfully imagined without undue fear. She also practiced imagining them again at home after she practiced her relaxation exercise each day of the intervening week; her mother agreed to describe the scenes to her. Also, during the third session, the therapist began to whisper the word *snake* to Melissa. Though this initially was somewhat upsetting, she rather quickly lost her fear reaction to the therapist using the word. She could not bring herself to use it, however.

During the fifth session, four more hierarchy items were presented. These were as follows:

6. Lying in bed and seeing a spider on the ceiling.
7. Lying in bed reading a book in which a boy jumps into a lake containing snakes.
8. Working at the kitchen counter when a spider crawls near.
9. Watching a television show in which people turn into giant lizards.

Also during this session, the therapist wrote the word *snake* on a piece of paper and gave the paper to Melissa face down. Melissa was instructed to use her relaxation responses to maintain calm and to turn the sheet of paper over when she felt she was ready to view the word. With about 8 or 10 attempts, Melissa was able to sustain her vision on the word *snake* without turning her eyes away. Finally, although it was only a whisper, she was able to read the word aloud—thus saying the word *snake* for the first time in 4 years. When asked about homework possibilities, Melissa volunteered that she would try to touch her mother's reptile-skinned shoes and handbag during the intervening week. Other homework included her writing the word *snake* on a poster and hanging it on her bedroom door so that she would see it daily. She was now instructed to use the relaxation tape only every other day and to try to relax on her own the other half of the time.

The sixth session began with Melissa proudly reporting that she had seen a spider in her house and, instead of "freaking out," had calmly walked out of the room and reported it to her mother. Much of this session was spent helping Melissa solve problems about how to handle the boys at school who liked to play pranks on her. The rest of the time was spent with the therapist drawing a very unreal-looking snake on a piece of paper. As with the word *snake*, Melissa was given the paper and could control when she chose to look at the picture. Eventually, she was able to look without averting her eyes. Her homework for the week was to draw a picture of "Elmer, the Wimpy Snake" and to compose a story about him.

During the seventh session, the therapist read to Melissa from an encyclopedia that described snakes and a variety of details about their existence; however, Melissa was not able to get herself to look at the photographs in the book. Her homework for the week was to use her own encyclopedia at home, have her mother cover the pictures of snakes with paper, and practice "peeking" at the pictures. In the eighth session she reported only partial success with this exercise, so the therapist presented Melissa with black-and-white copies of snake pictures. (Thus, they were somewhat realistic, but not so much as those in the encyclopedia.) The homework assignment for the week was to write a one-page report on the good qualities of snakes. She was also to draw her own realistic picture of a snake.

During the ninth session, Melissa reported not getting upset when one of the boys from school asked her about snakes. It was clear to her that he was trying to upset her, and she was proud of herself that she was able to control her reaction. The therapist and Melissa then walked to a nearby candy store and purchased a bag of "gummy worms." With coaxing and her practicing her calm responses, Melissa was actually able to eat one of the candies. Her homework assignment for that week was to take the remainder of the gummy worms home and distribute them around her bedroom clearly in sight. They were to remain there for the week. She was also to try again to view the snake photographs in the encyclopedia.

Both Melissa and her mother confirmed during the next session that she was doing well and had calmly handled situations that before would have "freaked her out." She was now able to use the word *snake*, was not afraid of watching television, and was not offering any resistance to going to school. Most of the session was spent with both Melissa and her mother discussing their feelings regarding a family friend's recent diagnosis of cancer. Melissa was given the homework assignment of both looking at the encyclopedia photos of snakes and visiting her friend's house in which there was a terrarium with a snake. In fact, she felt she would be able to go in the same room and look at it. It was agreed by all that three more sessions would be planned, with each spaced 2 weeks apart.

During these final sessions, Melissa continued to report increasing comfort at confronting situations that before had made her anxious or fearful. She was able to view realistic photos of snakes, and discussions turned to how she could utilize her coping skills to handle other anxiety-provoking situations. Although there had been doubt about it months before, Melissa decided she wanted to go away to a summer camp located in a very wooded area. Interestingly, her worry about camp was not whether she could manage her snake fears or whether she could tolerate the separation from her parents, but whether or not she might start menstruating while at camp. Thus, her unrealistic fear reactions were largely gone or under control, and she now turned her attention to developmental concerns.

General Issues in Using Classical Conditioning Procedures

Both relaxation exercises and systematic desensitization procedures require a degree of self-discipline that children often do not have. Thus, it is necessary to be creative in applying these methods in a way that meets the particular needs of the child being treated. In order to do this, it is necessary to do a thorough assessment, to get to know the child well, and to utilize the child's own stories, images, analogies, and the like whenever possible.

Because the developmental literature suggests that children younger than 8 or 9 years have limited imaging skills (Pressley, 1977), it is necessary to determine beforehand whether a child has the imagery capacity to engage productively in procedures such as relaxation training and systematic desensitization. Morris and Kratochwill (1983) suggest the use of an informal imagery test during the hierarchy construction phase. One way of doing this is to present the child a picture with many items in it. After the child is allowed to look at the picture for 20 seconds, he or she is asked to indicate on a blank of paper where each of the items was located. Another procedure involves describing a series of small scenes to the child, with the child instructed to imagine each scene clearly. When the child has the scene clearly in mind, he or she is to signal the therapist. Morris and Kratochwill (1983) suggest that those children who can get the scenes quickly in mind probably have the imagery skills necessary to undergo systematic desensitization. One element of imaging is to be able to sustain the image for a time; in order to test this in children, the therapist can begin by describing a scene for the child. Once the basic elements of the scene are described and the child reports having them in mind, the child is asked to provide further detail about the scene he or she is imaging. A child who can go on to add detail to the image is likely to be able not only to sustain the scene, but also to achieve a good degree of clarity.

It should be noted in discussing classical conditioning procedures such as relaxation training and systematic desensitization that there is some disagreement about the theoretical underpinnings of these procedures. Besides the typical reconditioning explanation, there are two other theoretical explanations that have received some credibility. One involves extinction—that is, anxiety reduction results from simply presenting conditioned fear stimuli that are not followed by the anticipated aversive consequences. Because fear reactions are often accompanied by avoidance behaviors, the individual does not come to learn that the anticipated aversive consequences may not occur or may be less aversive than anticipated. When confronted repeatedly with the feared object/event through either imagery or in vivo procedures, fear/anxiety is reduced when nothing aversive occurs.

A second explanation is that espoused by Goldfried (1971), which concentrates on the coping skills that individuals develop as they learn relaxation skills and how and when to utilize them. In this explanation, the presentation of the hierarcy items is less for counterconditioning purposes than for multiple opportunities to practice the coping skills (applying the relaxation skills to moderate anxiety). The Goldfried explanation of systematic desensitization as a self-control technique is attractive when one values bolstering the sense of control that clients have regarding their own lives. In order to enhance the self-control or coping qualities of systematic desensitization, Goldfried and Trier (1974) recommend altering some systematic desensitization procedures. Instead of asking the client to turn off the image once anxiety is experienced, Goldfried and Trier ask the client to keep the image in mind and to practice the relaxation skills until the scene no longer elicits uncomfortable reactions. Thus, the hierarchy images provide opportunities for the individual to practice coping skills.

The next chapter discusses two categories of behavioral procedures that were developed more recently than the operant and classical conditioning procedures discussed in this chapter. Social learning or modeling techniques and cognitive-behavioral therapy will be examined, with examples of how to apply them in work with children.

4
Behavior Therapy: Social Learning and Cognitive Therapies

T his chapter will examine the "newer" of the behavior therapy techniques. First, the variety of procedures that evolved from Bandura's social learning theory will be discussed, followed by cognitive-behavioral therapy procedures.

Social Learning Theory and Its Therapies

Albert Bandura is given most of the credit for what is called social learning or vicarious learning theory. Bandura's writings in the 1960s (Bandura, 1969; Bandura, Blanchard, & Ritter, 1969; Bandura, Grusec, & Menlove, 1967; Bandura & Walters, 1963) extended learning theory to assert that individuals learn not only from direct experiences, but also by observing others and the consequences they experience. By extending the possibility that one can learn from others' experiences by observing them, it was also suggested that individuals could be treated by having them observe healthy functioning models. Thus, a variety of procedures have evolved from social learning theory that are based on observing a model; these modeling methods are also called vicarious learning or imitative learning. It was only in the 1970s and 1980s that these procedures came to be consistently used in clinical settings. Social learning theory techniques have been employed with children's fears, phobias, and anxieties (especially animal fears and anxieties related to medical procedures) and social skills problems (social withdrawal, communication problems, and the like).

The basic social learning theory procedure is to have the child observe a model engaging in the behavior that is to be learned by the child. The model can be live or represented symbolically through film, videotape, or

91

audiotape. Often the model gradually approaches the feared object or uses approximations to the final desired behavior, much like in vivo desensitization and shaping procedures. Rimm and Masters (1979) list four possible outcomes for modeling techniques: (1) *acquisition* (the child is able to acquire new behaviors that were not previously in the child's repertoire), (2) *facilitation* (the modeling procedure enables children to use more appropriately behaviors that are already in their repertoire), (3) *disinhibition* (the modeling procedure allows the child to exhibit behaviors that were previously inhibited by anxiety or fear), and (4) *vicarious* or *direct extinction* (children reduce their own fear and anxiety reactions by observing someone else approach a fearful object or engage in an anxiety-provoking experience without negative consequences).

Acquisition of New Skills

When used to help children learn new behaviors (the acquisition function) the model demonstrates the desired behaviors in an appropriate context. If the behaviors are complex, the model will break them down into simpler segments that the child can understand. This form of vicarious learning is used mostly with children with social skills deficits—particularly shy, withdrawn children who lack the approach skills to engage interactively with other children. With this procedure, the child observes a model (usually another child) engaging in appropriate social approach behaviors, often while the therapist is providing a running commentary on what the model is doing and why. The child also sees the model receiving positive benefits from the approach behaviors as a result of other children responding well to the model's attempts to join in the group.

Although Bandura's theory would suggest it is not absolutely necessary in order for learning to occur, most therapists would then go on to have the child client perform the behaviors—that is, to combine the modeling procedure with behavior rehearsal. As the child practices the new behaviors, the therapist provides the child with feedback. Again, when complex behaviors are being learned, it is usual to request the child to make gradual approximations to the final behavior. This shaping procedure is often accompanied by social reinforcement (praise from the therapist or another meaningful person), and perhaps, for very young children, tangible reinforcement for each of the steps leading to the final set of desired behaviors. Lovaas and his associates have successfully used modeling to teach mute children language (Lovaas, Freitag, Nelson, & Whalen, 1967).

Other variants on this modeling procedure include the use of coaching on the part of the therapist (who directs the child in the attempt at new behaviors) and participant modeling, in which the therapist also models some of the behaviors alongside the child. Social learning procedures in the remediation of social skills deficits can also be utilized in a group format:

children can observe a competent model, then take turns "practicing" with one another. Whether the other children in the group participate in the feedback component or whether that function is reserved for the therapist depends on the abilities of the children in the group to give feedback in a constructive fashion. As with all the behavioral procedures that have been reviewed, the therapist has a final task of ensuring that the child is able to transfer what has been learned in the therapy setting to the real world. This often involves the cooperation of parents and/or teachers to set up opportunities to practice in one's environment and to provide the therapist with feedback about that practice. Obviously, it is even better if the therapist can participate in these real-life experiences himself or herself, at least in the early stage of transfer.

Facilitation of Learned Behaviors

Modeling procedures can also be used to strengthen or make more effective those skills that children already have in their repertoire. The use of modeling for children who are selectively shy and withdrawn is one application of this form of modeling. The procedure is similar to that described above for the acquisition of new skills. In this case, however, particular attention is paid to the situations in which already developed skills are inadequately used. For instance, children might be quite social and verbal with their family and around friends, but not so in the classroom, where they are reluctant to speak up or volunteer their ideas. The modeling presented to such a child would need to deal with the context of the classroom. As mentioned before, both shaping and reinforcement may further enhance the modeling procedure. O'Connor (1969) provides an example of a modeling procedure in which shy, withdrawn children were helped to become more outgoing and interactive.

Disinhibition and Extinction

In some cases, a child is capable of performing appropriate behaviors but has stopped doing so because of anxiety or fear. Thus, avoidance responses are abundant and prevent the child from engaging in desired behaviors. Modeling procedures can be helpful in this case by allowing the child to witness the model performing the desired behaviors without anything terrible happening. This desensitizes the anxiety or fear experienced by the child. Once the child's anxiety or fear level is diminished, the behaviors that were earlier in the child's repertoire can be performed with a little coaching.

This form of modeling may be enhanced by combining it with coping efforts on the part of the child. This would entail teaching the child relaxation responses or other calming responses that could be utilized while viewing the model and practicing the approach behaviors. Such modeling has been used with children's fears and phobias and in a preventive manner with children who are awaiting anxiety-provoking medical procedures, including dental fears (Melamed, 1979) and preparation for hospitalization and surgery (Melamed & Siegel, 1975). The medical community now commonly recognizes the utlity of preparing and educating children beforehand about the medical procedures they are to undergo. Children who have seen either live or filmed models undergoing a procedure have more information about what is to happen, may learn that the procedure can be endured with minimal discomfort, and can vicariously learn coping responses from the model. Although films regarding hospitalization, surgery, and intrusive procedures have been primarily directed toward the child, it is highly likely that parents also benefit from this experience. Anxiety can be contagious, and less anxious parents are likely to have less anxious children.

General Issues with the Use of Modeling Procedures

Both live and symbolic models have been utilized with children. Symbolic models have primarily been presented through film and videotape. Though symbolic models through imagery have been used with adults, there are few if any examples of its use with children. As mentioned before, the use of modeling procedures alone is seldom done clinically with children. The combined use of behavior rehearsal, coaching, participant modeling, coping skills, and reinforcement is common in one form or another.

There has been abundant research on the qualities of models that might enhance the effects of a modeling procedure. Perry and Furukawa (1980) reviewed this literature and determined that the effects of modeling procedures can be enhanced when the model used is viewed as similar to the child, is credible to the child, provides a coping model rather than a mastery model, and is viewed by the child as warm and nurturing. When considering models that are similar to the child, obviously a child model would be preferable to an adult. There may be some cases, however, in which the use of a child model is difficult; in such cases, an adult model may still prove useful. Other things to be considered when providing a model are similar age, gender, and race, although none of these factors have been found to be critical to success (Morris & Kratochwill, 1983). It would also be desirable to have the child view a model performing the desired behaviors in a situation similar to one that the child would face in real life. Finally, Bandura and Menlove (1968) found that the use of multiple models may enhance imitative effects.

Perry and Furukawa (1980) also found that it was best when the model was viewed by the child as credible and prestigious, although not so prestigious that the child could not identify with the model. Therefore, when using adult models, it would be useful to use a model that the child knows and respects (such as a parent, teacher, or therapist). When using a child model, there may also be enhanced effects when the model is someone the child respects. Because there is also some evidence that the model cannot be seen as too perfect, a coping model is preferred over a mastery model in most cases. The coping model is one who, through a graduated series of steps, is seen as overcoming the fear/anxiety or accomplishing something difficult. (This is in contrast to the mastery model, who seemingly is able to perform the feared or difficult behavior without much effort.) Coping models may be more effective for several reasons: children can identify more easily with them, and they provide the child a vicarious learning experience related to the active use of coping efforts. Finally, the child should see the model as warm and nurturing; this is probably most important if the model is an adult, and likely relates to the child experiencing the model as caring about him or her.

Bandura (1969, 1977) has also outlined qualities of the observer (in this case, the child) that may enhance the effects of modeling procedures. These include the child's being able to attend, to retain, to reproduce the behavior motorically, and to be motivated. Obviously, a child who has difficulty paying attention to the model well enough to learn would not be a good candidate for a modeling procedure. Thus, children who are very young or who have poor attentional skills may need to be treated with other methods. Furthermore, the child who has trouble remembering what was seen will not be well served with modeling procedures, although the memory capabilities might be enhanced by the therapist giving the child a running commentary on what is being observed. The third critical quality of the observer involves the ability of the child to actually perform the desired behavior. Thus, if the child cannot actually perform the desired behavior because of handicaps (either physical or mental), a treatment based on modeling would not be advised. In fact, if the child were not able to master the behavior even when it has been broken down into small, simple steps, then the therapist probably needs to establish a different treatment goal.

Even if the child is capable of attending, retaining, and reproducing appropriately, all is lost if he or she does not have the motivation for doing so. Thus, if a fear is so overwhelming that children are unable to force themselves to view the film, or if there are powerful secondary-gain effects that are stronger as positives than the fear is negative (for example, the attention of parents, getting out of doing difficult things), then the child will not be motivated to do the "hard work" of therapy. In this case, before a modeling procedure would be indicated, the child may need to be desensitized in another manner. If remaining fearful is reinforced in some way, then the secondary-gain effects that reinforce the avoidance behaviors should be the initial focus of treatment.

Finally, role playing and playacting can be useful techniques with children because of their "play" qualities. In role playing, the therapist might first demonstrate the desired behaviors while the child either observes or plays another role in the scenario. The child is then asked to assume a role that requires performing some of the desired behaviors. Social skills deficits might be particularly amenable to such methods. Another form of role playing, patterned after Kelly's "fixed-role" therapy (1955), involves asking the child to pretend to be someone he or she admires and knows would not have trouble performing the desired behavior. While pretending to be someone else, children may attain some distance from their anxieties or fears and so be able to perform more approach behaviors than if they were being only themselves. The therapist may also want to engage the child in a discussion of why and how this admired person is able to perform the desired behavior; such a discussion may bring to light coping efforts that can be utilized with the child.

There are many methods that have ties to social learning theory, and as was mentioned earlier, these methods are often combined with other behavioral techniques or more traditional therapy approaches. Which social learning methods are used and the medium by which they are conveyed to the child should be determined individually; only the therapist's creativity and ingenuity limit the possibilities.

Cognitive-Behavioral Therapy Procedures

In the mid-1970s there was a move by some behavior therapists to consider the role of cognitions in the learning and remediation of behaviors (Kanfer & Karoly, 1972; Mahoney, 1974; Meichenbaum, 1977). Thus, the area of congitive-behavioral therapy was established, and since that time, this particular aspect of behavior therapy has enjoyed a proliferation of methods. Underlying these methods is the notion that an individual's interpretation of environmental conditions can mediate subsequent behavior. Therefore, one child's interpretation of a dog's advance is that he or she is in danger; another child might interpret the same dog's advance as a friendly overture to play. Given the two different interpretations, we would assume that one child would retreat with anxiety and fear, whereas the other would be eager to pet the dog and play with it. If the first child can be helped to assess the threat of the situation realistically, or can be helped to feel more competent in handling the situation, anxiety and fear may well be reduced and appropriate behaviors displayed.

Similarly, it has been found that children can have distorted notions regarding the causes of events. Dodge (1985) has documented that aggressive, conduct-disordered children frequently assume that other children's interactions toward them are intentional and meant to harm them. For instance, while carrying his lunch tray to a table in the school cafeteria, Billy is bumped from behind by another child. As a result, Billy's milk is spilled, and he immediately turns around to kick the child who he believes has intentionally spilled his milk. On the other hand, James has a similar experience but does not automatically assume that the other child was malicious and intentional in bumping him. Thus, his response will be to gather relevant information about the situation before he makes a determination about intention. If aggressive children commonly share Billy's attributions about causality, then it is not surprising that they respond to their peers with aggressive behaviors. If these children can be trained to question their automatic assumptions and to delay reacting until important information has been gathered, the likelihood of their emitting aggressive and undesirable responses is diminished (Lochman, Burch, Curry, & Lampron, 1984).

Furthermore, the child whose cognitive and behavioral style is impulsive will not pause long enough to assess a situation fully and clearly before reacting (Meichenbaum & Goodman, 1971). This particular response style can then lead to behaviors that are poorly planned and have negative social consequences. This impulsive style, as well as distractibility, can lead to increased errors on tasks that require careful analysis and attention to detail. Performances on academic tasks are especially affected by an impulsive and distractible style. When children can be taught to slow themselves down, to think about the demands of the task, and to keep themselves focused on it, better outcomes occur (Kendall & Braswell, 1985).

Then there are children whose social skills and problem-solving efforts are inadequate because of an insufficient ability to assume the perspective of others (that is, understand how someone else feels or understand the situation) and to plan in a meaningful way how to resolve a dilemma. Programs that teach children to respond more empathically, as well as those that teach an organized method of social problem solving have been successfully utilized with children (Ellis, 1982; Spivack & Shure, 1982). Cognitive-behavioral therapy procedures that have been used with children who have problems with impulsivity/distractibility, fears and anxieties, misattributions, perspective taking, social relating, and problem solving will now be specifically examined. These procedures can be characterized as primarily involving *self-instruction* and *self-talk,* or *problem-solving skills and training.*

Self-Instruction and Self-Talk Methods

Meichenbaum and Goodman (1971) developed a method of instructing children to talk to themselves as an aid in maintaining attention and slowing an impulsive response style. In the most general terms, the steps to self-instructional training typically involve the following:

1. The therapist models the desired behavior while talking aloud about how to maintain concentration and to solve the problem.
2. The child is asked to imitate the therapist by talking aloud about how to perform the desired behvior.
3. The child is eventually asked to subvocalize while performing the desired behavior.

When the focus of self-instruction is to maintain attention and to slow an impulsive response style, the self-statements might include "Slow down," "Look at all the choices first before picking one," and "Keep your mind on the paper." Bornstein and Quevillon (1976) had disruptive children in a classroom repeat, "What does the teacher want me to do?" to themselves on a frequent basis. Self-talk methods have also been successfully used with delinquent behaviors (Snyder & White, 1979), to help preschoolers perform more independently (Bryant & Budd, 1982), and with academic problems (Brown & Alford, 1984; Lloyd, Hallahan, Kauffman, & Keller, 1991). These procedures can also be administered in the classroom setting by teachers (Weissberg & Gesten (1982).

Self-instructional methods also help children moderate fear and anxiety responses. In these cases, children are instructed to use self-talk that either enhances their sense of competence about their ability to handle the fearful situation or decreases the aversiveness of the situation in the eyes of the child. Competency-enhancing statements could include "I can do it," "I can be brave," and "This is a piece of cake." Statements that could be used to decrease the sense of threat from a situation are "The dark is fun," "The snake can't hurt me," and "Turbulence on a plane trip is normal." Some fearful children already use self-talk; however, the self-statements are fear enhancing (such as "The plane is going to crash," or "I'll never remember my lines, and the kids will laugh at me."). When the initial assessment determines that self-destructive cognitions are being used by the child, the new self-statements should be created to contradict and inhibit the anxiety-provoking cognitions. This, of course, requires a thorough assessment. Because cognitions are not observable events and are not easily accessed by others, self-monitoring by the child and interviewing the child are important sources of information about destructive self-statements.

When used to moderate fear and anxiety responses, self-statements are paired with behavioral rehearsal or in vivo experiences in which the child practices the self-statements while engaging in the feared activity. These methods have been used successfully to treat children with fears of the dark (Kanfer, Karoly, & Newman, 1975), nighttime fears (Graziano, Mooney, Huber, & Ignasiak, 1979), and dental fears (Siegel & Peterson, 1981). Dolgin and Jay (1989) also discuss the use of self-instructional methods with children who are undergoing medical procedures and who must cope with pain.

Meichenbaum (1986) delineates three steps to the development of a self-instructional program of intervention. The first involves helping clients become aware of the negative thinking that complicates their reactions. The second entails the generation of incompatible thinking through the use of overt (and eventually covert) self-statements. Finally, the client must apply the newly learned coping skills through either behavioral rehearsal or in vivo experiences. Self-instructional training is often only part of a package of intervention techniques that also includes self-reinforcement or external reinforcement, modeling, feedback, shaping, and relaxation training. For some clients, it is only after they are somewhat relaxed or calm that they can effectively employ the positive self-statements.

Cognitive Problem-Solving Skills Training

Spivack, Platt, and Shure (1976) found that children with social problems tended to have deficits in their social problem solving. Some of these deficits included a difficulty in generating alternative solutions, focusing too much on the end or goal rather than the process of getting there, not considering potential consequences to actions, difficulty in recognizing the cause of another's behavior, and reacting in an insensitive way to interpersonal conflict. As mentioned earlier, Dodge (1985) found that children with social difficulties overly attribute negative intention to others, and Kendall and Braswell (1985) implicated impulsivity as a problem to healthy social responding.

As a result of these problems in how a child thinks about social issues and their solutions, several organized programs have been established to teach children social problem-solving skills. The best known of these programs are those by Spivack and Shure (1982), Kendall and Braswell (1985), Lochman, Nelson, and Sims (1981), and Oden and Asher (1977). These authors offer manuals describing the particulars for implementation of their programs. Social problem-solving programs use step-by-step methods to achieve their goals of making children better at coping with the variety of dilemmas that arise in their relationships. As a group, these programs usually include some or all of the following components: accurate identification of the problem or interpretation of the situation; generation and evaluation of alternatives; empathy or perspective-taking training; self-instruction; self-reward; and self-monitoring. Behavioral rehearsal, videotapes, and hypothetical vignettes allow children to practice what they are learning, and eventually the methods are applied as part of in vivo situations. These social problem-solving programs can be administered individually or in groups.

General Issues in the Use of Cognitive-Behavioral Therapy Procedures

The philosophy behind most cognitive-behavioral therapy methods is to shift the locus of regulation of a child's behavior from an external source to an internal source. Thus, the development of self-control, coping procedures, and problem-solving skills are held as the primary goals. As such, these methods can be applied to specific, current problems, but their more general applicability to future coping and problem solving is intended. To enhance this possibility, the use of in vivo practice and the opportunity to practice the new cognitive skills in a variety of situations are invaluable.

Morris and Kratochwill (1983) and Kazdin (1984) have both reviewed the treatment outcome literature related to cognitive-behavioral therapy procedures. Both conclude that these procedures show interesting promise, but as yet have not been as well studied as more traditional behavioral methodologies. Because cognitive-behavioral methods often are presented in package programs, it is difficult to clearly discern the "active" treatment ingredients in the various programs. The cognitive-behavioral therapy area, however, has provided clinicians with a variety of techniques that can be combined in a unique and idiosyncratic manner for a particular client.

When considering which components to include in a child's treatment program, there are several factors to consider, such as the child's age and motivation. As cognitive-behavioral techniques rely heavily on self-control and self-administered procedures, a child must be motivated to carry out the program. Although external reinforcers can be used to enhance motivation, if there is not some degree of intrinsic motivation to engage in the treatment process, then cognitive-behavioral and self-control treatments may not be the treatments of choice. If a child's motivation for cooperation is questioned, that issue should be evaluated and possibly challenged before much time and effort is put into the establishment of a cognitive-behavioral program. A child's age becomes a factor in that very young children will have limited capacities to self-monitor, to self-reward, to take the perspective of another, to identify their own cognitive processes accurately, and to generate a number of alternative problem-solving responses. This is not to say, however, that forms of these procedures cannot be successfully used with preschool children. Shure and Spivack (1978) and Robin, Schneider, and Dolnick (1976) have applied social problem-solving methods to preschool and young elementary school–aged children.

Robin et al.'s "turtle technique" (1976) was originally intended for use in the classroom format, but can also be used with individual children. It will be discussed here in some detail as an example of a multifaceted, cognitive-social problem-solving intervention. The technique is primarily targeted at children who are impulsive, aggressive, and have difficulty coping with frustration; its goal is to promote self-control and effective problem solving. The curriculum is divided into three parts: self-control, relaxation training, and problem solving. To begin, children are told a story about a little turtle who seeks the advice of a wise old turtle regarding some problems it is having. The wise turtle proceeds to tell the young turtle that it has within itself the ability to manage these problems. At this point the children are taught to do the "turtle," which means to pull their head down between their shoulders, much like a turtle would do in its shell. They are told to hold their arms close to their bodies while doing this and to close their eyes. While in the turtle stance, the children practice simple relaxation responses (tensing and releasing muscle groups), followed by the use of a problem-solving procedure.

The problem-solving part involves the children generating alternatives, considering the consequences of various alternatives, picking an alternative and practicing it. Thus, they are taught to stop and reflect, minimize "bad" feelings, and then fix the problem. The children are taught to do the turtle when they are starting to feel upset, angry, or out of control. Initially, the children use stories, behavioral rehearsal, and prompting from the teacher and other children; there is also social reinforcement for the successful implementation of the turtle at the appropriate time. Other components of the program involve modeling, game playing, peer support, and monitoring.

Another cognitive-behavioral procedure—thought stopping—has been used in a limited way with children as well. There is a debate whether it primarily involves an aversive conditioning procedure or whether it is a self-control technique, but regardless of its mechanism of operation, thought stopping can have some applications with children. Wolpe (1973) is credited with developing thought-stopping methods as used today, although he credits Bain (1928) with being the first to suggest the use of such methods for thought control.

The primary use of thought stopping is with obsessions—troublesome thoughts that feel out of the control of the individual. The method involves having the client intentionally think the obsessive thoughts; when he or she reports that they are clearly in mind, the therapist yells out "Stop" or some other startling verbalization. This almost always will interrupt the obsession, and the client is then instructed to yell out "Stop" themselves when the obsession recurs. Over time, the client is allowed to whisper, then subvocalize the "Stop" command. This procedure is repeated many times until the client reports success at being able to stop the obsession at will. Variations on the thought-stopping procedure involve pairing the vocalization with an aversive stimulus (such as a pinch, or the snapping of a rubber band worn on the wrist) and the use of positive reinforcement after a thought has been discontinued.

Campbell (1973) reports an interesting application of thought stopping to the case of a 12-year-old boy who was having disturbing thoughts regarding witnessing the death of his sister. The thoughts would last for up to 20 minutes and were occurring an average of 15 times per day. The procedure used by Campbell involved the boy counting loudly backward from 10 to 1 when the disturbing thoughts occurred: at the count of 1, the boy was to switch his mind to a pleasant thought. Eventually, this procedure was done silently. The boy practiced each evening and was instructed to use the procedure during the day whenever the unpleasant thoughts came to him. During the first week of treatment, the incidence of thoughts was reduced from 15 to 3 per day, and after 4 weeks, the boy was no longer reporting any of the troubling thoughts. A 3-year followup revealed no recurrence of the disturbance. Others have used thought stopping with children for the treatment of obsessions (Kumar & Wilkinson, 1971; Yamagami, 1971); however, such work is infrequently reported in the literature and its effectiveness is not well studied.

Use of Multiple Behavioral Techniques

Throughout this chapter and Chapter 3, it has been mentioned that it is rare for any one of these techniques to be presented in isolation. Instead, it is more usual to combine a variety of behavioral techniques in a program, or to combine them with more traditional psychotherapy approaches. The following case report is presented as an example of the ways in which behavioral technologies can be combined to treat a complex problem.

Shulman (1978) reported the case of Donna, a 2 1/2-year-old child who made frequent and dangerous attacks on her 6-week-old twin sisters. These attacks were reported by the children's mother to occur as many as four or five times a day, and they included punching, throwing books and other things into the cribs, and poking a pencil at the babies. The attacks were most likely to occur when the mother was busy feeding or diapering one of the twins, during which time Donna would attack the other baby. The mother's spankings were ineffective in eliminating the aggressive behavior. Upon questioning, the mother admitted feeling overwhelmed and having little time to spend with Donna since the twin's arrival; the father refused to be involved in treatment and was described as having little contact with the children because of long hours at work.

The treatment program centered around Donna's obvious desire to gain her mother's attention. The mother administered the program at home with the therapist's guidance. Whenever Donna aggressed against the twins, she was to be given time out in her room for 5 minutes. She was to be told why she was being removed to her room, but no other punishment was to be given. Because the safety of the twins was a grave concern, a criterion for earning time out involved crossing over a taped line 4 feet away from the infants' cribs; Donna was not to cross this line without her mother's permission.

Along with the time-out procedure, a program was instituted to teach

Donna prosocial behaviors toward her siblings. A lifelike doll was purchased for Donna on which her mother was to model gentle and loving behavior by teaching Donna how to hold it, caress it, kiss it, clean it, and so forth. The mother was not to criticize Donna as she tried to imitate the behaviors. Praise and physical affection were used by Donna's mother for correct approximations toward the goal behaviors of affectionate and gentle behavior. Three training sessions were conducted each day, and these were introduced to Donna as the "dolly game." If Donna became aggressive or violent toward the doll, she was given one warning, after which the doll play was discontinued.

Next, Donna was asked to mimic with her doll her mother's behaviors when dealing with one of the twins. Thus, when the mother cleaned and powdered one of the infants, Donna would do similarly to her doll. Instruction, prompts, and praise were used by the mother during this phase. The final phase involved Donna being allowed to assist her mother in the care of the infants. Thus she was assisted in transferring her new skills to the babies under the watchful eyes of her mother. After 2 weeks, the masking tape was removed from around the crib, but Donna still required her mother's permission in order to play with the twins. Monitoring for a year revealed no further problems, and the mother reported being able to transfer what she had learned about using positives (instead of punishment) when teaching new behaviors to Donna.

The case of Donna illustrates the effective combination of a variety of behavioral principles and procedures. Time out was used as a punishment technique, whereas social reinforcement and attention were effectively used by the mother as rewards. Other procedures employed included modeling, shaping, coaching, and skill building. Clearly, not only the relationship between Donna and her siblings was affected for the better, but also that between Donna and her mother. Furthermore, parent training was accomplished as the mother was able to generalize specific concepts to other teaching situations she faced with Donna.

Closing Thoughts

Chapters 3 and 4 highlight an immense treatment and research literature. This coverage of behavior therapies focuses upon those that both are most frequently used and have the most research to support their effectiveness with children. Whether alone or in conjunction with psychotherapy and other approaches, behavior therapies have a place in the repertoire of the flexible and integrative child clinician.

5
Guides for Practice

The principles of psychotherapy and behavior therapy that were specified in the preceding chapters point out in broad strokes what the therapist does. In this chapter, attention will be given to the observations and points of view that help to guide psychotherapists in their work with children. Because it is usually helpful to have a name for an approach to psychotherapy, the designation *integrative psythotherapy* may be used to refer to the one described herein. For many years Thorne (1955, 1968) wrote of an integrative approach in clinical psychology, using the terms *integrative* and *eclectic* synonymously. Woody (1969) proposed "integrative psychotherapy" or "psychobehavioral therapy" for his method of treatment, which recognized the importance of both the relationship between child and therapist and the deliberate use of principles of learning; in a personal communication, however, he stated that he settled upon the latter designation for his method. At present there exists an effort to promote integration in psychotherapy through an organization, the Society for the Exploration of Integration in Psycotherapy, and a journal, the *Journal of Integrative and Eclectic Psychotherapy*. In the present context, *integrative* is used both in the sense of integrating what is of value from any area with relevance to treatment of a particular child and in the sense of helping the child and family to integrate or reconcile inconsistencies and denied aspects of themselves.

Goals

The writings of many therapists who emphasized the importance of the client-therapist relationship in psychotherapy (such as Allen, Axline, Rogers, and Moustakas) are characterized by eloquence, beauty, and often an inspirational quality. Perhaps in reaction to psychoanalytic writings, which stressed psychodynamics and an attitude of professional objectivity

104

and detachment toward the patient, their attention focused upon the personal qualities of psychotherapists and the things they did not do. These authors did not regard people as patients, but looked upon them with respect as clients. They did not do much, if anything, in the way of formal diagnosis, concentrating instead on understanding things from the client's frame of reference. They did not try to treat the client directly, but sought to create conditions that would enable the client to feel free to grow. They did not lead the client; they followed.

The goal of psychoanalytic therapy with children is to bring unconscious feelings and concerns into consciousness, thereby enhancing awareness of reality and weakening the influence of the past upon current functioning. In contrast, humanistic and Rogerian therapists aim to increase the child's self-confidence and self-esteem by conveying their respect for the child's abilities to deal with matters and solve problems effectively (Peterson & Burbach, 1988). These therapists see as their goal for psychotherapy the fostering of a process of growth. This growth is a natural process over which they believe psychotherapists have relatively little control and that in clients, for any number of reasons, has become aborted. They believed, however, that there were forces that could reinitiate constructive development when clients felt free and secure; the task of psychotherapists was to create conditions of safety and freedom that could be experienced by their clients. Thus, these therapists ascribe great importance to such personal attributes as friendliness and warmth, unconditional positive regard and genuineness, and faith in children's abilities to make decisions and progress.

A corresponding, though perhaps unnecessary de-emphasis appeared in these authors' writings concerning the therapeutic effectiveness of special treatment methods, techniques, and skills. This was based on the assumption that techniques foster a diagnostic, object-oriented, mechanical attitude on the part of the therapist toward the client (an attitude antithetical to the one desired) and dependency of the client upon the therapist (also undesired). Not surprisingly, Allen's approach was referred to as "relationship therapy"; Moustakas used the same name for his method, and Rogers (1961, p. 33) stated that "if I can provide a certain type of relationship (of genuineness, acceptance, and understanding), the other person will discover within himself the capacity to use that relationship for growth, and change and personal development will occur."

Though there is much in this view that is commendable—respect for the client's integrity has become an ethical obligation—it has unfortunately led some students of humanistic psychotherapy into the misconception that unconditional positive regard or freedom is equal to permissiveness. They see their goal as just being in a room with children and allowing youngsters to do almost anything they wish, whether it be smashing toys to smithereens or attacking walls with hammers and crayons. Usually, they pull up a chair in the corner of a playroom (out of what might be the line of fire), sit down, and smile benignly for about 50 minutes. If the child is playing quietly on the opposite side of the room, they may read a book or lapse into reverie. They believe they are being true to a humanistic theory by not asking the child a direct question and by never giving an injunction.

When it is called to their attention that they may have failed to respond with understanding to what their client has said or done, these therapists shrug their shoulders and say that if the behavior is important, it will come up again. They seem to feel it is easy to communicate understanding and that this is a relatively unimportant and unnecessary task; what is of paramount importance is to be friendly and nice. If the child does not return their friendliness, they say, "A relationship has not been established yet." They are sure that with patience *the relationship* will come about, and the child will somehow improve.

It should be clear that the principles of psychotherapy that have been delineated ask more of the professional psychotherapist than amiability and good intentions. The goal of the therapist is to be of help to clients in every way possible. This requires that therapists be aware of their responsibilities and their limitations, their competencies and their shortcomings, and indications for various techniques and methods of treatment.

The ideal goal for psychotherapy has been expressed in a number of beautiful ways: to love, to work, and to play well, with all that is thereby implied; to achieve self-realization; to be self-actualizing; to become a fully functioning personality; to experience self-discovery, self-fulfillment, happiness, and joy in living; to give of oneself to others, and thereby to gain satisfaction and importance from being of service to one's fellows (rather than by exploiting them); and to feel free, creative, and spontaneous. In actual practice, however, the ideal goal must be translated into concrete, rather mundane expectations. Parents are rarely interested in the self-actualization of their children, but they are concerned about whether their children are achieving in school according to their expectations. They may have little appreciation for spontaneity when their child is hyperactive. They genuinely want to know if their child is retarded and what this may mean for the child's educational and vocational attainments; it is often the responsibility of the child psychotherapist to tell them.

The assessment of the child helps the therapist to make the goals for psychotherapy more definite. It suggests forms of remediation that may be used, methods of treatment or behavior modification that may be appropriate, and limits upon what can be expected. If a child appears to be mentally retarded, there is little likelihood that psychotherapy will result in average intellectual functioning. If the child is autistic or psychotic, it is probably preferable to try a program of training attentional and social skills as a first step (Lovaas, 1987; Schopler, Short, & Mesibov, 1989). If the child is severely retarded in reading, tutoring in that subject might be provided when the child indicates a readiness to undertake it. Psychotherapy teaches children about themselves; it does not teach reading, writing, and arithmetic, and it should not be expected somehow magically to do so.

In general, the therapist's goal for psychotherapy in a particular case is based on an evalaution not only of the child, but of the parents and the circumstances. It is a sober prediction of what is likely to be accomplished. The therapist should believe there is a chance for some gain to be achieved; otherwise, there is little reason to offer therapy. The therapist also recognizes, however, that a prediction is made on the basis of information available at a certain time, and therefore with new information the goal may be reformulated to a more modest or more ambitious objective. For example, at one time it may be prudent to recommend that a child's deficiencies in reading be remediated through programs in perceptual-motor or psycholinguistic training; later, it may be learned that research has not found these programs to be effective in significantly improving reading achievement (Singh & Beale, 1988).

Accordingly, the therapist's goal for treatment should be regarded as somewhat tentative. It represents a judgment of what is believed to be achievable by a certain kind of treatment in a given case. This judgment is open to disconfirmation, revision, and surprise. It serves as a foundation for negotiation with the child, with the parents, and with other adults who are involved in order to help them set treatment goals that are relatively realistic and compatible.

The goals of the parents and the child are usually quite specific. Young children tend to express what they want in terms of implicit needs. They may say that they would like to see the therapist simply because they enjoy their time together, implying a need for a kind of attentive, understanding, accepting, and respecting adult relationship. Or they may say that they like to paint and make things from clay (a need for self-expression), or that they like the toys because they are so nice (a need for nurturance).

Older children will often indicate a wish for self-improvement: they would like to stop being so nervous, to do better in school, to be accepted by peers, to stop having nightmares, or to control their tempers. Preadolescents will talk of needing help in dealing with members of the family or persons in authority outside the family. They want to get along better with parents or teachers, to get parents to recognize their maturity and strivings for independence, or to be assertive without being offensive.

Some children during their initial contacts with the therapist cannot verbalize a goal and vehemently deny any need for help. That they have or have had problems is obvious, either by the nature of the referral or by their behavior with the therapist. A child who screams with terror and rage when separated from the mother, who has sexually molested other children, who steals repeatedly, or who sets fires and is enuretic either has difficulties now or has not dealt with difficulties effectively in the past. In either case, the therapist has the responsibility to try to be of help to this client. This may be accomplished by any of a variety of methods, including family therapy, counseling the parents, modifications in the environment, individual psychotherapy, training procedures, or behavior therapy. But if under these adverse circumstances therapists decide to offer individual psychotherapy, they make it clear to the child why they are extending these visits: that they have seen or been made aware of the existence of the child's problems; that this is what the problems are; that they know these problems are continuing; that they want to be of help to the child in dealing with them; that they know that the child does not want this help at this time; that both the therapist and the child's parents nevertheless feel an obligation to do what they can to see that things go better; and that the therapist hopes that the child, if in time she or he desires help, will feel able to tell the therapist about it.

Suzie was just such a child. She was 7 years old and was refusing to attend school. When first seen by the therapist she was clutching tightly to her mother, and she refused to accompany the therapist to his office. When brought there by her mother, she began to kick and bite her, crying and screaming because her mother wished to leave. After the separation took place, Suzie retreated to a corner and wept angrily, cursing the therapist and demanding to see her mother.

Suzie communicated that she had no problems by yelling, "Go to hell! I don't want you." Yet her problems were obvious; thus, in spite of her refusal of help, an effort was made to see if she could profit from individual psychotherapy. For the first few sessions she continued to be oppositional, to fight her mother, and to curse the therapist. Nevertheless, within a week or two she was attending school regularly, explaining that she did so in order to get out of the therapy visits. Moreover, she set a goal for the therapy: to control her temper and to get along better with her mother. Soon she was able to separate from her mother with no evident difficulty, and in her therapy sessions she was able to give verbal expression to her desire to be domineering and to control adults, as well as to her intense feelings of ambivalence toward both her parents. Her report card indicated marked improvement in her grades, and she reported great satisfaction from her successes and her peer relationships. She was what many professionals would think of as a very successful case.

The goal for psychotherapy that Suzie's mother had was to see her daughter return to school. Although she recognized that her daughter had a problem in separating from her, she did not find this troublesome; in fact, she saw this as evidence of being loved and was pleased by it. Therefore, it was necessary to get her to understand that she should disapprove when Suzie showed "affection" in this way and that she should help her daughter to develop other, more appropriate ways to express her feelings.

Like Suzie's mother, very few parents state what they want from psychotherapy in terms of what is often the therapist's goal: to see the child grow in self-assertiveness and the verbal expression of negative feelings. More often than not, they want their child to be made more obedient and submissive. They want him or her to become "motivated," usually for achievement in school, not appreciating the intensity of the child's oppositional motivation in view of the persistence of his or her self-defeating behaviors over the years. They want their children to talk with them and to listen to them, but they do not want them to be disrespectful—and they have a very low threshold for what constitutes disrespect. They want a child to stop a symptom, such as wetting the bed, even though it appears to be one of the few things in the world they are willing to let their child do.

Unlike many parents of previous days who saw their offspring as carriers of bad family genes, many parents now know or fear that their child is emotionally disturbed or mentally ill and that they may bear some responsibility for it. Most parents, like most therapists, want to be of help to the child and express this wish as their major goal. Nevertheless, they are apprehensive about being found at fault. Some deliver their child to the therapist like a broken piece of machinery that they will be able to reclaim after it has been repaired. Others ask the therapist for advice, but then neglect to implement it or distort it by their own fears and wishes; "allowing the child to refuse to do some things" may be translated into "letting him walk all over me," "negotiating privileges" into "running wild," and "asking your child for her opinion" into "having her make all the decisions."

Many parents want to know how seriously disturbed their children are and what the chances are that they can become "normal." The parents' judgments about these issues are best solicited by therapists before offering their own. On many occasions therapists will be pointing out to parents that although their children have problems that are of great concern to others and to them, relatively speaking these still are not what professionals would consider severe disturbances. This information can be a great relief to parents. Therapists can also honestly inform them that the majority of children who are seen in psychotherapy seem to benefit from it. Insofar as "normality" is concerned, what can therapists say? After ascertaining what the parents mean by their use of this term, the therapist's response will depend upon the assessment of the child's behaviors and condition. If the child is psychotic or autistic, for example, the parents can expect some improvement, but the gains may be few and slow in coming. If he or she is mentally retarded, they can expect better behaviors but a need for continued special educational programs.

Almost without exception, parents will ask for advice about how they can implement the goal and be of help to their child. Before responding to such a request therapists are wise to consider the following:

1. *Have you considered the health, the severity of disturbance, and the personality functioning of the parents?* Some parents suffer from illness, such as a heart condition, that make it difficult to recommend that they enter into stressful interactions with their child. Other parents may seem tenuously adjusted, so that their need is to be relieved of responsibilities rather than to be instructed in how to assume them. Very often, what the child requires is what the parents have found most difficult to provide because of their own needs, conflicts, and rigidity in functioning.

2. *Have you attended to the emotional tone or inflections of the question?* The parents may have asked for advice rhetorically, sarcastically, skeptically, or sincerely. Therapists would be foolish indeed to plunge ahead with their recommendations without first determining whether they are really wanted.

3. *Have you asked the parents what measures have already been attempted?* Failure to take this step may result in the therapist giving sound advice that the parents reject as already having been tried and proved useless.

4. *Have you asked the parents what they believe might be helpful?* Admittedly, some parents will feel this question is evasive, and others may protest that if they knew, they would not have asked the therapist in the first place. There is a third group, however, who will come up with ideas that are as good as any the therapist might have offered, if not better.

5. *Is advice what is now needed?* Perhaps this is the time for the parents to relax a bit and to stop pushing themselves to make over their child. They might welcome a comment like this: "You certainly have tried a lot of different things to help your child. What might be best now is to see what you can come up with as we continue to talk about your child in the weeks ahead. You've already learned some things, and you'll probably be learning more. Does that sound all right?" There are few parents who do not accept and respond favorably to this kind of comment.

In addition to parents, other adults must often be considered in connection with the goals for psychotherapy: school officials who may have initiated the referral, social workers from a juvenile court or foster care agency, and physicians. Although they too see their goal as being of help to children, this objective is sometimes in conflict with other goals. Their primary aim in referring the child may be to placate foster parents so the latter will not insist on the child's removal from the foster home, to ensure the smooth functioning of their institution, to dispose of the case inexpensively, to benefit the remainder of the classroom, and even to serve as a warning to the child's peers that misbehaviors will not be tolerated. Therapists become aware of conflicting goals when colleagues express resistance to the implementation of what seems to be the best possible treatment plan for the child (for example, the child's return to school or placement in a different foster home).

To illustrate, Alex was a 12-year-old of superior intellectual functioning who was doing exceptionally well in school. A good-looking boy who was in foster care for 2 years, he was referred by a child welfare agency because his behavior was so disruptive that his foster parents were threatening to demand his removal. To the therapist he denied having any problems and so relentlessly maintained an attitude of cheerfulness that, given the threatening circumstances, a denial of feelings of depression was suspected. Alex accepted the therapist's offer of help with the goal of trying to understand the reason for the dissatisfaction experienced by his foster parents with his behavior.

The social worker told the therapist that this was a good foster home for Alex, out in the suburbs with a superior school, which they hoped very much to retain. Moreover, the foster parents had only one other child in the home, a mildly retarded son (their own) of about Alex's age, so theoretically they could give Alex all the attention he might need. There seemed to be no reason for Alex to be such a problem for them. The social worker was beginning to suspect the foster parents might be unreasonable in their standards of behavior, since they refused to discuss their concerns with the therapist on the grounds that Alex had already given them more than enough trouble.

During his therapy sessions, Alex soon began to express his unhappiness in this foster home. From what he said, it was possible to gain the impression that his foster parents felt threatened by his excellence in school and his potential for achievement, since these were in marked contrast with the accomplishments of their own son and their expectations about his performance. Evidently they sought to compensate by finding fault with Alex about any triviality they could in order to make him appear less attractive.

The therapist met with Alex's social worker from the agency and shared these impressions. He was told that they were probably correct, but that the agency nevertheless wanted very much to keep Alex in this home because no other foster home was available and the agency was reluctant to lose these foster parents. Within a few weeks, however, what the agency wanted most to avoid came to pass: Alex's foster parents insisted that he be removed. Reluctantly, he was placed in an institution for children who were, for various reasons, without parents able to care for them. He was seen by the therapist for several weeks after this placement. During these meetings, Alex discussed his disappointment about what had happened and came to an understanding that allowed him to regain his self-respect. In the years that followed he continued to do well in school and was regarded as one of the outstanding children in the institution, being popular with peers and staff. Although the therapist and Alex came to be satisfied by this outcome, however, the therapist recognized that the foster care agency did not feel that the goal it had set for psychotherapy was met.

A similar disappointment with the results of psychotherapy occurred among the professionals who referred Ray, a moderately retarded adolescent who was suspended from school for being aggressive and for threatening his teacher. The supervisor of pupil personnel suspected a convulsive disorder and insisted the parents bring Ray for a thorough neurological and psychological evaluation before the school would think of taking him back. The neurologist could find nothing wrong, and now it was the psychologist's turn. Ray walked into the the therapist's office wearing a black leather jacket and a surly expression, glaring menacingly but saying nothing. The therapist explained why he was seeing Ray and asked in what way the client wanted things to go. Ray stated the he wished to return to school.

As he spoke, it immediately became obvious that Ray had a severe problem in articulation; the following impressions were formed more slowly. The menacing, surly expression turned out to be way of putting people off so that he would not have to talk, as well as helping him to seem to be in control of a situation when in reality he was afraid. Ray's "aggression" in school came about when his teacher yelled at him for standing up after being hit on the back of the head with a pencil. Ray sat down and glared menacingly at the teacher, who became afraid and locked the boy in a closet. When after a few minutes the teacher did not release him, Ray became frightened and began yelling to be let out. The teacher could not understand what Ray was saying and was afraid to open the door. In panic, Ray pounded and kicked at the door and knocked it down.

The therapist and Ray agreed that psychotherapy should be attempted and that an appropriate goal was to be honest in the expression of feelings and to try to put them into words, rather than actions or looks that could be misunderstood. When this goal was reached after about 3 months, the therapist had a meeting with Ray's teacher, his principal, and the supervisor of pupil personnel. The teacher, although he corroborated Ray's story, revealed himself to be an inexperienced, timid individual who felt overwhelmed by his work and was apprehensive about Ray once again being added to it. The supervisor of pupil personnel said that it was easier to get retarded students than to get teachers for the retarded; he wanted the therapist to provide an exemption from school for Ray on the basis of emotional disturbance. Ray could then "rest up" for what remained of the school year, attain the age of 16, and be encouraged to drop out. The therapist refused this suggestion. When the teacher pleaded that Ray needed individual handling, the therapist remarked that he thought that was what the teacher was supposed to be providing in his special class and what all teachers were trying to provide in every class. Ray's principal responded favorably to this remark and said that they would work something out. A week later, Ray returned to school.

Clearly there are times when psychotherapists and psychotherapy fail to please everyone. Parents may not be overjoyed when their child dares to be assertive, and teachers may not welcome into their classrooms children who were judged to be seriously disturbed. But the responsibility of therapists is to the children who are their clients: to do all that they can to be of help to them, and to act only so as to be in accord with this objective and further its attainment.

Ethics and Limits

Limits were discussed to some degree in Chapter 2 in connection with restrictions on the client's freedom to express feelings. Here consideration will be given to the place of limits in psychotherapy, to the handling of their violation, and to limits upon the therapist imposed by law and ethical codes and considerations.

Without limits there would be no freedom in psychotherapy. This may sound paradoxical, but there is an inherent contradiction in how freedom is perceived. When people do whatever they wish, they are perceived not as free, but as driven or impulsive. In order to be thought of as free, an individual must exercise choice with due regard for the circumstances and the reactions of others. Limits remind the client of the existence of the therapist as a separate person with oppositional standards, as well as defining the area or boundaries of freedom.

Of course, limits are reputed to do more than that; they are supposed to provide a feeling of security because they make clear what is allowed and what is not. Some children need to feel they are controlled externally before they can feel able to control themselves. Even when therapists are actually lacking the physical strength or inclination to subdue them, some youngsters will attribute such powers to them: "I don't want to tangle with you, 'cause I know you could beat me up." It is somewhat comforting to hear a hulking adolescent say this, though the therapist may feel obligated to point out the discrepancy between the perception and reality.

Some subtle limits deserve special mention. One is that the therapist does not subvert the purpose of play therapy. Play and the toys that are provided for the child's use are intended to serve as media of communication. Therefore, toys should be those that lend themselves to the expression of feelings and ideas, such as puppets, paints, clay, dolls of family members, guns, crayons, and blank pieces of drawing paper. They need not be elaborate, expensive, or brand new. The purpose of play psychotherapy is not to provide amusement for the child, not to entertain with the latest gadgets advertised on television, not to demonstrate that the therapist is a better provider than the parents, not to build models, not to offer training in any particular game, not to furnish decorations for the therapist's office, and not to prove that the therapist can win. In psychotherapy, the play materials and toys are there to help the child to communicate or express feelings and thoughts.

A second consideration with reference to limits is that they exist with regard to the therapist's knowledge, skills, and ability to be of help. There was a time during the 1930s and 1940s when the proponents of psychotherapy thought that almost anyone could be cured of almost anything using this method of treatment (Reisman, 1991) and when their claims and enthusiasm were so unqualified that a leading practitioner of the day, Gregory Zilboorg (1939), was moved to wonder whether some of his colleagues were overfixated with a belief in the omnipotence of words. Even today there is a tendency for some psychotherapists to commit themselves and their clients to a course of treatment with little or no assurance that psychotherapy will be effective for this particular problem. Though it is well and even necessary to have faith in the client's capacity for growth and in one's own ability to be of help, it is also ethically and perhaps legally (Klerman, 1990) required that therapists know their limits and the limits of their methods.

Any therapist who has practiced psychotherapy with an autistic or psychotic child has had a lesson in humility. Any therapist who has encountered a client who refuses help and who is determined to be uncooperative has had a lesson in humility. There are circumstances when it is necessary for the therapist to communicate respect for the client by acknowledging that the former has limitations. Psychotherapists should be able to communicate such a message without apologies and with dignity and self-respect.

A third limit upon child psychotherapists is that they must not find themselves identifying with their clients against the parents or other adults. This may manifest itself in the form of arguments with a professional colleague about whether they or the child is to blame for something or is telling the truth, or in the form of ridicule or undue criticism of parents. It may also show itself in coldness or detachment toward a responsible adult, or in a belief in the veracity of the child's perceptions and a wish to show others that the child loves the therapist, but not them. Such behaviors are, of course, in opposition to the attitude that the therapist, the parents, and professionals are working cooperatively to be of help to the child.

A fourth consideration is the set of legal restrictions imposed by the state in which the therapist works. Here the therapist must be aware of laws regulating the practice of psychotherapists. These laws do vary, but of pertinence are limits upon confidentiality. When certification and licensure laws for psychologists and psychotherapists were first enacted, there was an effort to make confidentiality within this professional relationship the same as that between lawyer and client. An attorney is not required to reveal anything communicated by a client, except to establish the existence of a professional relationship (that is, the lawyer must say the client was being seen). There were psychotherapists who felt that under no circumstances should confidentiality be violated to any extent, even to acknowledge in a court of law whether the person was a client of the therapist.

Even today the breaking of confidentiality remains a controversial issue, with some therapists arguing that to impose any limit upon what is confidential subverts the trust that should exist for clients in the relationship. Nevertheless, almost every state requires psychotherapists to break confidentiality if they have information that a child is being sexually or physically abused or that a client presents an imminent danger to the life or safety of someone else. Disclosure may also be required that is of relevance in a murder case or in a legal proceeding to determine mental competence. Mandatory reporting does seem to result in significant drops in such disclosures and may actually be counter productive (Berlin, Malin, & Dean, 1991), but it is likely to be continued.

The state of Colorado required psychologists to inform their clients of the therapist's professional credentials; treatment options; fees; probable duration of treatment; the right to seek other opinions; limits upon confidentiality pertaining to child abuse, suicide, and presenting serious harm to others; the right to be free of any form of sexual contact or exploitation; and the existence of a state grievance board and its address, should there be any complaint about the therapist (Handelsman, 1990). Although studies bearing upon the breaking of confidentiality and the informing of clients of its limits indicated few harmful consequences when this was done with respect for the client and in an effort to be helpful (Watson & Levine, 1989; Handelsman, 1990), the issue remained a conflicted one for many therapists.

This brings us to a fifth major limit, which is the therapist's adherence to a code of ethics and system of values. The American Psychological Association (APA, 1981) has periodically revised its code of ethics and undoubtedly will present many revisions in the years to come (APA, 1990 a,b; 1992). Still, there are certain ethical principles and considerations that are enduring. It is assumed that professionals seek to behave ethically and that unless their behavior is in flagrant violation, they may be acting out of ignorance or a misguided interpretation of the code. It also may be the case that there are conflicting principles within the code (for example, the principle not to do harm to one's clients may conflict with the principle to behave responsibly for the welfare of others or the society), or that the code may require behaviors that conflict with the therapist's values (a therapist may genuinely believe in a method of treatment even when there is little or no evidence to support its use; Steininger, Newell, & Garcia, 1984; Stone, 1990). This is merely to note that what is ethical is often a matter of interpretation and judgment, and that the ethical course is not always clearly and easily identified.

Ethics require that psychotherapists behave responsibly toward their profession, their clients, and the public; that they respect the rights and dignity of others; that they be aware of their limitations and strive to maintain and increase their competencies; and that they be honest in their dealings and representations. Ethical behavior requires that therapists present their services to the public in a modest and dignified manner and without guarantees of results, that they do nothing that would exploit their clients, that they not see children in psychotherapy without parental consent or legal sanctions, that they be aware of their own limitations in personality and training, that they unceasingly endeavor to advance their knowledge and skills, and that their actions be carried out with due regard for the law. Although there is some question as to when children can be regarded as having the same rights to treatment, informed consent, confidentiality, and decision making as adults, the error should be in the direction of according these rights to children rather than of assuming they are incapable of exercising them (Johnson, Rasbury, & Siegel, 1986).

Jim, an adolescent referred for psychotherapy after assaulting several women and stealing their purses, told his therapist he was becoming increasingly angry with his nephew and feared that "I just might explode and throw the little bastard out a window." The therapist wondered if Jim wanted to be placed in protective custody. Jim stated that he did not think that was necessary yet, but if he did, he would phone his probation officer and ask to be removed from his home. The therapist suggested he might discuss this with the probation officer so that if Jim phoned, his request would be taken seriously and given immediate attention. This was agreeable to Jim. The therapist consulted with a colleague, who believed it would be most prudent to hospitalize Jim because of the danger posed to the nephew. The therapist felt it imperative, however, to respect Jim's plan and his ability to act in accord with it. Within the week after Jim was informed by the therapist of the meeting with his probation officer, Jim phoned and requested his own removal.

In their meetings with children, psychotherapists may be called upon to represent reality and the legal consequences within society for certain proscribed behaviors. They try to make clear to their clients what is, not what ought to be or what might be nice or fair. Their aim is to help their clients to make decisions that are informed by the options that exist and the implications of those options. In so doing they seek not so much to communicate their values or to endorse the values of their society as to help their clients in articulating their own. Though they should refrain from stating their positions on issues, they must be careful not to seem to condone illegal activities or destructive wishes of their clients. To give a specific example, if a girl says she has begun to experiment with drugs, the therapist's responsibility is to assist her in understanding why she has divulged this bit of information, to assess her awareness of the hazards and uncertainties in persisting in this course of action, and to determine what, if anything, she wants to do about it.

Because what psychotherapists say and do can influence their clients, they must—even outside their meetings with them—exercise care in their conduct and public statements. There are limits upon their freedom that exist within and outside the therapy hour. To what extent the therapist should be guided by them is debatable (for example, should therapists endorse political candidates or take a stance for or against abortions?), but it is safe to say their effectiveness as professional psychotherapists is not greatly enhanced by achieving notoriety.

When therapists break limits, they soon become aware of the seriousness of their violations; clients and colleagues bring them to their attention. Some violations are so severe that formal reprimands, forced resignations from professional organizations, and loss of the privilege to practice result. When clients persist in breaking limits, however, the consequences are less clearly defined.

In most discussions of limits, it seems to be assumed that children will respond favorably to an admonition. If the child does not and continues to break the limit, Dorfman (1951) recommended that the therapist end the meeting. Ginott (1959) disagreed with this advice, although he did not say what the therapist should do under those circumstances. Bixler (1949) advised a four-step escalation process:

1. When a child threatens to break a limit, the therapist makes clear the wish or feeling and silently hopes that this recognition will be sufficient to prevent it from being translated into action.
2. When the child seems on the verge of breaking the limit or has just done so, the therapist states the intensity of the feeling or impulse but affirms that this behavior is not permitted. Ginott (1959) favored statements like "Books are not for tearing" and "Windows are not for breaking," but many therapists would probably say at this point, "Stop ripping the book!" or "Don't break the window!"
3. When the child repeatedly continues to break the limit, the therapist may be compelled to resort to physical control or restraint. The feasibility and success of this maneuver depend upon the size of the child in relation to the strength, size, and inclinations of the therapist. Unless the odds are greatly in the therapist's favor, this option should

not be entertained. Always remember that discretion is the better part of valor.

4. As an alternative to the above step, or in cases where the rebellion persists and combat fatigue threatens to overcome the therapist, the session is terminated.

All therapists would agree with Moustakas (1953) that limits are enforced with the therapist contnuing to communicate respect and acceptance of the child, though not of the prohibited actions.

Although Bixler (1949) reported several cases of boys who responded favorably to the imposition of physical restraint by the therapist, it is also possible to encounter youngsters who are terrified by being controlled or being made to submit to authority. If the setting of limits is a consistent feature of the meetings, the aims of psychotherapy are not likely to be achieved through these struggles, and it would be best if they could be avoided entirely.

Let us assume, then, that the only justification for therapists to employ physical restraint is in protecting children or themselves from injury—for example, preventing a child from banging her head on the floor or against the furniture during a temper tantrum, or grabbing her before she jumps off a roof. Should a child direct aggression against the therapist, the therapist may hold the youngster at arm's length or put some distance between them while trying to figure out what seems to be the trouble. Fortunately, such situations are rare. It is also extremely rare for a child to attack the therapist with the intent to inflict lasting hurt or damage; assaults are almost always sporadic, hit-and-miss (mostly miss) affairs from preadolescents.

There is little disagreement about employing Bixler's first two steps, but there is question about what to do with the child who persists in breaking limits. Keeping in mind that a purpose of psychotherapy is to help the client by the communication of understanding, respect, and a wish to be of help, it seems difficult to see how this purpose is served by a therapist running after a child from one session to the next and trying almost constantly to ensure no harm befalls either of them. Hyperactive or impulsive children referred for psychotherapy who reveal little ability to attend to the therapist and to exercise self-control might be better served by means of behavior therapy. Through behavioral techniques and procedures, assistance could be given to develop their self-control, attention, and concentration; then, perhaps, psychotherapy can reasonably be attempted.

The child under consideration here is the one who is ordinarily controlled but who now, for some reason, is breaking the limits. Usually this refers to a child who is smashing toys in the playroom, being aggressive toward the therapist, or trying to run from the session. In this case, the third step would be for the therapist to say something like, "You seem to be having a hard time controlling yourself today. If you don't stop, we're going to have to end our meeting."

If the child continues to break the limits, the therapist could say, "All right. We'll end our meeting for today, but I'll be seeing you again next week. Do you want to help me pick some of this stuff up before you go?" Some children will help the therapist to clean up or will wait quietly and watch; in either case these children demonstrate by this behavior that they wanted the meeting to end, for with its termination they assume self-control. The therapist communicates this observation to them and hopes they will express what is troubling them in words and that they will find the meeting easier or better next time.

Once out in the waiting room, the child may sit down quietly. Assuming the parent is not there and is expected, the therapist asks whether the child wishes the therapist to wait with him or her until the parent arrives. Whether or not the child wants the therapist's company, assuming continued self-control and appropriate behavior, when the parent does come the therapist should say nothing about the session being interrupted.

Some children, however, continue to break limits even after it is announced the session is ended. They may refuse to leave the playroom or office, continue their attack on the therapist or toys, or rush out into the halls or waiting room and create as much of a disturbance as possible. Perhaps they may dash to an office where their parent is being seen— which is just as well, because it fulfills the fifth step. When a child continues to break limits outside the playroom or office, the therapist should enlist the aid of the parent in imposing limits or removing the child from the building. A session with the parent can be interrupted with the following comment: "I'm sorry that I have to break into your meeting, but Mary [or whatever the name of the child is] has been having a hard time controlling herself today. Will you please come with me? I'll be seeing her again next week, but right now it would be best if you took her home."

If the child is not having a psychotic episode (in which case it may take several people to impose controls, and hospitalization may prove necessary), the parent is usually able to handle the youngster. It may be that the following week the child breaks limits again, however, precisely in order to end the meeting and to go home with the parent. Should this occur, suggesting that the sessions are less rewarding than what goes on outside them, the therapist can explore with the child and the parent the possibility of their being seen together. This may be structured as a temporary arrangement or as the treatment of choice (namely, family therapy). It offers the immediate advantage of making the therapist cooperative and the parent available to deal with the child's violation of limits, thus enabling the therapist to perform in a manner more congenial to the professional role and bringing into focus the parent-child interactions that seem to have been disruptive.

Communicating Person-Related Understanding

Person-related understanding refers to communications with content that conveys comprehension of the client's feelings, beliefs, or behavior. It is a major and definitive task of the therapist to offer this kind of communication consistently. Admittedly, communication takes place both verbally and nonverbally, and often the nonverbal message has more significance than what is actually said; however, our discussion will focus on verbal communication.

There are five types of statements that fall under the category of person-related understanding (Reisman, 1971). *Responsive* statements indicate by a simple word ("Yes"), expression ("I see," "Um-hmm"), or comment ("I understand how you feel") that the client's message or behavior is received and understood. *Empathic* statements paraphrase the client's immediate feelings, perceptions, and beliefs or make explicit what is implied by them. *Interpretative* statements point out possible relationships or connections between seemingly unrelated feelings, thoughts, and situations in the present, or note the influence of past events upon current behaviors. *Interrogative* comments or questions are requests for clarification, elaboration, or additional information. *Expository* statements consist of information, explanations, or authoritative presentations about the client's behavior, problem, treatment options, or possible courses of action.

As an illustration of these types, let us suppose that a child has painted a picture, turns to the therapist, and asks, "Do you like it?" The following are several different types of possible responses:

1. *Responsive:* "You want to know if I like it."
2. *Empathic:* "You're pleased, but it's important to you to know my opinion too."
3. *Interpretative:* "It seems to be kind of hard for you to be really satisfied with what you do unless a grown-up gives you a pat on the back."
4. *Interrogative:* "What would you do if I said that I didn't?"
5. *Expository:* "The important thing is what you think about your picture, not what I think about it."

Techniques for Communication

A number of therapists have offered suggestions or techniques for communicating understanding. In a training program developed by Beier, Robinson, and Micheletti (1971) for mental health aides to families, the following were some sound, specific recommendations:

1. Listen carefully and try to understand what the person seems to be saying and feeling.
2. Help to make the problem clear, but avoid giving advice or solutions.
3. When people blame themselves or someone else for something, point this out and consider the implications and consequences.
4. When people use personality characteristics as excuses for not changing behaviors, tell them that this is what they are doing.
5. When people try to use what has happened to them in the past as justification for not changing, direct their attention to the present and the courses of action that are open to them.
6. Note the ways in which the person tries to influence people and describe these ways. Ask how the person might act so as to cause others to react differently.

From his experiences as a therapist, Ginott (1965) gave two simple, yet profound suggestions to those who wish to improve their skills in communicating with children. The first suggestion was that messages be based on respect. Because psychotherapy is defined as the communication of person-related understanding, respect, and a wish to be of help, this bit of advice requires no clarification.

Second, Ginott urged that when the child describes a situation or event, the response be first to the feeling or the relationship instead of to the specific set of circumstances. For example, if the child says, "All the kids make fun of me; they tease me about my name," the therapist might respond to the feeling ("That makes you feel angry and hurt") or to the relationship ("So you don't figure you have too many friends," or "You wonder why your parents stuck you with a name like that"). Responding to the event, which might come later, would be to inquire about the conditions that lead to or follow the teasing, the children who do it, the child's reactions, and so on.

Ginott's second suggestion is similar to that offered by Dorfman (1951), who urged therapists to reflect the feeling tone in what the child says or does, rather than the content. Brammer and Shostrom (1960) also stressed the significance of reflecting feelings and gave several specific recommendations as to how this could be accomplished. Essentially, the therapist was to try to capture the underlying attitudes conveyed by the client; by expressing these feelings in words, the therapist made it possible for the client to become aware of these attitudes and so to alter them or the beliefs and behaviors connected with them.

Although they used the term *reflection,* Brammer and Shostrom emphasized that the therapist did not react in a passive and mechanical way like a mirror. The therapist had to be knowledgeable about human behavior and sensitive to its nuances in order to detect and respond to the feelings and attitudes implied by the client. Further, though they emphasized the giving of reflections, they advised therapists to employ countless variations upon this style of responding during their interviews so that their clients would not become bored, irritated, or amused by its use.

Another piece of advice they gave was to reflect feelings at the time the client expressed them, in words that could be understood by the client, and at the proper "depth," which is to say that the therapist should avoid giving farfetched interpretations to the client or making responses that are perplexing and apt to be rejected. These recommendations have a special urgency with children, who may suddenly shift topics or switch from one play activity to another. Accordingly, the therapist has to respond at the time that the child provides the information or feeling; a few seconds later and the therapist's response may no longer be of significance to the child, other than to suggest that the therapist is now out of touch with what the child is doing.

The tone with which therapists communicate their understanding of clients is very important. Ordinarily it should be calm, deliberate, and often somewhat tentative or inquiring. Unless the therapist intends to offer an exposition or pronouncement, the attitude to be communicated is that the client is to judge whether or not the therapist's understanding is accurate. In this way the therapist conveys respect for the client's integrity and places the ultimate responsibility for understanding on the client, which is where it belongs.

Psychodynamic Techniques

The two major psychoanalytic techniques are free association and dream analysis, but we are not going to discuss those. Our focus is on the depth of understanding communicated. When we consider the types of person-related understanding statements that could be made, it can be seen that the therapist might start with responsive or empathic comments, which are relatively close to the immediate situation and the client's behavior. These might then be followed by interpretative, interrogative, and/or expository remarks. This is to suggest that responsive or empathic responses are appropriate at first, but if the topic is not elaborated by the client, then the therapist might try other forms of understanding to help bring about further movement.

Menninger (1958) discussed a psychoanalytic technique that can be helpful for increasing the client's understanding and for moving the conversation when it seems to have reached an impasse. When the client discusses feelings that are related to current situations with people, the therapist explores the relevance of these feelings to their relationship. When the client mentions feelings toward the therapist, the therapist explores the occurrence of these feelings with other people in the past. When the client discusses feelings and attitudes toward people in the past, the therapist explores the persistence of these feelings and attitudes in current situations.

For example, a child might state that she is angry with her teacher because the latter criticized her work; the therapist might wonder if at times the child feels as though the therapist is being critical and hence feels angry with her. Assuming agreement with this remark and discussion of it, the therapist might then wonder whether there have been times in the past when the client has been angered by criticisms. After this topic is explored, the therapist might lead the child to consider how her sensitivity to criticism manifests itself in current interactions outside the school.

The use of this technique must be evaluated as to whether the child can participate in it and tolerate it. Although the followers of Melanie Klein have no hesitancy in making interpretation after interpretation to clients no matter how young, in general, probing or interpretative techniques should be used judiciously and cautiously. They are usually regarded as inappropriate with very young children or children whose contact with reality seems marginal and in need of strengthening.

Questioning the client so as to explore the past ramifications and origins of attitudes and beliefs is not thought to be especially necessary or effective by Rogerian and behavioral therapists. Systems of psychotherapy such as the Rogerian employ empathic and responsive types of communication almost exclusively. Even among therapists with an analytic orientation, responses of this kind are favored when dealing with children and adults who are psychotic (Federn, 1952). Many therapists therefore concentrate their energies on the mastery of empathic and responsive understanding and employ these responses fruitfully throughout their professional activities. Nevertheless, therapists who wish to consider the use of other techniques may be guided by the following psychodynamic recommendatons:

1. When the client's verbalizations or activities are loose and somewhat bizarre, the therapist should have the client try to examine the reality of the situation and reasonable steps for dealing with it.

Client: You don't like me. If you liked me, you'd tell me. How can you help me if you don't like me? You have to like me to help me, and you don't like me.
Therapist: I don't go along with what you said, but what is it that you want to do?

2. When the client's verbalizations and activities seem orderly, "rational," and controlled, the therapist should respond to what is fairly

obvious. Assuming that the client finds this response acceptable and nonthreatening, the therapist may then slowly proceed with the client in exploring the ramifications and origins of the behavior. This is based on Anna Freud's suggestion (1965) that the therapist in making interpretations should proceed from ego resistances to id content, or from surface to depth.

Client: (after a game of checkers) I won.
Therapist: You're very happy after your victory.
Client: Yes, I beat you.
Therapist: And that makes you feel pretty good, and powerful too.
Client: Sometimes I think I'm very strong.
Therapist: And that there are other grown-ups you could beat.
Client: I know karate. I'm little, but I could probably kill somebody if I hit him right. My father's big, but he doesn't know karate. He almost fell off our roof once. He was painting, and he got on a ladder and almost fell off.
Therapist: I guess it's kind of scary to feel like you could almost kill anybody, maybe even your own father.
Client: Yes.
Therapist: So you just sort of hold your feelings in and don't let anybody know.
Client: Yes, but now you know.

3. When the client expresses feelings of hopelessness and depression the therapist should try, after acknowledging these feelings, to point out the existence of an inconsistency that is positive and constructive.

Client: What's the use? Nobody cares. I can't do anything right.
Therapist: There are times when it seems hopeless. And yet here you are, so it seems as though you still have some hope that things can work out better.

The Silent Client

The discussion thus far has, by the nature of the medium of communication (the printed page), depended heavily on the client's words. In the actual psychotherapy situation, the therapist relies a great deal on nonverbal cues to influence and to give substance to the understanding of the person that is conveyed. Is there an emotional tone in what the client says? Is that tone in keeping with the content? Is the facial expression consistent with the client's communication? Do the body movements suggest tension or some subtle form of communication? These are some of the variables that the therapist considers in trying to help suggest the answers to two questions that are often raised in connection with psychotherapy with children: What does the therapist do if the child doesn't say anything, and what does the therapist do if the child just plays with the toys?

An absence of speech is associated with some disorders or constitutes the disorder in deafness, elective mutism, and autism. Such children are usually referred with their silence cited as one of their problems, so that the therapist expects little or no verbal communication in the initial contacts. Some children, however, come into the therapist's office and say nothing or spend a large percentage of their time with the therapist saying nothing, although it is known that they can and do talk elsewhere.

Axline (1947) described Rogerian play therapy with silent children, and her procedures are widely followed. Basically, she proposed that the therapist accept the child's silence and trust in the client's capacity to respond to the therapist's warmth, friendliness, and patient understanding. Cases were presented of children who sat quietly and said nothing, yet whose behavior outside the therapy hours was reported to have changed for the better and who later stated that they greatly valued the freedom they found with the therapist. It appears that one valid way for the therapist to handle the child who is silent is for the therapist to be silent as well.

A very dramatic and moving presentation of just such an approach with an adult female schizophrenic who was mute, entitled *Out of Darkness,* was shown on television in 1956. The psychiatrist began almost every session with his patient by announcing his availability to be of help, but stating that the time was her own to do with as she wished. She stood in silence, and he sat waiting patiently and calmly. After many such meetings, she spoke.

There are two sensible qualifications, however, before accepting the silence of the client. The first is that because silence is ambiguous, the therapist should try to determine why the person is not talking. Some children are quiet because they are resentful about seeing the therapist; some are frightened; some would like to talk but do not know what to say; and some really prefer to sit quietly rather than to do anything else. The second qualification is that the therapist should try to determine the client's feeling about the silence. The child may find the silence uncomfortable and stressful, not pleasant, but not know how to break it or recognize that other media of communication are available, such as toys and games. These determinations should be made whenever the child lapses into silence. Moreover, the therapist has to be sensitive to possible changes in the client's feelings about the silence as the meeting progresses (for example, being comfortable with it at the beginning but then growing increasingly uneasy about its continuation).

Many children will communicate by nods of the head or facial expressions that they agree or disagree with the therapist's comments. In this manner the child can respond to the therapist's empathic communications, and the therapist can arrive at some understanding of what the silence means. Often the child who is angry about seeing the therapist for the first time will begin to talk once this is understood and after there has been some explanation of the therapist's role and the purpose of their meetings. If the child indicates a wish to remain silent, however, the therapist accepts this decision but may point out that toys and various play materials are available as an alternative to sitting in silence should the child want to make use of them. If under these circumstances the child still sits quietly, the therapist also sits quietly, except to make some comment from time to time about the child's enjoyment of the silence, signs of fatigue, restlessness, or interest, and the approaching end of the meeting.

Brammer and Shostrom (1960) comment that there are occasions when it is advantageous for the therapist to be silent, even though the client may be willing to talk. By saying nothing, the therapist can give the client an opportunity to think and can slow the tempo of a conversation that shows danger of becoming too disorganizing to the client. They also suggest that the therapist's silence can compel a resistive client to assume responsibility for what is discussed, while conveying to quiet clients that they are persons of worth.

Nevertheless, despite the virtues ascribed to silence (it is, according to proverbs, "golden," and a condition to be desired by the wise and prudent) and the seeming ease of doing nothing, many therapists find it extremely difficult to contemplate sitting quietly with a child for about an hour.

Larry, for example, was a 12-year-old referred for lack of achievement in school, enuresis, and encopresis. These symptoms had persisted for some time. Larry had been underachieving throughout his school career, and he always wet his bed at night; however, he only recently began soiling his pants in school. His encopresis provoked the other children into calling him "stinky," alarmed his teacher about the consequences of promoting him to junior high, and prompted his parents into seeing a psychotherapist.

Larry had big blue eyes and spoke in a very soft voice. He seemed both embarrassed and amused by his symptoms. Although he claimed that he wished to be helped, there was nothing that he really wanted to do or talk about. He indicated that for many years his mother, his sister, and his teachers had been doing a lot of talking to him, and that with the therapist all he wanted to do was sit and enjoy silence. The therapist conveyed respect for this wish, and with that Larry fell silent. Every once in a while he would smile to show that he was enjoying the session, and every so often the therapist would reflect that feeling and get a nod.

This was the pattern for the next 20 sessions. Each week Larry would greet the therapist with a smile and state that he did not want to talk or do anything. Sometimes he would bring from home a game, a report card, or test papers. His mother would beam with pleasure at the therapist, because she was certain that the therapist was going to enjoy the game or take delight in seeing the report card or papers. Once inside the office, however, Larry would communicate that he did not actually want to show the therapist anything—that bringing the things was his mother's idea, but he preferred just to sit in silence. The therapist would then wonder why Larry did not tell his mother this in the first place and thus spare himself the trouble of bringing the materials to the office. Larry eventually thought that made sense, and from the 10th until the final meeting brought nothing.

During this time, Larry's mother reported steady improvement. He had stopped being enuretic and encopretic the week after psychotherapy began. His social adjustment, peer relationships, and schoolwork improved so markedly that he was going to be promoted with the rest of his class. He was standing up to his sister and expressing himself to his parents, an assertiveness that was new for him and was being welcomed by his family. These reports from the mother, more than anything else, helped Larry's therapist to appreciate the effectiveness of a treatment in which the client said and did virtually nothing that was obvious but enjoy his freedom to do nothing.

Termination was brought about when Larry and his family left to go on a summer vacation and the therapist moved out of the community. At the last meeting, Larry stated he was pleased by his sessions and that they had helped him a great deal. He thought he might like to see another therapist when he returned from his vacation, but he wanted to wait until then before making a final decision. Upon his return he decided to continue, because there were matters he had not as yet discussed.

The therapist who saw Larry believed that what was important in the psychotherapy was that at each meeting he established what Larry wanted to do and conveyed respect for this decision. He felt it was imperative not to assume that Larry wanted to be quiet each week or that he wanted to remain silent for the same reason on each occasion. In this way, every meeting was treated like a fresh experience. Rogerian therapists might say the freedom and safety provided in the psychotherapy were conditions needed by Larry to ennable personal growth. Analytic therapists might say that the understanding acceptance of Larry's obstinate refusal to do what adults expected of him was a corrective emotional experience (as compared to the way his parents may well have reacted when he refused to cooperate in toilet training), and this enabled him to be openly assertive and to abandon his symptoms. Behavior therapists might do a functional analysis of the situation and might find Larry was being rewarded for his assertiveness and new ways of behaving, while also learning to feel relaxed in the presence of adults and to be decisive with them. Whatever the explanation, what appeared to be essential was the therapist's communication of an understanding of Larry, respect for him, and a wish to be of help.

Communication in Play

Play can serve any number of functions. There are certain structured forms of play and therapist-child interaction that may aim to improve cognitive functioning (Harter, 1977, 1983), correct cognitive dysfunctions (Santostefano, 1984), or enhance self-esteem, (Jernberg, 1984). Our interest is in the consideration of play as a relatively unstructured or free medium for the child's expression of feelings and concerns.

The same principle of psychotherapy—that the therapist communicate respect and understanding—holds true for the child who engages primarily in play activities. Some children will play and not talk; some will talk to themselves or to the toys while they play; and some will be able to converse with the therapist, with the play materials as an aid or adjunct to the conversation. In general, the child's play with a particular toy or activity is to be regarded as a bit of communication, so that when the child changes to another toy or activity, this shift may be viewed as either a deepening of the "conversation" or an effort to avoid or change the topic.

The therapist's understanding of what the child seems to be communicating by play varies with the professional's theoretical background. Many therapists are analytic in their understanding and see the child's play as expressive of developmental impulses and conflicts (Freud, 1965). Finger painting, a messing and smearing activity, thus suggests an anal level of functioning and less control then does drawing a picture with crayons; feeding a doll with a bottle implies a more basic oral need than playing school. With the exception of therapists who follow the approach of Melanie Klein (1932) and give interpretations immediately to whatever the child is doing, however, most psychotherapists tend at first to make about the same kind of response, a comment about what is fairly obvious. Three examples of this sort of responsive understanding to play activities are as follows:

1. The child is painting a picture: ("You like to paint.")
2. The child uses a mother doll to feed a baby doll. ("The mother doll is feeding the baby.")
3. The child pounds away at a pegboard. ("You like hitting those pegs.")

When the child continues in the activity or intensifies or modulates it, the therapist then communicates empathic understanding:

1. The child continues to paint the picture. ("It gives you a good feeling to paint the sun shining and children at play.")

2. The child continues to have the mother doll feed the baby doll, increases the angle of pitch of the bottle, and forces it in the mouth. ("That mother is going to feed that baby, like it or not.")
3. The child continues pounding the pegs with gusto. ("You feel angry about something.")

As mentioned earlier, some therapists would continue to use empathic understanding as the child continues with the activity, whereas others might use interpretative or interrogative statements. Examples of the latter with the same three previous examples of play activities are as follows:

1. "That's what you'd like to have, a happy world."
2. "Are there times when it seems like your mother treats you that way?"
3. "What happened to make you feel so angry?"

A number of therapists have tried to describe what seems to be the essence of play therapy and to convey its complexity. Because child therapists are often with children who have little basis for comparison or judgment about what is going on, a therapist may do little or nothing and the child will not complain. Child psychotherapists require, perhaps even more than their colleagues who work with adults, a sense of responsibility and a capacity for critical evaluation. They may see children who flit from one toy or activity to another and who provide no verbal response to their comments. Would it be best to sit down and say nothing further? Is this child fleeing from a threatening adult? Is the child trying to communicate something that the therapist has yet to comprehend? Is the flurry of activities of no communicative sense whatsoever and merely a manifestation of the child's inability to be controlled and focused? Inside the room is a child who requires the therapist's understanding; outside are adults who await the therapist's judgments and recommendations.

Allen (1942) suggested that the process of play therapy consists of children working out their identities vis-à-vis their therapists. His observation sees psychotherapy as a process in which clients learn who they are, and this helps to make understandable much of what occurs in play therapy. For example, when a child orders the therapist to do something and the therapist reflects the child's wish but refuses to comply with it, what is made clear is that the child is a person with wishes and wants and that the therapist is someone else with different wishes and wants. It is hoped the child will eventually appreciate that though the therapist and other adults differ from the child in who they are and what they desire, they all can still accept and respect one another.

Moustakas (1953) suggested that during effective play therapy there is a progression in the child's expression of feelings. At first there is an undifferentiated, extreme, diffuse display of fear or hostility. Later, the fears or aggression become focused toward specific objects or persons. Still later in the process, feelings of ambivalence toward people are expressed. Finally there is a controlled, modulated communication of feelings about someone with an overtone of positive affect. It might well be added that with some children the process is reversed: they begin with the expression of only positive feelings toward people, proceed to the recognition of ambivalence, then express intense emotions of anger and hostility, and finally gain control over their affect in a full, rich sense.

Anna Freud (1965) saw within play therapy, as within psychoanalysis, a movement from surface to depth, from the interpretation of ego resistances or defenses to the interpretation of unconscious impulses, wishes, and fears. As the therapist communicates understanding to the child and makes what was "hidden" accessible to conscious thought and reason, there is a decrease in the client's level of anxiety or tension. Meanwhile the therapist is available to the child as a positive parental figure, and in the recapitulation of conflict situations offers new, constructive ways to experience and deal with them.

Whatever the framework of understanding of psychotherapists, they utilize it as appropriate in order to share their understanding of the moment with the clients they are trying to help. Given a choice between saying nothing and having the child wonder what the therapist is doing on the one hand, or saying something and being told by the child that it is wrong on the other, the therapist will do better to say something. Best of all, however, are those occasions when therapists communicate their understanding, respect, and wish to be of help and receive from their clients replies that begin with a deep, heartfelt "yes."

Some Questions and Answers

What Play Materials Are Desirable?

This depends upon the therapist and the purpose that the materials are supposed to serve. Let us begin by assuming that the purpose of the play materials is to serve as a medium of communication for feelings and concerns. Accordingly, toys should be selected that lend themselves to that purpose. Moreover, it can be expected that they will be subjected to hard use and even abuse, and therefore they should be sturdy, inexpensive, simple, and attractive. When broken, they should be repaired or discarded; it is not consistent with the communication of respect to present the child with an array of damaged merchandise. At another extreme, a therapist may only succeed in throwing a child into confusion by displaying a vast assortment of dazzling toys.

What is desirable is to have a small, nonoverwhelming selection of toys that appeals to a wide age range of children. Play materials can be used with clients regardless of age if they find this medium helpful in facilitating their communication. Federn (1952), for one, thought it possible that play therapy might be the treatment of choice for severe schizophrenics. Whitaker, Felder, Malone, and Warkentin (1962) reported games of checkers helped their adult schizophrenic patients to establish genuine contacts with their therapists. Mayers and Griffin (1990) found mechanical toys engaged the attention of elderly demented patients and increased their interest in their environment.

As an objective indicator of which materials to select, Lebo (1958) suggested that a "verbal index" for each be computed based on how many statements children made when a toy was used and the different emotions the toy elicited. This suggestion, commendable though it may be, has yet to be implemented. Most therapists prefer to rely on their experiences and judgment rather than on any objective measure when deciding which toys should be purchased. They favor toys representing the family, such as dolls and hand puppets; symbolic figures like witches, royalty, and animals; toys that permit the expression of aggression, such as pegboard and hammer, pistols, a punching bag or inflated doll, cars, airplanes, dump trucks, tanks, soldiers, and target sets; unstructured, creative materials such as paints, crayons, plasticene clay, pencil and paper, or a blackboard (which can accommodate a variety of emotions and concerns); games such as checkers, cards, ring toss, and chess; and a few miscellaneous things, such as doll furniture, a little broom, a rubber ball, and maybe some blocks.

Some therapists swear by certain toys or games (for example, Sorry, Candyland, Chinese checkers), and some have gone to the trouble to develop games of their own. Schaefer and Reid (1986) have presented a host of games for promoting communication (including a pile of cards on which each has a question like "What is something that bugs you?" or "What would you do if you had a magic wand?") for helping the child to learn to solve problems more effectively, for building self-esteem, and for fostering socialization skills. Some use toys and games to build controls and cognitive skills, for example, by assembling models and jigsaw puzzles. The list of purposes to which play can be put, and hence the toys and games that can be employed, is large.

Perhaps conspicuous by their absence are finger paints and a sandbox. Although many therapists believe them important and enjoy having them, they have been omitted in deference to the next question.

Who Cleans Up the Playroom?

Ginott (1961) proposed an ideal solution: neither the child nor the therapist has to clean the playroom, instead letting the maid do it. Unless the therapist is uncommonly fortunate or the playroom is seldom in use, however, it is not too probable that a maid will be available to tidy up between appointments. By default, this leaves either the therapist or child to do the cleaning, unless the therapist works in an organization where the mess can be left to the next therapist—a practice that would breed poor staff relationships and so is not really available as an option.

What usually happens is that the therapist sets aside a few minutes or more (depending upon the particular extent of devastation and disarray) toward the end of the hour to return the room to order. Some will ask the child to clean up, since after all the youngster is responsible for the mess: some will begin picking up the toys and ask whether the child will help; and others, after announcing that the time is almost up, will begin the task of restoration and see if the child voluntarily pitches in. In any case, if the child does not wish to help in this task, the therapist accepts this decision and does it alone. This is not without its treatment implications. By cleaning the room, the therapist presents the child with a model of appropriate behavior. Some children find it reassuring to see the room returned to a fairly neat condition, which seems to indicate to them that their actions do not have irreversible consequences. In addition, the child's participation (or refusal to participate) in the cleanup can be the first signs of cooperation with the therapist or, on the other hand, of a desirable self-assertiveness.

Sand and finger paints often require an inordinate amount of time for cleaning, though there are therapists who feel that these communication tools are worth it. This is a personal decision, since many children somehow manage to improve without throwing sand, smearing paint, or sloshing in water.

What If the Child Offers a Gift?

It may seem incredible, but there are times when children offer a present— often a picture, a marble, or some other inexpensive item—because they have been ordered to do so by some adult, and they actually want the "gift" for themselves. Therefore, the therapist must first reflect the child's feelings and determine why the present is offered. When it is not the child's idea, it is best to express appreciation for the gesture but to decline the present.

If a gift (which may only be a rubber band or a scrap of paper on which is written "I like you") is accepted, it should be kept, perhaps in a closet or desk drawer, at the very least until contacts with the child have come to an end. It is not uncommon for a child to ask months later to see the gift again. Few things can equal the pleasure and satisfaction that the child seems to experience when the old present is brought out of safekeeping.

Some children ask to have their gift displayed in the therapist's office, and some therapists feel no problem in complying with that request. Other therapists, however, find that such requests, if granted, foster competition and rivalry among the children that the therapist sees, stimulate unwelcome complications, and may provoke a child into producing a blizzard of presents so that everything else is buried. If therapists explain that it is not their practice to display gifts and that they intend to put them where they can be kept safe, children do understand and accept this explanation.

It may happen that a child, perhaps in order to punish the therapist, will ask to have a present returned. In this case the therapist, after establishing some understanding of what may be involved, complies with the request and communicates the following to the child: "I am going to return your present, but I want you to understand that once I give it back to you, it belongs to you and I do not want it back. Before you ever give me a present again, think it over carefully, because when you give something to somebody, it no longer belongs to you, but to that person. Therefore, if I ever take a present from you again, I will not return it." This limit is helpful with children who have the pattern of giving something mainly to place themselves in a bargaining position and to inflict pain and distress on the recipient when they demand its return.

Does the Therapist Allow the Child to Show the Office or Playroom to Siblings?

Yes, but the therapist is alert to the possibility that siblings may try to usurp the client's hour, or that parents may be trying to start another child in therapy now that the client shows signs of improvement. Therefore, it is best to allow the client to show the room, but not to permit siblings to play in it until the therapist has had an opportunity to assess the implications with the client and the parents.

Is Confidentiality the Same with Children as with Adults?

A basic fact about children is their dependence upon adults; either their parents or some other adult is legally responsible for them. During the assessment and during the course of psychotherapy, parents want to be informed about their child's condition and progress and to be told what they can do to be of help. They may be curious about what is being discussed or what activities are taking place in the playroom. They are bringing their child to the therapist, they are paying the bills, and they feel—with justification—that they are entitled to know whether their child is getting anything for their effort and money.

Honesty and discretion are exceedingly important in handlng confidentiality with children. Although some child therapists assert that "complete" confidentiality with the child "must be maintained" (Swanson, 1970), they usually go on to give exceptions, as indeed they ethically and legally must and as Swanson does when she noted that the therapist must break confidence if the child plans to commit a significant aggressive act. The following can be helpful guides in handling issues of confidentiality with children:

1. Although the child is the client, the parents have the authority to give or to deny the therapist permission to communicate about the case with others, such as school personnel. Without that permission, which is best obtained in writing on an appropriate form, the therapist should divulge nothing about the content of the contacts. Similarly, the parents may demand information about their child's treatment, unless they earlier agreed, again best in writing, to respect its confidentiality.

2. Before any breach of confidentiality—a meeting or discussion with parents, school personnel, or some other authority about the child— the therapist first informs the child about the meeting and its circumstances; ascertains whether there is anything in particular the child would like to have communicated; determines whether there is anything in particular the child does *not* want communicated; asks, when appropriate, if the child would like to attend the meeting; and states what is likely to be discussed and that in general confidentiality will be preserved. Of course, if the child wishes to attend the meeting, the therapist tries to see that this is arranged. After the meeting, there should be some discussion of it with the child.

3. Even when given permission by the client to discuss "anything," the therapist employs discretion. In general, should parents inquire about the content of the sessions, they are advised to request this information from their child. Should they respond that their child is reluctant to tell them, the therapist can suggest that it would then be best to respect this wish for privacy and that perhaps at some later date the child may be willing to share this information. If a special meeting with the parents is arranged at their request, it is of great importance that the therapist first determine what information they seek before volunteering anything.

4. When there are limits on confidentiality—for example, if the parents require the therapist tell them if their child is using drugs or engaging in sex— the child should be told of these limits, to the extent that this is possible and within the child's understanding. Such limits should be reasonable and acceptable to the therapist as being in the best interests of the child.

5. When therapists see children at the request of some agency, and a report of the meeting is expected, they begin the interview with their client by making this known (that is, the child is informed immediately that the contact is not confidential). It is the child's right and privilege to decide whether or not to cooperate with the therapist when in-

formed about the circumstances and its possible advantages and disadvantages.

How Are Fees Handled?

In many offices and agencies, fees are set by a clerk who is familiar with various third-party payments and who handles the billings. Regardless of the method of setting it, the fee should be established by the end of the first meeting with the parents, and there should be an agreed-upon understanding about payments. So long as the bills are paid within a reasonable time, there is no problem. If the bills are not paid, there is a problem, and professionals have different solutions for dealing with it.

The parents, not the child, are responsible for paying the bill, and they may not do so for valid reasons, such as loss of employment, unexpected expenses, or catastrophes in the family. More often than not, however, the parents do not pay the bill because they are dissatisfied with the service, are angry with the therapist, or have some need that they satisfy by receiving a statement each month.

The most common procedure is to ask the parents why they have not paid their bill. If they have legitimate reasons for being in arrears, an adjustment in the fee and an acceptable schedule of payment may be the happiest solution for all concerned. If the failure to pay represents a protest or a desire to have contact with the therapist, such a meeting with the parents should be arranged, with the goal not of collecting what they owe, but of addressing their problem.

When therapists are employed by an organization, their salaries are provided by their agency and usually have no relation to their billings. Under these circumstances it is expected that parents of many of their clients will pay low fees or nothing at all for their services, with the community or government paying the difference between what is collected by fees and the actual cost of operations. Such an arrangement makes it easy to forget that therapists are not donating their services out of altruism and goodwill.

Even in private practice with adults, it is tempting to both clients and therapists to deny the existence of the fee. Masserman (1953) suggested that such a denial helps the client to gain a feeling of self-importance, while the therapist may feel quite noble. With some children the denial is made easier because they may have little understanding of fees. This, however, should be discussed with children very early in the treatment when the mechanics for the meetings are being negotiated. Whenever possible, children should be informed that their parents will be paying for the therapist's services.

In a sense, the fee serves as an antidote to romanticizing about psychotherapy and as a form of motivation. Some children may want to hasten their treatment to relieve their parents of this financial burden, whereas some will see the cost as a way of punishng their parents. Some will confront the therapist by questioning why there should be payment for so little work. If therapists follow the principles of psychotherapy, they will be able to deal with these reactions and have clients who appreciate the efforts made on their behalf by both parents and therapists and who feel a measure of responsibility to reward these people.

6
Meeting the Child

Any specific method or technique that is used with everyone is bound to be inappropriate for someone. Even a benign technique like relaxation training may actually induce greater anxiety and tension for some clients (Lazarus & Mayne, 1990). Therefore, therapists must be skilled in a variety of procedures, knowledgeable about when each is best employed, and flexible in their implementation. Yet what also must be acquired with such preparation is the awareness that since each child differs from every other, each youngster and each family is a fresh experience for which the therapist is to some extent poorly prepared. Every child presents a new challenge to the therapist's understanding and ability to be of help.

In this chapter the first meeting with the child will be described, with special emphasis on the role of the therapist. Ordinarily, the therapist knows the name and age of the client, the nature of the presenting problem, and some basic information about the parents before meeting with the child. It may be that a diagnostic study or assessment of the child has been conducted and has led to requests for specific services, or the parents may have been seen for a number of interviews, thus providing a considerable body of data and impressions. Nevertheless, the therapist may wish to verify these impressions and to assess whether there have been changes since previous evaluations.

For example, Albert was a 5-year-old youngster referred for psychotherapy by a psychiatrist. Albert was a behavior problem in school. He would not follow directions, and he spat at his classmates and hit them. He had been tested by a school psychologist and was reported to be average in his intellectual functioning. Furthermore, the referring psychiatrist claimed Albert was depressed.

There was ample reason for depression. Albert was one of six children, of whom the eldest was 9 years old. His mother was on welfare, and his father, who was unemployed, lived nearby with his parents; he visited his family during the day or evening and left at night. Not surprisingly,

Albert was a thin child whose physical development did not seem to correspond with his chronological age. His speech was unclear, though some words could be understood, and he preferred to play rather than to talk so as to be able to demonstrate his skill in dribbling a ball. This accomplishment brought big smiles to his face, as did the possibility of seeing the therapist each week. The quality of his drawings suggested intellectual retardation, although this contradicted the results of the school psychologist's assessment. Moreover, his behavior with the therapist did not indicate depression.

Puzzled by these discrepant findings, shortly after the psychotherapy began the therapist met with the school psychologist and other school personnel. The therapist was told that Albert had been tested on the Stanford-Binet and had an average score, and that although no longer depressed, he continued to be a behavior problem for the teacher and the other students. As the psychotherapy continued, Albert ceased to be a behavior problem in school. At the same time it became more and more obvious that although Albert wanted very much to do well, he found it difficult to succeed in academic areas. In order to shed some light on this matter, the therapist readministered the Stanford-Binet and found that Albert was functioning in a moderately retarded range of intelligence.

A conference was then held at the school with Albert's teacher, the principal, the school psychologist, and the therapist. Everyone agreed that Albert was better behaved than he had been, but he was still unable to do the work in school. The teacher and the principal thought Albert to be retarded and in need of special help before going into first grade, but they were stymied by the school psychologist's finding of average intelligence. They wondered what the therapist thought.

The therapist reported a similar impression of retarded functioning and focused attention upon the school psychologist's assessment. When asked to produce the test protocol, the school psychologist allowed that his test results actually did not differ from those of the therapist. He went on to explain that he had added 15 points to Albert's score so as to compensate for the effects of cultural deprivation, and then 15 more points because Albert was emotionally disturbed. It was by benefit of these 30 additional IQ points and a generous interpretation of what constituted the average range of intelligence that Albert was reported to be of average intellectual functioning. With the revelation of this highly unorthodox and dubious procedure, school personnel were able to devise an educational plan for Albert that proved both satisfying and acceptable to him and to his parents.

Albert's case illustrates the point that information about their clients from other sources should not deter therapists from forming their own judgments. In making these judgments, they must remember that children may behave differently with them because of the special environmental situation that they present. The therapeutic setting would be expected to be unlike the circumstances in which symptoms were developed and manifested and evaluations were made. Thus, therapists cannot immediately discount impressions contradictory to their own, but must remain open-minded. They offer children their understanding, their respect, and their wish to be of help. How will a child perceive them? In what ways will a child respond to their offer?

The First Meeting

If the therapist is employed in a clinic or setting where another professional meets with the parents during the meeting with the child, it is customary for the two of them to go to the waiting room for their clients. There the therapist is usually introduced to the parents by the colleague who already has had some contact with the family, and he or she is then introduced to the child.

It will be assumed for the sake of simplicity of exposition, however, that the therapist is walking to the waiting room alone. Just from referral information, the therapist has probably entertained a number of hypotheses about what might be helpful for the client. Most reasons for referral have to do with molar or global aspects of behavior that can have differing etiologies. For example, failing in school can be brought about by learning disabilities, faulty teaching methods, opposition to demands of parents or teachers, compulsive overcontrol of hostile impulses, denial of reality, and environmental contingencies that do not help the child to do well. "Juvenile delinquency" is a legal term, and crimes are committed as a result of legitimate grievances and frustrations, as displacements of hostility, as a way of denying feelings of depression, as an attempt to bring about separation from a home environment that seems engulfing, as a means for asserting femininity or masculinity, and for the satisfaction of dependency needs, as well as because of ineffective parenting and a host of other explanations. There is rarely a shortage of plausible explanatons to suggest corresponding treatment strategies.

Some possible etiologies may not be pertinent to the child in question and so have been eliminated from the range of explanations. But it is likely, alas, that this early, tentative understanding will be modified or shattered the first instant that the client is seen. It is not uncommon for the child who has been described as "hyperactive, aggressive, and rude" to be found sitting quietly in the waiting room engaged in some constructive activity.

The therapist notes the placement of child and parent. Are they seated at some distance from one another, an arrangement that suggests a desire for estrangement? Is the child huddled close to the parent, indicating apprehension, dependency, and probably ambivalence when the huddling is intense and vigorous? Is the child playing away from the parent in what could be affirmation of independence, or is there a running to him or her every so often to solicit attention and approval, an act that suggests the persistence of dependence? Does the parent seem to ignore the child, possibly pointing to lack of training or inappropriate training in the child's development? Or do they sit side by side looking at a magazine in what is a fairly typical and positive pattern of behavior?

At this point, therapists introduce themselves to the parent(s) and pause in order to allow the parent(s) the opportunity to introduce the child. Some parents may become quite flustered during this pause because they do not know what is expected of them or how the therapist should be introduced. When that happens, therapists should save the parents from any embarrassment by turning to the child and introducing themselves: "Hello, Jane. My name is Dr. Reisman. We're going to be talking in my office while your mother waits out here."

There are several points that are made clear in this simple introduction. The first is that by using the child's name, the therapist indicates some knowledge about the child. The second is that by using a formal title and surname, the therapist emphasizes that this is a professional—not casual—relationship. Third, it is stated that communication is the major activity in which they are to engage, thus trying to allay any fear on the child's part about receiving shots or undergoing some other dreaded procedure. Finally, the child is told the location of the parent during their meeting in order to prevent or reduce any separation anxiety.

Younger children may make no response to the introduction but to look at the therapist or resume playing with a toy. When that happens, the therapist should take the child by the hand and say something like, "Let's go now." The two of them then march off to the office after the therapist tells the parent how long the appointment will last.

Older children, particularly adolescents, may shake the therapist's hand and say, "Pleased to meet you." It is usually best for therapists to inhibit the conventional response and not say they are glad to meet the client, since under the circumstances such a response strikes most adolescents as hollow and clumsy. A pleasant smile and nod of acknowledgment are sufficient, with some remark about going to the office signaling the time of departure from the waiting room.

Some children respond to the therapist's introduction with fear or anger. The child may draw closer to the parent or clutch at him or her, grasping tightly to a bit of clothing and refusing to look at the therapist. An older child may look at the therapist with much hostility and state emphatically, "I'm not going in." In such cases, the therapist observes the reaction of the parent. Does the parent smile weakly with a hint of pride and pleasure at this sign of filial attachment and devotion? Does he or she state with firmness that the child has nothing to fear and needs to talk with the therapist? Does he or she become disgusted and hostile to the child? Or does he or she look at the therapist and say, "Well, doctor, what do we do now?"

If the parent does not make an effort to promote the separation and if the child is hostile, the therapist turns to the parent and asks if he or she knows why the child is angry: "Jane seems to be angry about something. Do you have any idea about what it is?" Often the parent will say that he or she explained the visit to the child, and from that time on the child was opposed to the meeting. If there were any possible distortions in the parent's explanation ("You're going to see a doctor who wants to find out what's wrong with you," "You're going to take some tests," or "You're supposed to tell the doctor whatever's bothering you"), the therapist should attempt to clear them up for the child: "You don't have to talk with me if you don't want to. And now that you've come this far and are here, why not come into my office?" The therapist then pauses to allow the child to think it over. Most youngsters will decide, with a show of irritation and reluctance, to go with the therapist.

If the child seems frightened or clings to the parent, and the parent seems helpless, the therapist crouches at the level of the child, repeats the wish to see the child while the parent waits for them, then stands erect and tries to take the child's hand. If the child does not withdraw from the therapist's hand, the two proceed to the office. If the child recoils from the therapist or refuses to respond, however, the therapist is dealing with a difficult (though not uncommon) problem in separation. Suggestions for handling this will be discussed next.

Handling Problems in Separation

Not all therapists handle problems in separation in the same way. Some urge that the therapist forcibly, if necessary, separate the child from the parent in the waiting room and carry him or her kicking and screaming to the office. Obviously, this procedure is limited by the strength of the therapist and the size of the child.

Some advocate that the therapist respect the child's wish not to be seen and that the former either terminate the meeting and hope for the best at the next appointment or sit with the child in the waiting room. It is expected that by conveying understanding, respect, and a willingness to wait until such time as the child feels able to go to the playroom or office, the therapist will reduce the child's fear and arouse interest and cooperation (Axline, 1947).

The advantages of not forcing a separation are many. It is far less traumatic for all concerned to accept the child's decision rather than to combat it. Furthermore, it is consistent with the principles of psychotherapy to handle the situation in this way; the therapist communicates an understanding of the child, respect, and a wish to help by being willing to wait. An opportunity is provided for the child's growth during this period of acceptance of reluctance and apprehension, meaning that a decision to accompany the therapist (assuming that it comes eventually) represents some progress. Therefore the fact that the child has not been seen in the therapist's office or playroom does not mean that nothing is going on and that the client is not being helped. Just the opposite may be true: the most significant and meaningful part of the treatment for a child with a separation problem may occur in thus becoming able to effect a separation from the parent and in giving trust to a stranger.

These advantages would seem to be possible when the child has conflicted feelings about seeing the therapist, when the waiting room is relatively private, and when the parent is able to accept the child's and the therapist's behavior. If the child has no wish to see the therapist, however, then it is conceivable that acceptance will be construed as a rewarding of refusal and as capitulation and impotence on the part of adults. An indication that the child derives satisfaction from what is perceived as the frustration of the therapist is a triumphant smile or smirk that seems to say, "I have my mother, and there's nothing you can do about it." Given that reaction, it may be quite some time before the child is willing to go with the therapist.

Moreover when the therapist is employed in a clinic or agency where the waiting room is occupied by other clients and professionals, a calm acceptance of obstinate refusal can become a problem. The therapist's own clients who arrive early for their appointment will undoubtedly have some reaction. Other clients will observe this handling of the situation, and children, if present, will almost always intrude and react to it. Therefore, when the waiting room is public, the therapist may become unable to respond to the client with the same freedom that would be obtained in the office.

Furthermore, even if the therapist is comfortable in accepting the child's decision, other adults may interpret this as helplessness or ineptitude. In particular, this may be the feeling of the child's parents: they are paying for the therapist to see their child, and they are likely to believe this cannot be accomplished in the waiting room. In addition, it is probable that separation problems are the very reason they brought their child to the therapist, and they expect to see some dramatic achievement. Thus the parent may view the therapist's acceptance as giving in and as an inability to deal with the situation, especially if that is what they have had to do when the child has refused to separate from them. Moreover, if the parent has become involved in counseling with another professional, the child may prevent him or her from continuing with appointments that have become of significance both to the parent and to the therapist's professional colleague. Should the therapist fail to respond to these pressures to "do something," there is a danger not only that the child may be lost as a client but also that the antipathy of coworkers will be incurred.

On this basis, as well as the fact that what may be done may be construed as flooding or perhaps in vivo desensitizaton (Rachman, 1990), a case can be made for the therapist to intervene actively in bringing about a separation. It should be recognized that this is not psychotherapy, but a form of setting limits or training that may be therapeutic. In a sense the therapist acts to communicate the restriction that freedom can be allowed within the office or playroom, but that outside these areas there are constraints upon all concerned. Accordingly the therapist, in order to be of help and to enable the client to experience fully what the therapist has to offer, has to see the client in the professional's working areas. Further, it can be argued that by intervening, the therapist demonstrates to the child that there are limits and that the therapist is not afraid to deal with the child's fears and impulses, whereas the parents can see how their child can be controlled without dire consequences.

Let it be imagined, therefore, that the child shows no inclination to accompany the therapist from the waiting room and that the parent is making no effective effort to help the situaton. It seems rather clumsy, unprofessional, and needlessly distressing to force a separation on the spot in so public a place. It seems far better for the therapist to turn to the parent and say, "Let's all go to my office [or the playroom]. We'll see how Jane feels about it when she has a chance to see it." Immediately this places some responsibility on the parent to bring the child from the waiting room and to take an active part in the separation, demonstrates that the therapist has the situation somewhat under control, and transports the group into a setting with some measure of privacy.

Along the way to the office, the parent usually wonders what the therapist intends to do. If the aim is to see the child without the parent, a brief explanation such as the following is helpful: "When we get to my office I'll show Jane some of the toys there and try to talk with her. When it seems to be all right for you to leave, I'll let you know. Just go, close the door, and don't come back. We'll meet you in the waiting room when we're through, in about 50 minutes."

If the parent is supposed to meet with another professional while the therapist is seeing the child, it is customary for that therapist to accompany the group and to leave with the parent. In general, an appropriate time for the parent to leave is when the child seems to have left the parent by interacting with the therapist or playing with the toys. If the child is screaming and fighting with the parent on the way to the office because he or she is furious about the parent's "disobedience" in leaving the waiting room, however, the therapist might just as well separate them upon their arrival and allow the parent to escape to his or her appointment.

When the parent leaves, it is to be expected that the child will cry. Most often the child attacks the door in an effort to open it and rush from the office, but rarely do children attack the therapist. The therapist tries to (1) protect them both from being hurt; (2) prevent the child from leaving the room; (3) communicate an understanding of the child's fear, rage, and wish to be with the parent; (4) point out that they are supposed to meet and spend this time together, perhaps while the parent meets with someone else; (5) state the wish to be of help to the child and to discuss problems, of which this might well be one; and (6) indicate the availability of toys and play materials. With this kind of enforced separation, the majority of children stop crying within a few minutes, employ the session to advantage, and do not present so great a problem in separation at the second meeting, often leaving the parent without any special difficulty. Nevertheless, not every therapist is comfortable employing this procedure; as mentioned at the outset of this discusson, some prefer to wait it out until the child is able to separate without distress, however long that may be.

Although there are therapists who routinely handle separation problems by forcible interventions, arguing that at the very least these serve the diagnostic function of assessing the child's resilience and intensity of dependence, their use is contraindicated with psychotic children, where the child's reaction is likely to be catastrophic and prolonged. Moreover, if there is no compelling need to separate the parent from the child, it seems preferable for the therapist to act in accord with the principles of psychotherapy and to treat the family as a unit, either until such time as the case naturally comes to a conclusion or it is appropriate for the clients to be seen individually.

If the child is an adolescent or is of a size that would be injudicious for the therapist to attempt to restrain, a successful means for dealing with the separation problem is to turn to the parent and say, "Since Jane does not want to go to my office now, I think it would be a good idea for us to go there and make use of this time. Jane, I'm going to be talking with your mother for the next 50 minutes. If you would like to join us, my room number is 115, or you can get it from the receptionist."

This maneuver separates the parent from the child, demonstrates the time of the therapist is valuable and will not be wasted, and allows the child an opportunity to reconsider the refusal. The parent and the therapist can discuss the child's separation difficulty and ways of dealing with it during their meeting, which more often than not is interrupted by the appearance of the child.

In sum, when a child refuses to accompany the therapist, the latter should ask the parent to bring the child to the office or playroom. If it is feasible to leave the youngster alone in the waiting room and unwise to attempt force, the parent should be seen in order to discuss the problem and methods for handling it. A forced separation should never be attempted by the therapist in a public waiting room; when physical intervention is unavoidable, it is carried out in the therapist's office or playroom and only after careful consideration is given to alternatives (such as seeing parent and child in family therapy, parental counseling, or a patient nurturing of the client's ability to be independent).

Establishing Communication with the Child

Fortunately, most children accompany the therapist from the waiting room without any fuss. Before they leave, the therapist informs the parent how long the appointment will last, as a courtesy and an indication of respect for the parent's time (and thus for the parent). The therapist and child then depart.

Probably there is a playroom, although it may be that the therapist's office is sufficiently large to contain toys, play materials, and children's furniture, in addition to a desk and chairs. If the office does not double as a playroom, the therapist must decide where to go with the child. Usually older children (10 years of age and up) are taken to an office, whereas young children and those with difficulties in communication are taken to a playroom. With children known to be hyperactive and distractible, the therapist is wise to prepare the playroom by putting away some of the toys or by having just some play materials available in the office; this is to prevent overstimulation of the child.

It is better to assume that children can communicate verbally than that they cannot, so an effort should be made to engage the child in conversation before presenting the play materials. By so doing the therapist emphasizes the professional, helping nature of the relationship and may obtain straightforward accounts from children able to provide them. Therefore, unless it would be absurd to do so, the therapist begins by asking the child to be seated, pulling up a chair, and exploring the child's understanding of the situation. Many children have to be reminded of the name of the therapist, and one of us still fondly recalls the girl many years ago who, when asked, "And do you know what I am?" responded, "Chinese?"

There are four important questions that the therapist wants the child to address during this early stage of their contact: (1) What is your understanding of why you are here, and how do you feel about it? (2) What do you believe are your problems, and how do you feel about them? (3) What do you plan to do about your problems? (4) How can I be of help to you?

Throughout the conversation the therapist proceeds slowly and deliberately, attempting to clarify each point and being alert to any sign that the child is beginning to find verbal expression uncomfortable or burdensome. When the child does not seem able to participate meaningfully in a discussion, the therapist presents the play materials. Perhaps as the child plays, there will be opportunities to reach some answers to the four questions—if not in the first meeting, then little by little as the meetings continue. The important thing is not that these answers or other information be collected in a businesslike fashion, but that the message be communicated that the therapist is there trying to be understanding and of help to the child.

We are now going to consider two examples. In the first, a 12-year-old boy was referred for psychotherapy by his parents because "he said he would like to talk to a doctor about his problems after all these years, and we don't want him to miss this chance." Further information from the parents revealed their son was thought to be retarded in early childhood and received a diagnosis of infantile autism. He was in special classes throughout his years of schooling but was not retarded in basic academic skills. Indeed, his teacher reported he might be mainstreamed into a regular classroom except for his poor social adjustment and virtual isolation from peers. His parents, both college graduates, hoped that his wish for help might signal a desire for peer relationships, which if attained would permit them to pressure the school for a regular class placement. This, in turn, would create the possibility of their son's admission to an institution of higher education.

At his first meeting this youngster, Casey, never looked directly into the face of the therapist. He recognized the ambitiousness of his parents' goals for him, but he did not share them.

> *Therapist:* Well, Casey, your father told me that you had some problems and things that you wanted to talk about with someone. [The therapist gives a little background information to the child and deliberately broadens the scope of what might be discussed by saying "problems and things." He avoids saying "with me" but says "with someone," which is more accurate and allows the client to feel able to reject the therapist and yet still avail himself of psychotherapy.]
> *Client:* Yes. (*pause*) I don't like to play with children very much.
> *Therapist:* You don't like to play with children very much.
> *Client:* That's right.
> *Therapist:* If that's so, it's hard for me to see what the problem is, unless you want to change your feeling. But if you don't like to play with children, and I guess you don't play with them, then where is it a problem for you? [The therapist is trying to make it clear that his interest is to be of help to the client in what matters to the client.]
> *Client:* It's no problem for me, really. But my teachers and parents worry about it.
> *Therapist:* Suppose you tell me the things that bother you.

Casey went on to tell the therapist that he used to perseverate (it was most unusual to hear a 12-year-old use this term correctly), and that he used to become upset by changes and possible moves and alterations. He was particularly distressed when he overheard his father planning to convert a room over their garage into a bathroom. The therapist noted that Casey prefaced these problems by "used to," however, and he wondered what was troubling the boy now.

Casey explained that now he was frightened by crowds of people and loud noises. At a carnival there had been rides and shows that he would have liked to enjoy, but his fears had held him back. It was his feeling that he was missing things that were interesting, stimulating, and enjoyable, and he was angry with himself for allowing his apprehensions to restrain him. What he wanted was help in becoming less afraid so that his life could be enriched by taking advantage of the experiences his parents were willing to provide for him.

The second example involved Bill, a 10-year-old who was "gifted" but who was doing just passing work in school. His appointment was at 10:30 A.M. at the beginning of the summer vacation. He was seen in a playroom.

Therapist: Did your mother give you any idea as to why you were coming down here today?

Client: No, sir.

Therapist: Well, do you know where you are or what this place is?

Client: Well, I don't know exactly, but I know I'm in a psychology building. [The client is quite precise.]

Therapist: Um-hmm. This is a psychology clinic, and what we do is we see people who might be having some sort of problem—something wrong—and what we do is try to be of help to them if we can . . . and I was wondering what you feel is your problem.

Client: I don't know. I don't know what my problem is; my mom just brought me here today.

Therapist: Well, is this what happened? Your mother just said, "We're going to go down there, and you'd better come." [The therapist is trying to determine if the client feels overcontrolled by his mother.]

Client: No, it was more like a fight, because I was pretty tired this morning—and getting up at 6 o'clock in the morning—

Therapist: So you had to get up early. [The therapist is puzzled by the client's complaint, because the appointment is at 10:30 and the client lives nearby.]

Client: And I didn't want to get up—I was so tired—and I said, "Let me sleep a little longer. I don't want to get up so early." But I guess this is the only time you could give us. [The client is trying to arouse a bit of guilt in the therapist for the ungodly hour of the appointment.]

Therapist: But why did you have to get up so early? Because our appointment was at 10:30.

Client: Well, it was really 10:15. No, that's when we got here. Uh, about 9 . . . no, 9:30 . . . no, twenty to 10 is when I got up and had to eat breakfast . . . and I was so tired.

Therapist: So, you felt so tired this morning and wanted to lie in bed and didn't like the idea of coming down here. [The therapist decides it is better not to pursue the issue of time, since it is causing the client some confusion as he tries to extricate himself from a rash statement. Instead, the therapist focuses upon the feeling of fatigue as a possible justification for not wanting to be helped.]

Client: No, I was just so tired. [The client indicates some receptivity to meeting with the therapist.]

Therapist: Well, did you say to your mother, "Why do I have to get up? Where are we going? What are we doing?"

Client: No, sir. I forgot about the appointment time at 10:30.

Therapist: Did she say anything before this morning about why you were coming or what you were doing?

Client: No, sir.

Therapist: So you don't know at all what to expect here. No idea what we're going to do?

Client: No, sir.

Therapist: Well, you can see we're in a playroom with toys and things, paper and stuff.

Client: Yes, sir. Lots of toys over there.

Therapist: But what I'd like to do at first is talk with you a bit and find out your understanding of why you're here or what seems to be wrong. From what I can gather, Bill, your feeling is the only thing that's wrong is that your mother woke you up this morning and dragged you down here. Is that about right?

Client: Well, there is one other problem I have. She calls me a baby, and I guess I sort of am 'cause I don't know how to fight or anything. I can't fight at all.

Therapist: Um-hmm. Your mother calls you a baby.

Client: Just like the whole school. The whole school calls me a baby, but I don't know . . . if they got me mad enough, I could bust them pretty hard, cause these two eighth graders were picking on me and said they were going to throw me in a ditch, and I hit one of them right in the mouth and cut his lip. And they left me alone from then on. So, if they get me real mad, they get it.

Therapist: Um-hmm. So you kind of figure you're not really a baby. It's just that your mother calls you one, and I guess a lot of the kids do, too. And that's because you're not too interested in fighting.

Client: Yes, sir. And, uh . . . its because of that and because I have to take tranquilizers, 'cause I get real mad and hyperactive and sometimes I've gotten real mad at the teachers . . . and I can't help it and I don't know why.

Therapist: Well, when you get mad at the teachers, what do you do?

Client: I don't know.

Therapist: You mean it's a mystery. You really don't know what happens?

Client: Yes, sir.

Therapist: Then how do you know what happens? Do they tell you about it afterwards and say, "Bill, what you did! Wow!"

Client: They do. They say, "Nah, nah! Look at the baby!" And I've got a pretty good temper, too.

Therapist: Well, when you get angry at the teacher, can you recall the things that happen that make you angry? [The therapist is trying to determine what the provocations and contingencies in the situation might be.]

Client: No, sir. I forgot all about it after I get angry.

Therapist: So you don't know what it is that makes you angry . . . and you don't know what you do when you're angry.

Client: Right.

Therapist: Have you ever wondered what you do? Have you ever thought to yourself, "Gee, I wonder what I do when I get angry?"

Client: Yes, sir.

Therapist: Did you ever ask anybody?

Client: No. sir.

Therapist: Don't really want to find out. [Points out the inconsistency]

Client: Right. I'm kind of afraid to know what happened.

Therapist: What do you think might happen if you get really angry?

Client: If I got too angry I might—I'd probably—I don't know what I'd do. The teacher's desk might go flying through the air.

Therapist: You think if you got really angry, there's no telling how you might hurt somebody or what you might do.

Client: Right. And I don't know what I'm doing. I black out but I keep on doing it, like I'm still awake, but my mind blacks out and I don't know what I'm doing.

Therapist: And it's kind of frightening to you, in a way, to get to know what it is you might be doing.

Client: Yes, sir.

Therapist: I see. How long have you had these periods when you black out?

Client: Ever since I've been going to school. Five years. I'm in the fifth-grade.

Therapist: And is that why you take the tranquilizers?

Client: Yes, sir.

Therapist: And you take them every day?

Client: Every day I remember to take them.
Therapist: And you took them today?
Client: No, not yet.
Therapist: Forgot today.
Client: And I forgot two other pills I was supposed to take today.
Therapist: What are they?
Client: One 'cause I'm allergic to dust, and one 'cause I've got a cold.
Therapist: Oh, being allergic to dust—that must make it hard for you to play in dirt.
Client: No, only if it's dry dirt—real dry.
Therapist: So, you're able to play in dirt.
Client: Yes, sir, so long as it isn't dry and the dust doesn't come up.
Therapist: So you can play games, like baseball, if you want to.
Client: Yes, sir.
Therapist: Do you do that very much? Play games like baseball?
Client: No, sir. I don't like sports that much.
Therapist: Um-hmm.
Client: I like to just read and things like that.
Therapist: So you like reading. Any kind of books you especially like?
Client: Mystery books.
Therapist: Detective stories.
Client: Like the Hardy Boys and books like that.
Therapist: Um-hmm. Like to figure out who did it.
Client: Yes, sir. That's hard to figure it out, but finally you do.
Therapist: Um-hmm. Is that kind of your major interest, you might say—reading?
Client: Yes, sir. (*yawns*) [The nonverbal response suggests some inconsistency with the verbal.]
Therapist: Well, you mentioned having two problems. One is people say you're sort of a baby because you don't fight, and the other is that you're taking tranquilizers because you lose your temper. And yet you're also saying, aren't you, Bill, that when you do lose your temper is when you do fight. So, aren't you saying—don't you feel—that you're in a bind? That they want you to be one way and the other way at the same time.
Client: Yes, sir.
Therapist: What would you like to do? What would you like to be?
Client: I'd like to be where I could knock all the boys in my school to the moon . . . and leave them up there.
Therapist: Really like to let them have it.
Client: Yes, sir.
Therapist: What do they do, these boys, that bothers you so much? [The therapist is trying to determine if a goal around this issue can be negotiated.]

Client: Oh, they're—almost every single boy in my class is real mean to the girls and everything—and if I stand up for the girls, they say I'm a baby and things like that.

Therapist: So, one of the things that bothers you a great deal about the boys is—

Client: That they're mean to the girls.

Therapist: I guess you'd kind of like to protect the girls.

Client: Yes, sir.

Therapist: Any girl in particular you'd like to protect? [The therapist is fishing in psychodynamic waters.]

Client: No, sir. Just all of the girls, cause they're mean to them.

Therapist: Don't have any favorite girl?

Client: No, sir. Could I take my handkerchief out? 'Cause I do believe I'm going to sneeze. [The "allergic" reaction seems to serve to put this topic away.]

Therapist: OK. [The therapist does not want to be confrontative in this first meeting.]

Client: 'Cause if I do sneeze, I want to be ready. When I sneeze, I sneeze hard. My grandfather told me that that's the best way to sneeze.

Therapist: OK.

Client: Now I'm waiting for the sneeze to come. I can tell it's coming, 'cause my nose starts tickling.

Therapist: Um-hmm.

Client: I know I'm gonna. I don't know when.

Therapist: In the meantime, you want me to be quiet.

Client: No, you can talk if you want to.

Therapist: Um-hmm.

Client: (*blows nose*) Maybe that'll help the sneeze to come out easier. (*blows nose again*) It's coming. (*blows nose repeatedly*) You know, I bet it was one of those fake sneezes, 'cause it feels like it, and then I don't sneeze.

Therapist: Must be kind of a pain to feel like it, and then nothing comes. Not to be able to know when you do and when you don't.

Client: Right.

Therapist: I guess there must be a lot of things that are nuisances and irritations. And one of the things that's most bothersome is being called a baby.

Client: Yes, sir.

Therapist: And to the boys and to you, being a baby means not to fight, is that right?

Client: Yes, sir.

Therapist: And also being kind of nice to the girls.

Client: Yes, sir. That's what my mom thinks. Well, being nice to the girls, she thinks that's the right thing to do, but fighting—she thinks that's all right just as long as I don't start it. "Just finish it up," she says.

Therapist: So she wants you to fight.

Client: If someone starts the fight, yes, sir.

Therapist: What does she say to you?

Client: She tells me I'm supposed to fight.

Therapist: Does she yell at you if you don't?

Client: She gets real mad.

Therapist: Um-hmm, and what does she say then?

Client: "You're supposed to fight and not be a sissy." That's all she ever says.

Therapist: It sounds as if there are times when you come home and tell her what some of the boys did and why you might feel upset and instead of her saying, "That's too bad," or, "That's kind of tough, Bill," she says, "Why didn't you punch the guy in the nose?"

Client: Yes, sir.

Therapist: What are some of the things you kind of wish she would help you with or understand?

Client: I can't begin to tell you all of them.

Therapist: (*long pause*) You spend any time with your father?

Client: Yes, sir. I spend a lot of time with Mom and Dad. Dad can't do many things. He's had two heart attacks and he can't do real hard work, and mostly he sleeps when he comes home from work.

Therapist: I see. So there really isn't too much that the two of you do together.

Client: Right.

Therapist: What things do you do together?

Client: Well, right now we're building a wagon, and I don't know what we'll do after that.

Therapist: It sounds as though, because of his heart attacks, you've been told to go kind of easy with him. (*client nods*) Who told you that? Did he say that?

Client: No, it's just that I have to. Cause if he gets cut or anything he bleeds real easy, 'cause he has to take blood thinners.

Therapist: So you know he has a serious medical problem.

Client: Yes, sir.

Therapist: Who explained that to you? The doctor or—

Client: Mom and Dad told me. One day I came home and found him and he was having a heart attack. And he didn't want me to call the hospital, 'cause he said there'd be nobody to go with him.

Therapist: So you think he doesn't take good care of himself.

Client: Yes, sir. Look at all those toys over there.

Therapist: You'd like to go over and play with them.

Client: Yes. (*gets up and goes to toys*) You've got everything here. An

easel—I don't know why I didn't see them when I came in. You've got everything here. Just everything!
Therapist: You'd like to paint.
Client: No. You've just got everything here. Just everything! (*returns to seat*)
Therapist: Well, I'm going to be having a meeting with your mother and father. Would you like to be part of that meeting, because what we're going to be doing is talking over what we might be able to do to help. So, would you like to come to that meeting?
Client: Yes, sir. Mind if I stand up? I'm getting kind of hot.
Therapist: Oh, sure. OK, then, we'll let your parents know that you'd like to come to that meeting. We still have about 5 minutes. Would you like to take a better look at the toys?
Client: No, sir. I think I'd just like to walk around the room and look it over.
Therapist: OK.

The therapist had not decided by the end of this session what treatment method might be most appropriate. He hoped that such a decision would be facilitated by meeting with Bill and his parents and assessing their interactions.

In establishing communication with children, it is important for therapists to remember they are presenting their clients with a novel interpersonal situation. It is rare for adults to sit down with children and attend to what they have to say. Some young children may be most eager to please the therapist, but they may be unable to converse coherently about a given topic for more than a few sentences. Their speech may tumble out in a rapidly flowing stream of consciousness that can be most bewildering to the therapist, and even to the child if there is a persistent effort to make rational sense of it. Despite their wish to be ingratiating through the offering of verbiage, these clients are usually better served through responses to their occasional comments in play.

Other children, somewhat older, believe they are supposed to produce revealing and momentous incidents in their lives but find that they cannot. Neither do they feel comfortable in making use of the play materials, because they believe this would not be in keeping with their assigned task and thus signifies their failure. They look to the therapist to help them over this awkward period while they grope about for something to say. Here therapists must sensitively communicate their awareness of their discomfort, and they may casually suggest possible topics (such as school and sibling relationships) that are often problems for children.

Yet therapists must be alert to clients who plead for assistance only to reject it. In such instances, they make clear to the client that the conflict being experienced is self-imposed and that there is freedom to talk or not and to play or not. Should these children remain seated, silent, and wistful, it is helpful for therapists to communicate their recognition of the difficulties in arriving at a decision and of the wish to have the decision made by someone else. They assure these children, however, that what is of greatest importance is for them to make decisions for themselves. In this manner, a therapist gently but firmly refuses to allow the client to reject the freedom and the responsibility of psychotherapy and insists on a cooperative relationship.

It should be clearly understood that within integrative psychotherapy, therapists do not conceive of the establishment of communicaton with children as solely their problem and responsibility; it is also a responsibility of their clients. A child's outpouring of fears and concerns is no more a therapist's success than a child's silence is a therapist's failure. Psychotherapy is a cooperative endeavor, and its failures are brought about when cooperation has not been or cannot be obtained.

What have been presented thus far in this chapter are hints for gaining the client's cooperation and indications of its importance. It is among the responsibilities of psychotherapists to understand their stimulus characteristics, how their clients perceive them and respond to them, and whether they are participating in cooperative relationships. A first step in building cooperation is to establish what the client wants from psychotherapy and from the psychotherapist. This is in keeping with Principle IV: the therapist negotiates with the client a purpose or goal for their meetings. It is to this issue that our attention is next directed.

Establishing a Contract with the Child

Usually the psychotherapy contract is not a legal document, but an informal agreement between the therapist and client that they have a certain objective or goal in meeting with one another. As mentioned earlier, this objective must be valid—that is, it must be within the power of the client and the therapist to attain. Therefore the goal must not only be judged feasible, but also be independent of the influence of others not party to the psychotherapy.

Casey had a legitimate goal for psychotherapy. He wanted to feel less afraid and more able to undertake novel experiences. His parents, however, seemed to want something from psychotherapy—Casey's entrance into a regular classroom and eventually college—that was dependent on the decisions of authorities in schools and on achievements in courses many years into the future. It was necessary for the therapist to meet with the parents to clarify what they could reasonably expect from the treatment. This was accomplished by pointing out that though the therapist would be pleased to consult with school personnel, the latter determined school placements. Moreover, the therapist had Casey's permission to inform his parents of his goal. When told what their son wanted to attain, the parents could appreciate the value of his objective and adopted it as their own.

Goals that depend on the feelings and judgments of others—to be popular, to be liked by someone, to receive certain grades, to be promoted or to be saved from having to repeat a year in school—are not acceptable. Goals that are not the client's are not acceptable. The child who prefaces his or her aim with "My parents think I should" or "My teacher says that I should" is told that what is of concern here is what he or she wants. Goals that are outside the scope of psychotherapy—to do better in math, to be good in sports—are also not acceptable. Goals that are acceptable are those of personal self-improvement and self-undertanding.

Furthermore, it is acceptable to agree to work toward the definition of a goal. This may happen when children state they are unable to articulate a problem area or concern, but do feel a need to see the therapist and wish to identify what may be troubling them. Often this occurs when children report that the difficulties that led to their referral have been resolved, and yet they are uncertain about the adequacy of the resolution and their ability to cope with other problems.

It is also appropriate for therapists and clients to agree that their objective is to tell the parents they do not want to be seen in psychotherapy. Such a goal can come about when children maintain they have no problem and no idea why they are being seen. Their very presence in a therapist's office is inconsistent with their professed beliefs and raises the question of why they are there. To this, they usually respond that their parents brought them and insisted they come. The therapist's response is to wonder whether the client informed the parents of these objections. Sometimes children will say that they did not say anything, or that they did not make the effort because they knew it would be of no use. Their failure to communicate with their parents and their feelings of futility about such communications then emerge as an area of concern, and the proposal to work with a therapist so as to reject the service encapsulates a major human conflict in a highly engaging form.

Of course, there are times when children legitimately deny problems, or at least when this appears to express a constructive attitude. In assessing this possibility, therapists weigh the answers to the following questions: Does the child deny difficulties whose presence is obvious? Is a repudiation of problems an expression of hopelessness about their solution? Have reasonable steps been taken to modify objectionable behaviors, or is there resolve to undertake those steps? Is there concern that the parents have lost faith in the child's capacity for change and determination to prove them wrong? Is there a willingness to cooperate with the therapist in listening to the parents' side of the issue? Frequently, at a meeting with the family, negotiations occur between the parents and their child with the result that the child may decide to enter psychotherapy, or the parents may be encouraged to accept a trial period in which the child's progress without professional assistance can be evaluated. Whatever the outcome, therapists endeavor to be united with their clients in a cooperative venture in pursuit of their best interests.

It may also happen that children may be too young or developmentally immature to articulate a problem, or they may be reluctant to express a goal in other than a rudimentary form: "I want to come back," "I don't mind seeing you," "I like to play with your toys," or "I like you." Under these circumstances, therapists have a greater responsibility than ordinary to protect their clients from their dependence and compliance. In other words, the therapist must be prepared to decide on the appropriateness of psychotherapy and to represent the interests of the client with concerned adults; the therapist must judge whether the child should be seen, though parents and child may be willing to receive the service or though the child is willing but the parents are not.

The essential point of the contract is that it gives substance to the cooperative nature of the client-therapist relationship. It is possible to practice psychotherapy without a contract—indeed, since psychotherapy is merely the communication of person-related understanding, respect, and a wish to be of help, it conceivably could be practiced without a therapist—but it is preferable (and, in some states, mandatory) to have one. Until there is an agreement as to purpose, a first order of business in psychotherapy is the pursuit and negotiation of a goal.

Reluctant clients, those who are resistant to help but forced to try psychotherapy whether they want it or not, are common among a clientele of children. Many children are brought to the office of the therapist by adults who have resorted to threats or bribes. These youngsters may be frightened, angry, and contemptuous of the therapist. They know they do not want to be there, and they suspect the therapist will resort to cunning and guile to trick them into staying and revealing themselves.

Yet because psychotherapy depends upon cooperation, it can be argued that the "ploys" of the therapist with reluctant clients will not succeed when clients do not really want them to succeed. For example, Strean (1968) suggested enlisting the client's cooperation by proposing a clever reversal of roles: an adolescent may be asked to teach the therapist the ways of the delinquent or the best method to conduct psychotherapy with teen-agers. Deceptive tactics are questionable ethically, as can easily be imagined if the therapist is asked by the parents to explain why they are paying so their child can teach the therapist how to commit crimes. Furthermore, the use of deception and reactance techniques (the therapist's purported endorsement of maladaptive behaviors to arouse the client's negativism) implies that therapists have to outwit their clients and must seduce them into treatment and improvement, with a further implication of gullible clients and sly professionals. Even when this may be the case, it is a dubious basis for a relationship that depends so greatly on mutual trust. It is necessary to question whether therapists are ever justified in using deception with their clients.

Therapists are best advised not to set themselves against their clients' reluctance, but rather to align themselves in some constructive manner with what their clients do want. If they do not want psychotherapy, then in what way can the therapist help so that these clients do not find themselves in this awkward position again? If they are coming only to please a judge or some other authority and to avoid some threatened punishment, therapists, though sympathetic to their plight, cannot (in fairness to others who might use their services) allow themselves to be exploited. They must work to remove threats to their clients and determine if there is any valid basis for their contacts. When clients come in week after week despite a professed reluctance, then therapists must wonder, in view of this inconsistency, what it is clients do want or hope to receive from the service.

Frank certainly seemed to fit the designation of the reluctant client. An adolescent who was suspended from school on many occasions and adjudged a juvenile delinquent by reason of a series of thefts, he was brought to a therapist by his parents, who had been ordered by the court to do so. Frank claimed that he did not need help, that he had finally learned his lesson and would not steal again, and that he did not need a "shrink" because he was not crazy.

The therapist remarked that few of his clients would be thought of as crazy and that the issue was irrelevant. What was important was why Frank was there, since he obviously felt so strongly against coming. Why else, Frank grumbled, except that his judge had made it a condition of probation and his mother had dragged him down? Yet his mother, the therapist observed, was clearly no match for Frank in a fair fight. Perhaps along with his anger and resentment there was another feeling, maybe hope that the therapist might be able to do something that would be of help to him. Frank said nothing to this.

The therapist agreed that Frank had not been in trouble recently and that his intentions were in the direction that the judge and his parents seemed to want. But what of him? What did he really want? The therapist would check with Frank's parents and probation officer, see what they thought about his stopping the sessions, and report back to Frank at their next meeting. In the meantime, Frank could think things over and see whether there might be something he wanted help with from the therapist. Thus, the therapist reached an agreement with Frank: He would be willing to explore the reasonableness of Frank's termination, and in turn he asked that Frank be open-minded about getting something from psychotherapy.

At their next meeting, Frank decided he wanted help in being able to express himself to his parents and in not allowing them to shove him around.

Sometimes a child will present a problem or a variety of problems and will need a therapist's help to plow through this mass of information and transform it into a feasible goal. This occurred with Rick, a 12-year-old referred for setting fires and underachieving in school.

The fire-setting, though of greatest concern in the referral, turned out to be an isolated incident during which a friend of Rick's ignited some rags in a vacant lot. The fire was extinguished quickly, and there was no damage—or even the threat of damage—to any property, yet the police labeled Rick a "fire-setter." (Such a label can have serious consequences for a youngster, particularly when a residential placement is needed. Many institutions or homes for children will reject automatically any application that reports a history of fire-setting. Similarly, it is not uncommon to receive a referral of a child who is said to masturbate in school. Further investigation of what is meant by this frequently discloses that the child rubbed or pulled at the pubic area in an effort to relieve the discomfort of tight-fitting clothes.) Rick acknowledged poor performance in school, however, accompanied by severe nervousness.

Rick described a problem of diffuse, free-floating anxiety. For no identifiable reason, he found it difficult to concentrate or feel at ease. His hands trembled, he fidgeted in his seat, and he felt a strong urge to get up and walk about the classroom. Nor could he relax at home; sleep, when it came, seemed more like a struggle than anything else. This "nervousness" had existed as far back as he could remember, and he could offer no explanation for it. People had tried to help him in school, and an effort to provide relief by his pediatrician through the use of a number of drugs was also without success.

That Rick could offer no psychological explanation for his anxiety was inconsistent with the many traumatic events in his life. His mother had died of cancer a few years before the referral after a long and painful illness. His father was a mysterious figure whose source of income was vague and who wore sunglasses even inside the therapist's office; his major concern seemed to be to avoid incriminating himself and to do whatever would have to be done to ensure that he would not have to see the therapist again. Rick's recently acquired stepmother shared her husband's fondness for sunglasses and took refuge behind her newness to the family to shield herself from any responsibility for Rick's behavior.

The therapist speculated from a psychoanalytic perspective that Rick's anxiety stemmed from a weakness in the control of impulses, and that to probe for the origins of his conflicts could be expected to aggravate the anxiety. Fenichel (1945), in discussing spontaneous remissions, argued that symptom substitution would not occur if there were a reduction in anxiety, but would occur when symptoms were suppressed through force or intimidation. Therefore, what was indicated was somehow to reduce the anxiety. It was thought this could be best accomplished by training Rick in relaxation. Training in progressive relaxation not only would alleviate the anxiety but also was expected to increase Rick's feeling of being in control of himself, since this training depends greatly on the client tensing and becoming aware of various muscle groups throughout the body.

Rick was told there was a method for dealing with his anxiety that had not as yet been attempted: training him to feel relaxed. It required his cooperation in working with the therapist and in practicing the method at home. Also, the training would take up most of the time of the appointment, so there would be little opportunity for discussion. This pleased Rick greatly. Nevertheless, the therapist wanted Rick to know that if he did want to talk anything over with the therapist, time would be made available for that purpose.

The training in relaxation was eagerly accepted by Rick and received the endorsement of his parents. He was delighted by the first session, stating that he felt "light as a bird" and happier than he had ever been. His grades in school improved, and he claimed to feel in control of himself. The training stopped after ten sessions, with the client and parents highly pleased by the results and interested in no further assistance.

By now it should be clear that the contract need not be any lengthy or involved agreement as to purpose, and that it may be brief and quickly formed. Some examples are shown below.

Client 1: I can't control my temper.
Therapist: That's something we might work on.
Client 1: Yeah? OK.
Client 2. Yes, I'm still wetting my bed, but I don't think that's so bad.
Therapist: I see. You don't feel that that's really a problem for you, even though some people seem to be acting that way.
Client 2: Yeah. I wish they'd stop bugging me all the time. There's this counselor in school who keeps telling me I could do better . . . and my music teacher's after me, too.
Therapist: It sounds as though what you'd like to be able to do is to tell them to leave you alone without hurting their feelings.
Client 2: Yeah. And maybe you could help me stop smoking too.
Client 3: I don't know why, I just feel miserable. I sit in my room alone, and I begin to hear voices, and I feel like crying. Do you suppose we could figure out the reason?
Therapist: Maybe. We could try. And maybe while we're trying, things will begin to work themselves out.

In his discussion of technique, Federn (1952, p. 159) quoted a bit of advice he received from Freud: "He told me: 'Always have in mind that your patient should return the next day for treatment.'" By that Federn meant that the therapist should be certain to do the things that would ensure the client's continuance, such as avoiding or clearing up any misunderstandings and behaving in such a way that the patient did not feel rejected.

The possibility of inadvertently rejecting the client is not to be minimized. Some people are exquisitely sensitive to the slightest hint that the therapist may not want to see them again. A suggestion of time limits for the psychotherapy, while useful for some clients and perhaps unavoidable in settings such as schools (Osterweil, 1986), is contraindicated when clients have a history of being abandoned. Such a suggestion may provoke the client to reject the therapist before being rejected themselves. Yet the advice of Freud and Federn needs to be balanced by child psychotherapists with the awareness that many children they see are brought to them and have not requested their services. They have a responsibility to assess whether children are in need of psychotherapy.

For example, Allen, a 10-year-old, was referred by his mother, who described him as normal and well-adjusted. Though she saw nothing wrong with him, she thought it best to follow the suggestion of his principal to have him seen and evaluated for psychotherapy. The principal, a former army officer in charge of the military academy where Allen was enrolled, thought him a mediocre student and troublemaker.

Allen presented himself to the therapist in a polite, open, cooperative manner. He ackowledged that his grades in school had not been excellent (almost all B's), but claimed this was because he was trying to gain the acceptance of his classmates as an all-around fellow. Therefore he was concentrating, with the approval and encouragement of his parents, on developing his skills in football; in fact, he was attending that school because it had a football program for preadolescents. He claimed that he now regarded himself as "kind of silly" for allowing his studies to deteriorate and that he would improve his grades in the future.

He was not sure why the principal considered him a troublemaker. All that had happened was that he was standing in the hall when some other boy began yelling. His teacher had come out of the classroom in a fury, immediately spotted him, and without investigating the facts of the matter hit him over the head with a ruler and hauled him to the principal's office. The principal listened only to the teacher and suspended Allen. So far as Allen knew, this was his only "misbehavior," but ever since his return from suspension his teacher had been irritable with him and vigilant for any possible sign of mischief.

Allen's mother supported his account. Her son had never been a particular problem at home, and this was the first year he had experienced trouble in school. She and her husband were upset by "the knot raised on his head from the blow of the ruler," but since they wished him to remain at the school, they did not complain about it. They were aware that their son's grades were not outstanding, but believed they were good. What, they wanted to know, did the therapist think—should their boy be seen in psychotherapy?

Moustakas (1959) presented a case for children to be seen in play therapy as a routine means for the prevention of psychological problems and education in self-knowledge and social skills. He described a program in which children of nursery-school and kindergarten ages were seen in small groups as part of their usual schedule. Under such circumstances there is much to commend such an effort; however, when we are concerned with providing a service that is not routine but singles out a child for special attention (and, in this less than perfect world, possible stigma), when the family is required to pay for the service, and when the client who is being seen is receiving time that might be used by another client who is on a waiting list, the therapist cannot have as the goal of the first meeting just to ensure a commitment to psychotherapy. What, then, is a reasonable objective?

It seems best for the therapist to be guided in the first meeting by the aim of acting responsibly in achieving a cooperative relationship with the client. "Acting responsibly" refers to obligations not only to the client, but also to those who have been involved in the referral. Parents, teachers, principals, physicians have impressions of the client that were formed in situations unlike those presented by the therapist. They have information, and often they have made a heavy investment of their time in arranging for the arrival of the child in the therapist's office. The therapist should not arrive at a decision without taking into consideration and respecting the concerns and thoughts that led to the referral. Thus, in acting responsibly, therapists must take into account the wishes, judgments, and feelings of all the parties involved. They must remind the client of the involvement of persons other than himself or herself in the decision-making process, and they must try to enlist their clients' cooperation in the pursuit of a goal common to all and consistent with every impression.

Not all questions need to be answered, and not all decisions need to be reached in the first meeting, the second, or the ninth. It is not expected that the therapist is omniscient and perfect. Clients are understanding and accepting when the therapist says, "I'm not sure about that yet. Maybe it'll help to talk it over some more at our next meeting." Therefore, it is to be understood that the first meeting refers to a phase of a process that, regardless of its specific duration, has as its purpose to join in a shared undertaking by making explicit the client's understanding of the referral, feelings about it, and expectations about what may be accomplished.

7
Continuing Contacts

E very meeting with a client is a new experience, and although there is often continuity, the therapist should be prepared for radical shifts in direction and emphasis. A child may have been despondent and concerned about some problem in a previous meeting, yet now claim to be unconcerned and happy. A significant bit of information may have been exchanged that in the next meeting is alleged to have been forgotten or unimportant. A child who was cooperative and pleasant last week may be the same child who this week tries to torment the therapist and to wreck the playroom or office.

With some children, one session seems to blend into another with monotonous sameness. In every meeting Joan models with clay and paints, Frank plays checkers or chess, George fights with the puppets and toy soldiers, Larry wants only to play catch with the therapist, and Edith never appears to tire of a spelling game. The therapist begins to wonder whether progress is being made, whether clinical undertanding and sensitivity are dulled by boredom, and whether declining interest is produced by sameness or sameness is produced by declining interest.

Some children present similar pictures of themselves from meeting to meeting. Their sessions may not be dull—in fact, they may leave their therapists exhausted both physically and mentally by their demands—yet there does not seem to be any change. Every meeting with them becomes an ordeal for the therapist, who believes clinical techniques are being employed effectively but still is frustrated by the client's intractability. What is going wrong?

The changes that therapists expect to see are influenced by their theoretical orientations, namely, the understanding of behavior and personality functioning that they have at that particular time. Their understanding is based on their readings, training, attitudes toward and about human nature, personalities, and experiences. Perhaps they have come across a novel theory or recent experimental finding that has engaged their inter-

162

est and has modified or altered their expectations. It is reasonable to expect that over the years, their understanding of their system of treatment will be enriched and deepened by corroborative observations of human behaviors, so that they can view the progress of their clients in terms of both theoretical abstractions and specific occurrences. When trained to become sensitive to subtle modifications of attitudes and actions, however, even less experienced practitioners of psychotherapy are able to find and offer encouragement to parents and other concerned adults, taking their clues and encouragement from slight alterations in what children do, and even from drastic changes that superficially may seem to be for the worse.

Predicted Changes

For many clients, the onset of psychotherapy and the expectation that they will receive help afford an immediate reduction in anxiety and an alleviation of symptoms (Friedman, 1963). Quite frequently a client reports that the distressing problems of the first session have been eliminated, and that the therapist has worked a kind of magic. Hathaway (1951) referred to this sudden improvement as the "hello-goodby" effect, since it may be used by the client to justify an abrupt termination of the service. Behavioral therapists may be inclined to accept this recovery at face value, whereas psychodynamic therapists are apt to think of it as a form of resistance, implying a "flight into health" that is prompted by apprehension of the treatment. Nevertheless, even among analytic therapists there are those with an ego orientation who see resistance as a sign of the client's autonomy and desire for independence (Blanck & Blanck, 1974).

With children, immediate symptom reduction and a wish to terminate may be complicated further by the parents' phoning the therapist to cancel further appointments because of the improvement in the child's behavior. Although therapists respect these decisions, they are obligated to point out when they are inconsistent with decisions previously reached, such as if there was a mutual agreement about continuing appointments. Moreover, they must ensure that the child is aware of the parents' actions, and they must evaluate whether the child agrees with them. Therapists have a responsibility to their young clients under these circumstances to request an additional appointment, if for no other reason than to make certain that (1) the termination is not perceived by the child as a rejection and (2) it is understood by the family that the therapist's door remains open should the need for visits arise in the future.

To return to "typical" children who contiue in psychotherapy, however, there is symptomatic relief during the course of treatment. Almost immediately a lessening of anxiety may occur (on the part of the parents if not the child), and in the sessions that follow there are likely to be reports of "feeling better" and of "things going along a little better."

When behavioral approaches are employed, there are usually target behaviors that are expected to change in frequency. Not only are desirable behaviors expected to generalize beyond the training sessions, but steps are usually taken to bring about generalization and the maintenance of the behaviors. In psychotherapy there is less emphasis on training for particular changes and more on creating conditions that will enable the child to effect change. Specifically, psychotherapists expect that children will improve in their ability to control themselves, that they will progress from a rigid suppression of feelings or a tendency to act on impulses to being able to modulate the expression of emotions and wishes in accord with the demands and requirements of the circumstances. Aggressive and uncontrolled children become less impulsive, more patient and capable of delay, and less prone to emotional outbursts. Psychotherapy with such youngsters often presents parents with a picture of steady improvement.

In contrast, inhibited children can be expected to become more open in their emotional expression and more likely to give voice to their grievances. At times parents may be alarmed by their child's uncharacteristic relatively mild display of assertiveness, anger, or need. They may fear therapy has brought about a deterioration in their child's condition or that it fosters immoral, intolerable behavior. Fortunately, most parents are willing to see this "storm" through if given assurances by therapists that these changes are constructive, desirable, and likely to diminish in severity. Regrettably, however, there are parents who confess they prefer inhibitions and symptoms to "disrespect" and their child "acting like he doesn't love me anymore," and they may abruptly withdraw from psychotherapy during this phase.

It was mentioned earlier that Moustakas (1953) suggested children in psychotherapy at first express their hostility and fears in a vague, undifferentiated, but intense manner. Later they are able to be more specific about who and what it is they fear and dislike. As psychotherapy progresses, children's attitudes and emotions become less simple and one-sided and more complex and ambivalent. For example, at first the child may only express hatred or love for someone, then become capable of acknowledging that there are times when there is one feeling or another, and later come to a resolution of these inconsistencies by connecting feelings with the circumstances that bring them about and adopting a positive, tolerant, understanding attitude. Thus, children come to recognize that their parents do some things that frustrate and anger them, but for reasons that are consonant with their affection for them.

It should be noted that the description by Moustakas may be appropriate for the course of treatment of inhibited children, but not for youngsters whose referral problems are impulsiveness and aggression. These children express hostility too readily, feel their aggression is justified, and are untroubled by doubts and apprehension. In other words, they are already at a more extreme version of the first stage mentioned by Moustakas, with little indication they have ever had the self-control of an inhibited child. Accordingly, questions have been raised (Berkowitz, 1964, 1970) as to how much freedom should be allowed for aggressive children in psychotherapy to continue to be aggressive and whether the playroom should contain toys and materials that can be expected to elicit hostility during their visits. Empirical evidence suggests that the release of aggression does not serve as a catharsis but facilitates the release of still more aggression, and that children who are undercontrolled (Redl & Wineman, 1951) or who bully others should be handled by being seen in a setting where cues for hostility are minimized or eliminated, where limits are imposed upon their impulsivity, and where they are trained to respond to frustrations in more effective ways than by lashing out (Shore & Massimo, 1973).

Before any restrictions are introduced, however, the therapist should assess the "aggressive" child's response to the usual playroom. It is quite possible that the child may be able to express aggression in ways that promote communication and make clear conflicts and problems. Only if the therapist finds that the child's emotional expression leads to disorganization, disruptiveness in communication, or destructive effects upon their relationship should the aforementioned precautions be taken. But in no case can emotional release, in and of itself, be expected to guide the child to appropriate behaviors; that is one of the tasks of the therapist.

Psychoanalytic theory specifies a number of orderly changes in human development that can be related to signs of movement in psychotherapy (Freud, 1965). An understanding of these stages or this progression enables the therapist to estimate the child's level of functioning and to anticipate in what ways the client's behavior should advance to be age appropriate. Probably most sophisticated readers are familiar with the analytic notion that early in the child's life come conflict and preoccupation with being cared for and fed and gaining trust in a mothering person; that there follows concern about toilet training, establishing a sense of autonomy, and becoming willing to cooperate with authorities, even when they are frustrating and demanding; that next there is the oedipal situation, with attendant problems in jealousy, competitiveness, exercising initiative, and forming a positive relationship with both parents; that with the entry into school the child's interests should turn from the family to center on peers, teachers, learning, and a sense of competence and accomplishment from educational efforts; and that with adolescence there is a concerted groping toward identity, independence from parents, intimate relationships with peers, and the assumption of adult responsibilities.

With an analytic theoretical framework, a therapist would predict that a child would move from distorting and denying reality to being able to accept the world for what it is, from dependence on others to cooperation with them, from trouble with the control and expression of impulses to their modulated and socially appropriate discharge, from resistance to the demands of authorities to assertiveness when necessary and compliance when advantageous. The analytic position believes an important (though not always essential) element in this process is the uncovering of unconscious conflicts and concerns (Peterson & Burbach, 1988). Attempts to relate improvement to the process of gaining insight into one's unconscious and past, however, have not been very supportive of such an association (Wallerstein, 1989), though there was surprising support from an unexpected source: diabetic children seen in analytic therapy were better controlled in their blood-sugar levels as unconscious material emerged and was explored (Fonagy & Moran, 1990).

Rogerian therapists have emphasized changes in the self-concept of clients (Axline, 1947; Rogers & Dymond, 1954; Zax & Kline, 1960). The assumption is that clients at the beginning of psychotherapy view themselves negatively and that there are significant discrepancies between the kind of person they would like to be and the kind of person they believe they are; they are dissatisfied with themselves and probably with others as well. As treatment progresses, children are expected to begin to express genuine feelings of self-confidence and self-worth, while making more realistic appraisals of the kind of person they would like to be and the kind of person they are so that they will grow in their feelings of self-satisfaction. An important factor in bringing these changes about is the client's growing sense of responsibility for effecting personal change and exercising choice.

A case study (Reisman, 1968) of an adolescent seen for 50 sessions of psychotherapy measured changes in the client's ratings of the therapist and himself. As the treatment progressed, the client's ratings of himself became more positive while his ratings of the therapist became less positive, so that by termination the ratings were similar, positive, and relatively stable. These findings suggest that some clients can be expected to devalue (or perhaps more realistically appraise) the therapist during the course of psychotherapy.

Children may express their changing attitudes about the therapist and themselves by remarks such as "I guess you don't know everything," "Never mind! I think I'll handle it myself," and "These toys sure are old! Why don't you get some new stuff? I've got better things at home," as well as by comments about the latter's confidence and competence. In one sense, the entire process of psychotherapy can be seen as the child's struggle to establish an identity: an individuality as a person apart from, though dependent on, other persons (Allen, 1942).

Thus, therapists may note how children relate to them—whether in a dependent, domineering, withdrawn, or negativistic fashion—and may understand these modes of interaction as more or less effective attempts to sacrifice individuality for the sake of feeling secure (as would be the case with dependent and withdrawn behaviors) or as efforts to be assertive when essentially uncertain of their own identities (as is true of negativistic children, who determine what they want by first soliciting what someone else wants and then registering their opposition, or domineering children, who greatly fear being controlled by someone else).

Moreover, therapists are aware that such conflicts are not peculiar to children. The parents of their clients probably need assistance in deciding how much self-control and responsibility they can allow their sons and daughters. There may even be times when the assertiveness of children may provoke therapists to defend their individuality by imposing limits that, upon reflection, are difficult to justify. Yet it is a task of therapists to promote the growth of their clients as persons in their own right, and to that end they must respect (and encourage parents to respect) children's oppositional behavior and allow them many opportunities to formulate their own decisions.

Growth in self-understanding is one major change desired and valued in every system of psychotherapy. This gain in insight includes awareness of personal inconsistencies and their constructive resolution. Thorne (1968, p. 13) characterized the basic purpose of psychotherapy as, "to catalyze self-actualization by improving integrational status." But however the process may be conceptualized (Orlinsky, 1989), it must ultimately be recognized that therapists are dealing with individuals who have their own standards and expectations for what constitutes their progress. Some of these clients may be displeased by results that therapists regard as satsifactory, whereas other clients may be satisfied by levels of accomplishment that therapists believe fall short of their aims.

Implementing the Contract

The first meeting (or the first few meetings) with the child is (or are) relatively structured around the task of establishing the contract. Therapists have to assess clients and introduce themselves, to evaluate the child's understanding of the purpose of the contacts, and to find some service they can provide for their clients. For many children this degree of structure still affords them a freedom they have never before experienced with adults, and they move into the meetings that follow without any noticeable hesitation or reluctance. Other children may depend on the therapist to give them direction, and they may be surprised by—and flounder in—the relative lack of structure of subsequent meetings.

If a client waits for some direction upon entering a therapist's office or playroom, the therapist may remark that the client does not seem to know what to do but is free to do whatever may be wished: to play with the toys, to draw, to paint, to talk about anything, or to do nothing. There is often a moment's hesitation and wavering, and then the child begins by walking to the toys or talking with the therapist. The therapist responds by communicating an understanding of the child, respect, and a wish to be of help. This is psychotherapy, and this form of communication continues in response to the client's behaviors throughout the contacts that follow.

Suppose, however, that the child does not talk or play with the toys. What do therapists do when children stand in the room and say they do not know what to do, or sit down to talk and say they do not know what to say, or begin to talk about something that seems irrelevant? As we know, some therapists may have a variety of games and gimmicks to help deal with such awkward moments, but let us assume we are not going to resort to any of them. In general, we can regard whatever the child does as a form of communication to which the therapist can respond by communicating understanding, respect, and a wish to be of help. Further, once there is agreement about the purpose of the meetings, the behaviors of the child can be seen as either consistent or inconsistent with this purpose.

Therefore, when children are uncommunicative, their therapists can comment on the apparent difficulty being experienced by the child in getting started. They try to determine whether the client is uncomfortable with the hesitation or is making use of it to maneuver the therapist into assuming control for the hour. In either case the therapist may say, "You'd like me to give you some idea of what to say." Ordinarily, children respond to that statement with a smile of relief and say yes. Then the therapist reminds the client of their contract: "Well, just a few days ago you were worried about how things were going in school. Is that something that still bothers you?" If the child again answers yes, then the therapist may wonder why the client does not discuss a topic that is of concern. If the child answers no, then the therapist may wonder about this development and the way it affects the client's attitude toward treatment.

Some therapists prefer to reflect the child's wish for the therapist to provide direction, smile benignly, and say nothing. Or they may state with gentle firmness, "I suppose it might be easier for you if I told you what to do, but this is your time to do with as you wish. What is important is what you want to do." Usually a silence follows, and either the child will then enter into some activity or topic of conversation or there will be an open struggle with the therapist about who is to be responsible for assuming the lead: "I can't think of anything to say. I really don't know what to do. Why don't you tell me?"

It is important at this point to note that although the child seems to want something to say or do, the therapist has already made clear the availability of play materials and has stated the position of being interested in whatever the client wants to mention, including the discussion of those problems of which both are aware. Yet here is the client claiming to be at a loss, which is not consistent with what they know and the opportunities present. Perhaps this indecision and reluctance to assume responsibility should be a major focus of their meetings, and an aim of the therapist and client should be to work toward the latter becoming more decisive and independent.

As can be seen, therapists may take what seems to be a problem for the client (as indicated in the first few moments of their meetings), bring it into focus, and propose that part of the work of psychotherapy be to deal with it. The contract is thus flexible—capable of expansion and revision, yet with a structure that can be used to remind clients of their purpose. For example, a child may report that the original problem is gone or seems under control. The therapist accepts this bit of information and considers its implications with the client. If the resolution of this problem has been the goal of their meetings, the client may wish to substitute another goal or to direct attention to other matters that seem troublesome. Perhaps the child would like to see how things go for a while before deciding what to do about psychotherapy. The purpose of the meetings might then become to assess the stability and effectiveness of the client's recent adjustment. Or perhaps the child would like to end the meetings, in which case the therapist begins to explore this possibility by ascertaining how the parents might feel about it.

Another example involves the child whose talk or play seems irrelevant. It may be that a child comes into the therapist's office with homework and wants to do it; brings in a transistor radio, puts on the earphones, and starts to listen to music; or wants only to build plastic models or play solitaire. The therapist reminds the child of the purpose of their meetings, questions whether the child sees these activities as consistent with that purpose, and respects the client's decision once it is open and no longer unilateral. In other words, children who want to do their homework or whatever may not be in accord with their professed goals, but may do so once they recognize what they are doing and accept the responsibility for being unable at the moment to pursue their original objectives.

This means that children are free to be inconsistent or to break their contracts when they realize and appreciate that this is what they are doing and when they are aware of their therapists' continued understanding, respect, and wish to be of help. Moreover, this freedom can only be given temporarily. The therapist and child must work to resolve the inconsistency with the professional nature of their relationship. Such a stipulation is necessary because there are circumstances—a child ordered into psychotherapy as a condition of probation, readmission into school, or the receipt of some parental favor—where a therapist is in danger of being exploited by a client or used merely to gain some advantage while concealing from a third party that professional services are not being utilized. Under such conditions, therapists must eventually act in accord with their responsibilities to adults who are involved and to other prospective clients.

Axline (1947) stated that one of the principles of a Rogerian or humanistic psychotherapy with children is that the child leads the way and the therapist follows. This principle has a considerable amount of truth to it, and it is particularly helpful in encouraging therapists to be patient and to allow children freedom in their play and conversation. Specific educational programs or the reduction of specific symptoms are not the major goals of psychotherapy; one of the major goals is to work cooperatively with clients and to help them to accept their responsibility for the choices they make. Accordingly, it is better to see what directions the person chooses to take than to impose activities or topics that can be irrelevant or tangential to the client's needs. Yet freedom can become neglect, or an aimless indifference without any limits. It is more accurate to say that the child leads the way and the therapist notes the continuity of this action with what has gone before, its consistency or inconsistency with professsed goals, and its apparent meaning to the client at the moment.

Renegotiating the Contract

How many therapists prepare for the infinite number of variations possible in the meetings of psychotherapy? It has already been suggested that their understanding of personality or behavior enables them to see order and common threads through ostensibly different sessions. Moreover, it has also been indicated that to some extent the client displays similarities between one appointment and the next, as when a child tries to "work through" a conflict or plays repeatedly with certain toys in much the same way so as to gain a feeling of competence and control over some problem or behavior. Thus, on the one hand there is obvious consistency in what the client does, and on the other hand the therapist perceives consistency.

There is an additional consideration in that the therapist imposes consistency upon the sessions. At the beginning of each meeting, the therapist waits to see in what way the client wishes to make use of their time. Yet the therapist has expectations about what is appropriate based upon an understanding of the treatment or psychotherapy as a cooperative endeavor based upon their agreement or contract. Although open to change, the therapist strives to see that change is a product of mutual understanding and respect. Therefore, should the client attempt to make the relationship with the therapist competitive or parent-child, the therapist must comment on this effort to bring about an alteration. In a spirit of cooperation and respect for the child's needs at that moment, the child is allowed to make of the relationship whatever is desired, but this is done after noting what the needs are and any inconsistency of these demands. Within limits, everything is subject to change and negotiation by the client. In the final analysis, what provides stability and consistency to psychotherapy is the stability and consistency of the therapist who follows the principles of psychotherapy.

> *Client 1:* I still don't know what to say.
> *Therapist:* Kind of strange, isn't it? Here you are coming to see me about your problem in stealing, and yet you don't want to talk about it.
> *Client 1:* Yes. *(pause)* I still don't have anything to say. *(pause)* Do you play checkers? Let's play that.
> *Therapist:* It's easier to play against me than to talk with me.
> *Client 1:* I guess so.
> *Therapist:* OK.
> *Client 2:* You sit down over there, and I'll be the teacher.
> *Therapist:* I guess you'd like to push me around and be the boss.
> *Client 2:* Yes. Now keep quiet! Here's a piece of paper. You write down all these spelling words, and you'd better get them right.
> *Therapist:* I suppose it makes you feel angry to have to do all that work in school. You can tell me that, but I won't write down the words.
> *Client 2:* All right, you don't have to do it. But remember, I told you to keep quiet.
> *Therapist:* I can't promise to do that. It's my job to talk with you when there's something to say.
> *Client 2:* Oh, all right.
> *Client 3:* Let me sit in your chair, and you sit over there.
> *Therapist:* You'd like to feel like me for a while.
> *Client 3:* Yes.
> *Therapist:* All right.

Although analytic therapists may see a child four or more times a week—and there is evidence to suggest that such frequent sessions bring about more enduring changes (Heinicke, 1990)—the frequency of visits may be determined by what is customary in a particular setting, expediency, third parties, economics, and the lack of compelling evidence to do otherwise (Kazdin, Bass, Ayers, & Rodgers, 1990). For many parents, coming more often than a certain frequency presents a financial burden they are not able to assume. In addition, children who have to come to their sessions during their normal school hours present the complication of weighing the needs of treatment against their educational needs.

At times a child or adolescent will request more frequent or less frequent visits. Although there have been favorable reports of "dosing" the frequency (Zwick, 1960), acceding to these requests does not always appear to be what the client actually wants. It may happen that the adolescent granted a request to come every other week comes instead each week as usual, and the client who desperately wants more frequent visits cancels them because the crisis has quickly passed. What may actually be wanted is more a demonstration of the therapist's flexibility and willingness to accommodate the client than a change in appointments. Thus, it is best to give careful consideration to the reasons for the request and to what options or alternatives may be available. When this is done, clients usually decide to come at the frequency that was acceptable to them from the first.

It is expected that as the psychotherapy continues, a child will form a positive relationship with the therapist. Anna Freud suggested a number of techniques to ensure that positive feelings develop, since they are highly important to the success of analytic treatment. Among these techniques is doing things that will favorably impress the child, such as demonstrating superior skills and knowledge or interceding with others on the child's behalf so as to show power (Freud, 1946). Weiner supposed that a positive relationship would come about as a direct consequence of the therapist's understanding, genuineness, and interest in being of help (1970, pp. 364–369).

Yet for many children a growing fondness for their therapist presents them with a conflict. They see themselves as disloyal to their parents, and they are troubled by the fact that they can speak more freely with this "stranger" and behave more freely than they can with their own fathers and mothers. Parents may contribute to this problem by being jealous or upset if the child seems to enjoy the treatment or by making comments ("Why don't you paint pretty pictures like that at home?" "Did you talk to the doctor? Oh, you did!") that convey their disappointment at what is taking place in therapy and their resentment of it.

The best defense against such a development is for therapists to ensure that parents perceive the former as working with them for their child's benefit. When therapists are seen by the parents as aloof or as allied with their child against them, however, it is necessary to meet in order to clarify matters and to demonstrate concern about their feelings. The outcome of such a conference is often a renewed commitment to psychotherapy and a perceptible relaxation in tensions.

That psychotherapy often involves shifting demands and changes in purpose is illustrated by the case of Lionel, a 14-year-old who was suspended from school for being habitually late and disrespectful to teachers. Lionel's mother described him, somewhat unkindly, as a "big lummox" for whom the family made many sacrifices. He was a long-standing discipline problem and was sent to a military prep school, "but they don't want to take him back."

Lionel told the therapist his major problem was his 12-year-old sister. She always teased him, and he was sure one day he would explode and seriously hurt her. In comparison, the troubles at school were of little significance to him; therefore the therapist arranged to meet with Lionel and his sister. At that meeting his sister acknowledged teasing her brother, but explained that it was in retaliation for the things Lionel did to her, like putting pepper in her cold cream and ants in her bed. She agreed to stop the teasing if Lionel would leave her alone. Embarrassed by his sister's disclosures, Lionel accepted the terms for peace. That left him still suspended from school and unconcerned about it.

The therapist next met with Lionel and his parents. At this conference Lionel's father confessed he thought of his son as lazy and useless, but his mother hoped he would get into college on an athletic scholarship. Lionel was big and powerfully built, but he did have to graduate from school before he could go to college. Lionel agreed to go back and not "sass" the teachers; instead, he would see the therapist and talk over with him how he felt.

A phone call from the therapist to the school psychologist smoothed the way for Lionel's readmission. Each week Lionel came to see the therapist after school, and not once was he late. Moreover, he came on school holidays and during vacations. Soon he reported that his teachers were understanding and most encouraging to him; however, he wanted to continue meeting with the therapist because he liked having someone to talk with and because there were some matters he wished to clarify. This broad purpose served as his goal for the remainder of his psychotherapy. In that time Lionel decided not to go out for football and to concentrate on becoming a musician. He was not sure his troubles in school were ended, but he was sure there were one or two teachers now available to him who had his best interests at heart.

Transfer of Therapists

It often happens that children seen in psychotherapy experience the loss of their therapist. A therapist may leave for employment elsewhere, become sick, complete a period of training, or become pregnant. Whatever the reason, the question arises of whether it is better to bring treatment to a close or to transfer the client to another therapist.

In general, two major situations seem to exist when a child is considered for transfer. One is that the child appears to have made progress in treatment but still has problems, and the therapist wants to see this progress continue; perhaps a school psychologist whose time with the child is limited by the setting will believe some other therapist can pick up a case and explore problems in greater depth. The second is that the child has seemed to make little progress, and virtually all the original problems still exist.

Of course there are also the more routine kinds of transfer, in which a child may have been seen by a professional for only an assessment or in which a therapist, for whatever reason, thinks it better for the youngster to be seen by someone with different qualifications. Many of the issues appropriate to transfers from therapists who have worked with clients over an extended period of time are also germane to transfers when contacts were brief.

If children were footballs, it might make sense to think of them being lateraled from one therapist to another and carried over for a touchdown. But children are not footballs, and they do have feelings. The fact that they have put their trust in one therapist who has then left them will probably make them all the more hesitant to trust and confide in someone new. So when a child has progressed in long-term psychotherapy and is transferred to another therapist, two things are apt to happen, and neither is very productive for the client. First, the child goes through a "mourning" reaction in which the new therapist is compared unfavorably with the previous one. The original therapist had a great sense of humor, knew jokes and riddles, did card tricks, had a better assortment of toys and games, loved to go on walks, played badminton, provided soda and doughnuts, and had a closet stocked with an endless supply of goodies. From the child's description, this former therapist functioned like an ideal playmate and companion and did almost everything except practice psychotherapy. By contrast, the new therapist, who wants to help with problems, is cold and businesslike. Efforts to come to an agreement with the child about a purpose for their meetings are unpleasant to the client, because they remind him or her of persistent failings that may well have been avoided previously by filling the treatment hours with "fun and games."

Perhaps under the former circumstances the new therapist would have performed similarly, but it is now about a year of psychotherapy later. At the same time, the therapist feels an obligation to the departed colleague to continue psychotherapy, in spite of a growing conviction that termination would be the best course. Thus, evaluating the issue is not without conflict; however, the therapist's primary responsibility is to the client. At times this may take what appear to be very strange turns, as is true in the following case.

Al was in psychotherapy for 2 years while attending a special class for emotionally disturbed children. His therapist left in the middle of the school year to accept another position, and if for no other reason, a transfer to another therapist was necessary because a condition of the special class was that all its pupils be seen in individual psychotherapy.

At the time of transfer, Al was 10 years old. His problems were that he fought with other children, was a frequent truant, and had temper tantrums. He had an "excellent, warm relationship" with his previous therapist and was immediately disappointed by this new one. This new therapist did not laugh at his jokes and did not know how to play "Sorry." Moreover, the new therapist did not do magic tricks for Al's entertainment, seeking instead to reach an agreement with him about a purpose for their meetings. Al did not want to discuss his problems, and whenever the therapist mentioned them, the boy retreated into a closet and closed the door.

The therapist spoke with the social worker who was seeing Al's mother and learned that they had been talking about marital problems for over a year. Although Al's mother was concerned about her son's behavior, she was not doing anything about it, leaving that responsibility to the school and the therapist. In contrast, Al's father, a police officer, was unconcerned and had no complaints about his son's behavior. He saw Al as a modern Huckleberry Finn; he refused any participation in treatment, believing it foolish, but was kind enough to permit his wife and son to go ahead if that was what they wanted to do.

At a meeting with the school psychologist, the therapist learned that the teacher of the emotionally disturbed class was herself emotionally disturbed and was given this assignment to prevent her from harming normal children. It was also reported that the school disciplined Al in rather peculiar ways: whenever he was truant, he was suspended from school; whenever he had a fight, he was sent to the gym in order to "vent his hostility"; and whenever he threw a temper tantrum, he saw the school psychologist. His behavior was described as still very disturbed, and the school's only hope was that the new therapist would be able to carry on the good work of the old.

Meanwhile, back in the therapist's office, Al complained that if his father only had more power in the family, he would not have to be coming to treatment. He knew his father thought he was all right, and it was only because of his mother that he had to come. Furthermore, Al knew he was not learning anything in the special class and that he was falling so far behind he would require tutoring to achieve at grade level, something he really wanted. It seemed to the therapist that much of Al's misbehavior was brought about so as to be removed from a learning situation where success was difficult, if not impossible.

The therapist recommended to Al's mother that he be tutored in preparation for his return to a regular classroom. To the school, it was recommended that Al be returned to a regular class, that whenever his behavior was disruptive an inquiry be made as to the nature of his problems and the way in which he felt inadequate, and that he no longer be suspended from school or removed from the classroom as a punishment. With Al, the therapist suggested that their visits come to a close and that if he felt the need for the therapist's help, it would be made available to him. These recommendations were followed, and a year later the therapist was informed that Al was making a satisfactory adjustment in a normal class.

A second type of reaction of children transferred to a new therapist is to withhold confiding until they can be certain they will not be abandoned again. Children may bide their time for as long as they were previously seen in psychotherapy, waiting for the anniversary of the previous termination to pass without incident before being willing to trust and move forward again.

Although neither of these mourning reactions is an insurmountable obstacle in psychotherapy, they do confound the expectation that a transfer makes possible an uninterrupted course of treatment. A therapist who is leaving no doubt feels less guilty when given assurance that clients will be taken over by someone else, but the probability of complications requires serious consideration as to whether professional obligations are better discharged by termination than transfer. What needs to be weighed heavily in coming to such a judgment is if the desire for continuance is coming more from the therapist than from the client.

The transfer of a client who has gained little from psychotherapy has all the virtues of the unpromising. Since little was accomplished, little is expected, and any gains enhance the reputation of the new therapist. Even with no gains, professional colleagues may commend the therapist's courage in accepting a difficult case. Yet here, too, the question is whether transfer or termination is better for the client. What makes this determination more difficult than might be supposed is that the information provided may be incorrect, as the following case illustrates.

Bob was an 8-year-old who was excluded from school for 2 years because of "severe emotional disturbance." He was diagnosed as autistic and impulsive; for almost a year he attended a day treatment program for severely disturbed youngsters while being seen in individual psychotherapy. His therapist believed that her sessions with Bob had been a waste: each meeting he would sit on the floor of her office and act the role of Batman or else would run from the room, with her in full pursuit.

Obviously Bob needed help, but was psychotherapy the answer? Shortly after the beginning of his first session with his new therapist, Bob rose from the floor and dashed for the door. The therapist looked down the hall and saw Bob pause to see whether he was going to be chased. Instead of leaving the office, this therapist sat down. Within a few moments Bob appeared at the door, smiled, and threatened to run. The therapist continued to sit. Bob entered the office, and the therapist closed the door with this statement of limits: "Once our meeting begins, you're supposed to stay in the office. You seem to want me to run around after you, but that's not my job. We're supposed to stay in here." That was the last time Bob ran out of the therapist's office.

For several sessions Bob engaged in the "autistic" play described by his previous therapist. He sat on the floor and, using puppets and doll figures, staged a fight while constantly singing the music from the Batman television show, which at that time was very popular locally. This humming and singing would be punctured by various sound effects of bodies being punched and blasted and would last the entire session. At one meeting before Bob could get started, the therapist remarked: "You know, Bob, I have the feeling that you play Batman just to keep me out. You don't want me to get a word in. Well, you don't have to do that. If you want me to keep my mouth shut, tell me and I'll do it." Bob said nothing, but he did not play Batman or engage in any similar activity again.

The ease with which Bob abandoned his "impulsive" and "autistic" behaviors raised questions about his diagnosis. What became clear was that Bob did not want to talk about members of his family, though he did want help in improving his peer relationships. A psychological assessment indicated that Bob was functioning within a mildly retarded range of intelligence and that he had problems in visual discrimination and fine motor coordination. With improvements in his peer relationships, Bob returned to school in a program for children with learning disabilities.

Bob's was a situation bordering on the hopeless that benefited from the change of therapists. The new therapist not only handled Bob differently but, encouraged by Bob's favorable response to these changes, was able to come to a more optimistic assessment of his behaviors and prognosis. This is what all therapists must do when cases are transferred to them; they must take the information given to them about their clients with a grain of salt and arrive at their own formulations. They must also recognize the special complications brought about by transfers and then decide what may prevent or alleviate these problems for the child. In arriving at their decisions, they may find it helpful to meet with the client before the final interview has taken place with the previous therapist, or to handle the transfer like a new case—that is, to have a meeting or two with the child, parents, or family in order to assess the suitability of psychotherapy, to become acquainted, and to learn what they expect.

Testing the Therapist

While therapists strive to communicate their understanding, respect, and wish to be of help, and in the process may point out consistencies and inconsistencies in their client's beliefs and behaviors, there are corresponding activities on the part of children. Clients are also expressing feelings and are trying to communicate with their therapist.

Because everyone feels at the center of the universe, we regard our own words and activities as of the greatest interest and importance. For most clients it is a pleasant surprise to find an adult who seems to be in agreement with their appraisal, who listens to their words and attends to their actions. Some clients are suspicious of therapists, however, probably because they have had disappointing experiences with adults before. Before trusting again, they want to make sure therapists are what they seem to be.

In large measure the clients are right. Psychotherapists are too good to be true; they are not saints, and they are not perfect. There are times when they are inattentive and when they may be thinking about the last client they have seen instead of the one who is with them at the moment. When children set out to test their therapist, therefore, there are occasions when the therapist flunks. These tests take a number of different forms:

1. *The test of attention.* The child gives a lengthy and digressive account of some incident or television program. The therapist then is asked to answer questions about details presented at the beginning.

2. *The memory test.* The child tells the therapist the names of friends, enemies, and so on. A week or so later one or more names are mentioned, and the therapist is expected to know who they are.

3. *The anger-tolerance test.* The child tries to provoke the therapist to become angry. The therapist may be asked to play some game that the child contrives to win by hook or crook, or even through the cooperation of the therapist. Then the therapist is taunted about the loss. All therapists should be able to pass this test; one boy explained it to his therapist by saying, "I wanted to see if you'd lose your temper and be no better than I am."

4. *The test of love.* Does the therapist know that today is the child's birthday, and has a suitable gift been purchased? Where are the valentines, Christmas presents, and other tokens of affection? Here are situations where children want their therapists to be what they are not, and cannot be, for clients living within their own families—loving, beneficent parents. Therapists communicate their understanding of what the child wants and may need, but make clear that what they have to give are not presents and love but their understanding and wish to be of help. Most children respond to this statement of limits with "I know" or "I was just kidding," but nevertheless therapists may be forgiven and still experience a slight feeling of guilt.

5. *The rejection test.* Whenever therapists interrupt the continuity of their meetings (because of illnesses, vacations, conferences, or whatever), they risk having their clients feel rejected. Some clients are acutely sensitive to the least indication that their therapist may not wish to see them any longer; rather than be rejected, they reject their therapist by announcing they want their contacts ended. At such moments, therapists must quickly examine in their own minds what has happened and evaluate the reason-

ableness of the request. One index of unreasonableness is that the client may want the meetings ended immediately or at a time just before the therapist's scheduled interruption. Another indication that the request may be emotionally provoked is when it occurs seemingly out of context during the session and quite possibly in retaliation for a remark the therapist has made.

Under no circumstances should a therapist immediately accept a client's offer to terminate treatment. Therapists must always explore their clients' reasons and feelings about termination, particularly in relation to the contract and its goals. They should always offer their clients the opportunity to reconsider and to come to a decision at another meeting. Despite whatever precautions therapists take, there is usually a feeling of uncertainty about what has been decided, no matter what it is. About all that therapists can do is try to evaluate their performance honestly, hope that they have done their best for their clients, and try to do better for future ones.

6. *The test of confidence.* The child discloses a secret or bit of information to the therapist and waits to see the reaction. Will the therapist be alarmed, shocked, outraged, or indignant? Will he or she reject the client? Will the therapist run to tell the parents, the authorities, or the police? Of course, therapists should react in none of these ways; instead, they should try to discover the reason for the disclosure and the way, if any, in which the client feels the therapist might be of help with this information. An example of this test occurred with George, an adolescent, who reported that his 12-year-old sister would come into his bed at night and lie next to him. He wanted the therapist to discuss this situation with his parents and sister so that it would come to an end.

As a general rule, therapists must distinguish between tests that clients might reasonably expect them to pass and those where they could be expected to fail. If they are careless and inattentive, their clients have a legitimate grievance. If they are momentarily distracted by lingering concerns, they have the right to ask for their client's indulgence and forgiveness for a lapse. Assuming that therapists do not incorrectly claim perfection, they then have the privilege of pointing out that their client's indignation is based on a presumption, or wish, for infallibility or goodness. Let it be conceded, therefore, that therapists may disappoint their clients, in part because clients may demand more from therapists than can possibly be given. Let it also be recognized that if a client is determined that a therapist fail, the therapist will fail.

The following is an illustration of just such an engineered failure. Morris was a 200-pound adolescent who was very impulsive. He would run onto the roof of a clinic, wander into offices and steal from purses before his appointments, and try to con people out of money and candy after his sessions were finished. One day he arrived early for his appointment and began exploring the clinic in search of loot. The receptionist phoned the therapist and asked that Morris be found and returned to the waiting room.

When the therapist found Morris, he was going through a secretary's purse looking for candy. The therapist asked Morris to sit down. This request was refused. The therapist wondered whether anything was bothering Morris. This brought a laugh from him, and then he ran toward the therapist's office; however, he did not enter it but kept running down the hall to the kitchen of the clinic. There he began spilling hot coffee over the floor. When the therapist appeared, Morris ran back to the waiting room.

Back in the waiting room, the therapist asked Morris if he wished to begin his appointment early. Morris refused, but neither would be remain seated. The therapist suggested that since Morris seemed so oppositional, perhaps he did not wish to see the therapist that day. Morris said he was going to go home, and he left. A few minutes later, the therapist received a phone call informing him that Morris was bothering people on another floor of the building. Again the therapist located Morris and told him that he should either come for his appointment or leave the building. Morris said that he was going home, and the therapist walked with him to the street. A few minutes after the therapist had returned to his office, there stood Morris in the doorway.

The therapist said that Morris seemed to be having trouble making up his mind and asked him to leave. Instead, Morris jumped into the office. The therapist got up to evict Morris but, encountering resistance, turned from the client and closed the door. Immediately Morris lunged for the door. The therapist blocked his way and stated that since Morris seemed to be fighting with the therapist, perhaps they should try to figure out what was the matter.

Morris yelled at the therapist, "Get out of my way! I want to go home." The therapist braced himself against the door and suggested again that they talk. With that Morris fell to the floor of the office and began crying and screaming in a temper tantrum. He seemed to lose all control. His face flushed, tears flooded his eyes, and mucus streamed from his nose. He began kicking and thrashing and banging his head against the floor and baseboard. The therapist tried to cradle Morris' head so that he would not injure himself; as he did this, Morris grabbed his necktie in an effort to strangle him. There was a struggle while the therapist tried to loosen Morris' hold on his tie, which culminated in the tie's being torn. "Now will you let me go home?" Morris screamed. "I hate you, you son of a bitch. You're not my father. You're not going to change me."

After reflecting these feelings and encouraging Morris to pull himself together, the therapist said that Morris could leave. Morris ran from the office. The therapist phoned the parents to tell them that Morris had been upset and to urge them to contact him should there be any questions. Later they phoned to say that Morris had arrived home by taxi, saying that he would not go back to see the therapist. The therapist explained that it was most important that he see Morris again and arranged a meeting with the boy and his parents. At the meeting, the parents arrived without Morris. They explained that he did not want to come, and they did not want to force him. They thought it would be better for his sessions to end, and though he was still a burden upon them, despite everything they hoped Morris would some day be all right. Three years after this meeting, the therapist happened to meet Morris on the street. Morris said, "Hi!" and asked to borrow some money from the therapist so he could leave a tip for a waitress in a restaurant.

What can be learned from Morris? Did he suffer, as one psychiatrist suggested, a psychotic episode? Could the confrontation and physical struggle in the office have been avoided? Should the therapist have allowed Morris to leave almost immediately after his defiance was verbalized? Did the therapist act wisely by alerting the parents, or would it have been better simply to assume that Morris would come for his next appointment?

Almost every therapist sees a Morris, in the sense that almost every therapist has the experience of wondering what might have happened had a client been handled differently. Therapists learn from their clients, and it is to be expected that they are better therapists today than they were yesterday and that they will become even better in the future. It is said that surgeons bury their mistakes. Fortunately, this is seldom the case with psychotherapists; all that they usually have to do is learn from them. But it is also necessary for psychotherapists to recognize when they have done all that can be reasonably demanded of them, when they have practiced their method of treatment as artfully and skillfully as is humanly possible, and when a particular condition or person requires something other than the communication of understanding, respect, and a wish to be of help.

Signs for Termination

At the beginning of this chapter, changes that have been found to take place over the course of psychotherapy were mentioned. The presence of these changes—alleviation of symptoms, greater self-confidence, reports of improved social relationships and school grades—indicates that the need for psychotherapy may be coming to a close. Presumably the therapy has been going on for a time, and there have been suggestions from the client that things are looking up. The child's play has become organized and constructive, paintings are pleasant and optimistic, and interactions with the therapist convey a feeling of mutual respect.

There are other signs that termination may be near. The child may claim to be dealing with problems satisfactorily and wonder if the meetings with the therapist may be a waste of the latter's time. There may be a rummaging around during the session for something to talk about and a feeling of embarrassment about a shortage of things to say. A child may ask whether the therapist would like to help a sibling or a friend who now seems in greater need of help, or an attempt might be made to change the relationship with the therapist from a professional one to that of a friendship by asking the therapist to attend a school play or a party. The child may openly request that the meetings come to an end ("How much longer do I have to keep coming down here?" or "I don't think I need to come any more. When can we stop?"). It may also be that the therapist has come to the conclusion that the child has been helped and that while some gains may still be possible, it is better not to prolong the contacts in the hope of achieving additional improvement.

Probably, as Allen (1942, p. 269) commented, "There are no clear-cut signals for a therapist to follow in knowing when a child is ready to make such a plan [for ending therapy]." What Allen suggested is the element of uncertainty about the meaning of even a forthright request by the client for termination, in part because the therapist may be aware of continuing problems and in part because there is a need for faith in the client's development and further growth.

Yet despite misgivings and doubts, therapists ordinarily cannot wait for clients to announce with gratitude that they have been helped and changed for the better and that they are now ready to embark upon life's sea of troubles on their own. Such announcements come rarely. Instead, therapists must act with understanding, respect, and a wish to be of help to their clients in dealing with this new phase of their relationship. Ending involves separation, an affirmation of individuality, and a growing apart. Thus, it may evoke feelings of sadness and loss, as well as guilt, for both client and therapist. A client may feel guilty about no longer needing the therapist, whereas a therapist may feel guilty because the client has not achieved all that was hoped.

The first step in the termination process is for the therapist to decide to explore the client's interest in bringing their meetings to an end. If the child has asked when their meetings will stop, the therapist might respond, "You're kind of wondering about how long this is going to take." If there has been some subtle indication of the client's wish to end the sessions, the therapist could say, "From what you've just said, I get the feeling that maybe things are going along better for you now." If the child responds affirmatively, the therapist might say, "And so I guess you might wonder what that means as far as your coming here goes." If the therapist seeks to introduce the topic of termination, an opening is provided by some statement to this effect ("You've been coming to see me for some time now, and I wonder how you feel about it").

What therapists are trying to deterine is whether the client has a genuine interest in ending the sessions. They must be careful to avoid any suggestion that they wish to get rid of the client. Rather, they wish to convey that their objective is to come to an understanding of what the client wants and to make clear how they can help to achieve it.

Since in most situations children are referred by adults, therapists also have a responsibility to these adults and so cannot immediately acquiesce to a child's wish for termination. Even when children assert they want the meetings to end immediately, therapists must respond somewhat as follows: "I can understand how you feel, but what I have to do is check with your parents and see how they feel. I'll be doing that, and you can be doing it, too. Talk it over with them, and when we meet next week we'll have a better idea of what to do." If parents favor bringing the treatment to a close, the therapist inquires if they have any preferences about time. Customarily in long-term psychotherapy with an indefinite termination, a date about a month later is picked, and this bit of information is supplied so that the parents can react to it.

If they find it acceptable, the therapist is ready to resume negotiations with the child. The therapist discusses the conversation with the parents and asks whether the child's feelings about termination are unchanged. If they have remained the same, the therapist asks when the child would like the meetings to end. (At this point it is helpful to have a calendar handy.) Some children may say they want the meetings to end at once, conveying the feeling that they are hurt by the acceptance of their decision and wish to be rid of the therapist as soon as possible; these same youngsters, when told the meetings should continue for a while, will often then say that they would like the sessions to go on until they finish high school, get married, or attain some other milestone in their lives.

Although an extreme date into the future cannot be permitted, the therapist indicates a willingness to be flexible and tries to allow the child to make a decision by consulting with the calendar and appreciating how much time may still be available. Many children will pick a date that coincides with a birthday or another ending, such as the last day of school, that is 2 or 3 months into the future. If it is at all possible for the parents and the therapist to accept such a termination (what amounts to a brief period of time-limited psychotherapy), they should do so.

With that settled, children may feel both relieved and apprehensive. The question is raised as to whether the therapist will end the meetings on the date set no matter what happens, and even if there is a dreadful emergency. To this the therapist responds: "Of course not. If there is some sort of emergency, we can work something out. But even if there isn't any emergency, and even after we do stop and something comes up, you let me know. I guess you're kind of worried about whether you can ever see me again." If the child answers affirmatively, the therapist suggests that if something happens, the child should inform the parents so they can arrange an appointment, or he or she can feel free to call the therapist on the phone. The therapist may give the child a professional card or even a piece of paper with the office phone number; although many children are evidently pleased with this offer, few ever take advantage of it.

Once the issue of termination has been broached and discussed, no matter how skillfully and tactfully, it sends a chill through the relationship. It is a difficult effect to put into words, but the very air seems to cool and the client, despite a professed readiness for termination, appears a bit disappointed that the decision was accepted by the therapist. Although the therapist continues to follow the principles of psychotherapy, the ending phase is somewhat different from the beginning or middle. There may be an awkward, businesslike quality to the sessions, and clients may try to cram in solutions to every problem that they can think of in the remaining time. They may come in for their meetings each week as though nothing has happened, not mentioning the termination and discussing distant events in the future as if therapist and client will still be seeing one another when they occur. In contrast, many clients do not engage in denial, accept the termination, and work toward it with feelings of satisfaction and accomplishment.

This may be a difficult period for both therapists and clients. It is a period of disengagement. The beginning of psychotherapy affords limitless opportunities and ample time for engagement and dealing with problems, whereas this stage does not. Some therapists, impressed by its undeniable dysphoric qualities and uncertainties, are reluctant to take any responsibility for entering it and leave that decision entirely to their clients.

Yet the ending of psychotherapy can be the most exciting and challenging phase of treatment. Setting a termination date can catalyze clients into action, and it represents one of the few occasions in the lives of children when their opinions and decisions have to be considered by their parents. Thus, for many clients termination provides one of the singular experiences of psychotherapy. Their parents may have compelled them to seek help when they did not want it, but now they have reached a decision themselves, and the question is whether their parents will accept it.

This is the question that is implied by children who wonder how much longer it will be before they can stop: When will my parents (or adults in general) let me stop? Let us suppose the therapist meets with the parents and finds that they still have many doubts about their child's behavior. Perhaps they concede the child has improved, but they wonder whether the improvement will last, or they introduce new problems or bits of behavior that meet with their dissatisfaction and concern. They do not believe their child is ready to stop, and they want the psychotherapy to go on.

If this is the case, the therapist may meet with the child and try to reconcile the inconsistency between the client and the parents. Suppose the child agrees that the problems noted by the parents exist, but insists they are minor and can be handled without further contacts with the therapist; he or she still wants the meetings to end as soon as possible. Under these circumstances the therapist can propose a meeting with the child and parents in order to work out some agreement. Note that the therapist does not act in opposition to the child or to the parents, but strives to work in cooperation with them in reaching a mutually acceptable solution. At the family meeting the child will be confronted by the parents, who will express their doubts about the decision to end. In turn, the child will plead for the chance to be independent and will complain about their lack of faith. The task of the therapist is to make clear an understanding of both positions, so that in the process the parents and child can each appreciate the legitimacy of the stand taken by the other party.

Yet in this argument it is well to recognize that the values of the therapist are more likely to be compatible with the stand taken by the child than with that of the parents. After all, the parents are arguing against change and growth, they are predicting failure, and they are emphasizing what is negative about the child rather than what is positive. Nevertheless, the therapist must carefully evaluate their position, consider the problems and concerns they specify (and whether these are serious enough to justify continuance), the period of psychotherapy already completed, and the probable consequences for the child's self-concept, the parents, and the therapist of a contrary decision. Whatever is decided, the wishes of the child must in some measure be respected.

After the feelings of the parents and the child are expressed and acknowledged, there is often an impasse. Realistically, they may fail to reach a compromise because they lack an adequate understanding of what is involved. They may look to the therapist for assistance, who could offer the following: "You'd like to stop, and you're for continuing. Of course, stopping does not mean that you won't be able to get help. Perhaps this might be a reasonable solution; see how it sounds to you. Let's suppose we stop. What would that mean? You'd be giving Joe a chance to show you that he can handle things on his own. If he can't, you could say to him, 'Look, Joe, we gave you a chance, but it isn't working out.' And you know you can give me a call and get help from me. Does that sound fair to you, Joe? [If the child accepts this condition, the therapist turns to the parents.] Now, how does it sound to you?" It is very unusual for children and parents to reject a compromise of this kind.

At times, this type of meeting poses a crisis for the entire family and serves as a turning point in psychotherapy. This occurred with Ted and his parents. Ted had been referred for lack of achievement in school and for stealing his mother's undergarments. A 6-footer in his first year in high school, Ted had not been doing well in his studies since he was 10 years old. He had consistently rejected help and had accepted psychotherapy only because he himself was puzzled by his thefts.

What became clear during the course of his contacts in psychotherapy was the control that he felt his mother exercised over him and his seeming inability to please her. Although he could not explain why he had taken her clothing, such incidents stopped, and his grades in school improved. Yet his mother was not satisfied and silenced his complaints by telling him that he was aggravating her "nervous" condition. Ted finally concluded that he would have to get along in life without his mother's approval and that his work in school should be for his own benefit instead of being used as a weapon against his parents. He began to look outside his family and to his relationships with peers for acceptance. After several months he asked to terminate psychotherapy. His mother opposed this decision, because she felt that Ted was still obsessed with sex. She was certain that when he locked the door to his room he masturbated, and she still felt uncomfortable when he walked by her bedroom and saw her in her undergarments. (That she might close the door to her bedroom while dressing struck her as a novel, but potentially useful idea that deserved careful consideration.)

A meeting with Ted and his parents was arranged. At the meeting, Ted stated his position, and his mother stated hers. Unexpectedly, Ted's father began weeping. He saw himself as in part responsible for his son's problems by allowing his wife to exercise too much authority in the family and by neglecting Ted in order to concentrate on his business. He aligned himself with his son against his wife and announced that henceforth he would be responsible for disciplining Ted. Ted's mother literally collapsed; her voice, which had been stern and shrewish, became soft and compliant. She agreed to abide by her husband's decisions, one of which was that she should get dressed with her door closed. A termination date set for 3 weeks later was acceptable to all concerned, and both Ted and his parents seemed to benefit from their few remaining contacts.

An additional complication that sometimes arises in connection with termination should be mentioned. If a parent is being seen by a colleague, the therapist may be asked to delay the child's termination because it would disrupt the treatment of the parent. The argument may be that the parent is getting into meaningful material and requires the attendance of the child as an excuse for being seen; if the child stops, the parent will pull out just when he or she is close to involvement or constructive changes. Regardless of the specifics of the argument, it translates into "Will you keep the child in treatment longer than is necessary for the sake of the parent?"

Such a question assumes that psychotherapy is a condition like sunshine and rain, enveloping people and making them grow no matter how they feel about it. Thus, what can be the harm in sprinkling on some more respect, understanding, and help? The problem is that this communication is in response to a person, and for this client understanding means a recognition of the wish to stop, respect means accepting this decision, and help means implementing it, because implementation is within the therapist's power and responsibility. To continue treatment unnecessarily divorces psychotherapy from the client's feelings and accomplishments.

Nevertheless, a colleague may be quite distressed by a refusal to cooperate with what seems to be a reasonable request, and so therapists must be prepared to justify their actions. First, it should be suggested that parents be made to understand that their visits can continue after the child's visits come to an end; follow-up sessions can be recommended as a way of learning from them about the child's progress. Second, the harmful consequences to the child's self-respect, autonomy, and relationship with the therapist that could follow from postponing the request for termination should be made clear. Third, the advantages to exploring termination with the parent, such as hastening and focusing the treatment, should be mentioned.

In the final analysis, however, what therapists may face with their colleagues is what they must face with their clients and themselves: the many conflicting feelings about termination, about stopping obviously short of perfection, and about limits in being of help. For once an agreement to terminate is reached, both therapist and client are bound by the calendar to a supposition of strength as they go about their business in arriving at their final meeting.

8
The Last Meeting

J ust as every meeting with a client presents a possibility of a very different and perhaps novel encounter, so the closing of every session has aspects of a final interview in that therapist and client, regardless of what unfinished business remains, must go their separate ways. Ultimately they arrive at what they acknowledge is a last meeting and a final parting, presumably because the client has achieved as much as can reasonably be hoped to be accomplished from the sessions. Yet of course this tidy result, though true for the majority of cases, is not the basis for every termination. In our mobile society, it frequently happens that the parents or therapist may move to another community. Incomplete goals are mutually recognized, but the client may be reluctant to begin psychotherapy with someone else, or the parents may wish to see how their child manages without professional help. Often the illness of a parent or the impending birth of a sibling necessitates termination at what seems to almost everyone to be a most inopportune time. Another common reason for ending is simply a therapist's conviction that little more will be gained from continuance.

Accordingly, the last meeting between therapist and client is unique because it is regarded as a final separation, and it may be expected to elicit feelings that are a strange compound of apprehension, sadness, happiness, pride, humility, disappointment, optimism, guilt, and confidence. A client may have all those feelings; a therapist may also have them, and parents may share in the mixed emotions of the moment. Therapists, however, although sensitive to their own emotional reactions, cannot allow them to interfere with their professional responsibilities and judgment, which must be consistent in this meeting with what they were in the ones that led to it.

Personality theorists such as Otto Rank (1950) have recognized that separating—even when the occasion is marked by achievement and satisfaction—can arouse concerns about being independent and feelings of loss for the person with whom there was a relationship. Anxieties and worries are expected to make clients doubt the wisdom of their decision to terminate, and might bring them to ask for additional sessions. Under such circumstances therapists are mindful of certain realistic considerations.

First, in almost every instance, ideal goals have not been attained. Freud (1959a) described the dilemma of the therapist: an awareness that more might be done, though practicality dictates putting aside the task. The end of formal meetings, however, does not mean the end of analysis. The client is expected to have acquired skills that enable self-analysis to continue. Similarly, humanistic and behavioral therapists, among others, see treatment as a process of growth and behavior change that continues outside the treatment sessions and beyond them. The respect for the client's feelings, opinions, and decisions; the efforts by the therapist to afford opportunities and to encourage others to afford the client opportunities to make choices; the acceptance of attitudes, emotions, and thoughts—all these practices in psychotherapy are expected to promote individuality, responsibility, and an enduring process of personal reflection.

Some years after the analysis of Little Hans, Freud was visited by the young man who had that famous phobia in his childhood. Freud was pleased to see his former patient had grown into an apparently healthy adult. Though Freud would have liked to claim some credit for what happened, he found the young man could recall nothing of the treatment or the events that brought it about.

> So the analysis had not preserved the events from amnesia, but had been overtaken by amnesia itself. Anyone who is familiar with psychoanalysis may occasionally experience something similar in sleep. He will be woken up by a dream, and will decide to analyse it then and there; he will then go to sleep again feeling quite satisifed with the result of his efforts; and next morning dream and analysis will alike be forgotten. (Freud, 1959b, p. 289)

Freud's somewhat poetic example is designed to encourage therapists whose clients may be hard-pressed to attribute gains to their treatment. Note, too, Freud's acceptance of his former client's "amnesia." Therefore, despite a therapist's awareness that more may be achieved and despite a client's problems in seeing that anything has been accomplished, a therapist can have and convey, at the very least, the quite reasonable impression that the client has made (and is perhaps still making) some progress in the right direction.

Second, evidence is accumulating that positive expectations can have beneficial effects upon the course of various ailments (Robertson, 1991). Accordingly, the therapist should not communicate a negative or apprehensive expectation about the client's readiness for termination, but should instead be neutral or even positive. Throughout the course of therapy, and certainly in the last meeting, it is preferable to assume clients are able to deal with self-doubts and misgivings about their decisions than to presume they are weak (Rogers, 1951, 1980; Raskin, 1985); this very assumption of strength and competence may enable a client to be strong and competent.

Third, in many treatment interventions, generalization of effects and self-regulation or intrinsic motivation are planned (Gelfand & Hartmann, 1984; Johnson, Rasbury, & Siegel, 1986). Thus, parents and other responsible adults may be prepared to continue aspects of the treatment and to be of help to the child. At the same time, many clients are ready to accept personal responsibility for maintaining their gains and for acquiring desirable behaviors.

Fourth, there is evidence for the resilience of children in meeting life's challenges (Luthar & Zigler, 1991), for their continued progress in problem-solving and social skills (Kazdin, 1991), and for growth in self-understanding and interpersonal adjustment after treatment (Raskin, 1985; Rogers, 1980; Snyder, Wells, & Grady-Fletcher, 1991). These considerations argue that unless there is compelling justification to do otherwise, the meeting recognized by the parties concerned as the last meeting should in fact be the last meeting of the treatment.

Structure

The major and overriding consideration in the last meeting is that it is supposed to be the last meeting. There are not going to be additional opportunities for discussion or exploration, and when clients leave this meeting, the probability is very great that they will not be seen again. Therefore, in this session therapists cannot allow children to deny what is taking place, nor can they accept distortions about the finality of this meeting.

During the course of this session, therapists seek to determine their clients' feelings about the termination and about the effectiveness of psychotherapy. Their hope is that clients will report some gains from their contacts and so will have positive feelings about their experiences. This is what usually happens, but they must hope this even when they themselves can see little in the way of constructive changes, because they have a responsibility to help their clients to avoid discouragement and to find something positive and meaningful from their sessions.

This is not hypocrisy or self-justification. There is something to be gained from any experience. Even in rare instances when clients claim they have not changed and have acquired nothing, a therapist can still honestly say, "And yet in a way you have learned a little about what this is like. It isn't so strange to you anymore, so that if you do feel sometime in the future that you would like to try this again and are ready to profit from it, perhaps it will be a lot easier for you." If nothing else, remarks such as these may keep such clients from blaming themselves for failure and give them hope when, for some reason, they have not perceived their psychotherapy as beneficial.

If clients do not volunteer an assessment of their sessions, or if their evaluations do not address improvements in behaviors pertinent to their contracts, therapists should ask specifically about these matters. It is now or never, which means that for the therapist it must be done now. Yet this does not mean that therapists repudiate the principles of psychotherapy in order to conduct their assessment of treatment. If this information is given by clients without asking, so much the better. What it does mean is that therapists have a responsibility to themselves, to their profession, to the public, and to their clients to assess what has been accomplished.

When the client is met by the therapist for the last meeting, the therapist says nothing at first about the termination and allows the client the opportunity to bring up the subject. If the client seems at a loss for something to say or do, the therapist either reflects the client's difficulties in handling this final session or comments on the inconsistency between the many questions and feelings that might be expected in connection with termination and the client's silence. Should the client talk about matters or engage in activities unrelated to termination (perhaps a denial of the last meeting), after about 20 minutes the therapist may say something like, "You know, this is our last meeting (*pause*), but I guess there's not much you feel like saying about it. (*pause*) Perhaps you could let me know how you felt about coming down here." From there on, the therapist tries to determine the client's feelings about the contacts.

Reactions to Termination

Children may not say much about the termination and about their assessment of psychotherapy. In fact, some children may say nothing at all. With very young children or those who seem psychotic or severely disturbed, therapists may wonder if the child is aware of what is taking place or has any genuine response to the termination. Under such circumstances, there is a temptation to "let things ride" and not introduce the subject when the child shows no inclination to do so. To yield to this temptation would be a serious mistake. Therapists must not permit their own possible uneasiness about the last meeting to override their common sense and their responsibilites to their clients. Even when children seem oblivious to them, therapists must try to communicate the fact of termination on the chance that some part of the message will get through and prevent the client from feeling abandoned.

For example, Bob seemed to want little from his contacts with the therapist and appeared to gain little. On the day of their last meeting he ran into the therapist's office, climbed onto the windowsill, and drew the drapes so that he could not be seen. This was consistent with previous sessions in which Bob had refused to discuss anything that had to do with his family, consistently refused to talk with the therapist, and instead had used their time to play catch.

The therapist commented about Bob's wish to hide and to say nothing. This elicited from Bob the response of drawing the drapes more tightly shut. About midway through the hour the therapist mentioned the termination and tried to engage Bob in discussion about it, but received no response other than a firmer hold on the drapes. Then, with only a few minutes left in the meeting, Bob stuck his hand through the drapes and beckoned to the therapist to grasp it. This the therapist did; as he stood holding Bob's hand, Bob allowed the drapes to open slightly and reveal that he had been silently weeping. The therapist communicated an understanding of Bob's feelings, but the boy said nothing. Instead, he gently squeezed the therapist's hand. When the therapist announced the meeting was ended, Bob immediately released the grasped hand, wiped his eyes, left his perch, and ran from the office to his mother.

In contrast, Frank seemed happy about the last meeting. This former juvenile delinquent saw the termination as one more indication of his growing self-confidence and generally better adjustment. Throughout his contacts with the therapist he had been law-abiding and had taken pride in his improved grades and his growing interest in girls. Although he saw the therapist as a friendly, interested adult, he credited himself with making his positive changes. When asked to comment about what he had gained from psychotherapy, he thought for a moment and replied: "I used to go around with a chip on my shoulder, but I don't anymore. I found out that the only friends you get that way are other guys who think they're hot stuff, or as hot as you are, and it's no good."

What Frank meant was that he had been constantly trying to prove his masculinity. In the therapist's opinion a significant portion of the treatment had dealt with Frank's fear of homosexuality, and a turning point had occurred when he abandoned his aggressive competitiveness with other males and became able to work with them. Yet at the last meeting, none of this was mentioned. There was no need, because other things that Frank did believe were of importance to him incorporated and transcended that bit of information.

The last meeting with Suzie was of yet another kind. She walked in carrying a large plastic bag filled with water in which two goldfish swam. This was plopped down on the therapist's desk, and he was told to watch it so as to keep busy while Suzie took a last look at the toys with which she had played and the corner where she had screamed. Then she sat down to talk with the therapist and to look at her fish, a present she had received that day from her mother.

Although Suzie was aware of a number of changes that had taken place in her behavior, she was not happy about them. She spoke of them as if biting on a bullet, conveying the impression that she felt she had been compelled to make changes in order to escape from the clutches of the therapist. Though she acknowledged the therapist was not as bad as she originally thought, she reported that she found her meetings with him to have been distasteful, if not totally unpleasant: "I didn't like it [being seen in psychotherapy]. But it wasn't your fault. You tried hard to be nice, but I just didn't want to come. Now let's keep quiet and look at the fish."

Suzie has a valuable lesson to teach us. Some children may improve their behavior because they find psychotherapy so noxious a situation that they do whatever is necessary to be removed from it. Very often these youngsters are most frightened of their therapists, whom they see as powerful figures, capable of seeing through them and of changing them against their wills. The therapist's communication of understanding only seems to substantiate their belief in the extraordinary perceptiveness of this frightening adult. Some of these children are so unsure of themselves that they cannot risk any change, but others (like Suzie) come to accept that they both fear and want change, and so grudgingly are able to modify their behavior in desirable directions.

Other children may come to the last meeting and try during that one session to recapitulate everything they did during the entire course of psychotherapy. They may pick up a toy, start to play with it, put it down, begin to paint, go back to a favorite hand puppet, ask to play cards and checkers—in short, cram in as many activities as they possibly can. It is a session of nostalgia, and it is amazing how much some children remember of their meetings. They may ask to see a painting or a baseball card that seemed to be casually given some months earlier, not because they want it returned but because they want the pleasure of seeing it again for the last time.

There are children who express their feelings about termination most eloquently with the aid of paintings. One boy painted a bird flying from its nest in a tree: "He's grown up now, and he has to fly away. He's sad, but he's happy that he's big." Another boy painted a sailboat and a lighthouse: "The sailboat's pulling up anchor. It's time to go. It looks like there's a storm out there, but he can see the lighthouse and he'll be safe." A third boy, who painted many scenes of fighting and violence, at his last meeting produced a sunny landscape: "The war's over. The soldiers are going home, and the sun is shining. But before I go, I want to see all my pictures again."

Finally, some children profess to be indifferent about the last meeting. A therapist may learn that a client is hard-pressed to think of anything gained from these contacts other than "I liked missing school," "My mother would get me some ice cream after our meetings," or "I didn't have to take gym." If such an assessment by the client seems valid, a therapist would do well to consider whether the principles of psychotherapy were implemented. It is far better to hear, "I didn't get anything from it, but that's not your fault. You know, nothing against you personally. Maybe I wasn't ready for it yet." At least in the latter kind of assessment, the child was aware of the therapist's efforts to be of help and of a personal responsibility for bringing about change.

The Return of the Client

Some therapists make a strong argument against any possibility of seeing the client again. To suggest there may be a return visit, so the reasoning goes, is to suggest the client's weakness, which may be tantamount to bringing about a lack of confidence and resolve that results in breakdown and the need for further sessions.

This acute sensitivity to the client's presumed vulnerability to any hint of weakness is probably unnecessary in most cases. A return visit can be discussed matter-of-factly and treated as a matter of routine: "I think it would be helpful if you came in to see me again in about three months, just to let me know how things are going with you and your parents [or in school, or in practicing your relaxation]. How does that sound? Of course, if there's any problem that comes up that you'd like to see me about sooner, give me a call and we'll arrange an appointment."

Obviously, because there are differing reasons for termination and differing reactions to psychotherapy and to the last meeting, for some clients a follow-up visit would be welcome, whereas for others it would be inappropriate. If at the last scheduled session the client seems uneasy about never seeing the therapist again, it shows understanding to address this uneasiness by informing the client of the therapist's continued interest and availability. Such an option, though not always made explicit, is usually assumed by adults, but children may not be aware that it exists; they have to be informed.

Of course, if the client is so distressed at the last meeting that ending seems a mistake, it is best to acknowledge one's misgivings and to discuss this with the child and parents so that a follow-up visit can be scheduled "just to make sure everything is working out all right." If the principles of psychotherapy have been observed, however, an immediate follow-up should seldom prove necessary.

Occasionally a client will just "pop in" to see the therapist some time after termination in order to tell how things are going, in much the same way (and for the same reasons) that students will return to a school and inform former teachers of their progress. Some 4 years after his last meeting, Frank dropped in to tell the therapist that he was married and had become a father; he wanted the therapist to know that he was happy and was endeavoring to meet his responsibilities to himself and his family. Several months after his last visit, Michael returned to tell the therapist about the vocational program in which he was enrolled.

What is likely to happen more frequently than the unexpected, reinforcing casual visit is the contact of the therapist about clients who were not helped in psychotherapy and/or who are once again showing disturbed behaviors. In some instances the therapist may be asked for information by another mental health resource that has been approached by the family for help. At times the parents or the child may contact the therapist for additional assistance; under some circumstances, he or she may learn that a former client, presumed to be doing well, is in treatment with someone else. Usually the question that has to be considered most carefully is whether another attempt at psychotherapy with the therapist would be in the best interests of the client, or whether another treatment approach would have a better chance for success. The history of Leon illustrates these problems.

Leon was the pampered only son in a family where being a male was highly valued and in itself a success. Despite indications of superior intellectual functioning, Leon had never done well in school. As he grew older and as the demands made on him by teachers increased with advancing grade levels, he became more open in his refusals to do the work; ultimately he skipped classes entirely.

At home, Leon sought comfort in overeating. He attacked the refrigerator daily, consuming vast quantities of chicken soup and whatever snacks were available. When his mother tried to defend his waistline by interposing herself between him and the door to the refrigerator, he would punch her on the arms and shove her out of the way. Although both his parents claimed to be saddened by Leon's aggressiveness, his mother displayed her bruises as though they were badges of maternal devotion, while his father quietly conveyed the impression that hitting his wife was not such a bad idea.

When Leon was about 13, his parents sought help from a family agency because they were concerned that his deteriorating performance in school would prevent his going to college. For about a year Leon and his parents were seen in family therapy, but no improvement was noted. They were transferred to a child guidance clinic, where it was thought that separating the family members by providing individual therapy for Leon and counseling for his parents might help where family therapy had not.

One thing that soon became clear was that everybody in this family felt the only friend they had at school was Leon's counselor. This counselor, the therapist learned from consultations with him, actually disliked this family intensely and expressed his antipathy by indulging their self-defeating whims. Whenever Leon wanted, the counselor would permit him to miss classes and write excuses for him to the teachers; Leon thought he was the best, most understanding person around.

The therapist worked on getting the parents and the school to impose limits on Leon and to require his attendance in class, as well as on convincing Leon that indulgence was not equivalent to affection. By the end of the school year, things seemed to be going better. Leon was attending classes and passing his subjects. The school counselor was given a present by the parents for being so understanding, and the therapist was told that his help was no longer needed.

Six months after termination, however, the therapist was contacted by Leon's mother. Things once again were not going too well: in the middle of this school year, Leon was beginning to refuse to attend his classes and to do his assignments. He told his parents he felt his teachers did not like him, and so he refused to do any of their work. Fortunately, from his mother's perspective, the school counselor was still very understanding and had resumed writing excuses for Leon, but his mother was worried that he would never get to college at this rate. Meanwhile, Leon had become a religious fanatic. He spent much time in prayer and would challenge the parents to theological arguments. Now he would hit his mother if she did not properly observe the dietary laws of their religion. The mother saw her son's orthodoxy as a mixed blessing. The therapist scheduled an appointment to see Leon.

To judge from Leon's interview, the situation in this family seemed to be at a crisis level. Leon was going to school, but he was not doing any work; however, he justified his actions by claiming religious fervor. Though a psychodynamic explanation would emphasize a defense of himself from the growing demands of adolescence by withdrawal and asceticism, Leon presented the following plan for his future: he wished to drop out, to leave the public school system and its godless practices, and to enroll in a high school sponsored by his religion. This would require that he leave home and live at the theological school in a city several hundred miles away, where he would devote himself to learning God's law and prepare himself for a life of religious contemplation and service. His plan sounded acceptable to his parents, but that this indulged and pampered youngster might respond constructively to the highly competitive intellectual and emotional demands of such a school seemed most unlikely.

The therapist arranged a meeting with the parents during which he explained that he could not be optimistic about the prospects for psychotherapy with Leon unless a definite stand was taken by the parents. The problem was that Leon was uninterested in working with the therapist, and would remain uninterested so long as the parents were entertaining the possibility of sending Leon to this distant parochial school. He wondered what position the parents had taken; they replied that they were willing to make any sacrifice for their son, including giving him to God. The therapist explained that he felt Leon had little chance for success in a theological seminary, and he pointed out the probable advantages of taking a firm stand against this plan. The parents responded with little enthusiasm to the therapist, politely offering to think about what he had said. In closing, they added they were proud God had chosen their son, and though it made them sad, they were willing to lose him.

That was the last the therapist heard about Leon until a year later, when his mother phoned to ask for an appointment. In the meeting that followed she reported that quite a bit had happened to Leon during that year, which had been a bad one for the family. Despite the therapist's advice to the contrary, they had sent Leon to the parochial high school, and it had not worked out very well. Within a month they were getting calls that Leon was not doing his work and was socially maladjusted, and after only 2 months they were notified they would have to go to the school and bring him home. Once back, Leon refused to do anything. He was even angry with his religion because "the people there" had let him down.

A few months before contacting the therapist, the mother sheepishly confessed, she and her husband had taken Leon to a child psychiatrist, who had prescribed medication and made an attempt to involve him in psychotherapy. But Leon's mother was sure that the psychiatrist did not really like Leon, which was why the medicine and psychotherapy did not help. In fact, Leon seemed to get worse, and for a time the psychiatrist had him hospitalized on a psychiatric ward. Now he was back home, and not appreciably better; would the therapist see him again?

The therapist first tried to find out whether it would be better for Leon to continue his contacts with the psychiatrist. After speaking with all the parties concerned he learned that neither Leon, his parents, nor (most importantly) the psychiatrist wanted this. Second, he considered that he was due to leave the community in the near future. Third, he noted that since Leon was 16, he could be referred to an adult outpatient psychiatric clinic, and that being classified with adults might in itself be helpful to Leon. The therapist informed the parents of the imminence of his departure and scheduled an appointment with Leon in order to help develop a plan.

At the meeting, Leon stated he was not interested in being seen in therapy by any professional who did not like him, and he was sure most therapists either disliked him immediately or soon came to dislike him. Anyway, he felt particularly betrayed by the child psychiatrist, who had put him on some drug and thrown him into a hospital for no good reason. He did have his own plan, which did not require attendance at any school; a friend of the family had offered him a job in a grocery store. Leon thought it would be nice to work around food and wait on people. The idea of being seen in an adult clinic appealed to him, as did the possibility of being seen in group psychotherapy with adults. His problems, as he saw them, were that people didn't like him and didn't appreciate his fine qualities and that his parents were "too picky." He did concede that he might be able to use help in controlling his temper and in settling down to work.

Even if Leon's therapist had not been leaving the community, his continued involvement with this family would have been questionable. His recommendations had been disregarded by the parents, and worse than being wrong, he had turned out to be right. Now Leon and his parents saw in him an embarrassment and a reproach, and they found being with him difficult. Perhaps they felt that he knew them only too well. How else is one to explain that at the family's last meeting with the therapist Leon's mother hobbled in on crutches, begging to be excused from too much participation because of her physical ailments, and that at the end of the meeting she walked unaided out of the office, leaving her crutches at the therapist's desk? At any rate, Leon went to work in the grocery store and began group therapy, Leon's father promised the therapist he would allow his friend to pay Leon what he was worth instead of trying to subsidize his salary, and Leon's mother went home to think about whether or not she was satisfied.

Special Problems in Termination

Some parents evidence discomfort at the last meeting, at times because they have questions about their child's adjustment or because they themselves feel a need for help about matters that they are uneasy about discussing in the presence of their child. Although there are some therapists who maintain a rule against family "secrets" and for communication among its members about anything, an argument can be made that there are some issues that are best confined to adults, just as there are some feelings and thoughts of the child that should be confidential.

For example, the therapist had seen a 6-year-old girl because she was not achieving in school. Her grades and social adjustment improved during the course of the treatment, and at a meeting with the family everyone agreed that termination of her contacts was indicated. The parents, however, asked if they could meet with the therapist about "something personal." Rather than insist the parents be more specific about their concern, the therapist asked the child if this would be acceptable to her. She stated that it was all right with her so long as she would not be a subject of the meeting. Reassured by her parents that they had something about themselves they needed to discuss, the meeting was arranged. At that meeting the mother revealed that she and her husband had not been having intercourse for over a year, and the father revealed that he had been obtaining sexual gratification from a fetish with shoes.

A session with the parents may particularly be called for when their child is seriously disturbed and there are questions about the advisability of hospitalization or institutionalization. In general, there is no psychological disorder in childhood that in and of itself demands hospitalization or institutionalization; rather, a decision to place a child in an institution is based on the possibility that harm may be suffered by remaining in the present environment, that removal from the home is necessary in order to protect the child, or that the parents feel they are no longer able (or perilously close to being unable) to meet their responsibilities to their child. There are many truly pathetic situations that argue for such a recommendation or by law require its consideration: the abuse or exploitation of the child, the grave illness or death of the parents, the severity of a disorder gradually eroding the structure and effective functioning of the family, and so on.

Despite valid reasons that may be present for removing the child from the family, it is usually best for the therapist not to advise parents that removal or institutional placement is the only option available to them. Instead, the therapist should present institutionalization as only one of several possibilities and allow the parents to decide whether their child's removal from the home is the one they prefer. Even when the therapist exercises care in broaching this issue, it is so emotionally charged for some parents that they may distort and misrepresent what is told to them so that they can defend their image of being loving and devoted mothers and fathers.

This problem is illustrated in the case of Arthur, a 6-year-old who was diagnosed as autistic and brain damaged. Although he was mute, mentally retarded, blind, and hyperactive as well, an attempt was made to involve him in psychotherapy. When there was no improvement in his condition after a year, Arthur's parents asked their counselor if they could meet with their son's therapist. At this meeting they reported that their daughter, who was a young adolescent, could no longer tolerate Arthur and the demands and sacrifices imposed on her because of him. Moreover, the parents stated that their marriage was suffering greatly. They asked about Arthur's prognosis; after being told that, all things considered, it was not favorable, they inquired whether there were institutions that might be of help to children like their son.

The therapist mentioned several residential facilities and suggested the parents write for information, since each institution had its own selection criteria and waiting lists. Both father and mother said that the family had to be saved and that they were willing to do whatever was needed in order to provide Arthur with the best possible institutional care. They thanked the therapist for his assistance and concern. All in all, the matter seemed to have been handled well. Yet a week later the therapist was informed by a neurologist who had been seeing Arthur for an evaluation that Arthur's mother had asked, in great distress, to speak with him privately. She told him that the therapist recommended Arthur's institutionalization, which she and her husband considered to be a repugnant and unthinkable plan. The neurologist comforted her, recommended a brief hospital stay for Arthur so that a complete battery of neurological tests could be administered, and twittered over the therapist's mishandling of the case.

Arthur's parents and neurologist illustrate two very important points. The first is that therapists can do their best, seem to have a successful meeting, and still not have things work out right. Outcome is not a function of a therapist's efforts alone; what happens is a consequence of an endeavor involving more than one person. Evidently Arthur's parents broke down upon hearing the therapist's prognosis and gave expression to feelings and frustrations that they had not shared with anyone else, even with one another. After the meeting ended they were ashamed of what they had revealed, and they began to wonder what others would think of them if they took the obvious and public step of removing their son from their home. They pulled themselves together, denied their contemplated rejection of their son, and projected or attributed any such thoughts to the therapist. The neurologist might have recognized the defensive aspects of the mother's reaction by its extreme repudiation of a treatment plan that was not entirely unreasonable given her son's multiplicity and severity of problems.

The second point to be made here is that a professional should never believe what a client says about anyone, let along another professional, simply on the strength of the client's say-so. We are always dealing with perceptions, with how people perceive situations and other people. The reality of the situation and how other people perceive that same situation or themselves may each be quite different. Nevertheless, we accept the client's perception as valid information about how something is experienced; that is, we take what the client says and do not argue with it or dispute it, but never assuming it is the truth (put figuratively, we do not swallow it hook, line, and sinker). (By the way, a week later the neurologist confessed to the therapist that Arthur's mother had failed to bring him to the hospital for his thorough neurological evaluation.)

Although it is atypical for a therapist's remarks to be as completely distorted as they were by Arthur's parents, it is probably quite common for there to be some distortion, even of rather innocuous comments. When we get to weighty issues like removal from the home and abandoning children, parents may be expected to present their behavior in the most favorable light. It is not unusual for parents who wish to take steps to place their children in an institution to explain to their offspring that they are doing so only "because the doctor says it will be better for you." This absolution from responsibility may help the parents to live more comfortably with what they profess they were compelled to do, but it does not promote the child's trust or confidence in professionals trying to be of help in this difficult situation. When therapists discover that parents have resorted to such a deception with their child, they should act to see that honest communication exists among the parties concerned, even though this may be painful and unpleasant to assimilate.

On occasion, a therapist may receive a referral from parents or a foster care agency to see a child in psychotherapy so as to prevent institutionalization or removal from a foster home. When institutionalization is mentioned as a "dreaded" or "distasteful" possibility—but one that is threatening to be exercised—at the very outset of the case, it frequently happens that the natural or foster parents are at the end of their patience and more inclined toward removal of the child than toward any modifications in anyone's behavior in order to prevent the removal. Under such circumstances it is not unusual for the treatment to have to come to an end shortly after it begins because the parents demand the child's placement, even when he or she may be making satisfactory progress. Here therapists have a responsibility to children to help them to understand why they are being removed and that this result may have no relation to their current behaviors, being instead a consequence of the feelings of these parents that institutionalization may offer the best option for all of them.

With termination and the approval of the child and parents, and when it is indicated, therapists may arrange meetings with professionals or agencies involved in providing services to the family (schools, courts, child welfare agencies, and so on). Throughout Leon's treatment, for example, there were meetings with school personnel and representatives from social agencies who had contacts with the boy and his family. The purpose of these meetings is to see what can be done to enhance the child's or family's chances for maintaining gains and continuing to experience success. With this purpose in mind, therapists may offer to see the parents for a time; by helping them to accept and to deal with their child more effectively or to handle their own personal problems, a therapist may consolidate the child's gains and prevent a recurrence of disturbed behavior. These issues will be discussed more fully in the next chapter.

What is emphasized here is that in a last meeting, therapists continue to follow the principles of psychotherapy. Perhaps for this reason, many therapists prefer not to consider the last meeting as a special topic and to confine their remarks to a consideration of the "termination process," the "ending," or the "final stage of therapy." Ordinarily, however, there is a last meeting that is acknowledged as such by therapist and client, and which therefore requires a specific structure to bring about a certain closure in the treatment and a sense of what has been accomplished. For therapists, this means the client's feelings and concerns in the last meeting must be confronted and dealt with in an honest and constructive manner.

9
The Therapist and the Family

There is little controversy about the importance of the parents in psychotherapy with children and in the etiology and correction of many childhood disorders. There is disagreement about whether parents play a part in determining certain disorders, such as autism and schizophrenia, but there is no question that children have to be understood within their social context and that their family relationships have to be considered when trying to be of help to them (Fauber & Long, 1991).

Throughout this book there has been discussion of parents and family. At the beginning of his novel *Anna Karenina*, Tolstoy observed, "All happy families are alike; every unhappy family is unhappy in its own fashion." Yet the research indicates that unhappy families who bring their children for professional help have some commonalities. In general, the parents are unsure of themselves in their parenting roles and anxious and uncertain about whether their children will develop properly; moreover, if they experience the treatment as one more stress in a life already far too burdened with stresses, they are apt to withdraw themselves and their children prematurely from treatment (Kazdin, 1990).

Much has been written about working with parents and about being sensitive to their needs. Kessler (1988) examined some of the problems and considerations for therapists who work with atypical or uncommon parents, including those who are mentally ill, retarded, single-parent teenagers, or abusive. This chapter is addressed specifically to the work of the child psychotherapist in dealing with typical parents who refer their children for help, though Tolstoy's quote warns us against complacency and to be alert to the individual characteristics of every family.

The Normal Family

Within the United States and most other Western cultures, the family is nuclear in structure; that is, it is composed of parents and their offspring who have not assumed adult responsibilities. This type of family structure may be contrasted with that of the extended kin group, which typically contains three or more generations within one household. The extended kin group is associated with cultures that value tradition and elders (parents and grandparents), whereas the nuclear family is associated with cultures that value change, independence, individuality, innovation, and youth.

The structure of the nuclear family is suited to the demands of an urban, industrialized, expanding society. It has few members; hence, it has greater mobility than an extended kin group system. It can move to where opportunities exist, and its society expects it to move to where these opportunities exist. Although the culture professes to value children and human relationships, a greater value is placed on occupational demands. Parents and children are expected to give up their ties to friends and other family members willingly and to adjust readily if, for example, a parent's occupation requires that a move be made.

What is new tends to be valued by the nuclear family. A new product is assumed to be better than an old one, simply because it is the latest. Similarly, it is assumed that the new generation knows more than the old generation, that the beliefs and preferences of the parents are old-fashioned, and that new values are best. In other words, the nuclear family by its very structure breaks with the past and requires that children break from their parents and establish their own independent households. It is discontinuous, which is to say that it compels its members to seek their own identities. Our society does not expect children to follow in the footsteps of their parents; rather, it expects them to engage in "self-actualization" and to do their "own thing."

By its nature, then, the nuclear family undermines the authority of parents and family ties, and it promotes the development of insecurity and anxieties about identity. Children are encouraged to establish who they are not through their families, but by their own achievements. They must recognize and accept that their parents have their own individualities and their own lives to lead, and that the parental role in their lives is limited and of diminishing importance. Their parents have undergone a similar experience with their own parents, withdrawing from them and establishing their own homes. In the process, they have denied themselves the assistance that grandparents might have provided in the rearing of their children. Things change; people no longer do things the way they used to. There are new ideas about child rearing, new gadgets, and disposable products: "It (the nuclear family) lacks the security provided by time-tried customs and the unconscious assurance that the way in which the family lives is the proper way" (Lidz, 1963, p. 27).

As can easily be imagined, the "normal" nuclear family has its contradictions and paradoxes, which can be disturbing. It is dedicated to children, yet there is no question as to precedence when the needs of the parents for career advancement conflict with those of the children for emotional security and stability. It values individuality and independence but requires some degree of obedience and conformity in order to function effectively. It values freedom, initiative, and spontaneity while also esteeming respect for authority, following rules, and self-denial. In giving expression to their conflicting values and contradictory beliefs, parents are likely to bewilder their children, to feel guilty themselves, to say one thing but mean another, and to abruptly end arguments with their offspring with the angry admonition, "Do as I say and not as I do!"

As they grow older, the children of the nuclear family turn increasingly to peers for guidance in dealing with problems. So do the parents of the nuclear family, but they may also frequently seek advice from experts or authorities in the fields of child psychology or mental health. In a manner of speaking, the child psychotherapist fulfills some of the functions that used to be performed by grandparents.

The Roles of the Therapist

Professionals disagree about the role that parents should play in the treatment of their children and the role that therapists should play vis-à-vis the parents. Some therapists see parents as responsible adults who can provide reliable information about their children and can implement appropriate advice and recommendations without any problem or fuss. Other therapists see parents as probably most responsible for their offspring's disturbance and more in need of assistance than the children; such parents act in unconscious ways to sabotage the treatment, frustrate the therapist, and perpetuate the pathology. Yet another view, which is the one reiterated throughout this book, is that parents are a heterogeneous group who must perceive the therapist as working with them cooperatively for the welfare of their children.

Our view does not prejudge parents. It assesses each parent's individual strengths and weaknesses, assesses the contexts within which the family members function, and assumes by virtue of the referral that the parent has some interest in joining with the therapist to see that the child receives help. It is prepared to accept, however, that there are times when this interest is negligible and may easily be overshadowed by other fears and concerns. It emphasizes the responsibility of the therapist to understand, respect, and to join with the parent in being of help to the child. It contends that the principles of psychotherapy are employed in discharging this responsibility.

There has been much sound advice published on how the child psychotherapist should relate to parents. In 1930, Alfred Adler presented five recommendations that serve any therapist well (Ansbacher & Ansbacher, 1956, pp. 395–396):

1. Do not reproach or censure the parents for their child's pathology.
2. Remember that they are not entirely responsible for their child's behavior.
3. Avoid dwelling on what they are doing wrong, and instead concentrate on what they might do that would be constructive and helpful.
4. Enlist their cooperation, no matter what their imperfections, by telling them, "I can see that you are on the right track" (since, after all, they have come to see you).
5. Do not be authoritarian in giving advice or recommendations, but qualify your suggestions with "perhaps" or "maybe."

Adler's recommendations are predicated on the assumption that one is dealing with parents who are reasonable, cooperative, accepting of their child, and receptive to making changes in their behaviors. Essentially, this is the assumption that therapists have when they begin working with parents, and it is possible then to think of their own role as that of a consultant.

The Therapist as Consultant

Consultation may be described as an interaction process between two or more individuals, one of whom has a specialized area of knowledge that is sought and valued by the other(s). It differs from supervision (Reisman, 1980) in that the consultee maintains full responsibility for the work and has the power to reject the suggestions of the consultant. The aim of consultation is to promote the consultee's effectiveness in performing the tasks under consideration. It is not to increase the consultee's sense of personal well-being, though this may be a side effect of improved task effectiveness; nor is it to discuss the consultee's personal problems and feelings, though this may be necessary and the consultant should be sensitive to them. In other words, consultation is supposed to be a relationship between equals, and there have long been admonitions that consultants must take care to prevent their relationships from becoming like those of doctors and patients (Caplan, 1970).

Without too much difficulty, the roles of parent and therapist can be translated into those of consultee and consultant. The parent has a problem with a child and seeks the help of a specialist in child behavior and psychotherapy. Usually the parent does not present this problem as a personal or family problem, but rather as a problem of the child ("What's wrong with her?" "Why is he acting this way?") or a problem in task performance ("What am I doing wrong?" "How do I get him to mind?" "What can I do to help her?"). Ordinarily, parents do not expect to be involved in psychotherapy for themselves. They expect to receive advice, to maintain responsibility for their child, and to reject suggestions they think will not work. They believe that they know more about their child than the therapist does.

The task of the therapist-consultant is not to offer psychotherapy, to challenge the strengths of the parents and to inviegle them into treatment. As a consultant, the therapist aims to maintain the parents' confidence and to build upon their strengths. This is usually accomplished by first arriving at an understanding with the parents about the nature of their particular problem, then proposing and considering alternative ways of dealing with it. Often, in taking the first step, parents will themselves explore other options and obviate the need for the second step.

A parent may be concerned about temper tantrums in her 2-year-old, another about selfishness in her 3-year-old, a third about lying and stealing in a 4-year-old, a fourth about cross-gender behaviors in a 5-year-old, and a fifth about an adolescent's practice of masturbation. Simply hearing from a therapist that these behaviors are developmentally normal may be sufficient to alleviate the parents' worries about them.

The following is an excerpt of an interview that took place after a therapist was asked by a colleague to meet with the mother of an 8-year-old, Jimmy, who was being seen in play therapy. Jimmy's mother was raising a number of questions with her child's therapist, who thought it would be best if this parent could have her problems addressed by someone else. This excerpt is from the initial meeting with the consultant and deals with only one problem, though three were actually raised. Each of these problems appeared to be resolved to the mother's satisfaction by enhancing her understanding of it.

> *Consultant:* Well, where would you like to begin?
> *Client:* There are several questions I'd like answered, one being how much affection should a father show to a son normally in hugging and kissing a boy. This is a problem in our house.
> *Consultant:* I see. Your husband and you disagree in how much affection should be shown to Jimmy.
> *Client:* Well, maybe in a roundabout way. I see my husband needing to put his arm around Jim, and he just wasn't brought up like that. He believes love should be a depth love, which he has for Jim, but his outward affection. . . . It's hard for him to show it.

Consultant: So your feeling is he should try to be more open in the way he shows affection.

Client: Yes.

Consultant: And his is that as long as he has the feeling deep within himself, he figures that that might be the best thing. (*pause*) Well, is it your impression that Jim doesn't seem able to sense this?

Client: Jim outwardly reveals this. If my husband shows affection to me, he wants this shown to him, too. I want help in this, doctor. I want to know how to help him.

Consultant: Well, from what you've said it sounds as though your husband is saying to you, "Get off my back! I have a deep love for the boy." Is that kind of the way he is?"

Client: He just thinks it's sissy to show outward affection toward Jim.

Consultant: And you think there are times when Jim might welcome this from his father.

Client: Right.

Consultant: In talking about this with your husband, is his position that that's the kind of person I am and I can't change?

Client: More or less. And I want to know if this could be damaging to Jim, and how it would be damaging.

Consultant: Well, the first question is whether it would be, rather than how it would be.

Client: Yes.

Consultant: And from what you've been saying it sounds as though you do believe it would be. (*pause*) Does Jim himself complain about this at all?

Client: He'll make a remark like, "Daddy didn't kiss me this morning." It's jealousy in a way ... of the love between my husband and me. He doesn't know how to comprehend this.

Consultant: He doesn't? So what do you do?

Client: Well, I did tell my husband he shouldn't be afraid to show outward affection.

Consultant: So you feel this would make the bonds between Jim and his father stronger.

Client: Yes. I don't want Jim to feel rejected. He's been rejected so much, and Jim wants to kiss his father, and I just wonder. Should my husband kiss Jim every time he asks him to, two or three times a day?

Consultant: It sounds as though your husband doesn't feel he would like to.

Client: Yes. He doesn't want to.

Consultant: The issue here seems to be that your husband is saying, "I do like Jim, but I have a way of showing affection which makes me feel uncomfortable if I have to show it by kissing and hugging a boy." Now, I wonder, has he ever told Jim he feels this way about him, or

have you ever told Jim he feels this way about him?
Client: I'm trying . . . I'm trying by telling him that love is different between daddies and mothers, that mothers show more outward affection than daddies do.
Consultant: Well, what happens? Doesn't Jim buy it? Doesn't he believe it?
Client: Well, I think he's swallowing it a little.
Consultant: It would seem that you're attacking this problem in two ways. On the one hand, you try to encourage your husband to feel less uncomfortable in showing affection, and on the other hand, you're trying to get Jim to understand that his father shows his affection in different ways but still loves him.
Client: Right.
Consultant: Do you feel comfortable about the way this is working? Does it seem to be working all right?
Client: Yes, it is doing better now. I guess for a while I really forgot to tell Jim that mothers do show more outward affection than daddies.

What seemed to happen during this exchange was that the mother was reminded of an alternative approach to the problem. She had been focused on trying to change her husband, but then she recalled that she had also tried to explain her husband to his son, and that the latter method had been neglected. These parents have attitudes about sex roles that are dated, and it may be worthwhile to consider the circumstances when they might be questioned.

The last meeting with this mother, which was the eighth, serves to demonstrate the feelings that may occur in the final session of consultation and how the consultant handled them. The following excerpt is from the first few minutes of the session.

Client: Well, it's rainy today and it's kinda gloomy, and we got word this morning of the death of a real good friend, so . . .
Consultant: So it has been a very sad day for you, then.
Client: Yes, it is. Um . . . I did go ahead and tell Jim. I knew it would upset him, but I thought it would be better if he knew, and he bawled and squalled and was late getting off to school. So our day hasn't started off so good.
Consultant: It's been very upsetting to both you and Jim . . . very depressing.
Client: Yes, it's starting out that way. However, we see good things in store for us, too. Jim's grandmother is coming to visit with us this Saturday, and we're looking forward to Thanksgiving next week.
Consultant: So there are good things happening, too. . . . Well, this is our last meeting, and I don't know whether that comes under the

heading of brighter things in your day or gloomier things maybe, or maybe a little bit of both.

Client: Yes . . . there's a feeling of insecurity in knowing I won't have you to talk to, and yet there's a feeling of happiness because of the time I can spend in other ways. Time is so precious to me today.

Consultant: It makes you feel good, then, that there's this one sort of pressure on your time that's removed and you can do other things, and I guess . . . you mentioned some insecurity, too.

Client: Yes, it has really helped me considerably having you to talk to.

Consultant: Oh, in what way?

Client: I feel with you being educated to this problem, and I can find you as a friend, and I can talk these things out with you. There's so many people in the world that aren't understanding. For instance, last night my minister kinda got me riled up, wanting me to visit people new in the community. I didn't think he was very understanding. I'm usually good-natured, and they take advantage. When he asked, I just said no, but I felt like saying to him, "You start doing my work and then maybe I'll have some time to do yours."

Consultant: Well, I guess what you were trying to get across is that you have responsibilities right now and you don't feel able to take on any more.

Client: Yes, and the children do come first, and there are other people that can visit.

Consultant: I notice, too, that you might have been tempted to let him think that you were good-natured, but that now you kind of stand up for your rights.

Client: Yes. I just wanted to let him know the children come first.

Consultant: So you're trying to tell people what you do think when they step on your toes.

Client: Yes.

Consultant: Remember last week you mentioned how your husband took advantage of you, and how upset that made you feel, and maybe you're beginning to feel it's not such a good idea to be good-natured all the time.

Client: I'm beginning to believe you do have to make people see you do have rights.

Consultant: I see. (*pause*) In terms of some of the things you mentioned as problems when you first came. . . . Do you recall what they were?

Client: I remember I was upset about Jim and his father's relationship and about how much affection should be shown to Jim.

Consultant: And how has that worked out?

Client: Well, Jim doesn't seem to need as much affection, and that has taken care of it.

Very often in behavioral interventions we are dealing in consultation, with the parents assigned a significant role in providing the treatment or training. Sometimes it happens that the preparations for the intervention change the parents' perceptions of the problem. One example occurred when a mother phoned for help in dealing with her 5-year-old child's fear of dogs. Prior to a first visit, she was asked to get base rate data by recording how often each day her child exhibited the fear. A week later she phoned to say she observed a steadily declining frequency, and she subsequently phoned to say the problem seemed to have solved itself. Another example had parents complaining that their child "never listens to us." They were told to do a functional analysis, though not in those terms. The following session they reported that their child disobeyed less than they thought and listened more than they realized. Eventually they decided their child did not need help, and to be more careful to acknowledge his desirable behaviors.

There are times when the consultant role does not suffice, when a parent recognizes: "I know I shouldn't let this bother me, but I can't help it. Maybe it's me, not my child. Maybe I'm the one who needs help." To such a recognition, should the consultant bow out and the therapist role be introduced?

Some years ago, Sol Gordon would lecture about parent-child problems to audiences of parents and preface the period of questions and answers with an admonition: "You're going to ask me for advice and suggestions, and, all right, I'm going to give them to you. But I want you to promise me one thing. When I give you the advice and you don't want to take it, or you find out that you can't follow it, please ask yourself, 'Why not?' " This is a question that should be raised with many parents, for their difficulties in implementing relatively simple recommendations suggest personal problems that may require help.

To illustrate, a 10-year-old boy was referred for stealing. He repeatedly stole money from his parents, but what brought them to refer him was his thefts of money from the purses of teachers, even at Sunday school! These were middle-class parents (the father was a successful industrial engineer), and they were quite embarrassed by the actions of their son. The boy told the therapist that he had frequently asked his father for an allowance of 50 cents a week. His father had refused and told him to get a job, which was impossible at his age and in the suburban area where they lived. He doubted that he would steal if he could just have the allowance. When this was relayed to the parents they corroborated what their son had said, but the father again refused to give his son an allowance. The consultant pointed out the father's inconsistency in being willing to give a professional a fee for one session equal to more than a year of the modest allowance his son requested, yet the father still refused to give in. It was the mother who said she would speak with her husband and "try to bring him around." A week later she reported her husband had begun giving their son the 50 cents a week, and several months later the boy sent the consultant his class photo and a note of thanks.

It is not unusual for parents to be perplexed by their child's behavior, though their own contributions to it may be glaringly obvious to almost anyone else. They may also present therapist-consultants with many complex questions, some of which may actually be impossible to answer; therapist-consultants should be frank to admit this. When parents seek to explore their personal feelings and reactions, however, should therapist-consultants explain that their role with them is limited to their child's problem and its immediate ramifications, and that their personal feelings are best kept outside their area of consideration?

The aim in asking these questions is to make explicit the complications and very real problems that can occur when consultants try to adhere to a narrow conception of their role and to recognize the arguments for that narrow conception. For example, it is recommended that one way to prevent consultation from turning into psychotherapy is to respond to the remarks of the parent consistently in terms of their effects on the child, as follows:

Client: My parents were very strict with me.
Consultant: So that's why you're determined to treat your children differently.
Client: My husband and I haven't been getting along lately.
Consultant: And you wonder what effect this has on your son.
Client: At times I could scream, I get so upset and unhappy.
Consultant: That must make it all the harder to give your children the kind of attention they want.

Although the responses above are certainly possible and quite often effective in keeping the consultation focused upon the original problem rather than venturing afield into uncertain terrain, we are going to present a case for it to be appropriate—and even essential—to be sensitive to the feelings of the parents, to be understanding of them, and to communicate that understanding. Psychotherapy, as stressed repeatedly, is not a therapist-patient relationship of an extraordinary sort; it is a form of communication. When psychotherapy is defined and accepted as the communication of one person's understanding, respect, and wish to be of help to someone else, it becomes patently absurd to seek to exclude it deliberately from any human interaction. Moreover, when psychotherapy is understood as a form of communication, the distinction that is made between consultation and psychotherapy is blurred, if not lost entirely. As a form of communication, psychotherapy can be employed in consultation, and consultation can be employed in psychotherapy. This comes about because both terms can be understood in two different ways: as behaviors and as professionally provided services.

In psychotherapy, clients are concerned about and seek assistance to bring about changes in themselves. They usually feel personally dissatisfied, unhappy, and ineffective, and they trust their therapists to use whatever procedures may be necessary to promote their improvement and self-understanding. In the course of their contacts, the therapist or client may emphasize or focus upon the client's behaviors in certain situations or performance in certain tasks; at those times, it may indeed be difficult to distinguish what the therapist does from what is done by a consultant, trainer, or teacher.

The situation in consultation is more focused and circumscribed than it is in psychotherapy, where almost anything related to the client is open to discussion. A consultee wants to be helped in dealing with a specific problem. Consultees see the task or performance demanded of them as beyond their present skills but within their realm of competence; given a few pointers or suggestions, they believe they can handle it. They often believe they could have solved the problem if they had the knowledge of the consultant, or the time to acquire it. Thus, in seeking consultation they do not necessarily feel any personal inadequacy, and they are likely to resent any suggestion by the consultant that a personal deficiency is responsible for their needing help.

Essentially, this means that a therapist-consultant must be understanding of what the client expects and wants. Just because someone has been trained to be a psychotherapist does not mean that it is proper for that person to practice psychotherapy at all times with everyone. Not only would such behavior be inordinately demanding upon the person, but it would also not always be appreciated. In the consultation interview excerpt early in this chapter, the therapist-consultant began by asking Jim's mother, "Well, where would you like to begin?" Her response was to present her problem as one that did not question her behavior or feelings, but in which she questioned the behavior and emotional expressiveness of her husband. Her concern was not with herself, but with her performance in relatively narrow areas of her roles as wife and mother.

To illustrate this point further, during the same initial interview the other problems raised by Jim's mother involved her son's fights with his brother and the troubles that both boys had in doing their homework assignments from school. The second meeting was highlighted by a discussion of how to get the boys to eat their dinners faster so they could have more time to do their homework. The solution turned out to be that the mother either stop putting food on their plates that they did not like or stop insisting that they sit at the dinner table until they consumed everything. Obviously these mundane recommendations might occur to almost everyone, yet they were greeted by this mother as reve lations that were highly meaningful to her and that she took great de light in carrying out.

Also to be noted in the excerpt under discussion is that many of the consultant's responses communicate an understanding of the mother's feelings (that is, they are psychotherapy). The mother, however, did not elaborate upon her feelings; it seemed to be sufficient for her simply to have these feelings recognized. Moreover, she did not attempt to make the discussion more personal, and in fact she consistently steered it from herself to her husband or someone else. This was not challenged by the consultant, as it might well have been had the mother agreed to be seen for psychotherapy. Because their contract was for consultation, the consultant respected the mother's right to remain impersonal when she so chose. If this mother had begun to elaborate upon her feelings, or if she had expressed a need for personal help because of her inadequacies, then the therapist-consultant would have either renegotiated their contract or presented the option of referral to someone else for psychotherapy.

The following points summarize our position with regard to consultation:

1. In negotiating a purpose for their meetings, parents frequently express a goal in terms of increasing their understanding of their child's problem or disorder, its prognosis, and treatment options; community resources that may be available to assist them (such as parent groups with similar problems; Turnbull & Turnbull, 1990) and their child; and the reasonableness of their expectations for their child, in view of assessments of the child's strengths and weaknesses (Thompson & Rudolph, 1988). They may also request specific advice about how they can better deal with certain behaviors of their child. Neither they nor the therapist believe that personal help for the parents is necessary or indicated at this time.
2. When a therapist agrees with parents to work toward a circumscribed goal, there is a mutual obligation to respect this agreement.
3. During consultation, there will probably be times when it will be both appropriate and helpful for the therapist to respond with communications that constitute psychotherapy. Such communications do not alter the goal, but rather deepen and enrich it.
4. Many of the principles of psychotherapy are relevant to consultation and can apply to the performance of this function.

Another illustration: A mother and father contacted the therapist for help with their 14-year-old son, who had been diagnosed as autistic when he was about 3 years old. Over the years of the boy's childhood, his disorder manifested itself primarily in reclusiveness; he had no friends, despite his attendance in a public school. His teacher was concerned about his socially withdrawn behavior and, even though he was doing passing work for his grade, recommended he be retained rather than promoted into high school, where his social adjustment would be more of a problem. The question raised by the parents was whether it would be in their son's best interests to be held back for a year in hope of improving his social skills. How might the therapist proceed to provide consultation in this case? What recommendations might be given?

Treating Parents

There are occasions when therapists and parents may deem it advisable for the parents to be seen for psychotherapy, even though the presenting problem belonged to a child. This happened when Bob, a 12-year-old, was referred by his mother because he was doing poorly in school and running away from home. In his interview with the therapist, Bob stated that he was angry with his mother because she had chased his father out of their home and refused to take him back, and because he had no privacy now that he and his mother shared the same bedroom—and the same bed.

Sharing the same bedroom and sleeping in the same bed are two facets of parent-child togetherness that psychotherapists usually attempt to discourage as soon as possible. Therefore, when Bob's mother, Mrs. M., was next seen she was told it was inadvisable for herself and her adolescent son to sleep together, and that this was one of Bob's major complaints. Mrs. M. informed the therapist that she would take his recommendation under careful consideration, but that she lived in a three-room bungalow with a kitchen, a living room, and only one bedroom. Now that her husband was gone she felt more comfortable with Bob sleeping with her, instead of on the sofa in the living room. After she said this she began to cry. She was quite apologetic about her tears, even managing to laugh at how "silly" she was being. The therapist wondered whether Mrs. M. felt a need for help in view of the separation from her husband and the difficulties with Bob, and she said that she did. Accordingly, it was agreed that she would be seen for psychotherapy.

In offering psychotherapy to Mrs. M., the therapist had as a major consideration that this would be an effective way to be of help to Bob, who saw his problems as reactions to his mother's behaviors. That his explanation was not simply a defensive externalization of responsibility was suggested by the facts that his "disturbance" began shortly after his parents separated, by his mother's inability to comply with the simple recommendation that her son sleep outside her bedroom, and her obvious need to use Bob as a substitute for her husband.

Also, it should be noted that in this case Mrs. M. was experiencing distress about a current crisis situation involving her husband and her son. Frequently child psychotherapists encounter parents when they are experiencing problems with their children and feel their roles are in jeopardy; thus, the situation is often responded to as a crisis in which parental effectiveness has been questioned and the adjustments within the family are under threat. In many cases it is therefore possible for the parents and therapist to define a limited and definite goal for their involvement in the same way that the therapist negotiates a purpose for the meetings with any client.

Mrs. M. was seen once a week over a period of about 4 months. She was a plain, overweight, middle-aged woman, a sensitive, enveloping mother who cried when she was happy, sad, angry, or abused and who fought with all the strength she could muster to protect her pride and dignity from the wounds life inflicted—in short, a pathetic and courageous presence. What became evident was that she had not ousted her husband but instead been abandoned by him. From her accounts, only she and her son preserved the fiction that she discarded and spurned her husband. Everyone else saw things in a different light: "My neighbor told me that she saw my husband and this woman he's living with . . . some young woman who drinks too much, like him . . . at this amusement park over the weekend. He was hanging around with her even before he left. I'll never take him back. He'll probably get drunk and come begging to me, but I'll never take him back." And then Mrs. M. cried, again laughing with embarrassment at her tears.

Gradually, Mrs. M. came to admit to herself that her husband left her and made not only no effort to return but also no contribution to the support of his wife and son. She decided to be honest with Bob about his father, and she arranged things in their home so that Bob could have more privacy and would no longer sleep in her room. Bob responded to this disclosure and modification in his environment by trying to be of help to his mother and by doing better in his schoolwork. Mrs. M. also decided to return to employment as a secretary, to obtain legal assistance to compel her husband to shoulder some of his responsibilities to the family, and to lose weight. At her last meeting with the therapist she seemed frightened by the challenges that had followed her being truthful with herself, but she was determined to meet them and was pleased with the improvement in her son.

A quite different situation was presented by Mrs. B., the mother of 6-year-old Laura, who had elective mutism. Laura's problem of not talking to anyone outside her family was of particular concern to the school, where she simply sat all day without a word. Although at home Laura practiced her classroom assignments and talked almost incessantly, convincing Mrs. B. that her daughter was achieving at grade level and should be promoted, in school there was no evidence by which to gauge her progress. In the presence of a teacher Laura was immobilized; the result was that unless she changed her behavior, she would have to repeat the grade.

Both parents described their home life as idyllic, which made their daughter's problem all the more difficult for them to fathom. An attractive, middle-class couple, they had a comfortable home in the suburbs and a large family. Laura was the youngest of five children, and the first to give any sign of requiring professional help. Mr. B. was a loving father and generous provider who preferred watching television and being at home with his family to any other form of entertainment or relaxation. Mrs. B. was a devoted mother and housewife, dedicated to providing her family with home-cooked meals, fresh foods, and a bounteous array of desserts and snacks. Neither parent had any complaint with the other, and they could not understand why Laura's disorder came about. Since her problem manifested itself only outside the family, they supposed it had to do with something experienced in the outside world. Nevertheless, Mrs. B. agreed it might be wise to consider her family life in some detail with one therapist while Laura was seen by another.

In a few sessions, it became clear to the therapist seeing Mrs. B. that her resolute housekeeping and mothering constituted a reaction formation. Because the behaviors and values expressed by Mrs. B. are not too common these days and might even be regarded as qualities to be encouraged and emulated—who can dislike a clean house, a freezer filled with ice cream and snacks, and a plentiful supply of fresh-baked cakes, cookies, pies, and pizza?—the therapist had to be alert to the threat of his own fantasies interfering with his clinical judgment. One clue to the excessive and defensive nature of Mrs. B.'s behaviors was her remark that she worried greatly about the safety of her children: whenever they left the house, even to go next door, she insisted they phone her so she would know they had arrived safely. But what was most convincing was the increasing frequency with which Mrs. B. expressed feelings other than love for the members of her family:

> There are times when I get the feeling that they're all like a huge spider, closing in on me, suffocating me, sucking the blood out of me, demanding to be fed. . . . That dumb husband of mine just sits around all the time expecting me to wait on him. Why doesn't that big slob ever take me out? Why the hell should he, now that I think of it, when he's got me waiting on him hand and foot! Do you realize we never go out because he's so worried about the kids! Not even to relatives! Every Sunday they come to see us, and I'm expected to feed them. From now on, we're going to take turns.

Laura's therapist reported that she never spoke during their meetings, but she did use the time to play with clay and a dump truck. This therapist speculated that the child's immobility in school might be an overcontrol of aggressive impulses. Although Laura was still not talking within the class-room, there were indications of more cooperative behavior with the teacher. Meanwhile, Mrs. B. was taking a firmer and more self-assertive stand with her husband and her children. She also managed to convince Laura's teacher to grant a promotion if Laura could demonstrate that she had achieved grade-level work, and this demonstration was a success. At the final meeting with Mr. and Mrs. B. and the two therapists, Mrs. B. ar-rived before her husband, wearing a new fur coat and a broad grin. The coat, she explained, was a gift from her husband, to be worn when they went out in the evening. Upon his arrival, Mr. B. seemed a little flustered. He was carrying a gift-wrapped box, topped with a large bow ribbon, and this was immediately presented to his wife. Turning to the therapists, he confessed that this was an additional anniversary gift, which proved to be an electric carving knife.

A final illustration is provided by the case of Mrs. Y., who came for help for her overweight and underachieving son. Nevertheless, this prob-lem soon took a back seat to complaints about her medical condition. For some time Mrs. Y. had experienced stomach distress and abdominal pain. Her physician, after numerous examinations, informed her she had an "ir-ritable colon that is probably psychogenic." She was not sure what this meant, but she wanted it understood that her pains were not imaginary but very real. The therapist agreed to help her deal more effectively with her tension because until that was relieved, she would not be able to ad-dress her son's concerns.

First, the therapist explained to Mrs. Y. how stress and anxiety might contribute to her condition. An effort was made to enable her to deal with stress more effectively by practicing relaxation. Mrs. Y. found it virtually impossible, however, to relax for any length of time. She could not close her eyes, she could not tense her muscles, and she could not even sit back in a chair and begin to feel relaxed. What she could and did do at great length was talk about her pain and her bewilderment at why it was in-flicted upon her.

One day, after another procedure to induce relaxation failed and while Mrs. Y. continued her complaints about her abdomen, the therapist com-mented, "You know, I wonder what you would talk about if you didn't have your pain to talk about." This remark was prompted by the thera-pist's speculation that Mrs. Y.'s preoccupation with her pain diverted her attention from some other area of concern that was more personally threatening (that is, it may have been a displacement). Her response was immediate and dramatic. She appeared stunned, fell silent, and looked as if she were giving the question much consideration.

In the session of the following week Mrs. Y. announced she had been thinking about the therapist's comment. To her, it indicated that except for her pain her life was relatively empty: her profession was confining and no longer of interest to her; her children were relatively independent and no longer required her supervision; and her marriage was humming along on automatic pilot. What she needed to do, she decided, was to make some radical changes in her life. She had investigated the possibility of entering a training program that would prepare her for a new profession; it would begin in the next month. She decided that her son's weight and performance in school were his responsibilities, and she left it to him to determine if he wanted help with them. In all the excitement and exhilaration of that week she had little time to notice her pain. About 2 years later, the therapist met Mrs. Y. at a social gathering. She reported success in her new career, still found it difficult to relax, said her son was doing better in school, and remarked that though the pain came and went, it was not an interference. She also still remembered the therapist's comment and the impact if had upon her.

Treating the parents is often the focus of behavioral interventions when parental discipline or its lack are thought to contribute to the problems of children. Research has found that conduct disorders are associated with the parents' managing skills, and that training the parents to be more effective in their parenting or more clear about what they perceive as objectionable behaviors (Wahler, 1992) can be an effective intervention, even when the children themselves may not be seen in treatment (Fauber & Long, 1991).

On occasion, a very simple intervention can be helpful to the family. Alex, an adolescent, complained that his mother never appreciated what he did and always nagged at him for things he did not do, such as attend his classes at school and come home before midnight on school nights. In discussing this complaint with his mother, the therapist learned it was long-standing, but she felt being a single parent made it very difficult to do anything but attend to one crisis after another. The therapist proposed that Alex and his mother keep a daily chart of the tasks for which Alex was responsible and whether or not Alex's mother complimented him for his performance of each of them. They were also told to negotiate rewards and tasks, since Alex believed it might be a bit much to be thanked every time he emptied trash. This procedure was followed, and within a few weeks Alex and his mother reported sufficient improvements both at home and in school to no longer require monitoring of their interactions.

Reisman and Kissel (1968) conducted a follow-up of mothers and their children who were seen in a child guidance clinic for long-term clinic services. *Long term* was defined in this study as at least 20 interviews, and in this sample the mean number of sessions was 50. Out of 45 mothers who were potential respondents, 43 agreed to answer the questionnaire (an unusually high response rate, but it should be remembered that these mothers had long-term involvements with this clinic). Of the 43 respondents, 30 reported that their children had been helped by the clinic, whereas 35 stated that they themselves had been helped. Obviously there were 5 mothers who reported they had been helped when their children had not been, but the converse was not stated by anyone—that a child was helped, but the mother was not. Also of interest is that the mothers saw the help provided to their children in terms of changes in behaviors, whereas they saw the help they received in terms of gains in understanding. This study suggested that a child's behavioral improvement is more accessible and relevant to parents than changes in the child's psychological well-being (if the comments of the children were solicited, would they have reported changes in the behaviors of their mothers and gains in their own self-understanding?), and that the communication of understanding, respect, and a wish to be of help is not lost upon parents even when they do not sense that it has benefited their children.

The Therapist as Educator

It is not uncommon to find child therapists asked to meet with groups of parents and performing more or less in a tutorial or public relations role. The educational task may be to acquaint parents who are considering mental health services for their children with what they can expect should they decide to contact a private practitioner or an agency: what services are offered, what functions are performed by members of different disciplines, and what the routine procedures are. Alternatively, the talk may be about some aspect of parenting or childhood disorder.

Psychotherapy, behavior therapy, and other treatments come under the heading of secondary prevention, the amelioration of disorders that exist. Primary prevention refers to "preventing the *development* of disorders and promoting emotional well-being and psychological health" (Zax & Cowen, 1972, pp. 447–448). These goals are not mutually exclusive, but a reasonable argument is made that professionals should attempt to bring about constructive changes within organizations or the society so that the conditions that foster disorder are eradicated and policies that create a self-fulfilling citizenry are enacted (Jason & Glenwick, 1980).

Within the context of the principles of psychotherapy, primary prevention is somewhat addressed by urging that these principles be made known and implemented in relationships of all kinds, not only professional psychotherapy. Were people helped to communicate, under conditions where it was appropriate to do so, their understanding of others, their respect for them, and their wish to be of help, this world would undoubtedly be a better place. Changing environmental circumstances that elicit deviant behaviors (Principle VI) can afford help to large numbers of the population by eliminating institutional or social practices that are resented and perceived as unjust.

In other words, if people were made aware of the principles of psychotherapy and were encouraged to practice these principles, they might be expected to produce favorable effects on the mental health climates of their communities. And if professionals wished to have their skills produce the widest impact, they would direct some of their energies to the shaping of public policies and changes. For example, a therapist was asked by a principal to do something about the unruly behaviors of the children in his school. They were breaking rules about not talking in the halls and in the cafeteria in such numbers that they were putting a severe strain on the school's detention facilities. In this case, which might be preferable: a behavioral management program for the children, or a reevaluation by the principal and the faculty of their regulations?

A speakers' bureau is a time-honored service of mental health chapters and professional organizations. By contacting such bureaus, groups of parents can acquire a speaker who will address them about a topic of mutual interest. Ordinarily, these talks are not very long, and ample time is set aside for questions and answers and discussion. The primary goal of the speaker is to be informative.

In accepting such a responsibility, therapists are ethically obligated to assess their qualifications to deal adequately with the topic requested. Some topics may be controversial, both within and outside the profession. A topic frequently requested has to do with the reasons why children do not succeed in school. For years some professionals told the public that many children were academic underachievers because they were psychologically in conflict, emotionally disturbed, or unmotivated. Other professionals talk about learning disabilities, perceptual handicaps, minimal brain damage, and specific developmental disorders. Still others emphasize cultural deprivation, parental involvement in their children's education, inappropriate teaching methods and resources, poverty, the structure of the classroom, and the psychological climate of the school and community. Very likely there will be parents who will ask for clarification of these terms and who will wonder what conclusions have been reached within the profession and by the speaker. In agreeing to speak publicly, therapists assume obligations to their profession, the public, and themselves to present the best available information in a responsible manner.

Though the major aim is to convey information, there is frequently the hope that attitudes and behaviors of parents that are harmful to their children will be influenced for the better. The research in support of talks to parents has been questioned. Brim (1961) surveyed results and found some positive effects and no clear conclusions. Some 20 years later, evaluations of the research in this area continued to be encouraging, though critical: positive effects do seem to occur in the training of parents with some programs, but the measures of variables are of uncertain reliability and validity; control groups are seldom used; and there is rarely any follow-up to determine if the changes in the parents are lasting (Johnson & Geller, 1980; Rowbury & Baer, 1980).

Similar conclusions have been made after surveys of research with parent self-help groups and the use of the mass media to influence behaviors and attitudes (Peterson & Roberts, 1986), and of training programs used to increase the effectiveness of parents and teachers (Durlak & Jason, 1984). Nevertheless such programs do continue, and it can be argued that if they accomplish nothing else, they at least affirm the importance of certain behaviors, the disclosure of feelings and concerns, the child, and the role of the parents in affecting the child (Kessler, 1988).

Kahn (1968) conceded that merely presenting information to parents may not be especially helpful, but he believed that studies in industrial psychology afforded some clues as to what could make these talks more likely to bring about positive changes. One suggestion was that such talks be given to groups that have a continuing membership, rather than a group that assembles only to hear the speaker; continuity of the audience enables the information to be discussed and rediscussed by the members long after the speaker has left, thus providing opportunities for the repetition, clarification, and reinforcement of the message.

A second suggestion was to allow ample time not only for questions and group discussion, but also for the development of some group consensus about implications of the message for changes in behaviors. If the group is helped to participate in arriving at decisions about what behaviors and attitudes are desirable, it is more likely that changes will be effected. A third recommendation was that group members plan for time to hear reports about the results of their efforts to implement changes in attitudes and behaviors. Instituting this procedure makes it probable there will be efforts at implementation, allows the group to support one another in the performance of new roles, and rewards members who are successful.

These suggestions are relevant not only to the handling of public addresses, but also to group counseling of parents. There are a number of training programs for parents (including Gordon's Parent Effectiveness Training, which emphasizes the acquisition of empathic responding by parents, and Patterson's behavioral approach to assist parents in rewarding and disciplining their children), many of which have highly specific aims—dealing with parental separation and divorce, preparing the child for medical procedures, or coping with grief or certain transitions—and materials. Harman and Brim (1980) noted that the most effective parent programs require parental involvement for 1 1/2 to 2 years, hardly a casual undertaking by anyone, and a sobering reminder that although changes can be brought about in a single session, they are more apt to require a considerable investment and involvement.

More in the area of secondary prevention are therapists who meet with groups of parents who are in the process of applying for services for their children. These groups may be referred to as "orientation" or "intake" or by some other name, but they manage to serve a variety of purposes. They may enable the therapist to gauge the urgency of the problem and to offer some helpful bits of advice. In addition to their primary purpose of presenting an information package, such gatherings make parents immediately aware that other parents have similar concerns. This knowledge alone is often very reassuring and helps give parents some perspective on their difficulties. As one mother expressed it: "I guess when you hear the troubles that other people have, you remember what somebody said about troubles . . . that if they were like laundry and we could hang 'em all out on a line, everybody'd run to get their own."

Parents whose children have chronic problems may be helped by the therapist to band together into self-help groups. Such organizations exist for parents of autistic, learning disabled, and mentally retarded youngsters, and in some locales for conditions such as Tourette's disorder. These groups gather together to learn what is new in the field, to pressure funding bodies for treatment programs for their children, to sponsor educational conventions, to counsel one another and the general public about their needs, and to work with professionals to ensure that the disorders are given attention and support. Although it is not easy to document the effectiveness of parent self-help groups through research, there is no question of their importance in maintaining the dignity and self-respect of parents (Peterson & Roberts, 1986; Standifer, 1964). Child therapists should be knowledgeable about the parent organizations in their communities, since therapists may be of assistance to them, as well as their being of assistance to therapists and their clients.

Implicitly and explicitly, we have been emphasizing throughout this book the belief that most parents are responsible adults who wish to cooperate in doing what is best for their children. Some therapists take this conviction a step further and try to train parents to play a primary therapeutic role in modifying behaviors or treating their disturbed sons and daughters. It may be recalled that Freud (1959) did not actually treat Little Hans; he supervised by mail the father's analysis of the boy. Though Freud's pioneering effort was exceptional, there are systematic training programs to teach parents to function as psychotherapists and behavior therapists. Guerney (1964) described an educational program called "filial therapy," which aimed to train parents to serve as psychotherapists for their youngsters. The parents were trained in groups to perform Rogerian play therapy. Their progress was monitored, and once treatment of their children began, they reported regularly to the group for supervision and assistance. Similarly, behavior therapists, in order to modify undesirable behaviors as they naturally occur and to maintain gains achieved in their training programs, train parents to perform as behavior modifiers. Both the TEACCH program in North Carolina (Mesibov & Dawson, 1986) and Lovaas's program (1987) in California require the involvement and training of parents as cotherapists for their autistic children.

As already suggested, to some extent child psychotherapists play the role of educator with all the parents and children that they see, regardless of how they may conceive of their major role and function. In fact, if they are being responsive to the needs of their clients, it is difficult to see how they can avoid being at times a consultant, at times a therapist, and at times an educator. The demarcations between these different roles and functions are somewhat artificial and arbitrary. What is important is not that they be rigidly respected and adhered to, but that therapists be sensitive to those they serve and perform in accord with the principles of psychotherapy.

10
Family Therapy

Besides acting in a consultative role with parents and/or providing parents with their own therapy, therapists find many occasions in which it is beneficial to involve parents actively within the child's treatment. Fristad and Clayton (1991) interviewed the parents of 98 families who referred a school-age child for treatment at an outpatient psychology clinic; 89% had elevated scores on a measure of family dysfunction. Furthermore, the families of children being referred for conduct problems reported more family dysfunction than did the families of children referred for mood disorders. It is frequently the case that a child's psychological problems coexist with a variety of family problems. Where this is the case, involvement of the family in treatment is advisable.

Two family treatment formats will be examined in this chapter. The first format involves inclusion of the parents and/or other family members in all or many of the child's sessions; however, the focus remains on the child as the client, and the family sessions are spent facilitating the family as a whole in aiding in the diminishment of the child's problems. For instance, a child's fears may currently be reinforced by the protectiveness of the parents. To decrease the parents' protectiveness will ultimately diminish the secondary gain a child may be getting by being fearful. This type of family treatment might be referred to as working "from the inside outward" or from the child to the family (Ackerman, Papp, & Prosky, 1970). The second family treatment format is so-called traditional family therapy, in which the family as a whole is seen as the client, and the focus of treatment is not specifically on the child and the child's problems. Ackerman et al. (1970) refer to this form of family treatment as working "from the outside inward."

In both forms of family treatment, one of the ultimate goals is the alleviation of the child's presenting problems. The first approach focuses directly on the child's problem as an end in itself, whereas the second focuses on family dynamics and treats the child's problem as a manifestation of larger family problems (for example, a child may be acting out to divert the parents' attention from their own marital conflict). When the family problems are corrected, the child's problem is expected to diminish. One approach uses a magnifying lens that allows the highlighting of a specific element (in this case, the child) within the group, and the other uses a wide-angle lens that allows for viewing the entire system and how the various parts interact as a whole unit. Each of these approaches to involving family members in treatment has specific issues attached to it. In the remainder of this chapter, some of these issues will be examined.

Child-Focused Family Therapy

Child-focused family therapy can be initiated in two ways. Sometimes after the child has been seen in individual treatment for a while, the therapist decides that regular involvement of family members will be beneficial. At other times, the family is clearly and regularly involved in treatment (which is focused toward the child's problem) from the earliest phases of treatment.

Involving Family Members in Ongoing Child Treatment

When a child has been seen for some time in individual psychotherapy and there is a desire to include parents or other family members, it is important to prepare the child for this change. Sometimes the inclusion of family members is requested by the child; however, it is far more frequent that the therapist initiates the change. When the family treatment format is the therapist's idea, it is important to give the child a clear rationale for why the change in treatment formats is occurring. The rationale should ideally include elements that emphasize advantages to the child and minimize the child's anxieties about making the change.

Some of the common concerns children have about a change from individual treatment to a family treatment format are (1) that the child will no longer have the special attention of the therapist; (2) what information will be shared by the therapist with family members (confidentiality issues); (3) that the therapist will side with other family members against the child; (4) that information or half-truths the child has shared with the therapist will be contradicted by family members; (5) that family members will share negative things about the child with the therapist, thus causing the therapist to regard the child in a less favorable light; and (6) that other family problems that heretofore have not been a part of treatment might become involved (for example, parental alcoholism or conflicts). Although a therapist can assure the child about some of these worries (such as how confidential material will be handled), it is impossible to avert all of these concerns. The therapist, however, needs to be alert to the emergence of these issues and concerns both before and after family treatment has begun.

For children who have been in long-term individual treatment, there may need to be more time given to preparing the child for the change in treatment format. In such cases, it may be beneficial to have a formal termination of the one-on-one relationship with the therapist before changing to family treatment. Recontracting with the child is another important way for the transition to be made from individual to family treatment; certain goals of individual treatment may be assessed as completed, and new goals involving the family are established.

Obviously, the child is not the only one in the family who will be experiencing a change in the status quo as family treatment begins, and it is not only the child who may have reservations about this change. Thus, just as deliberate thought is given to introducing the change in treatment formats to the child, so should such preparations be given to the parents or other family members who will be included in treatment. Parents who have become comfortable with turning over the major responsibility for their child's treatment to the therapist may be reluctant to assume more responsibility for their child's problems. Other concerns that parents often have include that they will be blamed for the child's problem, that the therapist will be judgmental of their parenting or be able to see its inadequacy firsthand, and that family problems not identified previously may become known. One way of involving reluctant parents is to define their role as assisting the therapist in helping the child. Thus, they are viewed as experts on their own child and as potential assistants to the therapist in alleviating the child's problems. The initial joint family meeting should allow time for family members and the child to discuss their concerns about the new treatment format and for recontracting to take place. Each family member should have some basic understanding of her or his role in the treatment process and of the ways in which her or his presence is beneficial.

Finally, it should be noted that there are other versions of combining individual and family treatment than stopping individual treatment to do family treatment. These could take the form of alternating individual and family sessions, or meeting three times a month with the child and once a month with the family as a whole. (The reverse could also be true—meeting with the family three times a month and with the child once.) The therapist may want only parents and the identified child client involved in the family treatment and not siblings; in other cases, a sibling might join in the child's treatment (especially where the sibling relationship is one of the foci of treatment). In cases where parental separation or divorce is an issue, inclusion of the entire sibling system with or without the parents may be beneficial for at least a short period of time. Such meetings would allow the therapist to encourage the siblings to support one another during this difficult time for the family.

When discussing family therapy and involving parents in a child's treatment, it is important to realize that there are many configurations of parents and families in existence today. Thus, *parents* and *family* need to be flexibly defined to include those adults who function as parent figures to the child or those persons in the child's life who function as family members. Besides the traditional married mother and father, *parents* could be defined to include divorced parents who continue to co-parent, a mother and her live-in male friend who actively interacts with the child, biological parents and stepparents, and a single mother accompanied by a grandmother who lives with the family and is a primary caretaker of the child. There will also be many cases in which there is only one parent available. Additionally, although holding family treatment sessions with divorced parents is often complicated, in some cases it might be helpful. It is more likely, however, that separate family sessions would be conducted with the mother and child(ren) and the father and child(ren). Finally, some cultures have informal boundaries around the nuclear family and quite naturally include extended family members or even nonrelated persons as "family." The definitions of *parents* and *family* need to be individually determined on a case-by-case basis, and the therapist should be prepared to expand definitions beyond what is typical.

Involving Family Members in Child Treatment from the Beginning

Clarkin, Frances, and Glick (1981) provide an excellent discussion of how to make the decision about whether family treatment is indicated in a specific case. There are many cases in which a child's problem could be addressed most effectively in a family treatment format from the very beginning. The first is when the child is young, especially of preschool or early school age. With such young children, their reliance on their parents is intense, as is the impact the parents have on them. Because a young child is not as verbally capable as an older child, it is often from the parents that the therapist must learn how the child is doing from week to week. It is also with the youngest of children that treatment may primarily involve parent consultation and the training of parents in behavioral management principles. In fact, with the youngest of children and where the parents are relatively healthy and accurate reporters of their child's experience, the therapist may only meet with the parents. During these meetings, a plan can be constructed that the parents are to carry out at home with the child. Subsequent sessions are used to evaluate and modify, if necessary, the parent-directed plan until the presenting problem is managed. Examples of problem behaviors of young children that can often be treated through the parents without the therapist meeting the child include eating, toileting, sleeping, and separation problems.

The second situation in which the family treatment format is often beneficial from the very beginning involves child problems that include other family members. Thus, when relationship problems with family members are a primary part of the child's symptom picture, meeting with the entire family or pertinent family members instead of with the child alone may be the most productive format to use. Although beginning with such treatment does not usually require the degree of advance preparation needed when replacing a child's ongoing individual treatment (as described above), there still needs to be attention paid to providing all members concerned with a rationale for why the family treatment format is recommended.

The most common problems that arise in trying to get families to participate in family treatment from the beginning are in involving the father and involving the siblings. It is almost always the case that the mother initiates treatment for a child, and that the father is the family member who is most likely to resist involvement in family therapy. Sometimes father absences are due to practical issues, such as the scheduling of sessions when the father is working. Therapists need to be mindful and flexible, if possible, regarding scheduling at alternative times, as these times alone may allow a father or other family members to be included. Sometimes it is the case that the mother subtly discourages the father from attending. Perhaps she is aware that he has a different opinion of the problem than she does, or perhaps she feels it is her responsibility to take care of issues related to the children. If a mother hesitates to talk to the father about joining family treatment, the therapist may offer to do so. Even if the father continues to resist involvement in therapy, the therapist will have gathered some important diagnostic information from the interaction.

Sometimes fathers are defensive about attending family treatment because they have values against seeking outside help. This is particularly true in some cultures in which the father is viewed as the head of the house and the one to keep everything in order. Still other fathers regard issues with children to be their wives' purview; thus, their reluctance to be involved in a child's treatment is probably representative of their lack of involvement in the child's life in other areas. Getting such a father involved in family treatment may be a significant intervention in and of itself. In all fairness, many fathers are very willing to be involved in their child's treatment, and it is sometimes the case that the mother is hesitant to be involved. Teismann (1980) describes various convening strategies that can be utilized to get reluctant family members involved in family treatment.

Sometimes parents raise objections to the inclusion of siblings in family treatment. They often do not understand how the siblings' involvement will be beneficial, but once they have been given a rationale, it becomes a nonissue. Some parents, however, persist in their belief that siblings should not be involved. When this occurs, typically the first concern is that sensitive information that has not been shared with the sibling(s) will be revealed. An example would be sharing with younger siblings the parents' worry that a teenager in the family has been experimenting with drugs or has been sexually active. Such a concern on the part of parents may be legitimate, but sometimes it may be an overreaction. To determine if this is occurring and how to proceed, a separate meeting with only the parents and the therapist may be needed before it can be determined who will attend family sessions. Another type of objection raised to the inclusion of siblings occurs when particular children in the family are considered either "bad" or "good." In such cases, parents may be reluctant to "contaminate" a good sibling by exposing that child to the bad deeds and behaviors of a problem child.

A dynamic that is sometimes present in families in which there is a problem child is that the parents come to idealize the other child(ren); they do not have the emotional energy to deal with any more problems or the thought that their identified child's problems are symptomatic of family issues rather than issues specific to that one child. Usually non-problematic siblings are aware of the behaviors and issues of the problem sibling (and the conflictual interactions with the parents as a result), and these children are never quite as ideal as their parents want to believe. In fact, the idealization and scapegoating of children by parents probably gets played out in multiple interactions within the family and may contribute to the problems it presents.

If parents persist in resisting the idea that a sibling be involved, a therapist can proceed in several ways. The first is to allow the sibling not to attend family sessions, but again present a rationale for inclusion once issues come up involving the sibling or the family as a whole. A second strategy is to request the involvement of the sibling on a short-term basis (several sessions), with the primary aim being to collect diagnostic information and to get the sibling's view of what is going on in the family. After these initial sessions, it may be clearer to everyone whether the sibling should continue to be involved in future family sessions.

Although the therapist (and sometimes the family) may request that the family treatment format be used from the very beginning, there are times when it may be beneficial for individual child treatment to replace the family sessions or for individual child sessions to be conducted concurrently. This may be particularly true with older children, and with a child of any age who is having a particularly difficult time talking about issues in front of family members. It is also unfortunately true that family therapy has to be discontinued at times because of extreme psychological dysfunction in one or both of the parents. In such cases, they may not be able to contribute productively to family treatment.

Family-Focused Family Therapy

Family-focused family therapy involves treatment of the family system as a whole; this form of family treatment is often called "traditional" family therapy. In traditional family therapy, the family is the client, not the child. Maintenance (and, possibly, the cause) of the child's symptoms is seen as integrally tied to family functioning. Furthermore, it is believed that as family functioning is constructively enhanced, the child's symptomatology will decrease. Although traditional family therapy can be conducted without all family members present, it is usually preferred (and may be required) that all members of the family attend all sessions. Traditional family therapy is based on very specific conceptualizations that originate in systems theory.

Schools of Family Therapy

There are currently six major schools of family therapy: structural, strategic, family-of-origin (transgenerational), experiential, behavioral, and psychodynamic (Brown & Christensen, 1986; Hansen & L'Abate, 1982). The *structural model* is primarily represented by Salvador Minuchin (Minuchin, 1974; Minuchin & Fishman, 1981; Minuchin, Rosman, & Baker, 1978), and is so named because of the model's emphasis on the structure of the family. Structure incorporates such concepts as subsystems, boundaries, roles, enmeshment-disengagement, and rigidity-flexibility. The *strategic model* is represented by Jay Haley, Cloe Madanes, Paul Watzlawick, and Mara Palazzoli-Selvini (Haley, 1976, 1984; Madanes, 1981; Palazzoli-Selvini, Boscolo, Cecchin, & Prata, 1978; Watzlawick, Weakland, & Fisch, 1974). Strategic family therapy is very problem oriented, with the therapist devising various strategies to stimulate change in the family. This particular model is concerned primarily with symptoms, metaphors, hierarchy, and power and is probably best known for its controversial use of paradoxical and reactance techniques with families.

The *family-of-origin* or *transgenerational model* of family therapy is represented by the work of Murray Bowen, Ivan Boszormenyi-Nagy, James Framo, and Michael Kerr (Boszormenyi-Nagy & Framo, 1965; Boszormenyi-Nagy & Spark, 1973; Bowen, 1978; Framo, 1982, 1992; Kerr & Bowen, 1988). As its name implies, the transgenerational model is interested in how patterns of family interaction are passed down from one generation to the other. Though the intervention is necessarily in the present, understanding of this present is thought to be gained through examination of the past cross-generational dynamics and how they continue to be played out in the current generation. Triangulation, family projection processes, and differentiation are among the key concepts of the family-of-origin model. The *experiential model* of family therapy is based on the ideas of Virginia Satir, Carl Whitaker, and Walker Kempler (Kempler, 1981; Neill & Kniskern, 1982; Satir, 1967, 1972; Satir, Stachowiak, & Taschman, 1975; Whitaker & Napier, 1978). This model emphasizes the subjective feelings, values, and perceptions of family members; there is more focus on promoting growth and honesty among members than there is on eliminating symptoms. Issues such as affect, self-esteem, and clear, open communication are the basis of the experiential approach. This approach believes that each family member can contribute to better family functioning if that member is in touch with herself or himself, accepts responsibility, and honestly communicates with other family members.

The *behavioral model* of family therapy emphasizes the use of learning principles and behavioral management interventions. The primary representatives of this particular model of family therapy are Gerald Patterson and James Alexander (Alexander & Parsons, 1982; Patterson, 1971, 1980). Behavioral family therapy stresses restructuring through the altering of contingent interactions, especially by parent training and the use of homework assignments. Particular attention is paid to the family patterns that are maintaining or reinforcing dysfunctional behavior. *The psychodynamic model* of family therapy is based on the ideas of Nathan Ackerman (Ackerman, 1958, 1966; Bloch & Simon, 1982). This approach tends to focus more on intrapsychic variables than many other family therapy models; however, there is still an appreciation that the individual exists within the social context of the family. Giving interpretations, promoting emotional reexperiencing, and clarifying roles are the major procedures of the therapist in the psychodynamic model.

Each of these six schools emphasizes different aspects of systems theory in its own particular approach to family therapy. Recently there have been attempts to mesh various aspects of these schools into an integrated model (Breunlin, Schwartz, & Kune-Karrer, 1992; Lebow, 1984; Pinsof, 1983). The idea of an integrated model is attractive because there are many concepts that are held in common among the various schools of family therapy, and since an integrated model may be more effective than its constituents.

The Major Concepts of an Integrated Systems Theory

A system is a group of interdependent parts; in this case the family is the system, and the individual family members form the interdependent components. To understand systems theory one must look at the larger picture—the whole, instead of the part. The parts are examined in how they interact with one another within the system. The training of clinicians remains primarily individually focused, so that a switch to systems thinking often requires putting aside basically held viewpoints. Systems theory provides an ideology that has spawned a variety of procedures for therapy Although it is customary to utilize systems ideology while working with an entire family or a couple, it is possible to do "family therapy" with only one person present. This is because family therapy is a way of thinking about problems and change, and not merely a collection of techniques or methods.

Context

Individuals are seen as existing within particular situations and circumstances that influence their functioning. The family provides a context for its individual family members, and the neighborhood, culture, and socioeconomic status provide the family system a context within which it functions. Rather than emphasizing intrapsychic dynamics, systems theory examines how one's context affects one's functioning.

Related to the notion of context, systems theory does not have established notions of what is healthy and sick behavior. Behavior that does not "work" in one context (in other words, is sick), may work in another (and thus be healthy). For instance, parents whose rigid rules for their 14-year-old son do not allow him to do much socializing with peers outside of organized events may be regarded by some therapists as infantalizing and inhibiting the developmental process of their son. If their restrictions are viewed, however, within the context of an inner-city housing project in which gangs prey on young men, shootings are frequent, and people have to deal with the real threat of violence every time they step out their front doors, such behavior can also be seen as functional. Thus, for systems theorists, assessment includes looking beyond specific problems to the context in which they exist. Because behaviors are then relative, systems theorists tend to de-emphasize the formal use of diagnoses. Most diagnostic systems that are popularly used are nomenclatures for individuals and not systems: therefore, they cannot be applied easily to describe system functioning.

Furthermore, systems theorists see diagnostic systems as being fairly value laden. What the public sees as unhealthy, pathological behavior is, when viewed within the system or context in which it is occurring, not an individual's pathology but a system's dysfunction. An example is the teenager who has stopped attending school in order to care for younger siblings while her single-parent mother works. The school and truancy officer may label this child as unmotivated, defiant, and so forth. Her school absences are serving an important function for the family, however, and within the family there may be little concern that the teen's behavior is unusual. In cases like this, the child's behavior may never be seen as abnormal or problematic by the family until it comes under public scrutiny; even then, some families will still disagree with the external evaluator that there is anything about which to be concerned. With the systems theory model, behaviors and problems are viewed within a context that includes family, ethnic, racial, cultural, religious, and regional values. McGoldrick, Pearce, and Giordano (1982) provide an excellent discussion of the role of these contextually bound values in work with families.

When performing a contextual assessment, it is necessary to examine the variety of contexts within which a child exists. Figure 10–1 presents various levels of a contextual analysis. At the most minute level are the intrapersonal characteristics that are specific to the child; these could include such things as learning disabilities, chronic illness, gender, temperament, and social skills. At the next level, that of interpersonal dyads, the child relates to primary persons such as parents and siblings. The child, parents, and siblings exist in the transactional context of the family, which is the next level. The transactional level of analysis is the primary focus of most family therapists; the family at this level can be either nuclear or extended. There is a larger context in which the family exists: the environmental or ecological level of analysis, which contains cultural, ethnic, religious, racial and economic influences. Factors such as social support networks and stressors (father losing his job, a fire destroying the family's home, and the like) are also elements of the ecological level. It is important from a systems perspective to conduct a multicontextual analysis that examines assets and strengths as well as deficits and stressors at each of the various levels. As one examines the various levels of context, all information needs to be put in an even larger context, that of the developmental stage of the family.

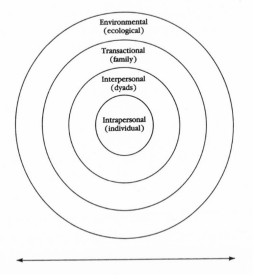

Figure 10–1
Levels of Contextual Analysis Within a Developmental Timeframe

Family Life Cycle

Just as the child has specific characteristics that are related to his or her age and developmental stage, so does the family. The family's developmental life is called the *family life cycle*. Its major stages are (1) forming a couple relationship (early marriage), (2) having a child, (3) families with preschool children, (4) families with school-age children, (5) families with teenagers, (6) families with children leaving home ("launching" families), (6) postparental families ("empty nest"), and (7) aging families (retirement). Each developmental stage brings normal changes and will require flexibility and accommodation on the part of the family. If the family can adapt to the new needs of family members at each stage, it will weather these transitions with a minimum of stress. If it does not adjust to new developmental needs, however, then conflict is likely. For instance, parental rules that worked effectively for 6- and 8-year-olds will not be as effective with 15-year-olds. Though one would expect some independence-dependence issues in any family with adolescents, in a rigid family these issues are likely to be much more conflictual. A family assessment would not be complete if it did not account for the particular developmental stage in which the family finds itself; what would appear to be pathological at one stage may be normal or expected at another stage. Carter and McGoldrick (1980) provide a detailed discussion of the concept of the family life cycle and its relationship to therapy with families.

An "out of time" (at the wrong chronological time in the family's life cycle) developmental change will usually cause more stress on the family system than one that occurs at an ordinary or predictable time. Examples would be the death of a parent while there are still children at home, or the pregnancy of a teenager. If either of these occurrences happened at another time in the family's life cycle, they would cause less stress. The death of a 35-year-old father will be experienced differently by a family than if he was 70 years old. Likewise, a daughter's pregnancy as a teenager is often extremely stressful for a family, whereas her planned pregnancy at 26 years may be an occasion for great celebration.

When examining family stressors, it is important to note that change is almost always a stressor for systems. Even positive change (the birth of a first child that was planned) requires accommodation on the part of family members. In this case, the excitement of the parents related to having their first child is offset by stresses on the parents' relationship (less private time as a couple, possible economic stresses as the mother quits her job, fatigue associated with sleepless nights, and so forth). Likewise, a promotion that brings more money into a family and allows for luxuries may also have negative consequences if the working parent has to handle more responsibility at work, put in more hours, and travel out of town on business. Thus, even positive changes need to be examined for possible stresses upon a family.

Causality

Causality, or what causes what, is a complex question for family therapists. Rather than espousing a linear causality model (in which A causes B), systems theorists think of multiple causalities and causality that is circular in nature. Figure 10–2 depicts a simplified example of circular causality. Because everyone is assumed to be affected by and affecting everyone else in the family, issues such as blame are regarded as unproductive. Family members, like most people, however, naturally think of causality in a linear way; thus, this is a difficult concept to get across to families. The tendency is to want to "discover" what the cause is, or who is responsible.

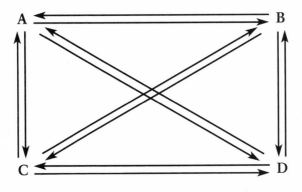

Figure 10–2
Models of Causality

Concepts that represent circular causality are reciprocity, interdependence, and mutuality. Because there is a belief that everyone is influenced by and can influence everyone in the family, various interventions that target different aspects of the family or different persons in the family may all have the same end result: a rock can be tossed in a pond at various points, yet no matter where it lands it will cause ripples throughout the pond. Although it is often more complicated, family therapy can be conducted with a few members or even with an individual. The essential element determining whether work with an individual or a subsystem will successfully bring about system changes is whether that individual or family subsystem is strong enough to withstand powerful forces within the family system that pull for the status quo or seek to minimize change.

Homeostasis

As used in family therapy, the concept of homeostasis is credited to the research group from the Mental Research Institute in Palo Alto (Watzlawick,

Beavin, & Jackson, 1967). Homeostasis is a process by which a family works to maintain the status quo. This process is activated when a family experiences anxiety and threat regarding possible or real change. Homeostatic mechanisms are critical and often are positive, as when a family weathers an acute crisis. In such a situation they serve to stabilize the family and eventually bring family functioning back to the norm. There are times, however, when a family's homeostatic mechanisms block change that would be beneficial and healthy for the family.

An example of such change would be that associated with normal developmental transitions. For instance, in a particular family, a mother has come to expect emotional support from her teenage son whenever she and her husband have a conflict. As the son prepares to leave the family to go off to college, his potential absence will unsettle the family dynamics, and various mechanisms will be played out that pull for the maintenance of the status quo. Perhaps the son will feel guilty and responsible for his mother (at her urging, if only covertly) and change his mind about leaving, deciding to work for a year to save up more money for college. Or the father will suddenly find an excellent job for his son within the community so that he can continue to live at home. In whatever way the homeostatic mechanisms get played out, the end result is that the son is prohibited from progressing in a developmentally appropriate manner. Homeostasis is also seen in the case of the child who is successfully treated in an inpatient program, yet loses all the gains that were made after being home for a while, eventually requiring another hospitalization.

As mentioned before, homeostatic mechanisms are not always negative for a system. In fact, a system requires both homeostatic (the pull for stability and the status quo) and heterogenetic (the pull for growth and change) processes. When the former predominates, the system is rigid in its problem solving and in dealing with change; however, when the latter predominates, the system can be chaotic and lack sufficient stability to allow family members a sense of safety. Healthy systems need to be able to provide both stability and growth.

Resistance

Although other theoretical models view resistance in various ways, the systems model would likely view it as anxiety and threat on the part of one or more persons in the system. This anxiety or threat triggers homeostatic processes that are against change and for maintenance of the status quo. A critical assessment task when doing family therapy is to determine the potential for resistance by each family member and the family as a whole. A thorough assessment would determine, for instance, what each family member would have to gain or lose if desired therapeutic changes were achieved. Resistance can come from unlikely sources, with an example being the mother who is presenting her family with complaints that her son is unmanageable and that her husband is never home to help her with the son. A possible therapeutic goal in this case would be to get the father more involved in parenting the son in both a positive and a restrictive way. For instance, therapeutic homework assignments can be devised to get father and son to participate in activities together while the father is also put in charge of the son's schoolwork done at home.

Though all this sounds positive and relieving of the mother's original complaints, it is possible that the mother may eventually be threatened by the developing closeness of her son and husband (especially if she does not have such closeness with her husband), or she may get anxious and sabotage the father's efforts to set limits on the son because she feels he is too strict. This example also illustrates the ripple effects that change in one part of a system can have on other parts of the system.

When dealing with systems, it is wise to appreciate the power of families to resist change (Anderson & Stewart, 1983). Even if the status quo is currently unsatisfactory for the family, at least it is predictable and does not require dealing with the unknown. A good therapist will anticipate anxieties and threats related to change, build in interventions to allay these fears, and anticipate that all in the family will be affected by even small changes in part of it. In the example given above, the therapist might have minimized the mother's anxieties by bolstering the parents' relationship and getting the parents to discuss mutually acceptable methods of dealing with their son.

Flexibility

As mentioned in the discussion regarding the family life cycle, there will be many events facing a family that will require adaptation on its part. It is through this accommodation that the family is able to deal with stress and proceed along the family life cycle; too much rigidity is manifested in poor problem solving and conflict management. This is often the case because the family persists in using the same processes that have not been successful in the past. These processes often occur with enough regularity that the family therapist can discern repetitive patterns that signal ineffective coping. Helping the family to change its ineffective, repetitive patterns is a major goal of family therapy. This is accomplished by educating (teaching alternative behaviors), pointing out patterns (interpreting), modeling (if family members are having trouble using the alternative behaviors), and by structured activities that require family members to behave differently. Olson, Russell, and Sprenkle (1979) refer to this flexibility/rigidity dimension as "adaptability" and have included it as one of three major dimensions in their family assessment instrument, the Family Adaptability and Cohesion Evaluation Scale (FACES). This instrument is one of the most popularly used family questionnaires and is currently in its third edition (Olson, Portner, & Lavee, 1985).

Communication

Another family variable that is very predictive of a family's ability to solve problems and cope with stress is communication. Family therapists believe there are multiple ways that family members communicate important messages, and that many of these ways are nonverbal in nature. There is often as much attention paid by the family therapist to what is said without words as to what is said with them. This interest in the subtle, covert methods of communicating and sending messages is compatible with an emphasis on the *process* as well as the *content* of family interactions. Thus, while the family therapist listens to the verbalizations that are shared by family members, he or she is as interested (or more so) in how the communications are sent, who speaks for whom, whether the communication is received or discounted, who aligns with whom on a particular issue, voice intonation, facial and body gestures, and so forth. Although more subtle and more difficult to catch, these nonverbal processes (metacommunication, or communication about a communication) provide valuable assessment information to the therapist working with a family.

Satir (1967) has discussed communication as open or closed, and as congruent or incongruent. Open communications are honest, sincere, and based on an individual's positive self-esteem. Families with open communications can tolerate differences and provide growth-enhancing opportunities for family members. In contrast, closed communications are defensive, critical, cautious and exist in a family that does not tolerate different opinions. If a family member should deviate from the family norm, then that family member is made to feel wrong, "crazy", or guilty. Thus, such a family will squash individual growth and independence.

Communications occur at two levels—overt and covert. When what is said (the overt process) does not match what is felt (as inferred from one's facial expression, or other covert processes), the communication is said to be incongruent. Many family therapists believe there is a significant positive relationship between incongruent communication processes and dysfunction in a family (for example, Satir, 1967). Congruent communications are those in which the overt and covert components match. For the receiver of the communication, congruent communications are less confusing and less likely to be misunderstood. It is important for the therapist to realize that he or she also communicates at multiple levels. Therefore, even though a therapist says, "No, I'm not angry that you missed your appointment", the wrinkled forehead or strain in the voice may well communicate otherwise to the family.

Family Structure

Family structure is a catchall term that incorporates many separate concepts (Minuchin, 1974; Minuchin & Fishman, 1981). Most basically, however, structure has to do with how the family is constituted, relates to one another, and defines roles. Six major elements of family structure will be discussed here. First, varying *boundaries* exist within and around families. There are boundaries around individuals that determine the degree to which one is private and independent in functioning relative to other family members. There are also boundaries around subsystems within families that likewise determine the degree to which others may enter or interact with this particular subsystem. Finally, there are boundaries around the family that determine how isolated and insulated the family is from its environment. Families with strong, rigid boundaries around the family unit are often isolated from external resources and interactions; the family functions as an island unto itself. On the other hand, the family with porous boundaries allows and benefits from interactions with the environment.

Boundaries mark *alliances* and *coalitions* within families. Most family therapists believe that certain coalitions or subsystems should have boundaries marking that particular group as important; for instance, the parental subsystem should have enough of a boundary that the parents can co-parent and solve their own problems without involving the children. Generational blurring occurs when boundaries mark a coalition that extends across generations within the family. When the mother weeps to her daughter about what a cad the father is, she is violating the boundary of the parental subsystem and including the daughter in this subsystem. The daughter more rightfully belongs in the sibling subsystem, and not "up" with her mother trying to function as a comforting spouse. Boundaries are generally considered to be best when they are not too porous (no sense of identity as a self or subsystem) or too rigid (isolated functioning).

A specific version of unclear boundaries involves the concept of *triangulation* (Bowen, 1978). Triangulation is the involvement of a person or thing in the conflict of two other persons that serves to distract or prevent the healthy resolution of the conflict by the two original parties. Generally, triangulation is seen as unhealthy and is to be minimized in families.

A common example of triangulation in families is when a child becomes involved in parental conflict. This involvement can take the form of the child taking one of the parents' sides, mediating the conflict, or distracting the parents by creating or being a problem. Another frequent example is when the mother serves as a go-between for her husband and the children; in this role, she carries messages back and forth between the husband and the children, keeping direct encounters between them to a minimum. This function gets activated when the mother worries about potential conflict between the father and the children, but the end result (despite the mother's possibly good intentions) is to prevent the father and children from resolving their conflicts and working out healthier relationships. It should be recognized that in families, the go-between may not only volunteer for the role but be actively recruited by the other two parties. The role of the go-between can be a very powerful one in a family; however, it is also a very heavy responsibility, as he or she works hard to minimize conflict and keep everyone happy.

The go-between is one of the informal *roles* that families may contain. Formal roles are those that are socially prescribed and obvious, such as parent, daughter, wife, and sister. Family members serve in multiple formal roles; thus, the girl is not only the daughter but also a sister, and the mother is not only a mother but also a wife. When the demands of various roles are in conflict, there will be tension within the individual and within the family. An example is the mother who has now remarried. Because the new stepfather is clearly more invested in his relationship with his wife than he is in parenting his stepchildren, the wife may feel that her wife and mother roles are in conflict, and at times the experience may be akin to having to choose between her new husband and her children.

Family members also have roles outside their families that can conflict with family roles. Thus, the teenager who would rather be a friend to his peers than a son to his parents will cause family conflict when he refuses to participate in the usual Sunday outing with his family in favor of some activity with a friend. There are also informal roles that family members play, including those of go-between, "bad" kid, emotional caretaker, black sheep, scapegoat, and the "fragile" one, among many others. Families will function better if critical roles are clearly defined, yet there must be flexibility in order to adapt to changing times and developmental needs of the family. The parents who could not understand their son's wanting to be with peers rather than with his family are rigidly assigning the son's role in a way that may have been more appropriate when the boy was younger.

Family *rules* are important to assess, as it is the rules of the family that regulate its functioning. As such, rules are integrally attached to power issues. Who makes the rules, who enforces them, and for whom they apply are all diagnostic questions to pursue. As was mentioned before under the section on developmental issues, rules must remain developmentally appropriate as children grow older. Families should have procedures by which rules are periodically evaluated and updated; in order for this to occur, the family system must allow for some degree of questioning of rules and for flexibility. At the same time, rules also need to be relatively predictable, as they provide stability. Rules that are made and not enforced are nonexistent and send very mixed messages to family members.

The issue of power and rules is most noticeable in terms of who in the family makes the rules. This is an area where it is most ideal for parents to work together to come up with reasonable rules with which both can live and, more importantly, that both can enforce. It is sometimes the case that one parent makes the rules and the other is expected to enforce them. If the enforcing parent does not agree with the rules, then there is ample opportunity for sabotaging them or for inconsistent enforcement. Children are quick to pick up on divisive parents and may try to take advantage of the situation. Children also learn when young to discriminate the situations in which rules apply and do not apply. Thus, even young children will soon realize that a particular rule applies when Dad is around, but not when Mom is alone with the child. In such a case, the therapist will hear the complaint from this mother that the child is "out of control," whereas the father has no trouble when the child is with him.

The rules that parents decide to have in their families are often influenced by their own upbringing. Especially when parents feel that their own parents' rules were too harsh or unrealistic, there may be a strong tendency to avoid being like their own parents, and in fact to go to the opposite extreme by having very few rules. Another influence on parental rules and enforcement is that often co-parents react to one another's styles. If a father considers that his wife is too harsh with the children, he may respond by being lenient because he feels sorry for the children and wants to compensate them. When his wife sees his leniency, she tries harder to impose limitations because she feels the children "are running wild." In such an interaction, one can see that over time, the co-parenting styles will become more opposite and extreme. Obviously, this is not an ideal situation for either the children or the parents.

It is also unfortunately the case that in some families the children make the rules, or at least decide whether they are going to abide by them. In such families the parents have a difficult time doing the "hard" part of parenting—setting limits, saying no, enforcing rules, and so on. Often this difficulty on the part of the parents is attributable to their own insecurity about themselves and their relationship with their children. A particularly insecure parent who desperately needs the child's love to compensate for low self-esteem or for feelings of being unloved by his or her spouse will hesitate to upset the child or make the child angry. Obviously, this sends messages to the child that it is all right to thwart the rules, as they will not be enforced. But it is also a heavy emotional burden for a child to carry; a child should not be held responsible for the self-esteem and emotional health of the parent.

Most families will have covert rules that govern some parts of family life. Though family members would deny there is a specific covert rule that is enforced, there would also be agreement that behavior is modified to accommodate the covert rule. An example of such a "silent rule" is that when Mom gets in one of her depressed moods, she is fragile and is not to be confronted about anything. In fact, at such times, all in the family

242 · *Principles of Psychotherapy with Children*

should do whatever possible to protect Mom from anything that might further upset her. Children in this family would likely say that no one has ever told them that their mother is fragile and in need of protection at such times; nevertheless, they would answer with something like, "That's just what you do in my family. Everyone knows not to bother Mom when she's feeling down." Another task of the family therapist is to bring these silent rules out in the open so that the family can examine them and determine whether, in fact, there is a necessity to have such a rule. Covert or silent rules can contribute to dysfunction within the family, because no one is allowed to question something that supposedly does not exist.

The final structural concept to be examined here is that of *enmeshment–disengagement*. Minuchin (1974) has discussed this concept as a continuum, with enmeshment on one end and disengagement on the other. In rough terms, enmeshment–disengagement represents families who are stuck together emotionally (enmeshed) or who are only loosely emotionally connected (disengaged). It is believed by family therapists that neither extreme is very functional, and that families at either extreme have predictable characteristics.

For instance, enmeshed families often have little tolerance for dissension within the family, are isolated from outside interactions, value blind obedience and loyalty, and use denial and projection as primary defenses. These families can look fairly ideal from the outside, but often start to have problems when the children are old enough to have opinions of their own or want to participate more with extrafamilial persons and activities. Dealing with conflict and anger are particularly difficult for these families; a family member is made to feel guilty and disloyal if that member questions the predominant family stance. Rules in such enmeshed families are often rigid and difficult to change, and roles are rigidly defined. In the enmeshed family, priority is given to family membership, with individuality given a lesser emphasis. Thus, dependency on the family is fostered, and independence from the family is discouraged.

The disengaged family, on the other hand, is a collection of individuals whose independence is primary over group membership. This is often not because these are healthy, independent individuals, but because the parents are ineffectual and have forfeited their positions as leaders of the family. As a result, individuals in the family learn that other family members are not necessarily there to meet their needs and cannot be counted on for this. There is thus an extreme lack of dependency in such a family, with the connections among family members being tenuous. Often these families are described as chaotic (having little predictability and leadership), constantly in crisis, and with children who are either out of control or dealing with matters that are beyond their maturity.

The most functional position for a family on this continuum is relatively in the middle. Such families have learned to balance the often conflicting needs of family membership and loyalty with individual growth and independence. In these families there is an interdependency and reliability that is experienced by members. Other members are there to help if needed, yet these families encourage and support the individual growth and development of their members, even if that means the individual is defining himself or herself as more than a member of the family. Across the family developmental life cycle, it will be the case that families may be more on the enmeshed side of the continuum when the children are young, and more on the disengaged side of the continuum when there are teenagers and young adults in the family. To be extreme on either side, however, is typically regarded as dysfunctional.

This particular concept needs to be carefully viewed within a cultural perspective. In some cultures (for example, Jewish, Greek American, or Hispanic), what might be considered unhealthy enmeshment may be the norm for that particular culture. Indeed, all of these family concepts need to be evaluated within their particular ethnic/cultural context; and as such, the norms discussed are relative.

Differentiation

One of the hallmarks of Bowen's (1978) family therapy is the concept of differentiation. Although enmeshment–disengagement is a concept that pertains to whole systems, the concept of differentiation is focused on the individual. Differentiation involves the ability of an individual within a family system to function as a separate real self. For Bowen, this means that the individual is not overly reactive to the family system. *Reactivity* is an emotional response that does not involve deliberation and choice; it is usually triggered by anxiety. In contrast, *responding* is primarily a rational response. The undifferentiated individual is very other directed, without an internalized sense of individual values and goals. This person reacts automatically on an emotional level to many family situations, and is extremely reliant on others for approval and a pseudo sense of self. The differentiated individual, on the other hand, is not on automatic pilot relative to reactions and does not merely react to external circumstances. This individual makes choices consistent with a sense of self and a set of values and goals. The differentiated person accepts responsibility for self and has a solid sense of self.

It is important to recognize that the concept of differentiation is more than one of independence versus dependence. In fact, often an individual moves away from the family in rather dramatic fashion and is seen as independent of the family. Bowen would say, however, that this person is "cutting off" from the family as an anxiety reaction—that the individual's need to isolate from the family is a very emotional one, not a rational one. In these circumstances, this is not true independence, and the individual will spend a lifetime continuing to react to experiences from the family, even though there is minimal direct contact. The person who has achieved some degree of differentiation may well make choices to be closely involved with the family; however, the quality of that involvement is on an adult-adult basis.

Furthermore, it is a choice and not a reaction to family-generated guilt or paralyzing dependency. A further aspect of Bowen's notion of differentiation is that individuals often select spouses who have similar levels of differentiation. Two persons who are relatively undifferentiated and who have both cut off from their familes of origin may well find solace in one another; however, because neither has a good sense of self and both remain very reliant on others for approval and a sense of self, each looks to the other to fulfill these needs. Obviously, over time the inability of each to meet these "illegitimate" needs of the other adds to feelings of resentment and frustration, and thus the relationship may fall apart. Another scenario for this particular couple would be for them to rely on their children to fulfill these empty spaces in their sense of self. This, of course, is an unrealistic burden to place on children, and ultimately such children evidence symptoms.

Family Projection Process

Another Bowen (1978) concept is that of the family projection process, also known by terms such as "family legacy" and "multigenerational transmission." The basic element of this concept is that families transmit to subsequent generations a variety of issues, values, and beliefs that may be beneficial or detrimental. A clear way to look at this process is to examine the destructive cycle of child abuse, which tends to exist across multiple generations of the same family. The original child abuse deprives a child of a healthy sense of self and an appropriate model for conflict resolution. This "wounded" child grows up to be a parent who is ill equipped to cope with the demands of parenting, thus continuing the intergenerational abuse.

In perhaps less dramatic forms, all families have some elements of the family projection process in effect. Another example is the son growing up in a family where he is clearly expected to follow in his father's and grandfather's footsteps and become a lawyer or take over the family business. If this son has personal interests and aptitudes that are consistent with this family legacy, then there will likely not be significant negative effects. If the son is interested more in artistic endeavors, however, and instead of law school or an MBA program wants to pursue his artistic interests, there is a likelihood of conflict in this family. Another example is the mother who learned that men were not to be trusted when her husband abruptly left her with two young daughters. She will transmit a variety of messages to her daughters, and thus these girls learn in growing up with this mother that they should function independently and never get too close to a man. A case in which the "legacy" is actually an opposite reaction is the father who intensely pushes his son to be the great athlete that he was never able to be; thus, the son is set up to fulfill a need of the father, not necessarily his own need.

The family projection process typically works through the silent and covert rules that were discussed earlier. This makes such processes very difficult to challenge and to examine. Identification and evaluation of these processes is another aim of family therapy, as these processes often are inappropriate for the current generation on which they are enacted.

Family Secrets

Covert rules and family legacies can be organized enough at times to constitute actual family secrets. These secrets can be known to all family members or to only part of the family. In either case, there are serious injunctions against sharing them with others, especially outsiders.

In one example of a family secret, the mother became pregnant by a man who left her after learning of the pregnancy. The father "rescued" the mother by agreeing to marry her and pretending that he had fathered the child. In return, the mother felt an incredible indebtedness to this man, which manifested itself in never challenging him and requiring the children to do the same. She lived in fear that if she upset him, he would leave her and tell of the "illegitimate" pregnancy. The children in the family, not understanding the source of their mother's subservience to their father, resented their forced obedience. This resentment grew as the children became older.

In this particular family, the oldest child, who had very low self-esteem and depression, was the problem. She always felt that her father liked her younger siblings better, and since she had no information to explain this experience, she assumed it was because she was unworthy of his love and attention. Furthermore, she was now entering her teen years and was constantly being bombarded by her mother about the dangers of dating boys. In fact, she was so intimidated by this indoctrination that she chose to isolate herself socially rather than face "scary" situations.

Family secrets can take many forms and even persist across generations. Berg-Cross (1988) differentiated between supportive, protective, manipulative, and avoidant secrets. Supportive secrets are those in which the family hides a failing or weakness of one or more of the family members. The parents agree, for example, to conceal that the father was actually fired from his job or that the mother had an abortion of an unplanned pregnancy. Sometimes supportive secrets are kept within the sibling subsystem, as when a sister promises not to tell the parents that her brother takes drugs or smokes.

Protective secrets are those that are kept from someone because it is deemed to be in their best interest not to know. It used to be common practice for parents to keep a child's adoption a secret, thinking that it was important for the child to feel a natural part of the family. This is not advised practice these days, but such a secret would be an example of a protective secret. Manipulative secrets are those which are kept covert for personal gain; thus, a son-in-law keeps secret his dislike for his father-in-law so that he can maintain a position in the family business. Avoidant secrets, meanwhile, serve to prevent the family from having to deal with unpleasant or anxiety-provoking issues. For example, a family may not share with the therapist that the daughter sleeps in the mother's bed and that the father sleeps in the daughter's room because they do not want to deal with marital problems.

Secrets are often associated with such predictable content areas as sex, money, crime, pregnancies, and illnesses. Though it is not always the aim (or even desirable) to uncover family secrets in therapy, at times their existence impedes progress. There will likewise be cases in which the therapist supports a family secret; for example, there may be no benefit at all to the children in a family discovering that the mother has had an abortion.

With this understanding of some of the theoretical concepts that order and define therapy with families, we are ready to consider the particulars of the work of the family therapist.

11
Conducting Family Therapy

The previous chapter provided a general overview of systems theory as it applies to family therapy. This chapter will discuss issues related to the practice of family therapy. Because no work with individuals or families will be very effective if it is not based in a thorough and accurate assessment, the topic of evaluation and assessment of families will be discussed first.

Assessment in Family Therapy

Family therapists generally take special time early in treatment to assess the individuals in the family and the family as a system. There is a strong belief among family therapists, however, in the necessity for ongoing assessment throughout treatment. In fact, some early interventions may well provide new and valuable assessment information that further refines subsequent interventions. In the family therapy model, assessment and intervention are seen as integrally related. Assessment is not completed after the first sessions, and in fact, premature closure of the assessment process is probably one of the leading causes of poor or mediocre treatment outcomes. Because family systems are complex and are constantly in flux, the therapist best regards assessment as a dynamic task that requires constant attention (Principle I).

Though the assessment of individuals can be complicated, the assessment of families is even more so. Not only must one have some basic understanding of the personalities and motives of each family member, one must also comprehend how the various individuals relate to one another and function as a whole. Although some family therapists emphasize assessment of individual members more (Bowen, Framo) or less (Haley, Minuchin), a thorough assessment includes attention to individuals as well as to the family system. Furthermore, it is our belief that the effective

247

child and family clinician is a generalist who has familiarity with a variety of conceptualizations regarding the development, manifestations, and maintenance of a variety of child and family problems. A national task force that examined issues and concerns regarding the training of child clinicians concluded that such clinicians must be experts in more areas of understanding than must adult therapists (Roberts, Erickson, & Tuma, 1985). The clinician who has developed a broad repertoire of understandings (in short, an integrative psychotherapist) will be open to examine each child's and family's unique characteristics and history. Thus, the therapist does not force assessment material into a narrow model and thereby ignore conflicting material and/or overemphasize supporting material. Just as there is a value in the family therapy literature that the best-functioning families are flexible, the best family therapists also have the capacity to be flexible.

Assessment Dimensions

Just what are the areas of information important to a thorough family assessment? Karpel and Strauss (1983) detail four dimensions of a family assessment: factual, individual, systemic, and ethical. This model of assessment is an excellent example of an integrated assessment approach that examines both individual and systemic variables.

The *factual* dimension includes the usual information that is gathered in a straightforward question-and-answer format. Ages of family members, relationships to one another, addresses, work/school information, educational backgrounds, financial information, marital status, and the like are all examples of factual assessment material.

The *individual* dimension involves the assessment of each individual family member relative to that person's feelings, motives, needs, stress level, strengths, weaknesses, defenses, and so forth. A significant component of an individual assessment is the potential for resistance from that individual. As was discussed in the last chapter, the most effective way to handle resistance is to anticipate it and account for it; thus, at the individual level, the therapist should discern what each family member's motive is for attending family therapy and what each member has to gain or to lose from the family's changing in predictable ways. In a system, one of the subtle potential losses that an individual might experience if the family dynamics change is loss of influence or power. When family relationships are being restructured as part of family therapy, such realignments may be good for the family as a system but very threatening to a particular individual within the family. Therefore, the individual assessment dimension includes characteristics of the individual as well as that individual's unique response to being a member of this family.

The *systemic* dimension of assessment relates to an examination of the relationship issues and larger system dynamics. The various family structural elements that were discussed in the previous chapter (such as coalitions, boundaries, rules, roles, and enmeshment) are examples of systemic assessment material. A thorough systemic evaluation would also include an assessment of the family's communication skills and style, the existence of scapegoating, triangulation, generational blurring, and so forth. Another part of a systemic evaluation is an assessment of the functioning of the primary subsystems within the family. Relevant assessment questions for the therapist to pursue (although rarely in as direct a manner as the factual information was obtained) regarding subsystems are as follows: (1) How are the parents functioning as both spouses and parents? (2) Is the sibling subsystem supportive of its members or competitive among itself? (3) Is there any extrafamilial person who functions as a member of a subsystem in this family? Other areas of assessment at the systemic level include how the family solves problems, how emotions are handled, how dissension and differences are tolerated, whether the family has supportive connections among its members, whether it allows members to function outside the family without being threatened, how desired behavior is encouraged and enforced, what typical disagreements are, and how time is spent.

The *ethical* dimension is one that has been uniquely emphasized by Karpel and Strauss, who feel it is also important to examine how various ethical and moral issues are manifested in a family. Some of the issues included under this dimension are entitlement and obligation, acknowledgement and claim, trust and trustworthiness, loyalty, fairness, vulnerability and risk taking, and accountability.

It is unrealistic to assume that all this assessment material will be gathered in one or two sessions; however, if the therapist is organized and has in mind the kind of information that needs to be collected (and the family is not in an acute crisis), several sessions will provide much of the basic assessment information on which the treatment plan is based. Again, it is important to point out that assessment is ongoing; the therapist should never consider it to be completed. What was accurate information early in the treatment process is no longer accurate as the dynamic family unfolds. It is also important to point out that assessment is conducted within the context of developmental expectations, both for the individuals in the family and for the family as a whole. Indeed, a thorough assessment will incorporate an examination of the various contexts that are external to the family but influence its functioning. Figure 10–1 depicts these other contexts.

Family Genograms

A frequently used assessment device for families is the family genogram. A genogram is a visual representation of several generations of a family; it is much more than a family tree, however, as valuable chronological, factual, and psychological information can be contained in a well-constructed genogram. Use of the genogram in family therapy was popularized by Bowen (1978), whose intergenerational perspective has interests in mapping dynamics and issues that are manifested from one generation to another. McGoldrick and Gerson (1985) provided a valuable and thorough resource on constructing, interpreting, and using genograms within family therapy. There are a variety of benefits afforded by a genogram:

1. The genogram provides a structure within which to collect factual information.
2. Construction of the genogram allows the "nervous" family some distance and structure, particularly early in family therapy.
3. The process of creating the genogram with the family may facilitate the shift from an individual focus to a family focus.
4. Because multiple generations are depicted, the genogram encourages families to view issues within the larger context.
5. Construction of the genogram may take the family back to a time when family members were happier and felt closer to one another.

Some of the process issues to attend to while generating the genogram are (1) who speaks for the family, (2) whether there are disagreements about some of the information and how are these disagreements handled, (3) what emotions are raised when certain topics or persons are discussed, (4) whether there are obvious cut-off persons within the family system, (5) who the most influential extended family members are, and (6) what constitute the legacies and intergenerational "unfinished business." Though important dates can be entered on the genogram, a separate, more detailed chronology often is developed alongside it.

Intergenerational patterns that become apparent most often relate to issues regarding losses, alcoholism/drug abuse, illegitimate births, divorces and marital problems, ethnicity and gender, education and employment, and religious influences. Coalitions and cut-off members can also be discerned from a well-constructed genogram. Although the therapist asks structured questions of the family in order to construct the genogram, there will often come up additional information of interest that the therapist should take the time to explore.

Other Family Assessment Methods

Besides the use of interviewing and genograms, there are now a variety of formal assessment measures that have been developed for use with couples and families. Many of these are self-report in format; others involve observational tasks.

Filsinger (1983) and Fredman and Sherman (1987) provide reviews of many of the family assessment instruments. Of the self-report measures, the most commonly used are the Family Cohesion and Adaptability Scale (FACES), now in its third revision (Olson, Portner, & Lavee, 1985), the Family Environment Scale (FES; Moos & Moos, 1981), the Dyadic Adjustment Scale (DAS; Spanier, 1976), the Marital Satisfaction Inventory (MSI; Snyder, 1981), the McMaster Family Assessment Device (FAD; Epstein, Baldwin, & Bishop, 1983), and the Family Inventory of Life Events and Changes (FILE; McCubbin, Patterson, & Wilson, 1985).

The most commonly used structured observational assessment methods are the Marital and Family Interaction Coding System (MFICS; Olson & Ryder, 1978), the Beavers-Timberlawn Family Evaluation Scale (BT; Beavers, 1985), and the Structured Family Interview (Watzlawick, 1966). With observational tasks, it is common to ask the family or the couple to engage in a behavioral task, which is videotaped. The particular elements of the interaction during the completion of the task are then coded later by the therapist. On a more informal basis, a family can be given a planning task ("Plan something that your family will do together on Sunday afternoon") that they are to complete as a family. While the family is engaged in the task, the therapist sits removed from the group and observes the variety of dynamics that are manifested: who the family spokesman is, how disagreements are handled, whether there is an ability to compromise, what unique communication patterns are, whether anyone gets left out of the discussion or task, whether anyone speaks for someone else or interrupts them, whether someone is discredited, what the prevalent coalitions are, and so on.

Family assessments can also be informal and consist solely of an interview format, or they can be any combination of interview and structured tasks (such as construction of a family genogram) or any of the variety of family assessment measurement tasks that are available.

Moving from a Child Focus to a Family Focus

Family therapists vary in regard to the extent to which they see it as necessary to take the focus off the presenting child and instead get the family to focus on larger family issues. At one extreme is Jay Haley (1976), who recommends working with the family's definition of the problem even if the therapist could see that there are larger systemic issues. At the other extreme is Virginia Satir (1967) and Murray Bowen (1978), who both would quickly move to a systemic level. Satir suggested that this switch from a child focus to a family focus is a subtle one that gradually occurs as the therapist works to involve everyone in the family in the discussion and activities; thus, before the family knows it, there is a more systemic focus. In contrast, though Bowen also worked to defuse the focus on any one individual (especially a child), he did so in a more educative way by providing the family with a rationale for the importance of examining systemic and even intergenerational influences. In between these two extreme stances is the position of honoring the family's concerns about a particular child's symptoms while also attending to larger systems issues.

Introducing the importance of also examining family issues can be a sensitive one for some families, whereas for others it is a very natural way to think about the situation. For relatively defensive families there are some fears attached to defocusing off the identified patient. These fears often relate to the family wanting to avoid confronting other, more sensitive issues, such as marital problems, family secrets, family violence, sexual abuse, or chemical dependency. At times the family's protectiveness is less avoidance of a particular topic than it is protection of (or fear of) a family member. An example is a mother's resistance to involve her husband in family treatment because of her fear that he will react angrily to any suggestion that he is not parenting appropriately and take out his anger on her and/or the children. Especially in families in which there is no permission for family members to question or criticize one another, working in a family format can feel very uncomfortable.

One way to minimize a family's discomfort is for the therapist to establish from the beginning that in order for family treatment to be effective, all members must feel free to express their opinions without fear of retribution outside the sessions. Even if such a rule is established, some family members will only gradually start to disclose sensitive material as they test to see if, in fact, the powerful members of the family will abide by the therapist's rule. It is important to remember that fear of talking in family sessions can be related not only to not wanting another family member to get mad but also to protecting a family member who is considered fragile and unable to bear hearing anything critical.

The opposite problem that family therapists face is the family that is destructively open about criticisms and disclosures. In such a family, the therapist must have enough control over the sessions and what happens in them so that no one member of the family is unduly scapegoated or hurt. Because negative emotions have often built up in a family before they seek outside treatment, the first session or two may be viewed as opportunities by family members to "dump" all their frustrations and criticisms about other family members. Though the therapist may need to allow some of this venting to occur in order to find out information and to promote a feeling that he or she understands how various family members feel, it is important that this form of destructive disclosure be contained. It is rarely productive for a child to hear a continuous barrage of accusations and negative personal evaluations from parents and siblings. The child has probably withstood similar assaults at home, and it is unproductive to allow a similar communication pattern to occur in the family sessions. Several ways that the therapist might control these negative outbursts are to limit talk time by any one member, to ensure that all members have an opportunity to speak, to force family members to use "I" statements and take responsiblity for what is being disclosed, and to get family members to move from blaming (reactive) to change (proactive) stances. Instead of staying stuck on the level of who did what to whom, one needs to promote a switch to the level of what can be done about problems now.

Regarding the issue of shifting the focus off the identified patient to the family, it is important for the therapist to use good clinical judgment to determine to what extent and how quickly such a shift can take place without unduly threatening the family. Though a particular family may resist efforts to examine larger family issues early in treatment, it may be that later, when members are more trusting of the therapist and the therapy process, there will be less resistance. Therefore, it is not unusual that whereas the therapist constantly has systems dynamics in mind, the overt focus of treatment is on the child's symptoms. Once these symptoms are reduced, it is often possible to recontract with families for a switch in focus to more family-related issues.

When parents are the ones who are resistant to defocusing off the child, the therapist can engage them in the family therapy process by including them as "experts" on their own child and as associates to the therapist in remediating the child's problems. Thus, they are not blamed for the child's problem but are instead recruited to be part of its solution.

Another tactic is to make a short-term contract (perhaps 3 to 5 sessions), after which there is a discussion of how to proceed. Knowing that their commitment to family sessions is limited may help some parents feel less threatened, and it is often the case that after these initial sessions are completed resistance to further family sessions is lessened. It is important to remember that it is not always the blamers who will resist moving to a family focus; at times, the scapegoat will also sabotage such efforts. This is particularly the case when the scapegoat is getting needed attention (secondary gain) from the role of "bad" family member or when his or her behavior serves to protect another family member by diverting attention from that member. Although most scapegoats are "recruited" by the larger system and wish to be rid of the role, there are some scapegoats who have actively campaigned for the position and will be resistant to giving it up.

Functions of the Family Therapist

Though the family therapist's role may vary from family to family, there are some predictable functions that are the responsibility of the therapist.

These include (1) establishing a working contract; (2) maintaining a safe, yet productive environment for therapy; (3) managing multipartiality, side-taking, and neutrality issues; (4) establishing ground rules; (5) challenging the family's status quo, interpretive set, and dysfunctional behaviors; (6) educating, modeling, mediating, and problem solving; and (7) empowering and reinforcing.

Establishing a working therapeutic contract with even one person can at times be complicated (Principle IV). Imagine, then, the potential for complexity as multiple persons become involved! In work with families, therapeutic contracting is often ongoing and occurs at multiple levels. Contracting can begin even as part of the intitial phone call as the therapist and the caller negotiate as to who will be present at the first session and when the sessions will occur. If fee and length of sessions are negotiable, then these, too, might be part of this initial contracting.

Once the first session is held, contracting occurs at a short-term and at a long-term level. An example of a short-term contract might be to agree to a three-session model in which a thorough assessment is to be conducted, after which there will be a session in which recommendations for how to proceed are shared. As mentioned above, this short-term contract might be particularly appropriate for the family that is feeling some resistance to committing to family-focused treatment over a longer time.

In its simplest form, a long-term contract is an agreement among all relevant members to work together over time on the problems that have been identified at intake, as well as those that might arise as therapy progresses. A more specific long-term contract would detail what problems are to be the focus of the intervention and how they will be addressed. Periodic review of progress toward the attainment of the contract goals is important, and such review sessions allow for new material and concerns to be raised. It is also the case that treatment outcomes are usually not so clearly specifiable; that is, a therapist may feel that certain treatment goals have been only partially met, whereas the family may be quite pleased with their progress and want to discontinue therapy at this particular level. In the establishment of treatment goals, it is important to be realistic, to recognize the limitations of both the family resources and the therapist, and to involve all members of the family in the discussion of and agreement upon the goals. To have all family members agree upon all goals is sometimes impossible; in such cases, compromising and including the goals of various persons are appropriate.

Maintaining a safe, yet productive environment for therapy can be a shared responsibility between the therapist and family members. Family members, however, are not always willing or able to appreciate that they can be destructive in their words and actions toward other family members, especially when emotions are high. No matter how directive or nondirective a family therapist may be, it is important that all present in the family sessions feel that the therapist is in control. It is by demeanor, firmness, honesty, respect, understanding, and confidence that a therapist is in charge in family therapy. The therapist should be able to manage whatever occurs in the therapy session in order that no one is physically or emotionally abused. If it is the case that the therapist cannot maintain control over a family member under such circumstances, then it is appropriate that the session be ended, with safeguards instituted to ensure the safety of persons once they leave the session. If the family's destructive behavior cannot be controlled over time, a family therapy format is an inappropriate treatment format for this particular family at this particular time.

Even when obvious destructive behavior is not present, it is still the function of the therapist to run family sessions so that members feel safe in disclosing and expressing opinions. Members who feel uncertain as to whether their words will be used to emotionally hurt them later or who fear retribution will be reluctant to participate openly and honestly in family sessions.

The therapist also needs to engender hope for change. Often families have lived with a problem for some time before seeking outside help. By this point, family members are often highly and negatively emotional, feeling helpless and hopeless about changing things, and pessimistic about the future. Although the therapist must never promote an unrealistic hope of change, it is important that he or she portray to the family that something can be done and that the therapist is capable of managing the situation. Whether this occurs even in the first session may well determine if a family comes back for a second session.

Managing multipartiality, side-taking, and neutrality issues is part of the decision of whether and when to support one or more persons in the family over others. Multipartiality involves the ability (particularly critical in the early stages of family therapy, in which rapport is being established) to connect with each member of the family. If done well, each family member will feel that he or she has a special relationship with the therapist, that the therapist understands him or her, and that the therapist is fair. Multipartiality is an ideal that parents strive for when raising children in the same family. Similarly, the family therapist strives to make all family members feel equally respected, understood, and special in their relationships with the therapist.

There are a variety of therapist behaviors that will encourage a sense of multipartiality. These include making sure all family members have an opportunity to talk and share their opinions (Principle II), putting restrictions on family members who would dominate family sessions, and having empathy and understanding for each member's position (Principle III).

Sidetaking is a valuable therapeutic technique; however, it needs to be carefully utilized so as not to impair rapport and a sense of fairness in the family. As a therapeutic technique, side taking can be used to balance out an unequal power exchange that is occurring in the family. For instance, if one family member is verbally overpowering another member, and thus not allowing the more timid member a chance to express an opinion, the therapist can interrupt the process and describe what is occurring, encourage the timid member to speak, and prevent others from interrupting while the reluctant family member does try to express an opinion. Sometimes side taking can occur in a productive way when the therapist sides with a teenager in explaining to the parents that their rules have not kept up with the advancing age of their child.

It is often advisable after taking a particular side that the therapist reassure the other party that it also has legitimacy. Thus, after telling the parents that the family rules are no longer appropriate for a 15-year-old, the therapist could turn to the parents and reiterate to them that he or she knows that they are good-intentioned parents, that they worry about their teen, and that it must be difficult to think of their child as growing up.

Sometimes side-taking occurs without the therapist making a deliberate choice to use it as a therapeutic technique. When this occurs, the therapist has probably been engulfed in the dysfunctional family dynamics and may be manifesting countertransference reactions. An example of this would be the therapist who is always siding with the teenager in a particular family, no matter what the issue. The therapist may be acting out leftover emotions and issues from his or her own adolescence, which may have been dominated by parents who were experienced as controlling and restricting. Thus, the therapist may find it natural to side with the teenagers in the families with whom he or she works; in contrast, the therapist who was a "good" teenager may find it more natural to side with the parents. Although side taking can be a powerful and effective therapeutic method, it must be rationally chosen with an equitable purpose in mind.

Neutrality is a stance in which the therapist refuses to become involved in the dynamics of the family, to take sides, or to do for the family what it should be able to do for itself. There will be many times that a family or members of a family will ask the therapist for direct advice about how to handle something. During some of these occasions, it will be quite appropriate for the therapist to give an opinion or offer suggestions. There are other times, however, in which it is best for the therapist to remain detached. In such cases, the therapist resists getting personally involved and thows the issue back to the family to resolve. When working with families who use triangulation efforts whenever significant conflict arises, the therapist may be most therapeutic by remaining detached from the conflict so that the two conflicting parties are forced to face one another and work

out the issue. There are times in the therapy of any family when the therapist will alternate among the various stances of multipartiality, side taking,
and neutrality. Each has an appropriate place in the family therapist's
repertoire, but each must be used judiciously.

The *establishment of ground rules* typically occurs early in family
treatment. There are some situations that are not easily anticipated, however, that may require rules. Common rules of family therapy include matters regarding attendance, family members talking one at a time, family
members not interrupting one another, and any type of violence not being
allowed. More idiosyncratic rules can be devised as needed when working
with a particular family. Thus, one family may need to be reminded not to
punish anyone at home for things said in the therapy session, or reminded
of how some therapeutic material should be treated confidentially.
Whenever appropriate, family members can be encouraged to participate
in identifying rules that will help the family get the most out of its sessions.
Ultimate responsibility for making and enforcing rules that apply to therapy sessions, however, rests with the therapist.

One function of the therapist is to establish rapport and to connect
with family members. Another function is quite the opposite: to *challenge
the family's status quo, interpretive set, and dysfunctional behavior*. This
confrontative function works best when the therapist has taken the time to
establish rapport and a sense of connection with the family. As was discussed in the previous chapter, a family's homeostatic processes resist
change; thus, a therapist needs to confront, "tickle the defenses," or raise
anxiety to get a complacent family to deal with difficult material and to attempt new behaviors. When a family's anxiety level falls too low, there is
not enough distress to stimulate an exploration of change. In such cases, it
may be necessary for the therapist to "shake up" the system enough for
members not to be satisfied with the status quo and to explore a more
functional pattern.

Minuchin (1974) has written about the need for a therapist to help get
a family unstuck by increasing the intensity within the family. One of the
means by which this is accomplished is to require the family to perform an
enactment—a verbal or behavioral exchange that highlights the ineffective-
ness of the family's current functioning. Thus, a child's belligerence to the
parents might be not only tolerated by the therapist but even supported or
exaggerated so it becomes clear to the parents that they are ineffective at
controlling their child. When they are able to drop their denial about their
parenting inefficiencies, they may be open to considering alternatives to
the behaviors they are using.

Just as some clients feel uncomfortable when sensitive topics are
raised, some therapists do as well. If this is to an extent that the therapist
avoids or minimizes sensitive material, then the therapist perpetuates the
family's dysfunctional manner of handling issues. When a therapist has

such a reaction, there is usually an unusual need on the part of the therapist to protect the feelings of some or all family members—a reaction typically embedded in the therapist's own unfinished business or countertransference reaction. If a family were capable of identifying, raising, and handling all their sensitive issues, after all, there would be no need for a therapist! Most families who present for treatment will need the therapist to help them, even to push them, to confront and to deal with uncomfortable material and to attempt new, anxiety-provoking behaviors. But even while pushing the family members, the therapist needs also to be supportive of them in order for them to tolerate the challenge and persist long enough to work it out.

It is typically the case that new therapists have supportive skills that are better developed than are their challenging and confronting skills. Good supervision can be very valuable to one's learning how to confront without either alienating a family or sounding wishy-washy. Supportive skills are important in the early rapport-building phases of family treatment, but challenging and pushing skills are what may eventually be necessary if significant change is to occur.

When a therapist challenges a family's interpretive set, the therapist is asking the family to consider the possibility that the way they have viewed a particular issue may not be accurate or the only way the issue can be viewed. Relabeling, reframing, and renaming are all similiar techniques by which the therapist attempts to offer an alternative (usually more benign or more positive) connotation for an important issue. Such therapeutic methods encourage families who have typically seen the world in black-and-white terms or in a rigid fashion to entertain more functional attitudes. When a child views her father as strict, controlling, and overly protective with the aim of making her life miserable, a relabeling that identifies the father as worried about the safety of his daughter provides a more benign interpretation of the father's behavior. This relabeling may be sufficient to defuse intense negative emotions in the daughter (particularly if the father can acknowledge his worry and sense of helplessness in regard to keeping his daughter safe), thus allowing for a dialogue to occur so that more appropriate rules can be established that are satifactory to the daughter.

Challenging a family's dysfunctional behaviors is usually accomplished by identifying such behaviors and associating the behaviors with negative outcomes and consequences. Although the family may not be able to recognize the role of some of their behaviors in leading to negative outcomes, they usually can agree that the negative outcomes are unsatisfactory. Thus, when the therapist is successful at associating or connecting the family's own behavior with undesirable or dreaded outcomes, the family may be more open to examining alternative behaviors. The family that externalizes blame onto persons or circumstances outside the family is one that may need to be confronted with the fact that some of its own actions are contributing to negative consequences. Only when this recognition occurs will a family start to accept responsibility for its actions and its ability to change. Offering interpretations, alternatives, and clarifications to families are other, more subtle ways to challenge interpretive sets and dysfunctional behaviors (Principle V).

A frequently exercised set of functions by the family therapist is to *educate, model, and mediate*. It is common for a therapist to provide the family with information about how it is responding or about better ways to handle matters. This educative function is critical, as many families are aware that what they are doing is ineffective, yet they do not know what else to do. When new skills are complicated or difficult to master, the therapist can aid in the family's learning by modeling the desired responses. Thus, parents who have difficulty establishing firm limits with a child can observe the therapist doing so, and then can try to emulate what they have seen. One of the most prevalent ways in which a therapist models for the family is in offering clear, honest, and congruent communications (Principle III) and encouraging the same from family members. Because most families who are in treatment have lost or never developed a good ability to compromise and work out differences, the therapist will often function as a mediator—particularly early in treatment until the family is able to take over this function itself. When mediating, the therapist needs to be concerned with the issues of multipartiality, side taking, and neutrality that were discussed earlier.

The final therapist function that will be discussed here is *empowering and reinforcing*. Because a family will often feel powerless and pessimistic about its abilities to solve its own problems, the therapist should utilize whatever opportunities are available to build up a sense of competence in the family. Empowering means that a therapist helps a family to function independently and to approach problems with new skills and confidence. Additionally, the therapist shows a respect for the competencies of the family: if he or she believes in the family, perhaps the family members will eventually believe in themselves. Though it may be far easier for a therapist to tell a family what to do, this short-term efficiency will not empower the family to be able to handle future issues that arise. Often it is well worth the extra time and effort to allow a family to develop its own problem-solving skills, as its members will need to utilize these after the family leaves treatment and no longer has the therapist available. Furthermore, even if a therapist has played a big role in the success of a family, it is always important to give that credit to the family. Successful family therapy occurs when the family leaves treatment feeling good about the progress *it* has made and its abilities to solve future problems.

A therapist can have strong reinforcing abilities for a family if rapport has been well established and the therapist has managed the issues of partiality successfully. Just as a child responds well to praise and encouragement, so does a family. If the therapist has become important to the family, he or she can have a powerful influence by being rewarding to the family. Obviously, such reinforcement by the therapist should be judiciously and sincerely used so as not to be construed as patronizing.

That the therapist matters to the family can be another therapeutic tool in the repertoire of the family therapist. The therapist, though, should never be in the position of wanting or needing the family's approval. When and if that occurs, the therapist has lost the leadership and neutrality role that is important to maintain control over the therapy process. Families will often offer praise to their therapist; this is acceptable as long as the therapist has not overtly or covertly solicited it, nor become reliant on it to feel good.

If the therapist needs the family's approval, it is a sure sign that good supervision or professional consultation is needed in order for the therapist to function more effectively and objectively. Just as parents should not look to their children for emotional support, nor should therapists look to their clients for encouragement and for feedback about their therapeutic competence. This sense of competence needs to come from within the therapist, sometimes with the help of supervisors or professional peers. No matter how experienced the therapist might be, each family can provoke idiosyncratic issues for the therapist. Thus, a therapist should always have access to professional supervision and/or consultation, be willing to examine his or her own role in the therapeutic process, and be a lifelong learner of new ideas.

Common Family Therapy Techniques and Methods

This section will briefly discuss the most prominently used techniques and methods in family therapy. If interested in their elaboration and development, the reader is referred to a variety of original sources, listed in the reference section of this and the previous chapter, that detail these methods.

Relabeling, Reframing, and Redefining

Often a family or members of the family will perceive or interpret a situation in an unnecessarily narrow, negative, or rigid fashion; this is particularly true of the problem(s) for which the family is seeking help. Just as a family can be "stuck" in repeating its own dysfunctional patterns, so can it get stuck in its perception of something. A family's perception of an event or circumstance is called an *interpretive set,* and it can greatly influence its willingness to entertain differing opinions and to work to resolve the matter. Thus, a useful technique is for the therapist to challenge the family mind-set in order to get members out of rigid positions that have proved unproductive.

For instance, parents who consider their son to be lazy and unmotivated will interact with him in primarily a negative manner about his schoolwork. If, however, the therapist perceives that there are other dynamics occurring for the son, such as his feeling too much pressure to achieve and his fearing failure (and thus being afraid to perform at all), it is useful for him or her to share these perceptions with the parents who can then, it is hoped, take a more constructive approach. Parents sometimes need to be instructed to view challenging (obstinate, in the parents' minds) behaviors by their child as an appropriate developmental exercising of independence and power. How, they might be asked, can restrictive and protective parents prepare their children to take care of and stand up for themselves if the parents make all the decisions for them? Such relabels often open the door for a useful dialogue to occur.

Most typically, relabeling and reframing allow a more positive connotation to be put on something previously thought of only as negative. There are also times, however, when a therapist may want to relabel something that is perceived by the family as positive or benign as something that is actually negative. For instance, parents with two sons, aged 9 and 11 years, presented their 9-year-old for therapy because of academic underachievement. It was clear after only a short time with this family that high academic achievement was a very strong value.

Thus, when the younger son did not live up to parental expectations, it was natural for them to think that something was wrong with the son and that he needed professional help. In this same family, however, it was discovered that both boys were sleeping nightly with their parents and that the older son was significantly encopretic. Neither of these issues were viewed by the family members as problems until the therapist relabeled them with a negative connotation. Negative relabeling is useful when a family denies a significant issue.

Another example of negative reframing occurred in a family in which the parents experienced much dissatisfaction and disagreement with one another; however, they refused to acknowledge their feelings and to face their conflicts. Their children lived in a very tense family but rarely saw their parents argue; instead, these parents used passive-aggressive or more subtle ways of handling their disagreements, including avoiding one another, scapegoating the children, having psychosomatic symptoms, and triangulating others into their conflicts.

The parents brought their family in for therapy because they could not tolerate the fighting that was going on among the children. The reframing the therapist used with these parents was that it was healthy for their children to be attempting to work out their conflicts openly (even if they were not very skillful at a it), but that it was *not* healthy for the parents to handle their conflicts by avoiding them. Thus, what the parents had viewed as negative (the kids' fighting) was reframed more positively, and what the parents felt was a positive way to handle their own antagonism was relabeled as dysfunctional. Whether used to diffuse strong negative emotions, correct misperceptions, or expand the family's current interpretive set, relabeling can be a powerful therapeutic tactic.

Restructuring Methods

As was discussed in the previous chapter, family structure is composed of a variety of concepts including boundaries, alliances and coalitions, triangulation, roles, rules, and enmeshment–disengagement. Restructuring methods involve challenges to the usual modes of transaction within the family. Minuchin and Fishman (1981) detail the various methods of restructuring families into more functional patterns of interaction. Among the most common restructuring methods are enactments, boundary marking, and increasing intensity (Colapinto, 1991).

Basically, *enactments* are the behavioralizing of transactional patterns. Enactments are set up by the therapist as a way for the family to "show" or "actualize" an issue, for instance, by discussing a conflictual topic between the parents. If the parents try to evade their task, the therapist gently brings them back to it. As the tension rises, one of the children interrupts the discussion by siding with one of the parents over the other (triangulation pattern). As a result, the parent who is now outnumbered turns on the interrupting child and begins a new conflict with him or her. In the process, the original conflict is forgotten.

Enactments can be used for diagnostic information (as in the above case, in which the triangulation and diverting patterns were recognized), or they can also be the means by which to encourage new behaviors by family members. In this case, the therapist might have stopped the child from interrupting the parental discussion, thus allowing the parents to pursue their disagreement. While the parents argue, the therapist might suggest how the interaction could proceed more productively. Thus, the parents might be encouraged to listen to each other more carefully, not to interrupt, to come up with compromises, and so forth. Once the parents have some success at resolving their own conflicts, the children's anxiety may be lessened. Therefore, the next time such a conflict arises, there may be less of a tendency for one of the children to interrupt the process and subsequently to become triangulated with the parents. Enactments allow the family to experiment with alternative, more functional ways of interacting and can be very powerful when they are well conducted. Enactments allow families actually to experience change as opposed to just talking about it.

Boundary marking is a tactic used by a therapist to encourage appropriate membership in coalitions, to foster connections among family members, and to reinforce the hierarchical nature of families. The means by which a therapist marks boundaries is to encourage members to be (or refrain them from being) involved in certain family transactions. Thus, an older sibling who is constantly chiming in with advice to the parents about how they should handle the younger sibling would be refrained from engaging in "parenting" behavior, while the real parents would be encouraged to form a strong, efficient parental coalition to deal with the behaviors of all their offspring. The clarification of rules and roles within the family and their appropriateness for the family circumstances can also be an important part of boundary marking.

Increasing intensity was a method discussed earlier to help a family become unstuck from a dysfunctional status quo existence. Challenging and confrontation are the primary means of increasing intensity, although encouraging members to take a transaction further than they usually do before they divert or avoid would also have that effect. It is this increased intensity that may motivate the family to examine new ways of perceiving and behaving. Obviously, once the intensity has been heightened, then the therapist can play another role in providing alternatives, modeling, educating, and so on.

Communications Training

When families have trouble communicating clearly and congruently, behavioral and/or emotional problems almost always follow. Communication is central to relationships; it is the medium through which people usually convey their needs, give feedback to others, solve conflicts, and convey affection. As such, it is not surprising that helping families correct their faulty communication patterns is a frequent goal of family therapy. In order for the family therapist to help a family with its communication, he or she first needs to recognize the problems in the family's communication efforts. This is typically accomplished in an informal manner by the therapist observing the process of communication among family members. It is not only the words that a family therapist attends to, however, because nonverbal communications can send louder messages than words.

In communication, there is a sender of a message and a receiver. Breakdowns in communication occur at a variety of points in the communication loop. The sender may not convey a clear message, or the message might have inconsistent elements (for example, the words are positive, whereas the facial expression is negative). The receiver may not hear the message as it was intended because of lack of attention, selective listening (hearing only what one wants to hear), or lack of respect for the sender of the message. After receiving a message, the receiver sends back a message based on what was received. If the information received was faulty, then the return message is going to be faulty as well, thus perpetuating a series of poor communications. When family therapists work with families on their communication skills, they focus on getting members to "say what they mean," not to send ambivalent or incongruent messages, and to get others' attention before sending a message. Eye contact, proper intonation, and consistent body gestures are important to the sender's getting the correct message to the receiver.

Additionally, the sender is asked to take responsibility for the message by using "I" sentences. This cuts down on the incidence of blaming and critical statements, which are not well received by listeners. The sender is also asked to pick the right time to communicate an important message. Asking one's mother for a big favor as she comes in the door from a stress-filled day is likely not to be the best time, if one wants to optimize the chances for a positive response.

From the receiver's viewpoint, issues that are stressed are active listening, checking out a message if it is unclear, giving appropriate nonverbal cues (giving eye contact, not yawning or looking away, and so on), not interrupting, and keeping an open mind while receiving the message. In family sessions, members are requested by the therapist to utilize these methods of communication.

When the communication process is breaking down, the therapist will intervene by asking the sender to repeat the message, asking the receiver to repeat back the message, checking for hidden meanings, and the like. The therapist can also serve as a model for good communication. Role playing and role reversals are also useful techniques for educating and modeling healthy communication skills.

Other communication issues that a therapist will have to handle include getting members to speak directly to one another, not to speak for one another or to talk over someone else, and not to speak through the therapist. Initial examples of faulty communication are typically pointed out by the therapist; if the same pattern recurs, he or she points it out again and suggests a correction. Ultimately the therapist will rarely have to interrupt the communication process, and will expect the family to identify and correct any faulty communication pattern on its own.

L'Abate, Ganahl, and Hansen (1986) list a number of problematic features of communication to be corrected in family therapy. They include abusive talk, better-than-thou postures, coercive behavior (bullying or nagging), personal avoidance (sulking, pouting, or ignoring), topic avoidance, excessive compliance, guilt induction, cross-complaining ("yes, but"), evasions (vagueness or incomplete sentences), interruptions, dogmatic generalizations (black-and-white thinking, use of *always*), mind reading (telling others what they think), spokesmanship (speaking for someone else), superreasonableness (avoiding feelings by using logic), straw-man discussions (creating a false issue or exaggeration), talking past the point of usefulness, overinclusions (excessive emphasis on past history, or dragging old hurts and resentments out), acknowledgment deficit (failure to acknowledge the other's correct statements), and reinforcement deficit (failure to encourage and praise).

Problem-Solving and Conflict Resolution

Closely related to communications skills is the family's ability to solve problems. Problem solving is based on good listening and speaking skills; if these are poor, the family is likely to have inadequate problem-solving abilities. Once communication is improved, the therapist can help the family apply its newfound skills to the resolution of problems and the negotiation of conflict. The typical steps in building problem-solving skills is to (1) identify the problem in a clear and specific manner; (2) communicate the issue to an appropriate person; (3) brainstorm alternative ways of solving the problem; (4) weigh the pros and cons of each alternative; (5) select the "best" alternative and try it; (6) evaluate the outcome of the attempted solution; and (7) go back to the other alternatives and start all over if it did not work. It is especially helpful to teach these problem-solving skills in actual family sessions. Once the family members have gained some degree of proficiency, they should be requested to use the same skills in structured ways at home.

Training families to resolve conflict often involves communication skills, problem solving, and intense negative emotions. Palomares (1975) detailed specific positive and negative strategies to resolve a conflict. These are as follows:

1. *Negotiating* (talking about one's position in the conflict and what can be done about it)
2. *Compromise* (both sides giving up something)
3. *Taking turns* (one person going first, and then the other)
4. *Active listening* (perceiving what the other person is saying and accurately paraphrasing it)
5. *Threat-free explanation* (communicating a position without threatening the other person)
6. *Apologizing* (being able to say that one is sorry without having to say that one is wrong)
7. *Soliciting intervention* (seeking a consultation from another source—a book, an expert, a prestigious other, and so forth)
8. *Postponement* (agreeing to wait for a more appropriate time to discuss the conflict)
9. *Distraction* (making something or someone else the focus of attention as a way of diffusing the conflict)

10. *Abandoning* (leaving the conflict situation if it cannot be dealt with and only more harm will result)
11. *Exaggeration* (giving an exaggerated interpretation of the conflict in order to enable participants to see its real components)
12. *Humor* (using humor that does not ridicule or insult can help reduce tension in conflict and thereby ease resolution)
13. *Chance* (using a technique, such as flipping a coin, where the resolution is literally given to chance often helps each individual save face)
14. *Sharing* (using reciprocity and equality in approaching the conflict)
15. *Violence* (verbally or physically abusing one another)
16. *Flight* (retreating internally or physically; the worst side effect from this approach is deterioration of self-esteem)
17. *Tattling* (attempting to enlist others to handle the conflict)

As can be seen, not all of these strategies are likely to lead to a satisfactory resolution for both parties. The last three may resolve the issue for one party, but leave the other party injured or dissatisfied. Obviously, this does not bode well for future conflicts between these two parties. The family therapist often uses the mediator function to facilitate the resolution of conflict.

As with problem-solving skills, conflict resolution skills are learned within the therapy sessions, then gradually practiced at home. One of the means to facilitate this transfer of learning into the family's day-to-day life is to prescribe specific tasks to be done at home.

Homework and Out-of-Session Assignments

As with the behaviorists, family therapists often utilize out-of-session assignments. This homework functions to give the family additional practice that may speed up progress, point out inefficiencies that remain when the family tries to use their new skills without the therapist's guidance (which then provides opportunities for correction), facilitate transfer and maintenance of these new skills into a more realistic setting than the therapy room, and allow families to practice more "private" behaviors that are difficult to replicate in the therapy room (such as getting a child to eat, or putting a child to bed). One of the ways to build a sense of competence in families is to give them opportunities to utilize what they have learned. When successful, families then have an increased sense of being able to manage similar issues that may arise in the future.

The first step is to describe clearly what the assignment is, provide a rationale, and demonstrate it or allow the family to rehearse it in the session. The instructions should be specific enough to make clear who is to do what, when, and how. The therapist should verify before the family leaves the session whether all members understand the instructions.

Particularly if they are complex, instructions for tasks can be presented in written form, with the instructions to be posted in a public place at home for all to see. The second step is for the family to attempt the homework assignment, and the third is for the family to report back to the therapist the particular successes or problems with doing the homework assignment.

At the second step there is the potential for all sorts of resistances to arise from family members. These resistances can be directed at doing the homework assignment at all, doing it as prescribed, or honestly reporting back the results of the at-home task. It is often helpful for the therapist to anticipate these possible resistances and either to address them in advance or to compose the assignment in such a way as to minimize the chances for error. Thus, when the task is being assigned, the therapist may ask the family, "If this homework assignment were not to work this week, what would be the most likely reason?" Getting the family to address possible stumbling blocks in advance may well preclude their happening. Other ways of minimizing resistances are to involve family members in the construction of the assignment, to provide a clear rationale for the importance of the assignment, to write instructions down, to make sure every family member understands everyone's role in the assignment, to prescribe a specific time for the assignment to be done (if the family is likely to avoid it), and to give the family a detailed form on which to record the success or failure of the assignment.

A common homework task is the home family session, which is an attempt by the family to hold a family meeting at home. Initially the agenda and purpose of the meeting might be very specific, but eventually the meeting can be held with less structure. At this point, family members can bring their issues forth at the meeting instead of having a specific, planned issue to discuss.

Home family sessions can be very useful early in treatment, when family interactions tend to be dominated by negative exhanges. The family can be instructed to set aside 30 minutes during the week in which family members have an opportunity to tell (without interruption or critique) other members about something positive, something that made them feel proud, an accomplishment, or some other topic. For some families, the time given to the home family session may be the only time the family gets together as a whole during the week, with the exception of the therapy session.

Later in treatment, as new skills are being acquired in therapy, home family sessions can be used to practice these skills. Finally, as treatment is starting to wind down, the therapist can space therapy sessions so that the family comes every other week. During the intervening week, the family is instructed to have a home meeting during the same time as they would have come to the therapy session. If the family struggles with such meetings, the therapist can request the family to tape-record the meeting so that the therapist can evaluate the meeting and help the family correct unproductive patterns.

Often the family will need to institute similar rules for their home family session as are used in the therapy sessions. These rules could include one person talking at a time, no interrupting, the use of "I" statements, the use of active listening, verifying messages, not speaking for one another, and so forth. As part of the termination process, the family therapist can eventually space sessions even further apart so that the family is meeting more at home than with the therapist. This gradual process of termination is particularly comforting to a family that has wavering confidence about its newly learned skills and whether it can function without the aid of the therapist.

It is always important to check on the outcome of a homework assignment if one is given. There are times that a family would prefer not to report back to the therapist; thus, it will be the therapist's responsibility to ask about the homework. If the therapist prescribes homework for a family, then fails to follow up at the next session, the disregard may be taken as a sign that the homework was not very important.

A final suggestion regarding the use of homework assignments is to start a family with assignments that are simple and relatively assured of success. If the intial assignment is complex and the family fails at it, it may be far more resistant to subsequent attempts by the therapist to use such tasks.

Just as in individual psychotherapy, there are many methods and techniques used by family therapists. The reader may access additional sources—Brock and Barnard (1988), L'Abate et al. (1986), and Gurman and Kniskern (1991)—for other techniques and procedures in family therapy.

Transcript of a First Family Session

A transcript of the first session with a family is provided in its entirety at this point. In reading the transcript, the reader should keep in mind the various roles and functions of the therapist: shifting from an individual to a family focus, contracting, and the variety of techniques (especially relabeling) discussed above. The reader should determine what alliances are in force, how power is exercised, if there are communication problems, and the family's strengths and weaknesses. This family consisted of a married couple (Dave and Beth C.) and their only child, a son named Tom who was 14 years old. They were referred to a community mental health center by a social worker at Tom's school after an incident in which Tom struck a teacher.

[The therapist sits facing the family of three who are seated in the form of a semicircle, with the mother to the therapist's left, the son in the middle, and the father to the therapist's right.]

Therapist: The first thing I'd like to do would be to hear from each of you what you think are the things going wrong in your family. [Therapist addresses no one in particular. The mother sighs.]

Father: Well, Tom's beating up on his teachers. That's really the worst of it. I'm not sure how you (*looking at mother*) feel about it right now, but I'd certainly say he's heading for a life of crime. [Father is visibly angry, yet trying to maintain control over his emotions.]

Therapist: A teacher was actually hit? Can you tell me about it?

Father: Well—the way I understand it, a teacher at school told Tom he was supposed to do something, and Tom didn't like it, so he popped him one.

Therapist: This is a male teacher?

Father: Right!

Therapist: And so the school became rather upset and you were called in?

Father: Well, my wife was called in. I was working.

Mother: Yes, umm, the principal was notified, and I went to the school. It sounds like Tom did have some part in this, but I got the impression that the teacher had some hostility toward Tom too, and I really, umm, umm, I don't know—I just feel that this school is really, umm, umm—I dunno. I just think they have the wrong attitude about teaching these kids. They act like it's a prison for these kids. You know, like in the cafeteria, you know, they have these—the kids can't even sit in the cafeteria without having these bars pulled across to keep them from, umm, you know, from wandering into the hallway. I just think it is a very unhealthy attitude.

Therapist: Which school is this?

Mother: This is [name of school].

Therapist: Sounds like you have some understanding of how it might have happened that Tom got so frustrated that he hauled off and smacked a teacher.

Mother: They just really have a very poor attitude. Now that this has happened, I think maybe we should just put Tom in a different school. I think that maybe . . .

Father: (*interrupting mother*) Attitude, schmatitude! The kid doesn't obey the rules, he gets in trouble. It's just like life!

Mother: Look, the people at that school just have the wrong attitude.

Son: Well, uhh, I just, uhh, the teacher's a jerk, a real asshole. He got on my case; he's been on my case. I guess he was in a bad mood and picked on the wrong guy, and I'd just had enough of him, so I turned around and smacked him.

Therapist: How has he been on your case, Tom?

Son: Oh, he doesn't like me. He hates my guts, and I don't like him and, uhh, and so he tries to bounce me around and he picks on me. So I just turned around and let him have it.

Therapist: How do you know that he doesn't like you? Does he do things to you?

Son: Oh, I dunno. He always, umm . . . like we're in class, and uhh, umm, other people are talking, but he'll call on me because I'm talking, while other people are talking.

Therapist: You get blamed for everybody else and get singled out? (*Tom nods*) Things must have really been building up for you to get you to the point where you actually smacked the teacher. Have things been pretty bad for you at school lately?

Son: No, uhh, just that guy who's a jerk!

Therapist: Un-huh. Is this the only teacher you have these feelings about?

Son: Well, uhh, I dunno that. I can't wait to get out of school.

Therapist: What grade are you in now?

Son: Eighth.

Therapist: So you have a while to go yet, huh? We'd better find out a way for you to learn how to tolerate the situation, because you have a few years in school yet. I imagine that this particular incident caused a lot of trouble for you at home, too.

Son: Uhh, yeh, well, Dad's been raggin' on me.

Therapist: Umm, yeh, it's pretty clear to me that he's a bit upset.

Father: I don't know about raggin'! I grounded him for a week. I wouldn't call it raggin'!

Therapist: Are you typically the one who disciplines Tom?

Father: The only one! I'm the only source of discipline. The kid gets rambunctious. He gets out of hand. Uhh, it takes a man's hand to keep him in line.

Therapist: (*to father*) You must not always be around him when things are going wrong. (*to mother*) What happens when your husband's not around, Mrs. C.?

Mother: Well, I dunno . . .

Father: (*interrupting mother*) He just runs rampant!

Mother: I just think that Tom's at that age when he's fighting a lot with his father. There seem to be a lot of angry feelings between the two, and I think it has a lot to do with his age. Umm, he's just looking for more independence, and umm, he's just getting into a lot of conflicts with Dave, and I think that has a lot to do with it. Umm, when Dave isn't around, umm, I think Tom usually, generally, behaves himself pretty well.

Therapist: What about those few times when he isn't doing something you expect of him?

Mother: Well, sometimes I'll ask him to do something and he won't. You know, but, umm, well, you know, I talk to him about it and everything, and umm, umm, he usually comes around to doing it.

Therapist: Umm. One of the things I know is that in families that have teenagers, there are often a lot of concerns about the rules in the family. Do you have any trouble with the rules that exist in your family, Tom?

Son: Rules?

Therapist: Do you have rules that are specified, that you're to follow? Any rules about chores or curfew or things of that sort?

Son: There's curfew, but when he (*looks at father*) isn't around I have more freedom.

Therapist: So most of the rules are Dad's rules?

Son: Yeh.

Therapist: How are you feeling about Dad's rules?

Son: I don't think they're necessary.

Therapist: What would happen in this family, Tom, if you wanted to renegotiate some of the rules, say like the curfew? How would you go about that?

Son: I dunno. Can't talk to him (*looking at father*). He blows up!

Therapist: So knowing that, what would you do?

Mother: Sometimes Tom talks to me about it and well, sometimes Dave gets kind of angry, and we sit down and talk about what's going on.

Father: I know how he renegotiates the rules . . . he hits the teacher with his fist. That's his idea of changing the rules. (*sounding angry*)

Mother: Well, this is the first time it happened.

Father: I know where he learned it, too.

Mother: I don't know what you're talking about. This is the first time that he did this.

Son: I donno . . . I don't think it would work . . .

Mother: Everybody is entitled to their mistakes. OK, it was wrong, you know. I think what we need to do is get him in a different school. I think that's what we need to do.

Son: Yeh, I'd like to go to a different school. This school sucks!

Therapist: Do you have some notions, Mr. C., about how Tom came to beat up his teacher?

Father: Yeh, I think so, because he's learning here that when I'm away that rules are something that you can get around, and he probably ran into someone who wouldn't let him get around those rules. And he has a very short temper, and the teacher didn't react like my wife and he got very upset about that.

Mother: Temper?

Therapist: (*to father*) What you're saying is that you're pretty strict with your rules. Has there ever been a situation in which Tom has hauled off and hit you?

Father: Oh, he's threatened to, but he stopped that quick!

Therapist: (*to mother*) Do you sometimes fear that they're (*gesturing toward Tom and father*) going to hurt one another when they really get going?

Mother: Well, sometimes Dave really does push Tom around a bit. You know, and I think that's where Tom gets it from.

Father: You can't say that. He gets it from learning how to manipulate you, when he sweet-talks his way around you.

Mother: He doesn't sweet-talk! I just can talk to him better than you can, that's all.

Father: But you don't get any results. You talk to him for 2 hours about taking the garbage out, and the trash is still there when I get home, and I have to drag it out myself.

Therapist: Do the two of you sit down and talk about how Tom's doing, how you're dealing with Tom, about the rules, in regard to Tom?

Father: I try to tell her, but it's not much help.

Therapist: You've tried to sit down and tell her what the rules should be? That's a bit different than having a discussion about it. Do you ever have a discussion where the both of you can share with each other your impressions and feelings about Tom?

Mother: Well, like I said, sometimes Tom, you know, wants to stay out later or something and I might, umm, try to talk to Dave about it, umm, and that sort of thing, umm, and it usually ends up in an argument.

Father: Sure, last week she wanted to let him stay out late one night, 3 days after he popped the teacher. That's what I'm talking about.

Therapist: Uh-huh. So it's real hard for the two of you to agree about how to deal with Tom. Have there been times when you really have been in agreement about how to handle him or some other of these situations?

Father: Well, I don't think we disagree much when Tom's on good behavior.

Therapist: And when did that change? (*long silence follows*)

Mother: Tom has always been kind of rambunctious.

Father: Junior high.

Therapist: Well, he's 14 now; a couple years ago, then?

Father: Yeh, 10 or 11, that's when he changed schools and started hanging out with the wrong crowd. I tried to tell him these weren't good people, but he picks his own friends.

Therapist: (*to Tom*) You've heard all this before, huh? (*Tom nods*)
Father: So he hangs out with punks, and has started to act just like a punk.
Therapist: (*to Tom*) So Dad doesn't agree with the friends you have? (*Tom nods*) Is this something you and Dad argue about a lot?
Son: Sure.
Therapist: Do you feel that he has been unfair about this?
Son: [Mumbles inaudibly. His head is hanging, and he looks very unhappy.]
Therapist: How do you feel about being here, Tom?
Son: (*deep sigh*) I don't get it.
Therapist: You don't get it? Why you're here, you mean?
Son: No, I think I understand why I'm here, but I'm still thinking it's not so important.
Therapist: You think a big deal is being made out of something that's not such a big deal?
Son: Yeh, I'll just go to a different school.
Father: You see? And I know where he gets that idea from. He runs into trouble, and he goes somewhere else.
Mother: I think it's a good idea.
Father: (*sounding angry*) Let him go to a school where they let him hit the teacher? Is there such a school? Let him go to a school where there are no rules? There is such a school?
Mother: No, a school where they try to understand him and take consideration for, uh, people differences, and uh, the fact that people don't need bars across the cafeteria and things like that.
Father: When they're throwing punches at you, they do. If you're gonna act like an animal, you're gonna get thrown in a cage.
Therapist: (*to Tom*) Have you thought about what it would be like to leave your friends, Tom, when you go to a new school?
Son: Leave friends?
Therapist: Uh-huh. Is that something you'd do pretty easily? (*Tom nods*) Do you have lots of friends?
Son: Yeh, pretty much.
Therapist: What did your friends have to say about this particular incident?
Son: You mean the teacher?
Therapist: Uh-huh.
Son: They were behind me.
Therapist: Were they in fact involved with this?
Son: No, not really. I mean, it was in the minds of some of my other friends, but, ah . . .
Therapist: Did this occur in the classroom or after school or in the hallways?

Son: After class.
Therapist: Your friends were saying, "Right on, Tom!"?
Son: Uh-huh.
Father: He doesn't understand that they set him up and that his friends are a little smarter than he is, because they're not the ones that got arrested for throwing a punch.
Therapist: Got arrested! Excuse me, I think I missed something.
Father: Okay, not arrested—stopped, taken out of the room . . .
Mother: (*to father*) See, there you go exaggerating again!
Therapist: What was the consequence at the school?
Father: Suspended for a week.
Therapist: (*to Tom*) So, a week's vacation, huh? What are you going to do? Is that week over already?
Son: No, I have a couple days left.
Therapist: How did you all decide to come here? (*looking at no one in particular*)
Mother: Well, the school counselor strongly recommended it. He thought that maybe there were some things that Tom needed to talk about with his family, ummm, and, ummm, I thought it was a good idea too, actually. I haven't been feeling real comfortable with the way things are at home.
Therapist: Can you tell me more about that?
Mother: Well . . . (*sigh, long silence*)
Therapist: Sometimes it's really hard to talk about families because it seems so personal. And you all may have experiences which are hard to talk about as well. I understand that.
Mother: Well, Dave and I haven't been getting along too well lately, either. I don't know, it's just that Tom being at the age that he's seeking more independence, and maybe this is causing some strain for us. But . . .
Therapist: Were you aware . . . Pardon me (*to Tom, who is fidgeting and looking away*), were you aware, Tom, that things haven't been so good between Mom and Dad?
Son: Yeh.
Therapist: How have you seen that? Are they arguing more, or what?
Son: They're arguing more now.
Therapist: Uh-huh. And Mr. C., do you agree with your wife that lately things haven't felt too good between the two of you, or that things haven't felt as good as they have in the past?
Father: Well, the only thing we really disagree about is bringing up Tom.
Therapist: Some of the things that Tom's doing are worrying you two. You feel that you and your wife can't get together?
Father: Well, uh, I think we have our problems.

Mother: Things do seem to have gotten a little more strained with Tom's being older.

Therapist: When you say that, it sounds to me like maybe things were a little strained before, but they're more strained now.

Mother: (*sighs*) Well . . . uh . . . (*silence*)

Therapist: People in families have different perceptions of how things are, and it doesn't mean that anyone is right or wrong, but I'm interested in hearing how each one of you sees the situation. That would be very helpful to me in trying to understand what's going on. I sense that when I asked that question, you weren't quite sure if it was OK . .

Mother: (*interrupts*) I'm not sure if we should discuss it in front of Tom. I feel a little bit uncomfortable, you know, uhh, talking about the problems between Dave and I. You know, I just feel a little bit uncomfortable talking about it.

Therapist: Yet Tom tells us that he's been very aware of these family issues. Were you surprised to know that he was aware of the situation?

Mother: Well, sure, we all live in the same house.

Therapist: But he may not be aware of some of the specific issues . . . this is what you are saying?

Mother: Yeh.

Therapist: In deciding to come here, were there other things besides helping Tom work it out with school, or the strain you've recently experienced in the relationship with your husband that you thought might be helped by coming here?

Mother: Well, I thought those were the main things. It's just this problem with Tom getting in trouble at school that made me realize that we needed to do something about this now.

Therapist: (*turning to father*) Mr. C., you seem to me to be a man of action. When things are going wrong, you want to step in and take control and get things back on track. As things have been going worse and worse with Tom, how does that make you feel? Are you . . .

Father: (*interrupting*) I don't like it. He's got himself in trouble, and he's not sure what this means yet. When you screw up, and you screw up real bad, you're gonna make a reputation for yourself, and you've gotta cover your face.

Therapist: It sounds like you're really concerned for Tom that he's really put himself behind the eight ball and may not be able to work his way out.

Father: Exactly! Let's face it, I'm not going to be here forever to take care of him. (*sounding less angry*)

Therapist: Is that what it's been feeling like lately, you're having to take care of him?

Father: Sure, when he gets into trouble, he needs to have some idea of how to get out of it. . . . (*inaudible*) Otherwise, the kid's gonna be a bum.

Therapist: What were your reactions when deciding to come to the center today?

Father: I had hoped to get some suggestions as to what would help Tom out.

Therapist: I'm glad that you said it that way, because I really am sensing that although you are pretty angry and upset with Tom, that basically you're here to find out how to help. I'm not sure that Tom experiences you that way.

Father: There's no doubt about that.

Therapist: Yeh, we don't help people we don't like or that we're so upset with. We help the people we care about.

Father: Well, I figure I'm responsible for him.

Therapist: It must be very frustrating to find someone that you're feeling responsible for not cooperating or holding the line.

Father: Well, uh, what can I say? It's a problem. We do the best we can, and you don't get back what you hoped for. (*to Tom*) You'll be 18 soon and you'll go off and be on your own, so between now and then I'll just have to be the best by you I can. But so far it's not working so good. (*sounding less angry and more depressed*)

Therapist: Sounds like you know from your own experience there, that after you're 18 and out on your own, things will be kind of rough.

Father: Well, uh, it wasn't that long ago.

Therapist: (*to Tom*) Does Dad ever talk to you about what it was like for him being 14?

Son: Sometimes . . . he really doesn't feel like talking much . . . He's always ordering me. He doesn't talk too much, he mostly screams.

Therapist: So when the two of you are having a conversation, it's mostly one way?

Son: We don't have any things to talk about.

Therapist: Is that new?

Son: I don't know . . .

Therapist: In the past, when your Dad was ragging on you, you just stood there and took it?

Son: He didn't used to rag on me so much. He wasn't around a lot.

Therapist: He was around a lot?

Son: Wasn't!

Therapist: He wasn't around a lot. Is he around more now?

Son: Yeh.

Therapist: (*to father*) Umm, did you have a job commitment or something earlier that changed?

Father: Yeh, I used to travel a lot more than I do now. I got a promotion, and I stick closer to home now.
Therapist: When was this?
Father: About 2 years ago.
Therapist: (*to mother*) Having Dad available at home more has changed things at home?
Mother: Well, it doesn't change things that much. Dave watches TV a lot. Usually when he gets home from work, he spends a lot of the time in front of the TV set. Except to eat dinner, of course. But sometimes he even eats that in front of the TV set.
Therapist: (*to father with a smile*) She's telling on you!
Father: (*to mother*) I don't always watch TV, for God's sake!
Mother: Dave, I think you watch a lot of TV.
Therapist: (*to Tom*) With Dad's being more available, do you and he, or have you and he, done some things together?
Son: There's a motorcycle we worked on.
Therapist: You both are mechanics?
Son: Uh-huh.
Therapist: Did Dad teach you?
Son: He and I started working on it.
Therapist: Does this continue to be, or has it been stopped?
Son: Oh . . . when he's not ragging at me . . . once in a while.
Therapist: So, when he's feeling good about you, that's when the two of you work on the motorcycle?
Son: Yeh.
Therapist: When was the last time you worked on the motorcycle? (*long pause*) It's been a while, huh?
Son: Uh-huh.
Therapist: (*to father*) When Tom talked about the two of you working on the motorcycle, it sounded like something that he enjoyed. How did you experience that?
Father: Well, I like working with my hands. I like working on it, but it's real hard to teach this guy anything.
Therapist: Why is that?
Father: He doesn't like to listen; he thinks he knows it all. It's just like . . .
Therapist: (*interrupts father*) Do you know that that kind of goes with the age to some extent? 14-year-olds typically think they know it all, to some extent.
Father: Well, uh, I don't know. He may think that, but once a 14-year-old thinks he can run around and hit a teacher . . . (*inaudible*) . . . and a 14-year-old thinks he can put on a muffler, and . . . (*inaudible*)
Therapist: You know, a difficulty parents with teenagers experience is how to deal with this kid who thinks he knows it all and still get him to learn rules or do things differently. Have you figured how to do

that with your own son?

Father: Well, I told him once that if you want to learn about motorcycles, you let me know when you're good and ready and I'll spend all the time you want. But if you're gonna carry on this way, I have better things to do. I shouldn't be trying to deal with these temper tantrums.

Therapist: Does that approach work with Tom?

Father: No, he thinks . . . that's what he calls raggin' on him. That's why I can't put up with this crap.

Therapist: Does he eventually come back to you and indicate that he wants your help?

Father: Uh, he used to . . . but not so much anymore. Not when he hangs out with those friends of his who break the law.

Therapist: Some of Tom's friends get into trouble with the law?

Father: Yeh.

Therapist: (*to Tom*) What do you think of Dad's ways of dealing with you?

Son: He pushes me and rags so much.

Therapist: What do you do when he's raggin'?

Son: I can't do nothing. He gets upset. (*sounding depressed*)

Therapist: Tom, you seem pretty mellow or pretty sad about this, just from looking at you. Are you feeling kind of down?

Son: Well, not really.

Therapist: Have you given a lot of thought to everything that's happening? Do you have some notions about why they happened, or what needs to be done about them?

Son: (*long pause*) If Mom and Dad didn't fight as much.

Therapist: That's something that would make you feel better, if that happened less?

Son: They're either not talking or they're fighting.

Therapist: So it's one extreme or another? (*pause*) So you're uncomfortable being in a house where either people are giving each other the silent treatment or they're yelling and screaming at each other. What do you do when they start fighting?

Son: Go find something to do, I guess.

Therapist: Go to your room or go outside or something?

Son: I hang out with the fellows.

Therapist: Do you have some notions why Mom and Dad are fighting more lately?

Son: I can't figure out what they do.

Therapist: Do you think that maybe you're the cause of some of the fighting? Are you feeling like you have some responsibility in this?

Son: They just can't figure out what to do with me, so they fight and argue about it. If they're not arguing, they're not talking.

Therapist: Well, maybe arguing is better than not talking.

Father: It beats hitting, anyway.

Therapist: (to Tom) It's my sense that you and Dad are the same way, that if you're not arguing, then you're not talking. Am I right about that?

Son: We talk.

Therapist: You talk to Dad?

Son: Not that much.

Therapist: You talk to Mom?

Son: Yeh, we talk a lot.

Therapist: Even when Mom's not talking to Dad, she's still talking to you . . . *(long pause)* Do you have a sense of what your parents are feeling about you? *(pause)* Disappointed?

Son: No, not really. Mom understands and Dad just likes to rag.

Therapist: I have a sense that you're not too happy with yourself . . . about what's happened.

Son: No, I'd just rather not think about it.

Therapist: Do you think that anything could be accomplished here?

Son: (long pause) Maybe we could figure out how to be more comfortable with this.

Therapist: Is that maybe one of the reasons why you agreed to come today?

Son: I came, because if I didn't, he'd bust my ass.

Therapist: You're a pretty big fellow. If you really didn't want to come, I'm sure there's no way that Dad could physically drag you in . . . *(pause)* Could it be worth your while to come here if you felt that maybe you could help Mom and Dad figure out how to make things better for them?

Son: Sure.

Therapist: And you hear their concerns were how to make things better for you?

Son: Uh-huh.

Therapist: One of the things that is true of families is that whenever anything is going wrong, even if it is only with one member of the family—because families are so close, and because they care about each other, when that person is in trouble, it kind of becomes the trouble of everyone. Everybody becomes involved and concerned. Because of that reason, I prefer to work with families together. It is fairly obvious that you, Mr. C. and Mrs. C., are very concerned about Tom. I'm also hearing that you have some additional concerns with regard to making things a little better for you in terms of how you relate to one another, perhaps around guiding Tom. I would propose that for the time being we meet together as a group of three. The goal would be for us to find out how everybody in the family can come up with the solutions to these problems that seem to be going on. Figure out how everybody can help everybody else out. I get a sense of caring, or else you wouldn't be here. You could have just taken him out of school and enrolled him in another school and said, "Forget that." But you're here, and that's a positive step, and it stems from wanting to make things different. It also tells me that you're in pain; that people aren't feeling too good about the situation right now. How would everyone feel to come back as a family, let's say for three more sessions, and we'll stop at that point and we'll see how things are going? We'll make a decision at that point as to what to do from there. Basically, I'm just getting to know your family. There may be lots of things you still want me to know and never had a chance to tell me, and you can do that next session. It will take a little time to get to know you and for you to tell me everything that's going on in your family. So basically in these first sessions, that's what we'd be doing.

Mother: Well, I think it sounds like a good idea. I'm for it.

Therapist: How about you, Tom?

Son: [He nods.]

Therapist: Mr. C.?

Father: Well, if you think it would help, we should certainly give it a try. The important thing is to put Tom back on the straight and narrow again. If it can help with that, we should do it.

Therapist: Well, therapy is one of those things, unfortunately, that there are no guarantees about. My initial impressions of your family is that a basic caring and love and concern for one another is there, which is usually a pretty good indicator for me that things can get better. (*pause*) Is this time OK with everyone's schedule?

Father: Well, I can take time off from work.

Therapist: It's possible for you to do that?

Father: Yeh.

Therapist: (*to Tom*) Dad must care an awful lot if he's willing to take time off of work. (*pause*) OK . . . I will see you, then, next Tuesday. Does anybody have any questions before we break up? I'd like you, Mr. and Mrs. C., to sign a release form so that I can talk to the school. Would that be OK with you, Tom?

Son: Sure.

Therapist: (*to Tom*) Who would be a good person to talk to at the school about what's been going on?

Son: One of my friends, if you want the truth.

Therapist: Well, that's a possibility. Do you think I could learn about the situation by talking to your friends?

Son: Sure.

Father: Can't talk to the teacher, because he's got his mouth wired!

Therapist: Maybe the social worker who you talked to, Mrs. C.?

Mother: I think that would be a good idea.

Therapist: OK. I'll have you sign a form which gives me permission to talk to the social worker. And, Tom, will you sign a form which gives me permission to talk to your friend? You might also want to tell him that I may be calling so that he doesn't freak out when there is a shrink on the other end of the telephone.

Son: Yeh, he'd freak out!

Father: Are you seriously going to talk to his friends?

Therapist: Sure. Do you have some concerns about that, Mr. C.?

Father: I don't know what good it would do.

Therapist: I don't know either, but we'll find out. OK? See you next week.

Special Issues in Conducting Family Therapy

Cotherapists

In both group and family therapy, the use of two therapists has become popular. Although it is often impractical (as staff availability and the family's financial ability may preclude it), when it is possible, there are some advantages to utilizing cotherapists with families. There are also a number of pitfalls, however, of which to be aware. The advantages to using cotherapists are that "two heads are better than one"; the two therapists can play differing roles with the family; they can model exchanges for the family that one therapist cannot; they may better manage a difficult or out-of-control family; having two therapists allows for the use of more techniques (such as one therapist removing the triangulated person to a separate part of the room or behind a one-way mirror while the other pushes the conflictual dyad to deal with their conflict more directly, using deliberate side taking); having two therapists better ensures that any one therapist's countertransference reactions would be less harmful to the therapy process; and the cotherapists can feel support from the other as they deal with difficult issues and emotions.

Though there are many reasons to use cotherapists, there are also some cautions to consider when utilizing such an arrangement. For the most effective cotherapist arrangement, the cotherapists should be relatively equivalent in status. Sometimes cotherapy is used as a way to train beginning family therapists; in such an arrangement, an experienced family therapist is paired with a novice family therapist. While this arrangement is helpful for the new family therapist's learning, it is often confusing to the family. It is clear to the family that the two therapists do not share equally in their authority to run the sessions, yet this may not be openly discussed. If such an arrangement is used, it would seem important to inform the family of the specific roles.

Other concerns regarding the use of cotherapists have to do with the particular therapists involved and whether they can work productively together. The most common problems that arise within the cotherapy relationship are (1) the two therapists being competitive with one another; (2) the therapists being overly protective of one another, and thus walking on eggs and avoiding negative feedback (this is a particular problem when a novice works with a more experienced therapist, who may also be the novice's supervisor); (3) there is poor trust between the therapists; (4) there is a domination/passivity pattern, (5) there are conflicts regarding who does the out-of-session "work" related to the case (paperwork, scheduling, returning phone calls, and the like); (6) the therapists develop an intense, perhaps intimate relationship that is not acknowledged as affecting their work together; (7) the therapists are not as spontaneous with their in-session reactions to the family because they wait for their partner's reaction; (8) each has a rigid theoretical orientation that is in conflict with the other's; (9) one or both therapists are defensive about receiving feedback or looking at personal contributions to the therapy process; or (10) there is not enough time to work on the cotherapy relationship and to plan for sessions.

Cotherapy can be a very positive and powerful arrangement when it works. It does take considerable effort on the part of the cotherapists, however, to ensure that issues are attended to and the relationship nurtured. When the cotherapy relationship suffers for any of the reasons cited above, it is probably in the best interests of the family that the cotherapy arrangement not continue. Although male-female cotherapists are the most common dyad, male-male and female-female cotherapists can also be effective. Decisions about who the therapists are and what characteristics they should have are clinical decisions and should be made with a particular family's needs in mind. Finally, it is important that the cotherapists have access to good supervision from a third party. Even the best and healthiest of therapists will face issues as cotherapists that are difficult to identify and resolve without the objectivity of an outsider to the relationship.

Consultation or Supervision

Having access to supervision or professional consultation is often necessary when working with families. There is probably no other therapy situation that provokes such personal reactions in the therapist as does working with families. More than working with individuals, there is the likelihood in working with families that among the multitude of issues and personalities will be some that provoke countertransference reactions in the therapist. Supervision or consultation is also needed because family therapy can be much more complex than working with only one individual; thus, the consultant or supervisor can provide another set of eyes and ears.

When supervision is most apparent is in the use of *live supervision* and *group supervision*. Both these forms of supervision have been popularized particularly by the family therapy movement. Live supervision involves the supervisor observing the session while it is occurring, usually behind a one-way mirror. It is also possible to conduct live supervision, however, from a far side of the therapy room or in another room through the use of remote television. In this format, the supervisor can function in various ways, including (1) observing the entire session and giving feedback to the therapist after the session is over; (2) observing the session, taking a break at a convenient stopping point in the session (usually midway or near the end of the session), and meeting with the therapist during this "break" to discuss what is going on and how to proceed during the remainder of the session; and (3) observing the session and interrupting whenever relevant information needs to be shared with the therapist. This latter procedure typically involves the use of bug-in-the ear equipment, a phone system that connects the therapy and observation rooms, or the supervisor actually knocking on the door of the therapy room. Although these interruptions may initially be distracting to families, if these procedures are routinely used, families become accustomed to them and actually consider the supervisor to be a legitimate part of the process.

Group supervision is conducted similarly, except that a team of persons who function as "not present in the room" cotherapists observe the session. As with the formats described above, the team can give feedback in a variety of ways, including at a break point, throughout the session, or at the end of the session. Functioning as a member of a live supervision team can be a powerful learning method for new family therapists; team members get to observe the session and give their imput without having to interact directly with family members.

Home Visits

There may be occasions in which the therapist might want to consider conducting family therapy in the family's home instead of an office. If appropriate, such home visits allow the therapist a firsthand look at the environment in which the family lives. Not only will the therapist be able to assess the living arrangements in the house or apartment, but the larger ecological context can also be evaluated. Sometimes when a therapist sees the neighborhood in which a family lives, it becomes clearer why there are certain issues within this family. While assessing the living quarters, the therapist can evaluate such issues as how privacy is handled in the family, space and overcrowding, the overall demeanor of the household (messy versus meticulously ordered), and how conducive the family quarters are to keeping children safe and stimulating them (for example, whether toys and books are available for the children to use).

Whether or not to do therapy in a family's home, or even to make a special home visit, should be a decision made after considering a variety of clinical information. Some families would welcome the therapist and take the willingness of the therapist to come to their home as a sign of caring and interest, whereas other families would become very defensive and threatened at the thought of the therapist encroaching on their private space. Families that are difficult to engage and who miss early sessions may be prime targets for home visits. Additionally, there are some families that are very intimidated by the thought of going to a professional setting. If the traditional methods of working with such families are ineffective, it is worth it to try alternative means of reaching them. The bottom line, however, is that the decision of whether to conduct home visits or home therapy needs to be considered uniquely for each family and the particular circumstances that they present.

Ethical and Professional Issues

Working with families can pose many of the same ethical and professional issues that are common to individual therapy. Doing family therapy, however, can raise other issues that are more specific to working with whole families. As was discussed earlier, the issue of contracting can get complicated when there are multiple persons contributing different goals to be included in the therapeutic contract. Should any one family member's agenda for treatment have precedence over another's? Though the parents certainly have greater status within the family to make family decisions, whenever possible the therapist should work to incorporate the various agendas that family members present. If these variant stances can be integrated and receive the consent of all family members, a major therapeutic intervention would have already occurred for many families who have not before been able to deal constructively with such differences.

Although it may not be legally required in all states, when signatures are required for the release of information or for permission to speak with collaterals, it is therapeutically advised to get the signatures of all family members concerned, including children. Additional problems around authority to release information arise when a family that was seen in therapy later has the parents getting a divorce. One parent may want the therapy record released, while the other parent does not. Again, a meeting with the opposing parties to work out a consensual agreement is advised; however, this is not always possible. This is one of those times when a legal consultation may be necessary.

Therapists who work with families should familarize themselves with the major aspects of family law that are in force in their particular state. Legal issues that frequently come up as one works with families are (1) mandated reporting of child abuse and neglect, (2) parental rights over consent to treat and consent to release information depending on custodial arrangements, (3) the rights of handicapped children to educational and mental health resources, (4) under what circumstances a child's or parent's right to confidentiality can be disregarded, and (5) the laws governing the hospitalization of a child against the child's wishes. Though it is often a wish of the therapist that these extraneous issues be kept out of the therapy arena, in reality they are often meshed with the work of therapy. Because a therapist cannot avoid dealing with these issues, he or she should be knowledgeable about and prepared to deal with them as they arise. If a therapist has a concern or question about how a legal or professional issue is to be handled, a consultation with another mental health professional is in order. In some cases, the consultation of a legal authority would also be advised.

Ethnic, Racial, Cultural, and Socioeconomic Issues

In work with families, the therapist needs to be ever mindful of the contributions of ethnicity, race, culture, and a family's economic status. Family therapists bring their own set of values, attitudes, and biases based on their own ethnic, racial, cultural and socioeconomic background to their work with families. The family therapist needs to be ever alert to the tendency to be *ethnocentric*—that is, to assume that others have had similar experiences and hold the same values and attitudes as the therapist. It is the responsibility of the therapist to get educated and to learn about the particular influences that various ethnic, racial, cultural and socioeconomic groups may manifest. As it is impossible to know everything about various groups, it is ultimately necessary for the family therapist to remain open to learning from each family the idiosyncratic values and attitudes that are integral to their being.

A therapist should never be afraid to admit to not being familiar with something; it is far better to ask to be educated than to proceed with ignorance, and it is also an ethical obligation. It is probably the case that therapists need to work harder at understanding those families that are different from the kind of family in which the therapist grew up. It is also possible, however, that when a therapist works with a family who shares a similar background, he or she overly assumes that the family thinks, feels, and reacts similarly to the therapist. Being a good therapist means to be open to learning, flexible to entertaining new ideas, and able to tolerate differences.

This book has emphasized principles of psythotherapy that guide therapists in the conduct of their work. But there is no substitute for the knowledge that is acquired when these principles are implemented in helping children and families. Serve them and learn.

References

Chapter 1

Allen, F.H. (1934). Therapeutic work with children. *American Journal of Orthopsychiatry, 4,* 193–202.

Allen, F.H. (1942). *Psychotherapy with children.* New York: Norton.

American Psychiatric Association. (1987). *Diagnostic and statistical manual of mental disorders* (3rd ed.). Washington, DC: Author.

Astor, J. (1989). A conversation with Dr. Donald Meltzer. *Journal of Child Psychotherapy, 15,* 1–13.

Barrett, C. L., Hampe, I. E., & Miller, L. (1978). Research on psychotherapy with children. In S. L. Garfield & A. E. Bergin (Eds.), *Handbook of psychotherapy and behavior change* (2nd ed.). New York: Wiley.

Bettelheim, B. (1967). *The empty fortress.* New York: Free Press.

Casey, R. J., & Berman, J. S. (1985). The outcome of psychotherapy with children. *Psychological Bulletin, 98,* 388–400.

Cummings, J. E. (1944). Incidence of emotional symptoms in school children. *British Journal of Educational Psychology, 14,* 151–161.

DesLauriers, A. M., & Carlson, C. F. (1969). *Your child is asleep; Early infantile autism.* Homewood, IL: Dorsey.

Despert, J. L. (1970). *The emotionally disturbed child.* Garden City, NY: Anchor.

Eysenck, H. J. (1961). The effects of psychotherapy. In H. J. Eysenck (Ed.), *Handbook of abnormal psychology.* New York: Basic Books.

Foa, E. B., & Emmelkamp, P. M. G. (1983). *Failures in behavior therapy.* New York: Wiley.

Freud, A. (1965). *Normality and pathology in childhood.* New York: International Universities Press.

Freud, S. (1959). Analysis of a phobia in a five-year-old boy. In *Collected papers, vol. 3.* New York: Basic Books.

Gelfand, D. M. (1969). *Social learning in childhood: Readings in theory and application.* Belmont, CA: Brooks/Cole.

Gerard, M. W. (1952). Emotional discorders of childhood. In F. Alexander & H. Ross (Eds.), *Dynamic psychiatry.* Chicago: University of Chicago Press.

Ginott, H. G. (1965). *Between parent and child.* New York: Macmillan.

Ginott, H. G. (1969). *Between parent and teenager.* New York: Macmillan.

Gurman, A. S., Kniskern, D. P., & Pinsof, W. M. (1986). Research on the process and outcome of marital and family therapy. In S. L. Garfield & A. E. Bergin (Eds.), *Handbook of psychotherapy and behavior change* (3rd ed.). New York: Wiley.

Haizlip, T., Corder, B. F., & Ball, B. C. (1984). The adolescent murderer. In C. R. Keith (Ed.), *The aggressive adolescent.* New York: Free Press.

Hood-Williams, J. (1960). The results of psychotherapy with children: A revaluation. *Journal of Consulting Psychology, 24,* 84–88.

Jersild, A. T. (1960). *Child psychology.* Englewood Cliffs, NJ: Prentice-Hall.

Jones, E. (1957). *The life and work of Sigmund Freud, vol. 3.* New York: Basic Books.

Jones, M. C. (1924). A laboratory study of fear: The case of Peter. *Pedagogical Seminary 31,* 308–315.

Kanner, L. (1943). Autistic disturbances of affective contact. *Nervous Child, 2,* 217–250.

Kanner, L. (1944). Early infantile autism. *Journal of Pediatrics, 25,* 211–217.

Kanner, L. (1960). Do behavioral symptoms always indicate psychopathology? *Journal of Child Psychology and Psychiatry, 1,* 17–25.

Kazdin, A. E. (1988). *Child psychotherapy: Developing and identifying effective treatments.* New York: Pergamon.

Kazdin, A. E., Bass, D., Ayers, W. A., & Rodgers, A. (1990). Empirical and clinical focus of child and adolescent psychotherapy research. *Journal of Consulting and Clinical Psychology, 58,* 729–740.

Kemph, J. P. (1964). The treatment of psychotic children. *Current Psychiatric Therapies, 4,* 74–78.

Kessler, J. W. (1966). *Psychopathology of childhood.* Englewood Cliffs, NJ: Prentice-Hall.

Klein, M. (1932). *The psycho-analysis of children.* New York: Norton.

Knowlton, P. (1967). Treatment and management of the autistic child. In M. Hammer & A. M. Kaplan (Eds.), *The practice of psychotherapy with children.* Homewood, IL: Dorsey.

Lapouse, R., & Monk, M. (1964). Behavior deviations in a representative sample of children. *American Journal of Orthopsychiatry, 34,* 436–446.

Levitt, E. E. (1957). The results of psychotherapy with children: An evaluation. *Journal of Consulting Psychology, 21,* 189–196.

Levitt, E. E. (1960). Reply to Hood-Williams. *Journal of Consulting Psychology, 24,* 89–91.

Linehan, M. M. (1980). Supervision of behavior therapy. In A. K. Hess (Ed.), *Psychotherapy supervision.* New York: Wiley-Interscience.

Lovaas, O. I. (1968). Some studies on the treatment of childhood schizophrenia. In J. M. Shlien (Ed.), *Research in psychotherapy, vol. 3.* Washington, DC: American Psychological Association.

Lovaas, O. I. (1987). Behavioral treatment and normal educational and intellectual functioning in young autistic children. *Journal of Consulting and Clinical Psychology, 55,* 3–9.

Masterson, J. F. (1967). The symptomatic adolescent five years later: He didn't grow out of it. *American Journal of Psychiatry, 123,* 1338–1345.

Miller, L. C., Hampe, E., Barrett, C. L., & Noble, H. (1971). Children's deviant behavior within the general population. *Journal of Consulting and Clinical Psychology, 37,* 16–22.

Moustakas, C. E. (1953). *Children in play therapy.* New York: McGraw-Hill.

Ollendick, T. H. (1986). Child and adolescent behavior therapy. In S. L. Garfield & A. E. Bergin (Eds.), *Handbook of psychotherapy and behavior change* (3rd ed.). New York: Wiley.

Rautman, E. & Rautman, A. (1948). Talking to a child. *Mental Hygiene, 32,* 631–637.

Reisman, J. M. (1971). *Toward the integration of psychotherapy.* New York: Wiley-Interscience.

Reisman, J. M. (1986). *Behavior disorders in infants, children, and adolescents.* New York: Random House.

Reisman, J. M. (1991). *A history of clinical psychology* (2nd ed.). Washington, DC: Hemisphere.

Robins, L. N. (1966). *Deviant children grown up: A sociological and psychiatric study of sociopathic personality.* Baltimore: Williams & Wilkins.

Rogers, C. R. (1951). *Client-centered therapy.* Boston: Houghton Mifflin.

Rogers, C. R. (1962). Some learnings from a study of psychotherapy with schizophrenics. *Pennsylvania Psychiatric Quarterly, 3–15.*

Ross, A. O. (1981). *Child behavior therapy.* New York: Wiley.

Shepherd, M., Oppenheim, A. N., & Mitchell, S. (1966). Childhood behaviour disorders and the child-guidance clinic. *Journal of Child Psychology and Psychiatry, 7,* 39–52.

Smith, M. L., & Glass, G. V. (1977). Meta-analysis of psychotherapy outcome studies. *American Psychologist, 32,* 752–777.

Smith, M. L., Glass, G. V., & Miller, T. I. (1980). *The benefits of psychotherapy.* Baltimore: Johns Hopkins University Press.

Staats, A. W. (1971). *Child learning, intelligence, and personality: Principles of a behavioral interaction approach.* New York: Harper & Row.

Tuma, J. M. (1989). Mental health services for children: The state of the art. *American Psychologist, 44,* 188–199.

Valentine, C. W. (1956). *The normal child and some of his abnormalities.* Baltimore: Penguin.

Volkmar, F. R., Bregman, J., Cohen, D. J., & Cicchetti, D. V. (1988). DSM-III and DSM-III-R diagnoses of autism. *American Journal of Psychiatry, 145,* 1404–1408.

Weiner, I. B. (1970). *Psychological disturbance in adolescence.* New York: Wiley-Interscience.

Weisz, J. R., Weiss, B., Alicke, M. D., & Klotz, M. L. (1987). Effectiveness of psychotherapy with children and adolescents: A meta-analysis for clinicians. *Journal of Consulting and Clinical Psychology, 55,* 542–549.

Wing, J. K., O'Connor, N., & Lotter, V. (1967). Autistic conditions in early childhood: A survey in Middlesex. *British Medical Journal, 3,* 389–392.

Witmer, L. (1919–1922). Orthogenic cases XIV. Don: A curable case of arrested development due to a fear psychosis the result of shock in a three-year-old infant. *Psychological Clinic, 13,* 97–111.

Zaslow, R. W., & Breger, L. (1969). A theory and treatment of autism. In

L. Breger (Ed.), *Clinical-cognitive psychology*. Englewood Cliffs, NJ: Prentice-Hall.

Chapter 2

Ackerman, N. W. (1958). *The psychodynamics of family life*. New York: Basic Books.

Ackerman, N. W. (1961). *Exploring the base for family therapy*. New York: Family Service Association of America.

Alexander, L. (1950). General principles of psychotherapy. *American Journal of Psychiatry, 106*, 721–731.

Alexander, J., & Parsons, B. V. (1982). *Functional family therapy*. Monterey, CA: Brooks/Cole.

Allen, F. H. (1942). *Psychotherapy with children*. New York: Norton.

Allen, F. H. (1962). Child psychotherapy. *Current Psychiatric Therapies, 2*, 41–47.

American Psychological Association (1992). Ethical principles of psychologists and code of conduct. *American Psychologist, 47*, 1597–1611.

American Psychological Association (1993). Guidelines for providers of psychological services to ethnic, linguistic, and culturally diverse populations. *American Psychologist, 48*, 45–48.

Ansbacher, H. L., & Ansbacher, R. R. (1956). *The individual psychology of Alfred Adler*. New York: Basic Books.

Argyle, M., & Henderson, M. (1984). The rules of friendship. *Journal of Social and Personal Relationships, 1*, 211–237.

Axline, V. M. (1947). *Play therapy*. Boston: Houghton Mifflin.

Barker, C., & Lemle, R. (1984). The helping process in couples. *American Journal of Community Psychology, 12*, 321–336.

Beck, A. T. (1976). *Cognitive therapy and the emotional disorders*. New York: International Universities Press.

Bell, R. (1981). *Worlds of friendship*. Beverly Hills, CA: Sage.

Bixler, R. H. (1949). Limits are therapy. *Journal of Consulting Psychology, 13*, 1–11.

Brammer, L. M., & Shostrom, E. L. (1960). *Therapeutic psychology: Fundamentals of counseling and psychotherapy*. Englewood Cliffs, NJ: Prentice-Hall.

Carkhuff, R. R., & Berenson, B. G. (1977). *Beyond counseling and therapy* (2nd ed.). New York: Holt, Rinehart & Winston.

Clarizio, H. F., & McCoy, G. F. (1970). *Behavior disorders in school-aged children*. Scranton, PA: Chandler.

Cowen, E. L. (1982). Help is where you find it: Four informal helping groups. *American Psychologist, 37*, 385–395.

Dorfman, E. (1951). Play therapy. In C. Rogers, *Client-centered therapy*. Boston: Houghton Mifflin.

Ellis, A. (1973). *Humanistic psychotherapy*. New York: McGraw-Hill.

Fiedler, F. A. (1950a). The concept of the ideal therapeutic relationship. *Journal of Consulting Psychology, 14*, 239–245.

Fiedler, F. A. (1950b). A comparison of therapeutic relationships in psychoanalytic, nondirective and Adlerian therapy. *Journal of Consulting Psychology, 14,* 436–445.

Freud, A. (1946). *The psychoanalytical treatment of children.* London: Imago.

Freud, A. (1965). *Normality and pathology in childhood.* New York: International Universities Press.

Freud, S. (1959). Analysis terminable and interminable. In *Collected papers, vol. 5.* New York: Basic Books.

Ginott, H. G. (1961). *Group psychotherapy with children.* New York: McGraw-Hill.

Glasser, W. (1965). *Reality therapy.* New York: Harper & Row.

Gurman, A. S., Kniskern, D. P., & Pinsof, W. M. (1986). Research on the process and outcome of marital and family therapy. In S. L. Garfield & A. E. Bergin (Eds.), *Handbook of psychotherapy and behavior change* (3rd ed.). New York: Wiley.

Hartup, W. W. (1975). The origins of friendship. In M. Lewis & L. A. Rosenblum (Eds.), *Friendship and peer relations.* New York: Wiley-Interscience.

Haynes, S. N., & O'Brien, W. H. (1990). Functional analysis in behavior therapy. *Clinical Psychology Review, 10,* 649–668.

Heinicke, C. M. (1990). Toward generic principles of treating parents and children: Integrating psychotherapy with the school-aged child and early family intervention. *Journal of Consulting and Clinical Psychology, 58,* 713–719.

Howard, K. I., Kopta, S. M., Krause, M. S., & Orlinsky, E. E. (1986). The dose-effect relationship in psychotherapy. *American Psychologist, 41,* 159–164.

Jackson, D. D., & Yalom, I. (1964). Family homeostasis and patient change. *Current Psychiatric Therapies, 4,* 155–165.

Kessler, J. W. (1966). *Psychopathology of childhood.* Englewood Cliffs, NJ: Prentice-Hall.

Klein, D. C. (1968). *Community dynamics and mental health.* New York: Wiley.

Klerman, G. L. (1990). The psychiatric patient's right to effective treatment: Implications of *Osheroff v. Chestnut Lodge. American Journal of Psychiatry, 147,* 409–418.

Lecky, P. (1969). *Self-consistency: A theory of personality.* New York: Anchor Books.

Levy, D. (1938). Release therapy in young children. *Psychiatry, 1,* 387–389.

Levy, D. (1939). Trends in therapy: III. Release therapy. *American Journal of Orthopsychiatry, 9,* 713–736.

Lippman, H. S. (1956). *Treatment of the child in emotional conflict.* New York: McGraw-Hill.

Melton, G. B. (1991). Socialization in the global community: Respect for the dignity of children. *American Psychologist, 46,* 66–71.

Menninger, K., Mayman, M., & Pruyser, P. (1963). *The vital balance.* New York: Viking.

Minuchin, S. (1974). *Families and family therapy.* Cambridge, MA: Harvard University Press.

Mitchell, K. M. (1974), Effective therapist interpersonal skills. In A. I. Rabin (Ed.), *Clinical psychology: issues of the seventies.* E. Lansing: Michigan State University Press.

Moustakas, C. E. (1953). *Children in play therapy.* New York: McGraw-Hill.

Moustakas, C. E. (1959). *Psychotherapy with children.* New York: Harper.

Nelson-Jones, R. (1990). *Human relationships: A skills approach.* Pacific Grove, CA: Brooks/Cole.

Palmer, J. O. (1970). *The psychological assessment of children. New York: Wiley.*

Parloff, M. B., Waskow, I. E., & Wolfe, B. E. (1978). Research on therapist variables in relation to process and outcome. In S. L. Garfield & A. E. Bergin (Eds.), *Handbook of psychotherapy and behavior change.* New York: Wiley.

Raskin, N. J. (1985). Client-centered therapy. In S. J. Lynn & J. P. Garske (Eds.), *Contemporary psychotherapies: Models and methods.* Columbus, OH: Merrill.

Reisman, J. M. (1971). *Toward the integration of psychotherapy.* New York: Wiley-Interscience.

Reisman, J. M. (1979). *The anatomy of friendship.* Lexington, MA: Lewis.

Reisman, J. M. (1982). Friendship and psychotherapy. *Academic Psychology Bulletin, 4,* 237–246.

Reisman, J. M. (1986). Psychotherapy as a professional relationship. *Professional Psychology: Research and Practice, 17,* 565–569.

Reisman, J. M., & Shorr, S. I. (1980). Developmental changes in friendship-related communication skills. *Journal of Clinical Child Psychology, 9,* 67–69.

Reisman, J. M., & Yamokoski, T. (1974). Psychotherapy and friendship: An analysis of the communication of friends. *Journal of Counseling Psychology, 21,* 269–273.

Rogers, C. R. (1951). *Client-centered therapy.* Boston: Houghton Mifflin.

Rogers, C. R. (1957). The necessary and sufficient conditions of therapeutic personality change. *Journal of Consulting Psychology, 21,* 95–103.

Rogers, C. R. (1961). *On becoming a person.* Boston: Houghton Mifflin.

Rogers, C. R. (1962, Summer). Some learnings from a study of psychotherapy with schizophrenics. *Pennsylvania Psychiatric Quarterly,* 3–15.

Rogers, C. R. (1980). *A way of being.* Boston: Houghton Mifflin.

Rosen, J. N. (1964). Direct psychoanalysis. *Current Psychiatric Therapies, 4,* 101–107.

Ross, A. O. (1959). *The practice of clinical child psychology.* New York: Grune & Stratton.

Ross, A. O. (1981). *Child behavior therapy.* New York: Wiley.

Satir, V. (1967). A family of angels. In J. Haley & L. Hoffman (Eds.), *Theories of family therapy.* New York: Basic Books.

Satir, V. (1968). *Conjoint family therapy.* Palo Alto, CA: Science & Behavior Books.

Schmeideberg, M. (1960). Principles of psychotherapy. *Comprehensive Psychiatry, 1,* 186–193.

Schofield, W. (1964). *Psychotherapy: The purchase of friendship.* New York: Prentice-Hall.

Shaw, F. J. (1948). Some postulates concerning psychotherapy. *Journal of Consulting Psychology, 12,* 426–431.

Singer, E. (1965). *Key concepts in psychotherapy.* New York: Random House.

Staats, A. W. (1971). *Child learning, intelligence, and personality: Principles of a behavioral interaction approach.* New York: Harper.

Stone, A. A. (1990). Law, science, and psychiatric malpractice: A response to

Klerman's indictment of psychoanalytic psychiatry. *American Journal of Psychiatry, 147,* 419–427.

Strean, H. S. (1968). Choice of paradigm in the treatment of parent and child. In M.C. Nelson (Ed.), *Roles and paradigms in psychotherapy.* New York: Grune & Stratton.

Strupp, H. H., Fox, R. E., & Lessler, K. (1969). *Patients view their psychotherapy.* Baltimore: Johns Hopkins University Press.

Strupp, H. H., & Hadley, S. W. (1979). Specific vs. nonspecific factors in psychotherapy. *Archives of General Psychiatry, 36,* 1125–1136.

Szurek, S. A. (1967). Principles of psychotherapy. In S. A. Szurek & I. N. Berlin (Eds.), *Training in therapeutic work with children.* Palo Alto, CA: Science & Behavior Books.

Truax, C. B. (1970). Effects of client-centered psychotherapy with schizophrenic patients: Nine years pretherapy and nine years' post-therapy hospitalization. *Journal of Consulting and Clinical Psychology, 35,* 417–422.

Truax, C. B., & Carkhuff, R. R. (1967). *Toward effective counseling and psychotherapy.* Chicago: Aldine.

Weiner, I. B. (1970). *Psychological disturbance in adolescence.* New York: Wiley-Interscience.

Weisz, J. R., Weiss, B., Alicke, M. D., & Klotz, M. L. (1987). Effectiveness of psychotherapy with children and adolescents: A meta-analysis for clinicians. *Journal of Consulting and Clinical Psychology, 55,* 542–549.

Weisz, J. R., Weiss, B., & Denenberg, G. R. (1992). The lab versus the clinic: Effects of child and adolescent psychotherapy. *American Psychologist, 47,* 1578–1585.

Whitaker, C. A., Felder, R. E., Malone, T. P., & Warkentin, J. (1962). First stage techniques in the experimental psychotherapy of chronic schizophrenic patients. *Current Psychiatric Therapies, 2,* 147–158.

White, R. W. (1964). *The abnormal personality.* New York: Ronald.

Wolberg, L. R. (1967). *The technique of psychotherapy, part 1* (2nd ed.). New York: Grune & Stratton.

Woody, R. H. (1966). *Behavorial problem children in the schools.* New York: Appleton-Century-Crofts.

Zuk, G. H. (1971). Family therapy during 1964–1970. *Psychotherapy: Theory, Research and Practice, 8,* 90–97.

Chapter 3

American Psychiatric Association Task Force on Behavior Therapy (1974). *Behavior therapy in psychiatry.* New York: Aronson.

Bandura, A. (1969). *Principles of behavior modification.* New York: Holt, Rinehart & Winston.

Bandura, A. (1977). *Social learning theory.* Englewood Cliffs, NJ: Prentice-Hall.

Barkley, R. A. (1990). *Attention deficit hyperactivity disorder.* New York: Guilford.

Barrios, B. A., & O'Dell, S. L. (1989). Fears and anxieties. In E. J. Mash & R. A. Barkley (Eds.), *Treatment of childhood disorders.* New York: Guilford.

Bellack, A. S., & Hersen, M. (1977). The use of self-report inventories in behavorial assessment. In J. D. Cone & R. P. Hawkins (Eds.), *Behavorial assessment: New directions in clinical psychology.* New York: Brunner/Mazel.

Bellack, A. S., & Hersen, M. (Eds.) (1988). *Behavorial assessment: A practical handbook.* New York: Pergamon.

Cautela, J. R., & Groden, J. (1978). *Relaxation: A comprehensive manual for adults, children, and children with special needs.* Champaign, IL: Research Press.

Ciminero, A. R., Calhoun, K. S., & Adams, H. E. (Eds.). (1986). *Handbook of behavorial assessment* (2nd ed.). New York: Wiley.

Cone, J. D., & Hawkins, R. P. (1977). *Behavorial assessment: New directions in clinical psychology.* New York: Brunner/Mazel.

Crary, E. (1979). *Without spanking or spoiling: A practical approach to toddler and preschool guidance.* Seattle, WA: Parenting Press.

Dunlap, K. (1932), *Habits: Their making and remaking.* New York: Liveright.

Epstein, L. H., & Squires, S. (1988). *The stop-light diet for children.* Boston: Little Brown.

Fine, M. J. (1973). *The teacher's role in classroom management.* Lawrence, KS: Psych-Ed Associates.

Goldfried, M. R. (1971). Systematic desensitization as training in self-control. *Journal of Consulting and Clinical Psychology, 37,* 228–234.

Goldfried, M. R., & Merbaum, M. (1973). *Behavior change through self-control.* New York: Holt, Rinehart & Winston.

Goldfried, M. R., & Trier, C. S. (1974). Effectiveness of relaxation as an active coping skill. *Journal of Abnormal Psychology, 83*(4), 348–355.

Graziano, A. M., & Mooney, K. C. (1984). *Children and behavior therapy.* New York: Aldine.

Hartmann, D. P., Roper, B. L., & Bradford, D. C. (1979). Some relationships between behavioral and traditional assessment. *Journal of Behavioral Assessment, 1,* 3–21.

Hersen, M., & Bellack, A. S. (Eds.) (1981). *Behavioral assessment: A practical handbook* (2nd ed.) New York: Pergamon.

Jacobson, E. (1938). *Progressive relaxation.* Chicago: University of Chicago Press.

Johnson, J. H., Rasbury, W. C., & Siegel, L. J. (1986). *Approaches to child treatment.* New York: Pergamon.

Jones, M. C. (1924). The elimination of children's fears. *Journal of Genetic Psychology, 7,* 382–390.

Kanfer, F. H., & Karoly, P. (1972). Self-control: A behavioristic excursion into the lion's den. *Behavior Therapy, 3,* 398–416.

Kanfer, F. H., & Saslow, G. (1969). Behavioral diagnosis. In C. M. Franks (Ed.), *Behavior therapy: Appraisal and status.* New York: McGraw-Hill.

Kazdin, A. E. (1984). *Behavior modification in applied settings* (3rd ed.). Homewood, IL: Dorsey.

Kestenbaum, C. J., & Williams, D. T. (Eds.). (1988). *Handbook of clinical assessment of children and adolescents, vols. I & II.* New York: New York University Press.

Koeppen, A. S. (1974). Relaxation training for children. *Elementray School Guidance and Counseling, 9,* 14–21.

Lazarus, A. A. (1960). The elimination of children's phobias by deconditioning. In

H. J. Eysenck (Ed.), Behavior therapy and the neuroses. Oxford: Pergamon.

Lazarus, A. A., & Abramovitz, A. (1962). The use of emotive imagery in the treatment of children's phobias. Journal of Mental Science, 108, 191–195.

Mahoney, M. J. (1974). Cognition and behavior modification. Cambridge, MA: Ballinger.

Mash, E. J., & Terdal, L. G. (1982). Behavioral assessment of childhood disorders. New York: Guilford.

Meichenbaum, D. (1977). Cognitive-behavior modification. New York: Plenum.

Milby, J. B., & Weber, A. (1991). Obsessive compulsive disorders. In T. R. Kratochwill & R. J. Morris (Eds.), The practice of child therapy (2nd ed.). New York: Pergamon.

Morris, R. J., & Kratochwill, T. R. (1983). Treating children's fears and phobias: A behavioral approach. New York: Pergamon.

Mowrer, O. H., & Mowrer, W. M. (1938). Enuresis: A method for its study and treatment. American Journal of Orthopsychiatry, 8, 436–459.

Novaco, R. W. (1978). Anger and coping with stress: Cognitive behavioral intervention. In J. P. Foreyt & D. P. Rathjen (Eds.), Cognitive behavioral therapy: Research and application. New York: Plenum.

Ollendick, T., & Hersen, M. (Eds.). (1984). Child behavioral assessment. New York: Pergamon.

Parkinson, R. W. (1985). Growing up on purpose. Champaign, IL: Research Press.

Patterson, G. (1976). Living with children (2nd ed.). Champaign, IL: Research Press.

Pavlov, I. P. (1927). Conditioned reflexes (G. V. Ansep, Trans.). London: Oxford University Press.

Phillips, D., Fischer, S. C., & Singh, R. (1977). A children's reinforcement survey schedule.

Pressley, M. (1977). Imagery and children's learning: Putting the picture in developmental perspective. Review of Educational Research, 47, 585–622.

Salter, A. (1949). Conditioned reflex therapy. New York: Capricorn.

Shirk, S. R., & Phillips, J. S. (1991). Child therapy training: Closing gaps with research and practice. Journal of Consulting and Clinical Psychology, 59(6), 766–776.

Siegel, L. J., & Smith, K. E. (1991). Somatic disorders. In T. R. Kratochwill & R. J. Morris (Eds.), The practice of child therapy (2nd ed.). New York: Pergamon.

Skinner, B. F. (1948). Walden two. New York: Macmillan.

Skinner, B. F. (1953). Science and human behavior. New York: Macmillan.

Smith, R. E. (1973). The use of humor in the counter-conditioning of anger responses: A case study. Behavior Therapy, 4, 576–580.

Stumphauzer, J. S. (1977). Behavior modification principles. Kalamazoo, MI: Behaviordelia.

Tuma, J. M. (Ed.) (1985). Proceedings: Conference on training clinical child psychologists. Washington, DC: American Psychological Association.

Walker, C. E., Milling, L. S., & Bonner, B. L. (1988). Incontinence disorders: Enuresis and encopresis. In D. Routh (Ed.), Handbook of pediatric psychology. New York: Guilford.

Watson, J. B. (1913). Psychology as a behaviorist views it. Psychological Review, 20(2), 158–177.

Watson, J. B., & Raynor, R. (1920). Conditioned emotional reactions. *Journal of Experimental Psychology, 3,* 1–14.

Wolpe, J. (1958). *Reciprocal inhibition therapy.* Stanford, CA: Stanford University Press.

Chapter 4

Bain, J. A. (1928). *Thought control in everyday life.* New York: Funk & Wagnalls.

Bandura, A. (1969). *Principles of behavior modification.* New York: Holt.

Bandura, A. (1977). *Social learning theory.* Englewood Cliffs, NJ: Prentice-Hall.

Bandura, A., Blanchard, E. B., & Ritter, B. (1969). The relative efficacy of desensitization and modeling approaches for inducing behavioral, affective, and attitudinal changes. *Journal of Personality and Social Psychology, 13,* 173–199.

Bandura, A., Grusec, J. E., & Menlove, F. L. (1967). Vicarious extinction of avoidance behavior. *Journal of Personality and Social Psychology, 5,* 16–23.

Bandura, A., & Menlove, F. L. (1968). Factors determining vicarious extinction of avoidance behavior through symbolic modeling. *Journal of Personality and Social Psychology, 8,* 99–108.

Bandura, A., & Walters, R. H. (1963). *Social learning and personality development.* New York: Holt, Rinehart & Winston.

Bornstein, P., & Quevillon, R. (1976). The effects of a self-instructional package on overactive preschool boys. *Journal of Applied Behavior Analysis, 9,* 179–188.

Brown, R. T., & Alford, N. (1984). Ameliorating attentional deficits and concomitant academic deficiencies in learning disabled children through cognitive training. *Journal of Learning Disabilities, 17,* 20–26.

Bryant, L. E., & Budd, K. S. (1982). Self-instructional training to increase independent work performance in preschoolers. *Journal of Applied Behavior Analysis, 15,* 259–271.

Campbell, L. M. (1973). A variation of thought stopping in a twelve year old boy: A case report. *Journal of Behavior Therapy and Experimental Psychiatry, 4,* 69–70.

Dodge, K. A. (1985). Attributional bias in aggressive children. In P. C. Kendall (Ed.), *Advances in cognitive-behavioral research and therapy, vol. 4.* Orlando, FL: Academic Press.

Dolgin, M. J., & Jay, S. M. (1989). Pain management in children. In C. J. Mash & R. A. Barkley (Eds.), *Treatment of childhood disorders.* New York: Guilford.

Ellis, P. L. (1982). Empathy: A factor in antisocial behavior. *Journal of Abnormal Child Psychology, 10,* 123–134.

Graziano, A. M., Mooney, K. C., Huber, C., & Ignasiak, D. (1979). Self-control instruction for children's fear reduction. *Journal of Behavior Therapy and Experimental Psychiatry, 10,* 221–227.

Kanfer, F. H., & Karoly, P. (1972). Self-control: A behavioristic excursion into the lion's den. *Behavior Therapy, 3,* 398–416.

Kanfer, F. H., Karoly, P., & Newman, A. (1975). Reduction of children's fear of the dark by competence-related and situational threat-related verbal cues. *Journal of Consulting and Clinical Psychology, 43,* 251–258.

Kazdin, A. E. (1984). *Behavior modification in applied settings.* Homewood: IL: Dorsey.

Kelly, G. A. (1955). *The psychology of personal constructs, vol. II.* New York: Norton.

Kendall, P. C., & Braswell, L. (1985). *Cognitive-behavioral therapy for impulsive children.* New York: Guildford.

Kumar, K., & Wilkinson, J. C. M. (1971). Thought stopping: A useful treatment for phobias of "internal stimuli." *British Journal of Psychiatry, 119,* 305–307.

Lloyd, J. W., Hallahan, D. P., Kauffman, J. M., & Keller, C. E. (1991). Academic problems. In T. R. Kratochwill & R. J. Morris (Eds.), *The practice of child therapy.* New York: Pergamon.

Lochman, J. E., Burch, P. R., Curry, J. F., & Lampron, L. B. (1984). Treatment and generalization effects of cognitive-behavioral and goal-setting interventions with aggressive boys. *Journal of Consulting and Clinical Psychology, 52,* 915–916.

Lochman, J. E., Nelson, W. M., & Sims, J. P. (1981). A cognitive behavioral program for use with agressive children. *Journal of Clinical Child Psychology, 10,* 146–148.

Lovaas, O. I., Freitag, L., Nelson, K., & Whalen, C. (1967). The establishment of imitation and its use for the development of complex behavior in schizophrenic children. *Behaviour Research and Therapy, 5,* 171–181.

Mahoney, M. J. (1974). *Cognition and behavior modification.* New York: Plenum.

Meichenbaum, D. H. (1977). *Cognitive-behavior modification.* New York: Plenum.

Meichenbaum, D. H. (1986). *Stress inoculation training.* New York: Pergamon.

Meichenbaum, D. H., & Goodman, J. (1971). Training impulsive children to talk to themselves: A means of developing self-control. *Journal of Abnormal Psychology, 77,* 115–126.

Melamed, B. G. (1979). Behavioral approaches to fear in dental settings. In M. Hersen, R. Eisler, & P. Miller (Eds.), *Progress in behavior modification, vol. 7.* New York: Academic Press.

Mealamed, B. G., & Siegel, L. J. (1975). Reduction of anxiety in children facing hospitalization and surgery by use of filmed modeling. *Journal of Counseling and Clinical Psychology, 43,* 511–521.

Morris, R. J., & Kratochwill, T. R. (Eds.). (1983). *The practice of child therapy.* New York: Pergamon.

O'Connor, R. D. (1969). Modification of social withdrawal through symbolic modeling. *Journal of Applied Behavior Analysis, 2,* 15–22.

Oden, S. L., & Asher, S. R. (1977). Coaching children in social skills for friendship making. *Child Development, 48,* 495–506.

Perry, M. A., & Furukawa, M. J. (1980). Modeling methods. In F. H. Kanfer & A. P. Goldstein (Eds.), *Helping people change* (2nd ed.). New York: Pergamon.

Rimm, D. C., & Masters, J. C. (1979). *Behavior therapy: Techniques and empirical findings* (2nd ed.). New York: Academic Press.

Robin, A. L., Schneider, M., & Dolnick, J. (1976). The turtle technique: An extensive case study of self-control in the classroom. *Psychology in the Schools, 1,* 449–459.

Shulman, M. (1978). Love training: Behavior therapy with an aggressive child. *Behavior Therapist, 1*(5), 16–17.

Shure, M. B., & Spivack, G. (1978). *Problem-solving techniques in child-rearing.* San Francisco: Jossey-Bass.

Siegel, L. J., & Peterson, L. (1981). Maintenance effects of coping skills and sensory information on young children's response to repeated dental procedures. *Behavior Therapy, 12, 530–535.*

Snyder, J. J., & White, M. J. (1979). The use of cognitive self-instruction in the treatment of behaviorally disturbed adolescents. *Behavior Therapy, 10, 227–235.*

Spivack, G., Platt, J. J., & Shure, M. B. (1976). *The problem-solving approach to adjustment.* San Francisco: Jossey-Bass.

Spivack, G., & Shure, M. B. (1982). The cognition of social adjustment: Interpersonal cognitive problem solving thinking. In B. B. Lahey & A. E. Kazdin (Eds.), *Advances in clinical child psychology, vol. 5.* New York: Plenum.

Weissberg, R. P., & Gesten, E. L. (1982). Considerations for developing effective school-based social problem-solving (SPS) training programs. *School Psychology Review, 11, 56–63.*

Wolpe, J. (1973). *The practice of behavior therapy* (2nd ed.). New York: Pergamon.

Yamagami, T. (1971). The treatment of an obsession by thought stopping. *Journal of Behavior Therapy and Experimental Psychiatry, 2, 133–135.*

Chapter 5

Allen, F. H. (1942). *Psychotherapy with children.* New York: Norton.

American Psychological Association. (1981). Ethical principles of psychologists. *American Psychologist, 36, 633–638.*

American Psychological Association. (1990a). Ethical principles of psychologists. *American Psychologist, 45, 390–395.*

American Psychological Association. (1990b, June). Ethical principles revised. *APA Monitor, 21, 28–32.*

American Psychological Association (1992), Ethical principles of psychologists and code of conduct. *American Psychologist, 47, 1597–1611.*

Axline, V. M. (1947). *Play therapy.* Boston: Houghton Mifflin.

Beier, E. G., Robinson, P., & Micheletti, G. (1971). Susanville: A community helps itself in mobilization of community resources for self-help in mental health. *Journal of Consulting and Clinical Psychology, 36, 142–150.*

Berlin, F. S., Malin, H. M., & Dean, S. (1991). Effects of statutes requiring psychiatrists to report sexual abuse of children. *American Journal of Psychiatry, 148, 449–453.*

Bixler, R. H. (1949). Limits are therapy. *Journal of Consulting Psychology, 13, 1–11.*

Bramer, L. M., & Shostrom, E. L. (1960). *Therapeutic psychology: Fundamentals of counseling and psychotherapy.* Englewood Cliffs, NJ: Prentice-Hall.

Dorfman, E. (1951). Play therapy. In C. Rogers, *Client-centered therapy.* Boston: Houghton Mifflin.

Federn, P. (1952). *Ego psychology and the psychoses.* New York: Basic Books.

Freud, A. (1965). *Normality and pathology in childhood.* New York: International Universities Press.

Ginott, H. G. (1959). The theory and practice of "therapeutic intervention" in child treatment. *Journal of Consulting Psychology, 23, 160–166.*

Ginott, H. G. (1961). *Group psychotherapy with children.* New York: McGraw-Hill.

Ginott, H. G. (1965). *Between parent and child.* New York: Macmillan.

Handelsman, M. M. (1990). Do written consent forms influence clients' first impressions of therapists? *Professional Psychology: Research and Practice, 21,* 451–454.

Harter, S. (1977). A cognitive-developmental approach to children's expression of conflicting feelings and a technique to facilitate such expression in play therapy. *Journal of Consulting and Clinical Psychology, 45,* 417–432.

Harter, S. (1983). Cognitive-developmental considerations in the conduct of play therapy. In C. E. Schaefer & K. J. O'Connor (Eds.), *Handbook of play therapy.* New York: Wiley.

Jernberg, A. (1984). Theraplay: Child therapy for attachment fostering. *Psychotherapy, 21,* 39–47.

Johnson, J. H., Rasbury, W. C., & Siegel, L. J. (1986). *Approaches to child treatment.* New York: Pergamon.

Klein, M. (1932). *The psychoanlysis of children.* New York: Norton.

Klerman, G. L. (1990). The psychiatric patient's right to effective treatment: Implications of *Osheroff v. Chestnut Lodge. American Journal of Psychiatry, 147,* 409–418.

Lebo, D. (1958). A formula for selecting toys for non-directive therapy. *Journal of Genetic Psychology, 92,* 23–34.

Lovaas, O. I. (1987). Behavioral treatment and normal educational and intellectual functioning in young autisic children. *Journal of Consulting and Clinical Psychology, 55,* 3–9.

Masserman, J. H. (1953). Faith and delusion in psychotherapy. *American Journal of Psychiatry, 110,* 324–333.

Mayers, K., & Griffin, M. (1990). The play project: Use of stimulus objects with demented patients. *Journal of Gerontological Nursing, 16,* 32–37.

Menninger, K. (1958). *Theory of psychoanalytic technique.* New York: Basic Books.

Moustakas, C. E. (1953). *Children in play therapy.* New York: McGraw-Hill.

Peterson, L., & Burbach, D. J. (1988). Historical trends. In J. I. Matson (Ed.), *Handbook of treatment approaches in childhood psychopathology.* New York: Plenum.

Reisman, J. M. (1971). *Toward the integration of psychotherapy.* New York: Wiley-Inerscience.

Reisman, J. M. (1991). *A history of clinical psychology* (2nd ed.). Washington, DC: Hemisphere.

Rogers, C. R. (1961). *On becoming a person.* Boston: Houghton Mifflin.

Santostefano, S. (1984). Cognitive control therapy with children: Rationale and technique. *Psychotherapy, 21,* 76–91.

Schaefer, C. E., & Reid, S. E. (1986). *Game play: Therapeutic use of childhood games.* New York: Wiley-Interscience.

Schopler, E., Short, A., & Mesibov, G. (1989). Relation of behavioral treatment to "normal functioning": Comment on Lovaas. *Journal of Consulting and Clinical Psychology, 57,* 162–164.

Singh, N. N., & Beale, I. L., (1988). Learning disabilities: Psychological therapies. In J. L. Matson (Ed.), *Handbook of treatment approaches in childhood psy-*

chopathology. New York: Plenum.

Steininger, M., Newell, J. D., & Garcia, L. T. (1984). *Ethical issues in psychology.* Homewood, IL: Dorsey.

Stone, A. A. (1990). Law, science, and psychiatric malpractice: A response to Klerman's indictment of psychoanalytic psychiatry. *American Journal of Psychiatry, 147,* 419–427.

Swanson, F. L. (1970). *Psychotherapists and children.* New York: Pitman.

Thorne, F. C. (1955). *Principles of psychological examining: A systematic textbook of applied integrative psychology.* Brandon, VT: Journal of Clinical Psychology Press.

Thorne, F. C. (1968). *Psychological case handling, vols. 1 & 2.* Brandon, VT: Clinical Psychology Publishing.

Watson, H., & Levine, M. (1989). Psychoherapy and mandated reporting of child abuse. *American Journal of Orthopsychiatry, 59,* 246–256.

Whitaker, C. A., Felder, R. E., Malone, T. P., & Warkentin, J. (1962). First stage techniques in the experimental psychotherapy of chronic schizophrenic patients. *Current Psychiatric Therapies, 2,* 147–158.

Woody, R. H. (1969). *Behavioral problem children in the schools.* New York: Appleton-Century-Crofts.

Zilboorg, G. (1939). Overestimation of psychopathology. *American Journal of Orthopsychiatry, 9,* 86–94.

Chapter 6

Axline, V. M. (1947). *Play therapy.* Boston: Houghton Mifflin.

Federn, P. (1952). *Ego psychology and the psychoses.* New York: Basic Books.

Fenichel, O. (1945). *The psychoanalytic theory of neurosis.* New York: Norton.

Lazarus, A., & Mayne, T. J. (1990). Relaxation: Some limitations, side effects, and proposed solutions. *Psychotherapy, 27,* 261–266.

Moustakas, C. E. (1959). *Psychotherapy with children.* New York: Harper & Row.

Osterwell, Z. O. (1986). Time-limited play therapy: Rationale and technique. *School Psychology International, 7,* 224–230.

Rachman, S. J. (1990). *Fear and courage.* New York: W. H. Freeman.

Strean, H. S. (1968). Choice of paradigm in the treatment of parent and child. In M. C. Nelson (Ed.), *Roles and paradigms in psychotherapy.* New York: Grune & Stratton.

Chapter 7

Allen, F. H. (1942). *Psychotherapy with children.* New York: Norton.

Axline, V. M. (1947). *Play therapy.* Boston: Houghton Mifflin.

Berkowitz, L. (1964). Aggressive cues in aggressive behavior and hostility catharsis. *Psychological Review, 71,* 104–122.

Berkowitz, L. (1970). Experimental investigations of hostility catharsis. *Journal of Consulting and Clinical Psychology, 35,* 1–7.

Blanck, G., & Blanck, R. (1974). *Ego psychology: Theory and practice.* New York: Columbia University Press.

Fonagy, P., & Moran, G. S. (1990). Studies on the efficacy of child psychoanalysis. *Journal of Consulting and Clinical Psychology, 58,* 684–695.

Freud, A. (1946). *The psychoanalytical treatment of children.* London: Imago.

Freud, A. (1965). *Normality and pathology in childhood.* New York: International Universities Press.

Friedman, H. J. (1963). Patient-expectancy and symptom reduction. *Archives of General Psychiatry, 8,* 61–67.

Hathaway, S. R. (1951). Clinical methods: Psychotherapy. *Annual Review of Psychology, 2,* 259–280.

Heinicke, C. M. (199). Toward generic principles of treating parents and children: Integrating psychotherapy with the school-aged child and early family intervention. *Journal of Consulting and Clinical Psychology, 58,* 713–719.

Kazdin, A. E., Bass, D., Ayers, W. A., & Rodgers, A. (1990). Empirical and clinical focus of child and adolescent psychotherapy research. *Journal of Consulting and Clinical Psychology, 58,* 729–740.

Moustakas, C. E. (1953). *Children in play therapy.* New York: McGraw-Hill.

Orlinsky, D. E. (1989). Researchers' images of psychotherapy: Their origins and influence on research. *Clinical Psychology Review, 9,* 413–441.

Peterson, L., & Burbach, D. J. (1988). Historical trends. In J. L. Matson (Ed.), *Handbook of treatment approaches in childhood psychopathology.* New York: Plenum.

Redl, F., & Wineman, D., (1951). *Children who hate .* Glencoe, IL: Free Press.

Reisman, J. M. (1968). Ratings of self and therapist: Two studies. *Psychiatric Quarterly Supplement, 42,* 116–123.

Rogers, C. R., & Dymond, R. F. (1954). *Psychotherapy and personality change.* Chicago: University of Chicago Press.

Shore, M., & Massimo, J. (1973). After ten years: A follow-up study of comprehensive vocationally oriented psychotherapy. *American Journal of Orthopsychiatry, 43,* 128–132.

Thorne, F. C. (1968). *Psychological case handling, vol. 1.* Brandon VT: Clinical Psychology Publishing.

Wallerstein, R. S. (1989). The Psychotherapy Research Project of the Menninger Foundation: An overview. *Journal of Consulting and Clinical Psychology, 57,* 195–205.

Weiner, I. B. (1970). *Psychological disturbance in adolescence.* New York: Wiley-Interscience.

Zax, M., & Klein, A. (1960). Measurement of personality and behavior changes following psychotherapy. *Psychological Bulletin, 57,* 435–448.

Zwick, P.A. (1960). Gauging dosage and distance in psychotherapy with adolescents. *American Journal of Orthopsychiatry, 30,* 645–647.

Chapter 8

Freud, S. (1959a). Analysis terminable and interminable. In *Collected papers, vol. 5.* New York: Basic Books.

Freud, S. (1959b). Analysis of a phobia in a five-year-old boy. In *Collected papers, vol. 3.* New York: Basic Books.

Gelfand, D. M., & Hartmann, D. P. (1984). *Child behavior analysis and therapy* (2nd ed.). New York: Pergamon.

Johnson, J. H., Rasbury, W. C., & Siegel, L. J. (1986). *Approaches to child treatment*. New York: Pergamon.

Kazdin, A. E. (1991). Effectiveness of psychotherapy with children and adolescents. *Journal of Consulting and Clinical Psychology, 59,* 785–798.

Luthar, S. S., & Zigler, E. (1991). Vulnerability and competence: A review of research on resilience in childhood. *American Journal of Orthopsychiatry, 61,* 6–22.

Rank, O. (1950). *Will therapy and truth and reality*. New York: Knopf.

Raskin, N. J. (1985). Client-centered therapy. In S. J. Lynn & J. P. Garske (Eds.), *Contemporary psychotherapies: Models and methods* (pp. 155–190). Columbus, OH: Merrill.

Robertson, M. (1991, June 30). Positive thinking theory gets a boost from science. *Chicago Tribune,* sec. 5, p. 3.

Rogers, C. R. (1951). *Client-centered therapy*. Boston: Houghton Mifflin.

Rogers, C. R. (1980). *A way of being*. Boston: Houghton Mifflin.

Snyder, D. K., Wells, R. M., & Grady-Fletcher, A. (1991). Long-term effectiveness of behavioral versus insight-oriented marital therapy: A 4-year follow-up study. *Journal of Consulting and Clinical Psychology, 59,* 138–141.

Chapter 9

Ansbacher, H. L., & Ansbacher, R. R. (1956). *The individual psychology of Alfred Adler*. New York: Basic Books.

Brim, O. G., Jr. (1961). Methods of educating parents and their evaluation. In G. Caplan (Ed.), *Prevention of mental disorders in children*. New York: Basic Books.

Caplan, G. (1970). *The theory and practice of mental health consultation*. New York: Basic Books.

Durlak, J. A., & Jason, L. A. (1984). Preventive programs for school-aged children and adolescents. In M. C. Roberts & L. Peterson (Eds.), *Prevenion of problems in childhood: Psychological research and applications*. New York: Wiley-Interscience.

Fauber, R. L. & Long. N. (1991). Children in context: The role of the family in child psychotherapy. *Journal of Consulting and Clinical Psychology, 59,* 813–820.

Freud, S. (1959). Analysis of a phobia in a five-year-old boy. In *Collected papers of Sigmund Freud, vol. 3*. New York: Basic Books.

Guerney, B., Jr. (1964). Filial therapy: Description and rationale. *Journal of Consulting Psychology, 28,* 304–310.

Harman, D. & Brim, O. G. (1980). *Learning to be parents*. Beverly Hills, CA: Sage.

Jason, L. A., & Glenwick, D. S. (1980). Future directions: A critical look at the behavioral community approach. In D. Glenwick & L. Jason (Eds.). *Behavioral community psychology*. New York: Praeger.

Johnson, R. P., & Geller, E. S. (1980). Community mental health center programs. In D. Glenwick & L. Jason (Eds.), *Behavioral community psychology*. New York: Praeger.

Kahn, R. L. (1968). Implications of organizational research for community mental health. In J. W. Carter, Jr. (Ed.), *Research contributions from psychology to community mental health*. New York: Behavioral Publications.

Kazdin, A. E. (1990). Premature termination from treatment among children referred for antisocial behavior. *Journal of Child Psychology and Psychiatry, 31,* 415–425.

Kessler, J. W. (1988). *Psychopathology of childhood* (2nd ed.). Englewood Cliffs, NJ: Prentice-Hall.

Lidz, T. (1963). *The family and human adaptation*. New York: International Universities Press.

Lovaas, I. O. (1987). Behavioral treatment and normal educational and intellectual functioning in young autistic children. *Journal of Consulting and Clinical Psychology, 55,* 3–9.

Mesibov, G. B., & Dawson, G. (1986). Pervasive developmental disorders and schizophrenia. In J. M. Reisman (Ed.), *Behavior disorders in infants, children, and adolescents*. New York: Random House.

Peterson, L., & Roberts, M. C. (1986). Community intervention and prevention. In H. C. Quay & J. S. Werry (Eds.), *Psychopathological disorders of childhood* (3rd ed.). New York: Wiley.

Reisman, J. M. (1980). Child psychotherapy. In A. K. Hess (Ed.), *Psychotherapy supervision*. New York: Wiley-Interscience.

Reisman, J. M., & Kissel, S. (1968). Mother's evaluation of long-term clinic services. *Bulletin of the Rochester Mental Health Center, 1,* 13–17.

Rowbury, T. G., & Baer, D. M. (1980). Applied analysis of preschool children's behavior. In D. Glenwick & L. Jason (Eds.), *Behavioral community psychology*. New York: Praeger.

Standifer, F. R. (1964). Pilot parent program—parents helping parents. *Mental Retardation, 2,* 304–307.

Thompson, C. L., & Rudolph, L. B. (1988). *Counseling children*. Pacific Grove, CA: Brooks/Cole.

Turnbull, A. P. & Turnbull, H. R. (1990). *Families, professionals, and exceptionality: A special partnership* (2nd ed). Columbus, OH: Merrill.

Wahler, R. G. (1992). *Trials and tribulations in the parenting of conduct disordered children*. Paper presented at Midwestern Psychological Association Convention, Chicago.

Zax, M., & Cowen, E. L. (1972). *Abnormal psychology: Changing conceptions*. New York: Holt, Rinehart & Winston.

Chapter 10

Ackerman, N. (1958). *The psychodynamics of family life*. New New York: Basic Books.

Ackerman, N. (1966). *Treating the troubled family*. New York: Basic Books.

Ackerman, N., Papp, P., & Prosky, P. (1970). Childhood disorders and interlocking pathology in family relationships. In E. J. Anthony & C. Koupernik (Eds.), *The child in his family* (pp. 241–266). New York: Wiley-Interscience.

Alexander, J., & Parsons, B. (1982). *Functional family therapy.* Monterey, CA: Brooks/Cole.

Anderson, C. M., & Stewart, S. (1983). *Mastering resistance: A practical guide to family therapy.* New York: Guilford.

Berg-Cross, L. (1988). *Basic concepts in family therapy.* New York: Haworth Press.

Bloch, D., & Simon, R. (Eds.). (1982). *The strength of family therapy: Selected papers of Nathan W. Ackerman.* New York: Brunner/Mazel.

Boszormenyi-Nagy, I., & Framo, J. (Eds.) (1965). *Intensive family therapy: Theoretical and practical aspects.* New York: Harper & Row.

Boszormenyi-Nagy, I., & Spark, G. (1973). *Invisible loyalties: Reciprocity in intergenerational family therapy.* New York: Harper & Row.

Bowen, M. (1978). *Family therapy in clinical practice.* New York: Aronson.

Breunlin, D. C., Schwartz, R. C., & Kune-Karrer, B. (1992). *Metaframeworks: Transcending the models of family therapy.* San Francisco: Jossey-Bass.

Brown, J. H., & Christensen, D. (1986). *Family therapy: Theory and practice.* Monterey, CA: Brooks/Cole.

Carter, E. A., & McGoldrick, M. (Eds.). (1980). *The family life cycle: A framework for family therapy.* New York: Gardner.

Clarkin, J. F., Frances, A. J., & Glick, I. D. (1981). The decision to treat a family: Selection criteria and enabling factors. In L. R. Wolberg & M. L. Aronson (Eds.). *Group and family therapy: 1981* (pp. 149–167). New York: Brunner/Mazel.

Framo, J. L. (1982). *Exploration in marital and family therapy.* New York: Springer.

Framo, J. L. (1992). *Family-of-origin therapy: An intergenerational approach.* New York: Brunner/Mazel.

Fristad, M. A., & Clayton, T. L. (1991). Family dysfunction and family psychopathology in child psychiatry outpatients. *Journal of Family Psychology, 5*(1), 46–59.

Haley, J. (1976). *Problem-solving therapy.* San Francisco: Jossey-Bass.

Haley, J. (1984). *Ordeal therapy.* San Francisco: Jossey-Bass.

Hansen, J. C., & L'Abate, L. (1982). *Approaches to family therapy.* New York: Macmillan.

Kempler, W. (1981). *Experimential psychotherapy with families.* New York: Brunner/Mazel.

Kerr, M. E., & Bowen, M. (1988). *Family evaluation.* New York: Norton.

Lebow, J. L. (1984). On the value of integrating approaches to family therapy. *Journal of Marital and Family Therapy, 10*(2), 127–138.

Madanes, C. (1981). *Strategic family therapy.* San Francisco: Jossey-Bass.

McGoldrick, M., Pearce, J. K., & Giordano, J. (Eds.) (1982). *Ethnicity and family therapy.* New York: Guilford.

Minuchin, S. (1974). *Families and family therapy.* Cambridge, MA: Harvard University Press.

Minuchin, S., & Fishman H. C. (1981). *Family therapy techniques.* Cambridge, MA: Harvard University Press.

Minuchin, S., Rosman, B., & Baker, L. (1978). *Psychosomatic families.* Cambridge, MA: Harvard University Press.

Neill, J. R., & Kniskern, D. P. (Eds.). (1982). *From psyche to system: The evolving therapy of Carl Whitaker*. New York: Guilford.

Olson, D. H., Portner, J., & Lavee, Y. (1985). FACES III: Family Adaptability and Cohesion Evaluation Scales. In D. Olson, H. McCubbin, H. Barnes, A. Larsen, M. Muxen, & M. Wilson (Eds.), *Family inventories* (2nd ed.). St. Paul, MN: Family Social Science, University of Minnesota.

Olson, D., Russell, C. S., & Sprenkle, D. H. (1979). Circumplex model of marital and family systems II: Empirical studies and clinical intervention. In J. Vincent (Ed.), *Advances in family intervention, assessment, and theory*. Greenwich, CT: JAI.

Palazzoli-Selvini, M., Boscolo, L., Cecchin, G., & Prata, G. (1978). *Paradox and counterparadox*. New York: Aronson.

Patterson, G. R. (1971). *Families: Applications of social learning to family life*. Champaign, IL: Research Press.

Patterson, G. R. (1980). *Coercive family processes*. Eugene, OR: Castilia.

Pinsof, W. M. (1983). Integrative problem-centered therapy: Toward the synthesis of family and individual psychotherapies. *Journal of Marital and Family Therapy, 9* (1), 19–36.

Satir, V. (1967). *Conjoint family therapy*. Palo Alto, CA: Science & Behavior Books.

Satir, V. (1972). *Peoplemaking*. Palo Alto, CA: Science & Behavior Books.

Satir, V., Stachowiak, J., & Taschman, H. A. (1975). *Helping families to change*. New York: Aronson.

Teismann, M. W. (1980). Convening strategies in family therapy. *Family Process, 19*, 393–400.

Watzlawick, P., Beavin, J. H., & Jackson, D. D. (1967). *Pragmatics of human communication: A study of interactional patterns, pathologies, and paradoxes*. New York: Norton.

Watzlawick, P., Weakland, J., & Fisch, R. (1974). *Change: Principles of problem formation and problem resolution*. New York: Norton.

Whitaker, C., & Napier, A. Y. (1978). *The family crucible*. New York: Harper & Row.

Chapter 11

Beavers, R. (1985). *Manual of Beavers-Timberlawn Family Evaluation Scale and Family Style Evaluation*. Dallas, TX: Southwest Family Institute.

Bowen, M. (1978). *Family therapy in clinical practice*. New York: Aronson.

Brock, G. W., & Barnard, C. P. (1988). *Procedures in family therapy*. Boston: Allyn and Bacon.

Colapinto, J. (1991). Structural family therapy. In A. S. Gurman & D. P. Kniskern (Eds.), *Handbook of family therapy, vol. II* (pp. 417–443). New York, Brunner/Mazel.

Epstein, N., Baldwin, L., & Bishop, S. (1983). The McMaster Family Assessment Device. *Journal of Marital and Family Therapy, 9*, 171–180.

Filsinger, E. E. (Ed.). (1983). *Marriage and family assessment*. Beverly Hills, CA: Sage.

Fredman, N., & Sherman, R. (1987). *Handbook of measurements for marriage and family therapy.* New York: Brunner/Mazel.

Gurman, A. S., & Kniskern, D. P. (Eds.) (1991). *Handbook of family therapy, vol. II.* New York: Brunner/Mazel.

Haley, J. (1976). *Problem-solving therapy.* San Francisco: Jossey-Bass.

Karpel, M. A., & Strauss, E. S. (1983). *Family evaluation.* New York: Gardner.

L'Abate, L., Ganahl, G., & Hansen, J. (1986). *Methods of family therapy.* Englewood Cliffs, NJ: Prentice-Hall.

McCubbin, H. I., Patterson, J. M., & Wilson, L. R. (1985). FILE: Family Inventory of Life Events and Changes. In D. Olson, H. I. McCubbin, H. Barnes, A. Larsen, M. Muxen, & M. Wilson (Eds.), *Family inventories.* (2nd ed.). St. Paul: Family Social Science, University of Minnesota.

McGoldrick, M., & Gerson, R. (1985). *Genograms in family assessment.* New York: Norton.

Minuchin, S. (1974). *Families and family therapy.* Cambridge, MA: Harvard University Press.

Minuchin, S., & Fishman, H. C. (1981). *Family therapy techniques.* Cambridge, MA: Harvard University Press.

Moos, R. H., & Moos, B. S. (1981). *Family Environment Scale manual.* Palo Alto, CA: Consulting Psychologists Press.

Olson, D. H., Portner, J., & Lavee, Y. (1985). FACES III: Family Adaptability and Cohesion Evaluation Scales. In D. Olson, H. McCubbin, H. Barnes, A. Larsen, M. Muxen, & M. Wilson (Eds.), *Family inventories* (2nd ed.). St. Paul: Family Social Sciences, University of Minnesota.

Olson, D. H., & Ryder, R. (1978). *Marital and Family Interaction Coding System (MFICS): Abbreviated coding manual.* St. Paul: Family Social Sciences, University of Minnesota.

Palomares, U. (1975). *A curriculum on conflict management.* La Mesa, CA: Human Development Training Institute.

Roberts, M. C., Erickson, M. T., & Tuma, J. M. (1985). Addressing the needs: Guidelines for training psychologists to work with children, youth, and families. *Journal of Clinical Child Psychology, 14*(1), 70–79.

Satir, V. (1967). *Conjoint family therapy.* Palo Alto, CA: Science & Behavior Books.

Snyder, D. K. (1981). *Marital Satisfaction Inventory (MSI) manual.* Los Angeles: Western Psychological Services.

Spanier, G. (1976). Measuring dyadic adjustment: New scales for assessing the quality of marriage and similar dyads. *Journal of Marriage and the Family, 38,* 15–28.

Watzlawick, P. (1966). The Structured Family Interview. *Family Process, 5,* 256–271.

Index